T0378039

The Neuroscience of Language

The Neuroscience of Language offers a remarkably accessible introduction to language in the mind and brain. Following the chain of communication from speaker to listener, it covers all fundamental concepts from speech production to auditory processing, speech sounds, word meaning, and sentence processing. The key methods of cognitive neuroscience are covered, as well as clinical evidence from neuropsychological patients and multimodal aspects of language including visual speech, gesture, and sign language. More than eighty full-color figures are included to help communicate key concepts. The main text focuses on big-picture themes, while detailed studies and related anecdotes are presented in endnotes to provide interested students with many opportunities to dive deeper into specific topics. Throughout, language is placed within the larger context of the brain, illustrating the fascinating connections of language with other fields including cognitive science, linguistics, psychology, and speech and hearing science.

Jonathan E. Peelle is an associate professor in the Center for Cognitive and Brain Health at Northeastern University, with appointments in the Department of Communication Sciences and Disorders and the Department of Psychology. He has taught undergraduate and graduate courses on the neuroscience of language; speech, language, and hearing science; cognitive neuroscience; and functional brain imaging. He is a reviewing editor for *eLife* and *Neurobiology of Language*, and former reviewing editor for *NeuroImage* and *Language, Cognition and Neuroscience*. He has authored more than eighty papers on the neuroscience of language and is currently the chair of the Society for the Neurobiology of Language.

Cambridge Fundamentals of Neuroscience in Psychology

Developed in response to a growing need to make neuroscience accessible to students and other non-specialist readers, the *Cambridge Fundamentals of Neuroscience in Psychology* series provides brief introductions to key areas of neuroscience research across major domains of psychology. Written by experts in cognitive, social, affective, developmental, clinical, and applied neuroscience, these books will serve as ideal primers for students and other readers seeking an entry point to the challenging world of neuroscience.

Books in the Series

The Neuroscience of Expertise by Merim Bilalić
Cognitive Neuroscience of Memory by Scott D. Slotnick
The Neuroscience of Intelligence by Richard J. Haier
The Neuroscience of Adolescence by Adriana Galván
The Neuroscience of Suicidal Behavior by Kees van Heeringen
The Neuroscience of Creativity by Anna Abraham
Cognitive and Social Neuroscience of Aging by Angela Gutchess
The Neuroscience of Sleep and Dreams by Patrick McNamara
The Neuroscience of Addiction by Francesca Mapua Filbey
Introduction to Human Neuroimaging by Hans Op de Beeck and Chie Nakatani
The Neuroscience of Sleep and Dreams, 2nd edition by Patrick McNamara
The Neuroscience of Intelligence, 2nd edition by Richard J. Haier
The Cognitive Neuroscience of Bilingualism by John W. Schwieter and Julia Festman
Fundamentals of Developmental Cognitive Neuroscience by Heather Bortfeld and Silvia A. Bunge
Cognitive and Social Neuroscience of Aging, 2nd edition by Angela Gutchess
Cognitive Neuroscience of Memory, 2nd edition by Scott D. Slotnick
The Neuroscience of Language by Jonathan E. Peelle
Neuroscience of Attention by Joseph B. Hopfinger
Introduction to Human Neuroimaging, 2nd edition by Hans Op de Beeck and Chie Nakatani

The Neuroscience of Language

Jonathan E. Peelle

Northeastern University

CAMBRIDGE
UNIVERSITY PRESS

Shaftesbury Road, Cambridge CB2 8EA, United Kingdom

One Liberty Plaza, 20th Floor, New York, NY 10006, USA

477 Williamstown Road, Port Melbourne, VIC 3207, Australia

314–321, 3rd Floor, Plot 3, Splendor Forum, Jasola District Centre, New Delhi – 110025, India

103 Penang Road, #05–06/07, Visioncrest Commercial, Singapore 238467

Cambridge University Press is part of Cambridge University Press & Assessment, a department of the University of Cambridge.

We share the University's mission to contribute to society through the pursuit of education, learning and research at the highest international levels of excellence.

www.cambridge.org
Information on this title: www.cambridge.org/highereducation/isbn/9781009245272

DOI: 10.1017/9781009245296

© Jonathan E. Peelle 2025

This publication is in copyright. Subject to statutory exception and to the provisions of relevant collective licensing agreements, no reproduction of any part may take place without the written permission of Cambridge University Press & Assessment.

When citing this work, please include a reference to the DOI 10.1017/9781009245296

First published 2025

A catalogue record for this publication is available from the British Library

A Cataloging-in-Publication data record for this book is available from the Library of Congress

ISBN 978-1-009-24527-2 Hardback
ISBN 978-1-009-24530-2 Paperback

Additional resources for this publication at www.cambridge.org/Peelle

Cambridge University Press & Assessment has no responsibility for the persistence or accuracy of URLs for external or third-party internet websites referred to in this publication and does not guarantee that any content on such websites is, or will remain, accurate or appropriate.

To Murray Grossman,
mentor, colleague, and friend,
who taught me more than anyone about the neuroscience of language.

Contents

Figures

Preface

As a researcher, one of the things I've appreciated most about language research is how many other areas of science it comes into contact with: memory, decision-making, acoustics, audiology, linguistics … the list goes on. One of the joys of teaching students about the neuroscience of language has been to make connections with other areas of their lives, and I've enjoyed trying to convey this enthusiasm and some of the many fascinating facets of human language throughout this textbook.

The chapters are written so that they can be read in any order, although the first three chapters provide background in terminology and methods that is assumed in subsequent chapters. When I teach this class, I mostly go in order (with some skipping around at the end).

One difference you may notice between this textbook and some others: I have broken with textbook tradition and included a great deal in endnotes. I had several inspirations for doing so. First, for people new to the field – that is, the intended audience of the book – filling the main text with parenthetical citations is not particularly meaningful, and I worried it would actually distract them from the main points. However, having done my best to simplify the text, I wanted to be sure both to give credit where it's due – the endnotes include primary references to support claims made in the text – and to offer interested readers not only more details (and interesting tangents) but also some commentary based on my own perspective. My goal is that the main text is readable and understandable without ever reading an endnote, but that endnotes will be useful and interesting for readers who want a bit more. One teaching strategy that works well is to review specific studies during lectures, or assign research articles as additional class reading, to highlight specific aspects of research. In addition to sources noted in endnotes, each chapter includes a handful of suggestions "for further reading" that can be used for these activities.

Another way in which I have broken with textbook tradition is that I have included a number of figures that I've created myself, including figures summarizing brain imaging results. (It is relevant to note at this point that I am not an artist.) I've modeled these figures from what I would include in a lecture – for example, what I might draw on a blackboard while explaining a concept.[1] As with the written text, these figures are meant to convey main ideas in a consistent visual format, and should not be taken as a substitute for referring to primary research. I envision a useful strategy is to supplement these simplified figures with specific examples of research results in class. The figures I created for this book are available from https://osf.io/geqb6/.

The boxes included throughout out are intended to highlight specific concepts that complement the main text. In many cases, they introduce new and complementary topics, and contain endnotes with additional information. One possibility – which I have done in my own teaching – is to assign small groups to dig into one of these "tangential" areas and read one or more of the references appearing in a box or endnote, giving them an opportunity to dive a little bit deeper into an area, supported by the background of suggested readings and context provided by the textbook.

Some of the boxes also include stories of real people whose life experience relates to the neuroscience of language. To those who allowed me to share their stories: thank you! Your contributions have helped make this book richer and more personal. To the readers, I would like to point out that most of the people I interviewed are people I have had contact with in real life, and I suspect many of *you* also know people with interesting stories about the neuroscience of language. As you read this book it may be worth thinking about whether there is someone in your own circle whose experience you can learn from.

To all my colleagues in the field: thank you for all of your wonderful contributions to our understanding of the neuroscience of language, and please forgive my oversimplifications (and, no doubt, mistakes). I have aimed to present enough information to give readers a broad understanding of some of the biggest issues in the field and prepare (if they so choose) for further and deeper study. I have very specifically tried *not* to present every experimental finding or theoretical viewpoint, even very good ones, to prevent information overload. I have also avoided certain paradigms and analysis approaches that I judged too complicated for an introductory text, no matter how compelling. I am very aware that many laudable studies are not included here and I'm sorry if yours is among them.

Note

1. During my PhD, I had the good fortune to be taught foundations of neuroscience by Eve Marder, who during her lectures notoriously avoided PowerPoint slides in favor of colored chalk (described eloquently in Marder, 2000). And now you have a concrete example of one of the ways I use endnotes in this book.

Acknowledgments

This book was not written in a vacuum and I am deeply grateful to all who supported and encouraged me during its writing.

I am grateful to Scott Slotnick, who first approached me about this project, and Stephen Acerra, Jackie Grant, and the rest of the team at Cambridge University Press, who not only brought the book to completion but made it better along the way. Their encouragement, feedback, and patience were instrumental throughout the process.

I am also incredibly grateful to my colleagues in the field of cognitive neuroscience, particularly the neuroscience of language, for their thoughtful research and interactions. I have benefited incalculably from prior review papers, chapters, talks, and personal interactions over the last 20-plus years. I am particularly indebted to my primary mentors – Art Wingfield, Murray Grossman, and Matt Davis – who taught me about science, speech, and language, and even more importantly, about being a kind and thoughtful human being.

I have included experiences of actual people to help illustrate everyday experiences related to language processing. The stories and people are all real, although some details may have been changed to provide anonymity. I am deeply grateful to everyone who took the time to speak with me and let me share their story.

I am also grateful to authors of academic software that has helped me to both learn neuroimaging analysis and provide some of the figures in this book, including (but not limited to) Chris Rorden for his wonderful MRIcroGL (and its predecessors, MRIcro and MRIcron), the SPM development team at the Wellcome Centre for Human Neuroimaging, and the FSL development team at Oxford University. Developing this software, publishing methodological articles on the underlying algorithms, sharing the code, and organizing workshops and training opportunities has benefited countless scientists through the years.

The book was improved at all stages by many people who provided helpful feedback, especially Kristin Van Engen, Kristen Allison, Drew McLaughlin, Kate McClannahan, Erin Meier, Emily Myers, and Jamie Reilly. I am indebted to their thoughtfulness and useful suggestions. I am also grateful to many lab members, students, friends, and family members who took the time to read and proofread sections of the book.

Finally, I am grateful to Abram Van Engen for convincing me that writing a book was a good idea, and to my family for their constant love and support.

CHAPTER ONE

Introduction: Transferring Ideas from One Brain to Another

1.1 The Speech Chain

If you read a story about a superhero who could transmit their thoughts into another person's brain without any physical contact, you might think it was a little far-fetched. But in fact, that's exactly what happens during spoken communication: I can take an idea from my brain and place it in your brain. Of course, this brain-to-brain transfer does not require mystical powers – it happens using our body's ability to produce and detect subtle variations in air pressure, and our brain's exquisite ability to harness these processes. But the overall feat remains remarkable, even though we experience it on a daily basis.

Language itself is fundamental to human experience, both as individuals and as a species. But language is also intimately related to other domains of science that have historically been studied in isolation, including memory, emotion, sensory processing, decision-making, and motivation (to name a few). The neuroscience of language is thus a useful microcosm of human experience that transcends traditional boundaries between disciplines. As we will return to in Chapter 10, language is truly a whole-brain activity.

Although I touch on other forms of language processing, the focus of this book is on spoken verbal language – that is, on human speech. Various forms of vocal communication are present in many species, and in humans spoken communication is evolutionarily older than written communication. Many theoretical considerations are similar across different modalities of language, including spoken, written, and signed language. Thus, a firm grounding in spoken communication provides a vocabulary of terms and ideas that translate well to other aspects of language. However, it is important to recognize there are many different modalities of human language, of which speech is just one (a theme we return to in Chapter 9).[1]

A cartoon overview of spoken communication, modeled after the original "speech chain" from Denes and Pinson (1993), is shown in Figure 1.1, and loosely informs how this book is organized. Spoken communication begins with an idea in a talker's head, which is then translated into acoustic vibrations using their mouth and vocal folds (a process that involves monitoring their own production via auditory and somatosensory input). These sound waves travel

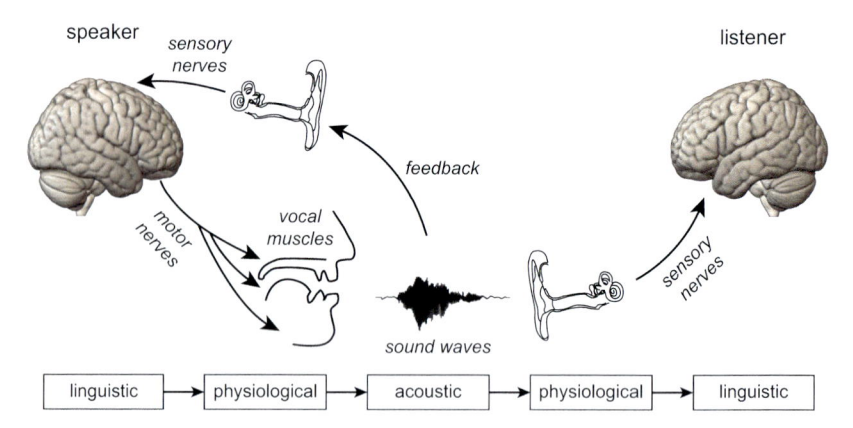

Figure 1.1 Schematic of the "speech chain" (after Denes and Pinson, 1993). To transfer an idea to a listener, a speaker controls their body in a specific way to produce air vibrations that we experience as sound. These travel to the auditory system of both the listener (who will, hopefully, extract the intended meaning) and the speaker (who can check to make sure they produced the sounds they intended). https://osf.io/geqb6/ (CC-BY).

through the air and may be mixed with environmental noise or otherwise degraded before reaching the ear, and auditory system, of the listener. After traveling up a complex and interconnected ascending auditory pathway, the now-transformed acoustic signal is processed by cortical auditory and speech regions to extract meaning (which we experience as "understanding" what a talker has said). Given the rapid rate of speech, the above process must happen very quickly, and also continuously (at least during extended listening, such as in a conversation or lecture). Throughout the rest of the book, we will examine these stages of the speech chain in greater detail.

1.2 Levels of Speech Processing

Linguistics is the study of language; branches of linguistics deal with topics including speech sounds, concepts, how words are combined, and comparisons of language attributes across cultures. Psycholinguistics specifically deals with how the mind processes language – the psychological facets of linguistics – and thus focuses on the perceptual, cognitive, and linguistic operations required for language. Researchers interested in the neuroscience of language are influenced by both of these traditions, as well as by thinking in neuroscience and psychology more broadly. To understand the terminology in

Table 1.1 Key levels of speech processing.

phoneme	Smallest meaningful speech unit.
syllable	Unit of speech that combines to form words (for example, a consonant–vowel pair).
morpheme	A meaningful linguistic unit that can't be divided up into smaller units. A word like "dog" is a morpheme; so is the "s" at the end of "dogs." A free morpheme can occur as a separate word, whereas a bound morpheme cannot stand on its own.
lexical	At the level of a word, including word meanings and grammatical function.
sentence	A grammatical unit composed of one or more clauses.
discourse	Language unit longer than a single sentence, including the function of language in conversation more broadly.

the rest of the book and research papers you read, a preliminary understanding of some basic terms will be useful. These are listed in Table 1.1.

An enduring challenge to our understanding of how the brain understands language is creating a mapping between terms used in different fields. Sometimes different terms refer to a similar underlying concept; other times *similar* terms refer to *different* concepts.[2] Clear and explicit definitions are useful to keep close at hand.

It is also worth considering how existing linguistic and psycholinguistic frameworks have influenced areas of research in the neuroscience of language. For example, from a language-centered background, it makes sense to identify neural mechanisms underlying phonemes, syllables, and morphemes; from a strict auditory neuroscience perspective, however, it might make more sense to think about amplitude fluctuations and the acoustic complexity of the signal. Combining these perspectives is one of the most challenging facets of the neuroscience language but can also be one of the most rewarding.

1.3 Challenges of Spoken Language Processing

Before we get too far into the neuroscience of language, it's useful to think about some of the challenges listeners need to overcome for successful communication to occur (many, though not all, of which are shared to some degree across different modalities of language and, indeed, across other cognitive domains).

1.3.1 Categorical Perception

Categorical perception refers to the general phenomenon in which things that are technically not identical are perceived as being linked together as the same *kind* of thing. For example, at some point you almost certainly learned what a chair is. In fact, you developed a concept of "chairness" that goes beyond any particular example of a chair that you encountered. As a result, you probably find it easy to recognize whether a piece of furniture is a chair or not, even if you have never seen it before. Importantly, your concept of CHAIR (I use all capitals to denote concepts, rather than particular words) encompasses different types of chair: an office chair, a dining-room-table chair, an easy chair, and so on. You have learned a category of objects that share certain features and label these items "chair" – you don't think, well, this one is 100 percent of a chair but this other one is a little different so I'll say it's just 70 percent chair.

Now, for a speech example. Let's say you have four friends and you ask each of them to say the word "dog." Each of your friends has a different body – specifically, a different vocal tract, vocal folds, mouth, and so on – and thus the acoustic vibrations coming out of their mouth when they say "dog" are going to be different (that is, the acoustic signals are not identical). Nevertheless, as a listener, you will have no trouble understanding that they are saying "dog." In other words, you have mapped four different sounds onto the same category (in this case, "dog"). This is sometimes expressed in terms of a "many-to-one" mapping, because a large number of acoustic sounds need to be associated with a single category (in this case, a word).

The field of speech research has many examples of categorical perception as studied in a laboratory setting. In one classic paradigm, listeners are played a series of sounds and given two choices: For example, did you hear a "pa" or a "ba"? Unbeknownst to the listeners, the sounds they hear vary continuously between "ba" and "pa" (that is, the acoustic signal varies in equal steps between a continuum that moves from 100 percent "ba" to 100 percent "pa"). However, the responses that people make show a classic sigmoidal function (see Figure 1.2), indicating that "ambiguous" sounds (acoustically between "ga" and "ba") are more likely to be heard as *either* "pa" or "ba" – that is, they are perceived as belonging to a category (in this case, listeners of English know that "pa" and "ba" are both possible options). Perhaps most importantly, people struggle to discriminate tokens that fall within a category but *are* able to discriminate tokens that fall between categories. The learning of these speech categories during childhood, and how listeners transform a continuous acoustic space into a discrete word space, have long intrigued speech scientists.[3]

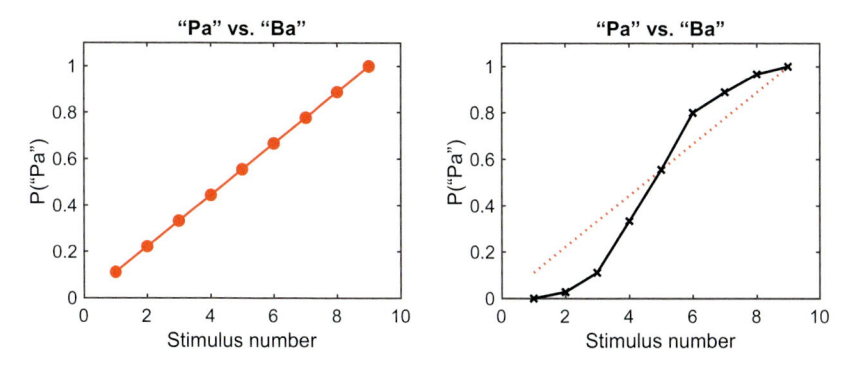

Figure 1.2 Categorical perception of speech is demonstrated by a lack of linearity in how listeners perceive speech. For example, in this cartoon example, the acoustic signal changes in equal steps from "pa" to "ba" (stimulus 1 = 100 percent "ba," stimulus 9 = 100 percent "pa"). The probability of a listener reporting "pa" – P("pa") – is plotted on the y axis. *Left:* If our perception were true to reality, the probability of choosing "pa" or "ba" would also change equally (red line). *Right:* In real life, listeners tend to choose *either* "pa" or "ba," which is why the curve is steeper in the middle than on the ends. Compare the black line (what listeners tend to do) with the dotted red line (equal change in perception). https://osf.io/geqb6/ (CC-BY).

1.3.2 Time-Constrained Understanding

Although estimates vary, spoken conversation generally happens at a rate of around 140–180 words per minute (which corresponds to 2–3 words every second). Speaking rate can be substantially faster than this if a talker has rehearsed, is reading from a prepared text, or the speech has been edited (for example, for a TV show or podcast).[4] Listeners must therefore rapidly map the continuous acoustic signal presented to their auditory system to the words they are interested in understanding. Importantly, in live contexts, a listener does not have the opportunity to slow down the incoming speech: The speaking rate is controlled by the talker, not the listener. The next time you attend any large event with a single speaker (such as a lecture, ceremony, religious service, or similar event), take a moment to consider how quickly the speaker is producing speech, and how in control of this you feel, as a listener. You can do the same thing next time you watch a show.[5] Now compare that experience to what you are doing right now when you read this text. Here, you are controlling your own eye movements across the page. If you don't understand a sentence, you can go back and read it again. For example, if I use an unusual word that makes you lour,[6] you might pause, even if the word is entirely cromulent.[7] Or, if you need a second to pause and think (or read an endnote), you can take it whenever you like. Spoken language is thus fundamentally constrained in time in a way that reading is not.[8]

What are the consequences of these time constraints? The need for rapid analysis pressures listeners to make use of all available cues to aid perception. These might include predictions about upcoming words based on prior content and defaulting to common interpretations when ambiguity arises. The heavy reliance on context and prediction is often helpful but can also hinder understanding when unusual (or at least, unpredicted) utterances are encountered.

1.3.3 Flexibility

In the midst of the drive to rapidly map acoustic signals onto previously learned sound categories comes another challenge: namely, the need to be flexible.

Recall that a challenge of categorical perception is the many-to-one problem that requires a listener to perceive different acoustic signals as belonging to the same speech category. However, *which specific* speech sounds get mapped to a speech category is not as straightforward as one might think. Earlier, we encountered the example of different people saying the same word; already, as a listener, we need to accommodate that variability so that we aren't confused when someone new starts talking (fortunately, you could meet a stranger and probably understand them if they said "dog," even though you had never heard them speak before). Our ability not only to accommodate variability in a general sense but also to adjust our perception to match a specific talker suggests that perceptual categories are not set in stone but have some degree of flexibility. Exactly how listeners implement this flexibility is not always clear.

Furthermore, no matter how flexible we are as listeners, there are some situations in which our understanding of speech will start to falter. For example, consider listening in the midst of background noise (think about a crowded restaurant, sporting event, or having the bad luck of sitting next to an air-conditioning unit during a lecture; listening to someone with an accent that is unfamiliar to you; or listening to digitally altered speech, such as a podcast at 1.5 times normal speed). In such situations you might find yourself missing words and not entirely understanding what a talker is saying. However, in many (though not all) of these cases listeners are able to adjust to challenging speech signals over time, a process usually framed as **perceptual learning** or **adaptation**. There is no clear boundary between "normal" flexibility in listening and perceptual learning, but generally the ease and success of perception plays a role. So, for example, when you understand all of your friends saying "dog," there is no additional adjustment required: Your perceptual system is already accommodating this level of variability and you are very accurate at understanding what you hear. However, if you listen to a podcast at twice normal speed, you might find that after a minute of listening you are able to catch more words than when you started – or you might understand the same amount but find it less effortful – reflecting some perceptual learning.[9]

The overall point is that listeners need to be flexible, both in the moment (to accommodate little variations in speech sounds) and over a longer time period (to accommodate greater challenges to perception).

1.3.4 Multimodal Integration

As noted in Section 1.1, most of this book deals with auditory speech (or more specifically, "auditory-only" speech). As listeners we frequently want to understand language that is solely in the auditory modality (radio, podcasts, phone calls, a passenger in the back seat of our car, to name a few real-life examples). However, in many instances even "auditory" speech occurs across modalities, most commonly involving visual speech information in addition to auditory information. It has long been appreciated that being able to see a talker's mouth can improve speech recognition, especially in the presence of background noise (covered in more depth in Chapter 9). Interestingly, some of the information provided by auditory and visual speech signals is redundant, and some is complementary. At a basic level, auditory and visual information are necessarily separated, because they are processed by different sensory organs, and thus enter the brain through different pathways. There is no question that auditory and visual speech information *are* combined – simple behavioral experiments reliably demonstrate this fact – but the *way* in which they are combined continues to be a matter of active investigation. (Visual speech information is not the only type of nonauditory information listeners use. For example, gestures – a visual, but nonspeech cue – are also commonly used during conversational speech and tend to align with important acoustic cues.)

1.4 Major Themes

Throughout the remaining chapters in the book I will refer to a few major themes – central ideas that crop up in different contexts. This list is certainly not exhaustive, but it provides a starting point to think about important threads that run through different areas of language processing (and thus different chapters). By necessity, individual research studies need to investigate fairly specific questions, and the details of these studies are critically important to understanding the findings. At the same time, I hope these overarching themes encourage us to think about the big picture: What have we learned about language, or human cognition generally? One nice exercise is to return to these themes for reflection or discussion after each chapter: Although some will relate more obviously than others to each chapter, most chapters touch on several of these themes.

1.4.1 Stability versus Flexibility

Memory, in all its forms, is extraordinarily important for helping us to efficiently navigate our environment. When I was growing up, we had three cats, who got their dinner about five o'clock every afternoon. As soon as they heard the can opener, all three would come running so they wouldn't miss a morsel of food. Similarly, if you've ever had a bird feeder in the yard, you can see how quickly the neighborhood birds (and squirrels) learn that it provides a reliable source of food and they stop by to benefit. Remembering their past experience saves the animals from having to forage at random every time they're hungry, preserving that time and energy for other activities.

In some ways, language is no different. To efficiently communicate, we have collectively agreed upon a set of words that refer to particular concepts (and other words that help piece those together). If we each somehow invented our own personal language, it might be useful for helping organize our *internal* thoughts and plans. But the most obvious benefit of language comes from interpersonal communication: By developing a shared vocabulary, we can quickly communicate ideas (sometimes even very complex ideas) to others. As noted in Section 1.3.3, the need for a shared set of sounds we can use to communicate drives both the need for stability (we need to remember those specific sounds) and flexibility (we need to understand different talkers in different situations).

1.4.2 Language Processing Benefits from Prediction (or Context)

In the previous section I gave some examples of how speech comprehension is constrained by time, and thus how the rapid extraction of meaning is required during communication. Although there are no doubt a number of strategies listeners use to facilitate rapid language processing, many fall under the broad category of "prediction." That is, the average literate adult may know about 40,000 words,[10] but not all are equally likely to occur at any instant. Expectations about the next word to be heard will be influenced by the current social or environmental setting, preceding linguistic context, and acoustic cues in connected speech (among other things). The use of context to constrain perception – and specifically, to predict the upcoming speech signal – is fundamental to spoken language processing.

1.4.3 Language Processing Relies on Both "Bottom-Up" and "Top-Down" Processing

As typically used, **bottom-up processing** refers to sensory-driven computations carried out by the brain. For example, when photons of light hit the retina, a neural signal is created in the eye. The neural signal is completely explained by how the photoreceptors (light-sensitive cells) in the eye react to incoming sensory information. By contrast, **top-down processing** reflects non-sensory influences, including our expectations, memories, attentional state, and so on, that can alter the processing of incoming sensory information. Top-down influences are clearly demonstrated in the context of attention: If I provide a cue that indicates the spatial location of a flash of light, you will see it more rapidly than without the cue. The photons hitting your retina are identical, but your attentional state helps you to process that information more efficiently. In reality, the relative weight of bottom-up and top-down information is not always clear, and it may well be that dividing behavior into these two categories is an oversimplification.[11] Because of this ambiguity, I am tempted to always use quotes when describing these two positions – I will avoid doing so to keep the page cleaner, but you might want to imagine the quotes being there anyway. The degree to which our language understanding is driven by sensory information compared to other types of processing, and the degree to which this changes with context, is a recurring theme.

1.4.4 The Neural Organization of Language Processing Is Hierarchical

During everyday communication, language enters the brain through sensory regions that are also responsible for processing all of the nonlanguage things in our environment. That is, the auditory system that processes your friend saying "good morning" is also responsible for making sense of a dog barking, a car horn honking, and a running faucet from the next room. From here on, though, processing diverges, and increasingly complex forms of language processing are engaged, corresponding to different regions of the brain (particularly along the temporal lobe, and into the frontal lobe, covered in more detail in Chapter 3). The type of information processed at each stage changes and becomes less and less dependent on the original sensory input. In addition, the reciprocal wiring of the brain means that "higher" levels in the hierarchy can influence the processing at "lower" levels. The type of hierarchical organization I've described is hardly unique to language; rather, it seems to be a general organization principle of the brain. However, it plays a critical role in how we think about computations and constraints during language processing.

1.4.5 Language Processing Depends on the Task That People Are Doing

As listeners, it is critical that we can distinguish different speech sounds. For example, "bat" and "pat" are both valid words in English, with different meanings, and so we need to be able to tell them apart. Now let's say that I would like to conduct an experiment to study speech perception; I play a sound and ask listeners to indicate if they hear a "ba" or a "pa" (often referred to as a two-alternative forced-choice task, also abbreviated 2AFC). At first glance, this experiment might seem to transparently tap the same processes listeners use when understanding speech (distinguishing between a /b/ and a /p/ is required to distinguish between "bat" and "pat"). In reality, however, the task demands are very different. My experiment is using isolated speech sounds rather than words; moreover, I am asking participants to make an explicit decision about what they hear (that is a **metalinguistic** decision – a decision *about* language). Even though the decision might be an easy one, it still requires participants to consider options and make a conscious choice (and probably press a button to indicate the decision, requiring motor processing) – cognitive processes that are typically not present in everyday conversation. If I identify brain regions that respond to this sort of task, how sure am I that these are indeed what listeners do in the everyday world? Carefully controlled studies play an important and necessary role in helping us understand language. At the same time, we need to be aware of the specific task listeners are doing and the degree to which this affects our conclusions.

1.4.6 There Is No "Language Network"

Don't get me wrong – of course, some brain regions are more important for language function than others. Clinically, this is highlighted most obviously by the fact that only some types of brain damage lead to **aphasia** (severe language difficulty). However, this important (and undisputed) clinical observation, coupled with a general focus on localizing cognitive functions, has encouraged a mindset that often results in discussion of "the" language network, which is inaccurate. There is no single language region, language center, or even language network: We know beyond a doubt that the parts of the brain recruited to understand language are different depending on the specific type of language being processed and the specific task required. Although I address this issue most directly in Chapter 10, it is worth keeping it in mind any time we are thinking about identifying brain regions supporting language processing.

1.4.7 Some Forms of Language Processing Are Lateralized

Lateralization of function refers to the left or right hemisphere of the brain being more specialized for a specific process than the other. In its most extreme form, a completely lateralized function would be supported *exclusively* by one hemisphere. In practice, even if one hemisphere dominates a particular process, the other hemisphere usually also contributes. The term **hemispheric dominance** is sometimes also used, and may convey a more graded sense of distinction than "lateralization."

Foundational studies in lateralization of function were conducted on patients who had some, or all, of their corpus callosum severed. The **corpus callosum** is a bundle of white matter tracts that connect the left and right hemisphere (discussed more in Chapter 3).[12] In the mid twentieth century it was discovered that for some patients with epilepsy, severing the corpus callosum provided relief from recurrent seizures.[13] Importantly, in patients with a severed corpus callosum, each hemisphere of the brain was still able to function, but information does not flow freely between them. These patients are sometimes referred to as "split-brain" patients.

A series of classic experiments conducted in the 1960s by Roger Sperry, Mike Gazzaniga, and colleagues relied on organizational principles of the visual system to provide information to one hemisphere but not the other. Specifically, if you look straight ahead at a point on a screen and don't move your gaze, everything to the left of where you are looking will be processed by the right visual cortex; everything to the right of where you are looking, by the left visual cortex. Thus, if a word is shown on the right side of a screen, it is transmitted to the left visual cortex, and thus easily processed by the rest of the left hemisphere (but not the right hemisphere). Researchers can thus present tasks to either the left hemisphere, or the right hemisphere, by presenting items on the left or right side of the screen.

Relevant for our discussion on language, in one of many demonstrations, Gazzaniga and colleagues (1965) presented a series of words and objects to the right or left visual field of one of these patients. In the author's words: "it was only those stimuli that fell in the right visual half-field that were acknowledged and described verbally." This pattern of responses suggested that the left hemisphere was dominant for language processing (or at least speech production); because items in the right visual field were processed by the left hemisphere, the patient was able to verbally describe them. By contrast, words presented to the left visual field were processed by the nonverbal right hemisphere, and therefore the patient was not able to verbally describe them. These and other demonstrations helped reveal the remarkable extent to which each hemisphere of the brain can act on its own. They also led to popular notions of "left brain" versus "right brain" thinking. In the context of language, as we'll see, there is certainly evidence for lateralization, but it is not always as clear-cut as these early studies might lead one to expect.

1.5 Summary

- Spoken language proves a mechanism to convey information to others through a complex coupling of motor, sensory, and cognitive processes.
- Understanding spoken language provides a scaffolding of important considerations across all modalities of language.
- Major themes are threads that weave through the fabric of individual chapters, including: stability versus flexibility; language processing benefits from prediction; language processing involves both bottom-up and top-down processing; the neural organization of language processing is hierarchical; language processing depends on the task people are doing; there is no "language network"; and some forms of language processing are lateralized.

Notes

1. It is also important to recognize how bias toward one modality of language communication might affect users of other modalities – for example, having a spoken language bias might discourage use of sign language in deaf children born to hearing parents.
2. Flake and Fried (2020) discuss the challenges of terminology in the context of measurement (p. 461): "Transparency regarding the (theoretical and operational) definition of the construct – as well as regarding the motivation for selecting a measure – helps prevent thinking that two instruments measure the same construct because they have similar names (i.e., the *jingle fallacy*) or assuming that two measures assess different constructs because they have different names (i.e., the *jangle fallacy*)." Trying to be clear about definitions can help avoid at least some of the jingle-jangle confusion.
3. Like many things in science, the truth is actually a bit more complicated. Historically, most categorical perception experiments of the type I have described in the text have used what is often referred to as a "two-alternative forced-choice" (2AFC) procedure. In other words, on every trial, the participant is forced to make a choice from among two options. In contrast, Kong and Edwards (2016) used

a continuous measure of categorical perception by using a visual analog scale. Participants were given a line with endpoints marked for two choices (for example, "d" and "t"). After hearing a speech token listeners were instructed to click anywhere on the line to indicate how close the sound was to a "da" or a "ta." The authors found that responses were generally consistent with a gradient representation (rather than a strict categorical representation), and that individual listeners differed in their degree of gradiency. Kapnoula and colleagues (2017) extend this work, though also finding generally similar results across visual analog scale and 2AFC versions of phoneme categorization tasks. A comprehensive discussion of issues of gradiency in speech perception is found in Apfelbaum and colleagues (2022). Despite these nuances, given that speech sounds and words are limited in number, the importance of speech categories is not going away any time soon.

4. Although some people tend to talk more quickly than others, speech rate can vary over the course of a conversation even for a single talker. Miller and colleagues (1984) found substantial variability within and across thirty different talkers, even within a single conversation (on the order of hundreds of milliseconds per syllable). Stine and colleagues (1990) measured speaking rate of TV shows, which ranged from 101 to 191 words per minute (of course, current norms may differ from what was true in 1990).

   On a somewhat related note, Mehl and colleagues (2007) investigated whether there are gender differences in the number of words produced, given long-standing assumptions that women are more talkative than men. They used an electronically activated voice recorder to sample speaking in 396 talkers and found that over the course of a day women in their sample spoke an average of 16,215 words, and men 15,669 words – a negligible (and not statistically significant) difference.

5. Where electronic media are concerned, of course, listeners often *do* have the opportunity to go back and experience something again. And even in live conversations, listeners also have some tools at their disposal for slowing a speaker down, such as social cues (looking grumpy or confused) or asking the speaker to slow down or repeat themselves. The main point here is that these options are not always available, and in many instances are impractical (at a lecture or a large classroom, listeners are typically at the mercy of the speaker). The situation for speech thus fundamentally differs from that for reading, where the ability to reread text is the norm (not the exception).

6. The Oxford English dictionary defines lour as: "To frown, scowl; to look angry or sullen."

7. As related by Merriam-Webster, *cromulent* first appeared on *The Simpsons* on February 18, 1996, in the episode titled "Lisa the Iconoclast." Some of the schoolchildren are watching a film about Jebediah Springfield, the founder of their town, which ends with him saying solemnly: "A noble spirit embiggens the smallest man." One teacher comments to another that she had never heard the word "embiggen" before moving to Springfield, to which the other teacher replies: "I don't know why. It's a perfectly cromulent word."

8. Reading also happens rapidly, and readers are notoriously efficient at using prediction and context to facilitate rapid language processing. My point here is just to highlight unique aspects of listening.

9. I spent part of my PhD researching adaptation to time-compressed speech (Peelle and Wingfield, 2005). In that work, we played people speech that was over 600 words per minute, resulting in rather poor intelligibility. However, we found that over the course of about 20 sentences, young adult listeners improved their understanding from about 20 percent correct to 40 percent correct (older adults improved somewhat less). This finding sparked my interest in perceptual flexibility and how we might be able to use this to improve communication success.

10. Estimating vocabulary size is fundamentally a tricky thing to do, as it is impractical to ask people to list all the words they know (even if they could list them all – which they couldn't). There are also challenges with definitions of "vocabulary" and what it means to "know" a word (and even what a "word" is). Brysbaert and colleagues (2016) attempt to clarify some of these issues and estimate that a 20-year-old native speaker of American English knows about 42,000 words. But other researchers (using different approaches and/or definitions) estimate anywhere from 16,000 to 200,000 words (D'Anna et al., 1991).

11. In the context of visual processing, Kinchla and Wolfe (1979) have proposed "middle-out" processing that relates to the specific properties of a stimulus. In many cases, it indeed seems that our perceptual systems act flexibly depending on the specific task we are doing.

12. Although the corpus callosum is the *primary* means to transfer information between the left and right hemispheres, there are other white matter tracts and subcortical connections that also allow information to reach both hemispheres even without a corpus callosum. However, these pathways are smaller and less efficient.

13. Vaddiparti and colleagues (2021) provide a history of callosotomy, noting that the first callosotomy was performed in 1936 by Walter Dandy. However, the first callosotomy for management of epilepsy was performed in 1939 at Strong Memorial Hospital in Rochester, New York, by William P. van Wagenen (1897–1961), chair of neurosurgery at the University of Rochester. He had hypothesized that severing the corpus callosum might control epilepsy based on observations in earlier patients. As noted by Mathews and colleagues (2008), van Wagenen was assisted by Andrew J. Akelaitis, a psychiatrist who evaluated patients' pre- and postoperative functioning. In the 1960s, Roger Sperry and Michael Gazzaniga (a PhD student of his) spearheaded a series of experiments on patients who underwent callosotomies, using sophisticated testing to reveal differences in processing between information available to the left and right hemisphere (e.g., Gazzaniga et al., 1962, 1965). In 1981 Sperry shared the Nobel Prize in Physiology (with David Hubel and Torsten Wiesel) for his work on split-brain patients.

Further Reading

Gazzaniga MS, Bogen JE, and Sperry RW (1965) Observations on visual perception after disconnexion of the cerebral hemispheres in man. *Brain* 88: 221–236.
> Example of studying differing biases of the left and right hemisphere by studying patients with a severed corpus callosum.

Holt LL, Peelle JE (2022) The auditory cognitive neuroscience of speech perception in context. In: *Speech Perception* (Springer Handbook of Auditory Research, vol. 74) (Holt L, Peelle J, Coffin A, Popper A, Fay R, eds.), pp. 1–12. Springer. http://doi.org/10.1007/978-3-030-81542-4_1.
> Provides a brief historical overview of approaches to studying speech perception, and the opportunities that come from studying speech from a neuroscientific perspective.

Poeppel D (2012) The maps problem and the mapping problem: two challenges for a cognitive neuroscience of speech and language. *Cognitive Neuropsychology* 29:34–55. https://doi.org/10.1080/02643294.2012.710600.
> Lays out several challenges facing researchers interested in understanding the neuroscience of language, including how to formulate formal links between fields that do not have a large, shared vocabulary.

CHAPTER TWO

Methods of Cognitive Neuroscience

To appreciate the experiments that inform our understanding of how the brain processes language, we need to understand something about how the data are collected. Although many behavioral approaches also feature heavily in the neuroscience of language, these frequently rely on tasks that are fairly easy to intuitively understand (such as pressing a button when a target is heard, indicating whether a sentence is grammatically correct, or providing a definition for a word). By contrast, most people do not have an intuition for how we measure human brain activity, nor what the limitations and advantages of different methods are. This chapter provides a general introduction to the main methods of human neuroscience that appear throughout the remainder of the book. However, before we understand how to measure activity in brain *regions*, we first look at how individual neurons communicate.

2.1 The Neuron and the Action Potential

Neurons are the cells in the brain primarily responsible for processing, storing, and communicating information. Although we don't have space for a full treatment of how neurons function, a basic understanding is very useful for understanding what types of brain signals human neuroscience methods can measure (and what types they can't).

There are something on the order of 86 billion neurons in a human brain,[1] composed of several subtypes that have different properties and functions. However, because human brain imaging is not able to differentiate these cell types, we won't cover them here.[2]

A typical neuron is shown in Figure 2.1. A neuron's function is strongly influenced by electrical charges (specifically, the difference in electrical charge between the inside of the neuron and outside of the neuron, or **membrane potential**). Processes called **dendrites** receive inputs from other cells, which affect the electrical charge in the *cell body*. Inputs can be excitatory (raising the membrane potential) or inhibitory (lowering the membrane potential). The inputs have the most effect on the **axon hillock**, located at the transition of the cell body to the **axon**, a long projection from the cell body. When a neuron receives enough

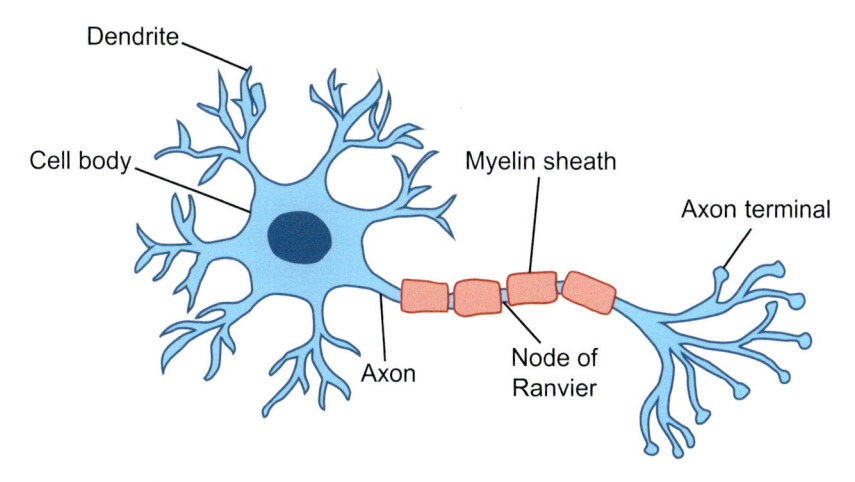

Figure 2.1 Schematic of a neuron. Dendrites receive signals from presynaptic cells; these signals are integrated in the cell body. If a sufficient number of excitatory signals are received, an action potential is triggered, which travels down the axon away from the cell body. When the action potential reaches the axon terminal, a signal is sent across the synapse to a postsynaptic cell (not shown). https://osf.io/geqb6/ (CC-BY).

excitatory input, it fires an **action potential**, an electrical signal that travels down the axon of the neuron and sends a signal to another neuron.[3]

In vertebrates (including humans), axons are surrounded by **myelin**, a fatty material that wraps around the axon and acts to electrically insulate it. The insulating properties of myelin mean that electrical current can travel further given the tiny diameter of the axon than would be possible without insulation. Because it is fatty, myelin appears white to the naked eye, and thus axon bundles are referred to as **white matter**. Cell bodies, which lack myelin, appear gray, and are referred to as **gray matter**. Ion channels are concentrated in the **nodes of Ranvier**, spaces between myelin where the membrane is relatively exposed.

The connection between two communicating neurons is called a **synapse**, and neurons can therefore be classified as presynaptic (the "sending" neuron) and postsynaptic (the "receiving" neuron). Neurons do not physically touch; there is a space, called the **synaptic gap**, between them. The signal between neurons is most often sent by releasing a chemical known as a **neurotransmitter** from the end of the presynaptic neuron, which travels across the synaptic gap before being taken up by the dendrites of the post-synaptic neuron, where it affects the membrane potential. Neurons thus typic-ally communicate through a combined electrical-chemical signal, occurring at dizzyingly fast speeds and with meticulous precision. It is important to recognize how densely interconnected neurons are in the brain: A neuron does not receive input from one or two presynaptic cells, but from thousands. This allows a single neuron's activity to reflect the activity of many thousands of cells due to how it integrates the inputs it receives.

Because of the necessity of the action potential to initiate communication with another cell – that is, it is the action potential that triggers neurotransmitter release – action potentials are integral to neural processing. However, they are not the only signal that can be measured, and complementary signals may reflect complementary processes. For example, the **local field potential (LFP)** reflects the average membrane potentials across a large population of neurons, and fluctuations in LFPs play an important role in coordinated neural activity.

As neurons are more active they require more oxygen, which is provided through blood vessels that proliferate throughout the brain. Thus, as neural activity increases, more blood flow is needed to keep up. To be efficient, blood flow does not change equally over the entire brain, but in a regionally specific way: That is, if one area of the brain is very active, blood flow increases to that area, but not elsewhere.[4] Because the parts of the brain where neurons are more active strongly correlate with changes in blood flow, the blood flow response (usually called the **hemodynamic response** – *hemo* for blood and *dynamic* because it's changing) can be used as a proxy for brain activity (see Section 2.2.4).

2.2 Methods of Human Neuroscience

In this section I review the primary methods used to study the structure and function of the human brain. You will encounter these methods throughout the book and may wish to refer back to this section to remind yourself about them. Before getting into specific methods, though, let's first look at the types of information various techniques can provide.

2.2.1 Spatial and Temporal Resolution

No brain imaging method is perfect; each has advantages and disadvantages. One useful way to think about how to categorize different methods is to consider each approach's spatial and temporal resolution. **Spatial resolution** refers to the size of the "units" that can be distinguished. For example, a neuron is approximately 10 microns in diameter. A method with 10 micron spatial resolution would be able to distinguish different neurons from each other; a method with 15 cm spatial resolution would only get a single picture of the

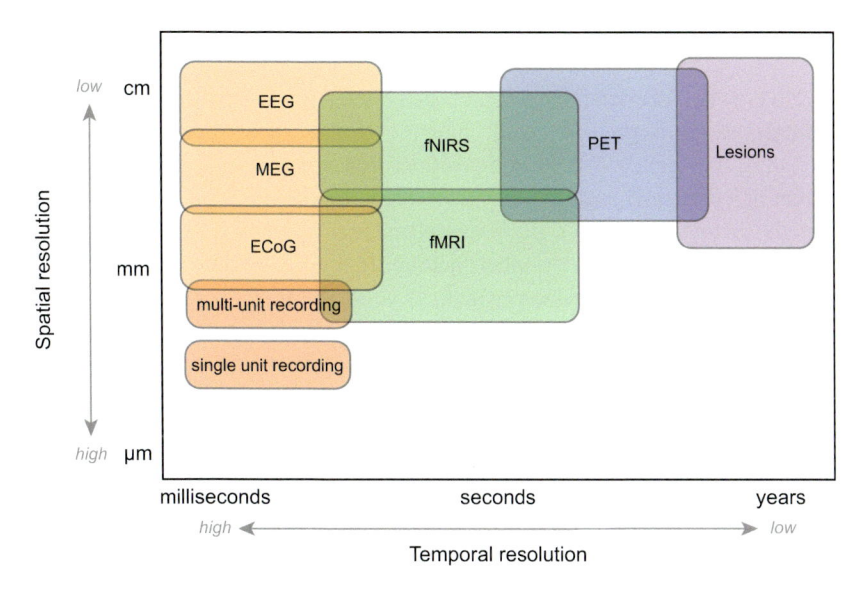

Figure 2.2 Methods in human neuroscience offer many tradeoffs, including in spatial and temporal resolution, as illustrated by this schematic. https://osf.io/geqb6/ (CC-BY).

entire brain. (Approaches for human brain imaging all lie between these two extremes.)

Temporal resolution mirrors this idea, but with respect to time rather than space. A method with millisecond temporal resolution would be able to distinguish brain events occurring milliseconds apart; one with a temporal resolution of three seconds would not (but would be able to distinguish events occurring many seconds apart).[5]

Because different types of functional brain imaging capture different signals, they vary in their spatial and temporal resolution, illustrated schematically in Figure 2.2 (some version of which appears in nearly every cognitive neuroscience textbook). Although it's an imperfect relationship, many people conceive of popular functional brain measurements as being better at spatial resolution, but having relatively poor temporal resolution (for example, functional magnetic resonance imaging [fMRI]), or having better temporal resolution, but relatively poor spatial resolution (for example, **electroencephalography [EEG]** and **magnetoencephalography [MEG]**). As you go through the selection of methods it is worth thinking about where each method falls on this figure, and what consequences this might have for our understanding of the brain.

2.2.2 Structural Brain Imaging

As covered in more detail in the next chapter, there is a link between anatomical features of the brain and neural function that is evident on many levels, including the brain's overall composition. For example, the amount of gray matter in a particular region of the brain might depend on some combination of genetic factors, a person's life experience, and whether they have had any neurological disease (among other factors). If it turns out the amount of gray matter relates to brain function (which, as you will see, it does), then knowing about the structural characteristics of the brain can inform us about its function.

Historically – that is, before the middle of the twentieth century – it was only possible to look at brain structure by examining the brain directly after some-one was dead. Take, for example, the famous neurologist Paul Broca (1824–80) (also discussed in Chapter 3). Broca famously had a patient who had difficulty producing speech, and Broca was interested in how language function was organized in the brain. But it wasn't until after the patient passed away that Broca was able to visually examine the patient's brain, and link what he saw about the location of the patient's brain damage to the behaviors Broca had observed. Over the last century, tremendous technological advances have provided us with the ability to noninvasively look at brain structure. In particu-lar, noninvasive structural brain imaging has provided the opportunity to get more rapid access to information about brain structure in a greater number of people. In addition, different types of structural brain imaging have also provided types of information not visible with the naked eye, opening up new avenues for linking brain structure and behavior.

One of the first imaging techniques for measuring brain structure was **computed tomography (CT)** scanning, developed in the 1970s.[6] In a CT scan (sometimes referred to as a "cat" scan), X-rays are sent from a tube toward the body, and a set of detectors measure what passes through the body. The X-ray tube rotates and the information from different angles can then be reconstructed to produce a virtual three-dimensional image.[7] Computed tom-ography scans produce images that are poorer resolution than can be obtained with more modern structural magnetic resonance imaging (MRI) approaches. However, they are still used in many clinical contexts and are possible to collect even in people who cannot get an MRI (for example, because of an implanted medical device).

Developed in the 1970s and 1980s, MRI has long been the core technique for structural brain imaging.[8] Structural MRI images (Figure 2.3) generally pro-vide high spatial resolution (around 1 mm × 1 mm × 1 mm), and sufficient image contrast to distinguish different tissue types found in the brain (including gray matter, white matter, and cerebrospinal fluid). There are many different

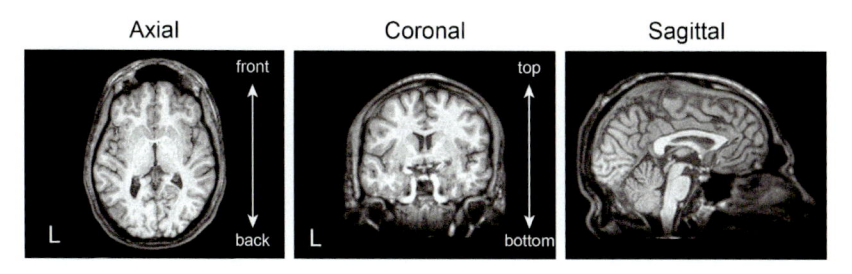

Figure 2.3 An example structural MRI image in three views: axial (viewed from the top), coronal (viewed from the back), and sagittal (viewed from the side). This example shows a T1-weighted MRI image on which gray matter is darker than white matter. Cerebrospinal fluid (CSF) is black. https://osf.io/geqb6/ (CC-BY).

types of structural brain images, but the most common is a T1-weighted image (the name referring to a specific property of the signal being measured).

For cognitive neuroscientists, the primary contribution of structural brain imaging is that it helps establish a link between brain and behavior. There are various terms for this; I typically use **lesion-symptom mapping** to describe the process of relating brain damage to changes in behavior. However, linking brain structure and behavior does not require "damage" but can also be done using individual variability in various brain structures. As with most other applications of human brain imaging, such an approach relies on strong assumptions about the regional localization of cognitive function (covered in detail in the next chapter). **Cortical thickness analysis** and **voxel-based morphometry** are both approaches that look at regional differences in gray matter, for example in relation to demographic factors (such as age or sex), clinical profiles (patients vs. controls), or cognitive/behavioral measures (for example, memory ability). Across many domains, greater amounts of gray matter in specific regions are associated with differences in behavioral performance. Thus, structural brain imaging provides a way to quantify relationships between various aspects of brain structure in helping understand the link between environment, genes, and behavior.[9]

Given that neurons communicate with each other by sending information along axons, the path that axons take has been of great interest to neuroscientists. Two common questions are (1) where do axons go?, and (2) how healthy is an axon? A method useful for answering both of these is diffusion-weighted imaging (DWI), developed in the 1980s. Although there are many types of DWI, perhaps the most common is **diffusion tensor imaging (DTI)** (Figure 2.4). Diffusion-weighted imaging capitalizes on the fact that axons

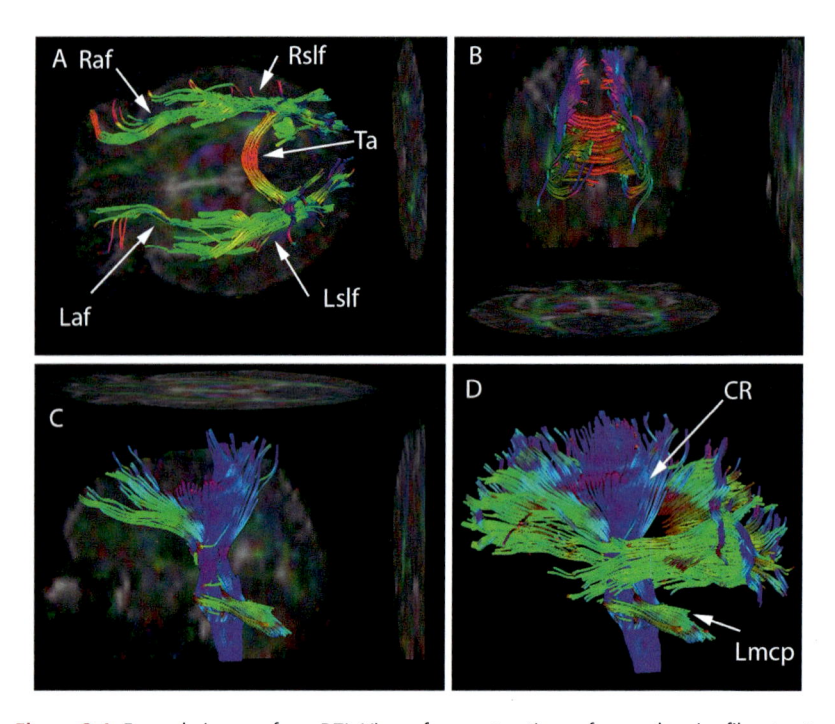

Figure 2.4 Example images from DTI. View of reconstructions of several major fiber tracts based on diffusion imaging, displayed with slices showing colorized maps. By convention colors indicate direction of the tract (green: anterior-posterior; blue: superior-inferior; red: left-right). Regions include right arcuate fasciculus (Raf), left arcuate fasciculus (Laf), right superior longitudinal fasciculus (Rslf), left superior longitudinal fasciculus (Lslf), coronal radiation (CR), and left middle cerebellar peduncle (Lmcp). Courtesy of Dr. Aaron Filler and distributed under a Creative Commons Attribution-Share Alike 3.0 Unported license.

are surrounded by myelin, a lipid-rich material that is hydrophobic (it repels water). Diffusion tensor imaging uses MRI to estimate the movement of water molecules. If nothing is in the way of a water molecule, it doesn't stay perfectly still but moves about randomly in three dimensions.[10] (One term for being equal size in all directions is *isotropic*, which will come in useful shortly.) Because axons are hydrophobic, however, water molecules tend not to diffuse across axons, but tend to move *along* the axon. The level of isotropy (or lack of isotropy; *anisotropy*) of water molecules can therefore provide an indirect measure of white matter in the brain. A commonly derived measure from DTI is **fractional anisotropy (FA)**, which simply quantifies the degree to which movement in a voxel is not isotropic; higher FA values correspond to more directional motion, which we interpret as reflecting more myelin. Fractional anisotropy values are thus often interpreted as reflecting white matter "integrity," and are lower in patients with diseases known to affect myelin. The process of estimating where axons go is called *tractography* and relies on a computer models that fits the direction of movement across multiple voxels. White matter tracts defined with DTI are not actually individual axons but instead reflect the likely position of bundles of axons. (Single axons are too small to be identified with DTI, which commonly has a voxel size of 2 × 2 × 2 mm. However, tractography images such as those in Figure 2.4 may evoke connotations of individual axons.)

2.2.3 Functional Measures of Electrical and Magnetic Activity

It is probably intuitive that if a substantial part of brain signaling relies on electric activity then measuring electrical changes in the brain can tell us something about neural function. An electrode is simply something that conducts electricity; when connected to a meter, it can be used to measure electrical current. From a measurement standpoint, the most straightforward way to measure brain activity is to insert an electrode directly into the brain. Tiny electrodes have long been used for single-cell recordings, either by placing them on or near a neuron (extracellular recording) or penetrating the cell wall and recording electrical activity inside the cell (intracellular recording).

Unfortunately, inserting an electrode into the brain tends to damage brain cells, and thus is not done in human studies unless clinically necessary. One area of medicine which has historically required detailed recordings of brain activity for clinical purposes is epilepsy. **Epilepsy** refers to a group of neurological disorders characterized by recurring seizures, reflecting periods of abnormal electrical activity in the brain. Epileptic seizures can interfere with normal brain activity, including motor control and other cognitive functions. For many people, epilepsy is well controlled with medication. However, in cases where medications are not able to control seizures, surgically removing the part of the brain where the seizure originates can sometimes be an effective treatment. Thus, it is important to accurately identify both the part of the brain where seizures originate and also parts of the brain responsible for abilities such as language, damage to which should be avoided during surgery. One approach for performing this kind of brain mapping involves placing electrodes on the surface of the brain (or occasionally, using depth electrodes that go deeper into the brain). **Electrocorticography (ECoG)**, also known as intracranial EEG (iEEG), refers to data collected in this manner. Electrodes are inserted through a surgical hole in the skull and placed on the surface of the brain in the area the neurosurgeon needs to study. The spatial localization of ECoG is therefore relatively good in that, because the electrodes are directly on the surface of the brain, signals are strongest from the electrode nearest to brain activity being measured. The spatial resolution depends not only on how closely spaced the electrodes are but on the degree to which electrical activity travels through the brain. The spatial resolution of ECoG is typically considered to be on the level of several millimeters. The temporal resolution is also excellent, typically 250–1,000 Hz (1 Hz = 1 sample per second; 1,000 Hz = 1,000 samples per second = 1 sample every millisecond).

One disadvantage of ECoG is that only limited portions of the brain can be simultaneously measured. Electrode placement is driven by clinical needs; typically, the general region where seizure activity is suspected is already known, and electrodes are placed there. So, for example, in one patient electrodes might cover the left lateral temporal lobe, but not anywhere else; in a second patient, they might perhaps cover portions of the frontal cortex and part (but not all) of the temporal lobe. Thus, to characterize activity across the entire brain, data must be combined from many patients. However, even then, in two patients with the "same" region covered, the electrodes are likely not placed in *identical* locations, and combining data across participants is therefore not always straightforward. In practice, ECoG data is nearly always restricted to some portion of the brain.

A final caution in interpreting ECoG data is that it typically comes from patients who have severe epilepsy (or other brain disorder necessitating invasive electrical recording). Years of prolonged abnormal brain activity is likely to have caused some reorganization in the brain, and so, in theory, results obtained from ECoG may not match what would be obtained in a neurologically healthy person (were we able to record from their brain). However, it is standard practice to exclude data from electrodes that show seizure-related or otherwise abnormal activity, and ECoG localization commonly matches that identified using other methods. So, although in theory we need to be careful about assuming that patient findings are also true in neurologically healthy people, in most cases conclusions about localized activity identified with ECoG indeed seem to generalize very well.

By far the most common approach to measuring electrical brain activity in humans is **electroencephalography (EEG)** (Figure 2.5). Rather than placing electrodes on the surface of the brain (as in ECoG), in EEG electrodes are placed on the scalp. Because the head conducts electrical current, electrical activity in the brain can be detected from these scalp electrodes. Typical EEG systems have between 32 and 128 electrodes spread out evenly over the participant's head. Hair is not very electrically conductive (that is, electricity

a)

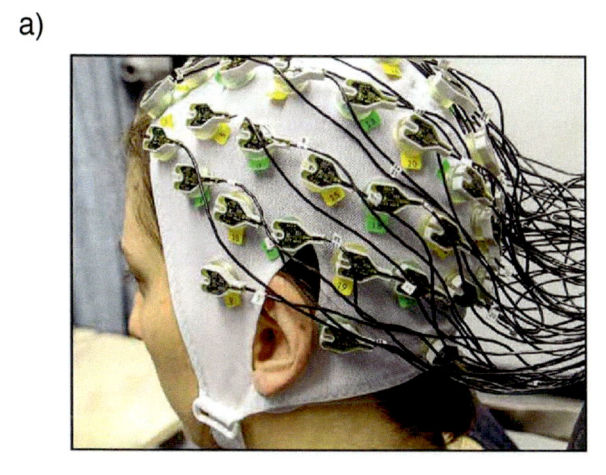

b)

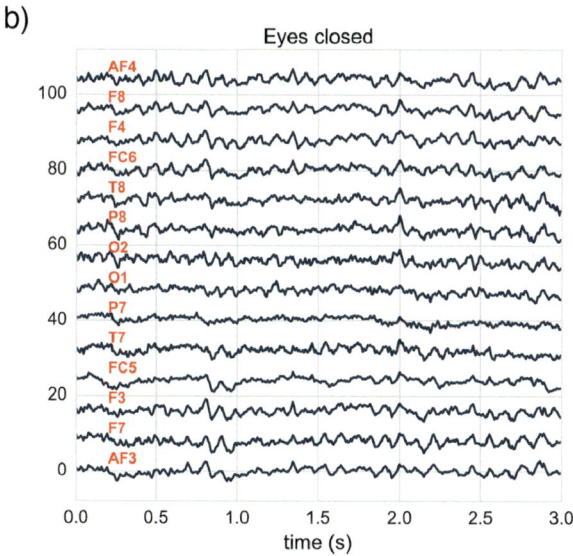

Figure 2.5 Electroencephalography. (a) EEG cap with electrodes (Pacharra et al., 2017, CC-BY). (b) Example recordings from 24 EEG channels (Morán and Soriano, 2018, CC-BY).

does not flow through hair easily), so most systems use either a conductive gel or saline solution on a participant's head to help the electrode get a strong signal. Electroencephalography has excellent temporal resolution, typically sampling the brain's electrical activity at a rate between 250 and 1,000 Hz.

A significant challenge for traditional EEG is **source localization**: That is, given the pattern of electrical current detected across electrodes, what is the part of the brain – or the parts of the brain – responsible for the signal? You might think this is straightforward, because surely the electrodes (also called channels) with the strongest signal are going to be nearest the part of the brain generating the signal. However, electrical current spreads through conductive surfaces, including the scalp. The current spread means that any given electrode might be picking up a signal from a distant brain source. In fact, the **inverse problem** in EEG refers to the fact that any given pattern of electrical activity detected at the scalp could arise from multiple underlying patterns of brain activity: Mathematically there is no single solution. (For a simple example, imagine you have a microphone which you use to record a faint beep. Did you capture something making a soft beep right next to the microphone, or a very loud beep that happened far away? The loudness of the recording, alone, can't tell you.[11]) There are three common solutions to this challenge. One is to use topographical patterns of activity to infer localization. For example, if I play a short beep, and see an EEG response that has a particular spatial pattern, I might conclude (reasonably) that this pattern reflects activity in auditory parts of the brain. If I do another task, and see the same pattern, I might then interpret the result as "auditory" activity. Although the logic makes sense, the "topological pattern" approach is not foolproof – we already know that different patterns of brain activity can give rise to similar patterns of scalp-measured electrical activity. Other approaches actually try to provide a quantitative estimate of where the brain activity underlying EEG data is located – often called a "source" or a "generator" – based on the EEG data itself (possibly with the aid of structural brain information). These methods may model one or more explicit generators or provide distributed estimates of where generators would likely reside.[12] Although the inverse problem means that the source of EEG signals is always somewhat uncertain, the spatial resolution can generally be considered on the scale of centimeters.

One interesting property of electricity is that electric currents induce magnetic fields – specifically, in a direction perpendicular to that of the electric current. If you have taken physics you might remember the "right hand rule": Imagine placing your right hand around a wire carrying an electrical current. If you point your thumb in the direction of the current, the magnetic field around the wire flows in the direction your fingers point. **Magnetoencephalography** (Figure 2.6) takes advantage of these electrically induced changes in magnetic fields to indirectly measure brain activity. To do so, it uses tiny sensors – superconducting quantum interface devices (SQUIDs) – to detect small changes in the magnetic field around the brain. Current MEG devices require

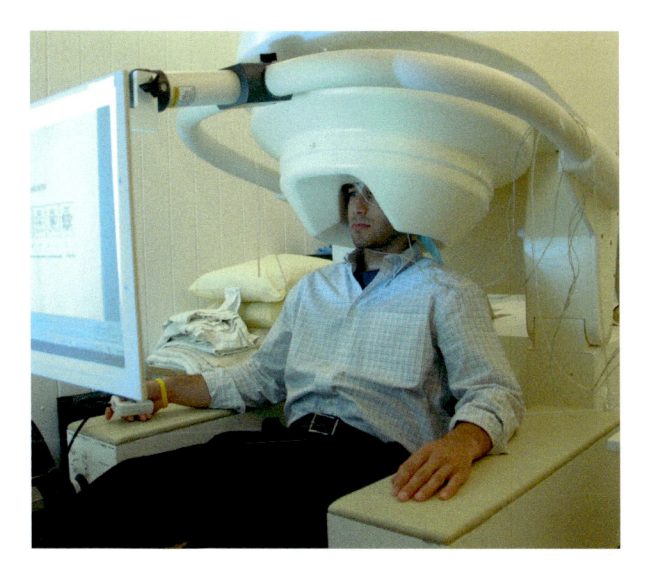

Figure 2.6 Magnetoencephalography (MEG). The sensors (SQUIDs) are contained in a cap around the participant's head. Courtesy of the National Institute of Mental Health, National Institutes of Health, Department of Health and Human Services.

SQUIDs to be supercooled using liquid helium (colder detectors are more sensitive to magnetic field changes).

Because the changes in magnetic field parallel changes in electrical activity, MEG measures a comparable signal to EEG and has a similar temporal resolution of 250–1,000 Hz. And, because the MEG sensors lie outside the head, similar to EEG, source localization is also a challenge for MEG, and deep sources are difficult (or impossible) to detect. However, there are some key differences between MEG and EEG. Notably, MEG relies on magnetic (rather than electric) fields. Unlike electric fields, which are affected by the skull and scalp, magnetic fields pass through unchanged. The reduced interference simplifies modeling for source localization and may provide more accurate estimates of sources than available for EEG. The spatial resolution of MEG is several millimeters to a centimeter.

2.2.4 Functional Measures of Blood Flow

Since the early 1990s **functional MRI (fMRI)** (Figure 2.7) has provided a means to measure local changes in blood flow corresponding to brain activity. (See Box 2.1.) The most common type of fMRI in research settings is usually

Raw fMRI data   Group fMRI results

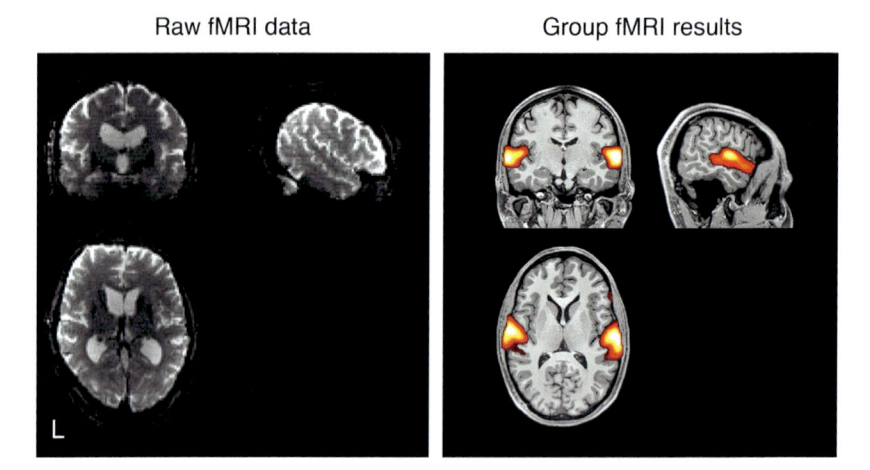

Figure 2.7 *Left:* A single volume (that is, a three-dimensional picture) of a brain acquired with fMRI. *Right:* A color map generated from statistically analyzing fMRI data from a task in which people heard spoken words, overlaid on top of a structural brain image. In displays of fMRI data, the color overlays typically reflect a statistical value, which is interpreted as brain activity. https://osf.io/geqb6/ (CC-BY).

Box 2.1 How closely do hemodynamic measures match neural activity?

In many fMRI studies – including all of those mentioned in this book – the researchers conducting the studies are primarily interested in neural activity. That is, answering the question: What part of the brain is engaged when someone is performing a particular task? The signal provided by fMRI or fNIRS is used as a proxy for neural activity. However, because methods that rely on blood flow, including fMRI, only *indirectly* assess brain activity, a common question is how similar blood-flow-related measures are to more direct measures of brain activity. In other words, how confident are we that fMRI signals reflect neural activity?

Electrophysiological measures have long been central to neuroscience, and the most accurate electrophysiological readings come from placing an electrode into the brain. Different types of electrodes can be used to measure signals such as single-unit activity (i.e., action potentials from a single neuron), multi-unit activity (action potentials from multiple neurons), or local field potentials (the summed electrical changes across a large number of neurons).

Box 2.1 (cont.)

Some of the most informative work linking hemodynamic and electrical measures is done using animals in which the two can be simultaneously recorded; researchers are then able to directly evaluate how closely various measures line up.

A foundational study in this regard was conducted by Niko Logothetis and colleagues (2001). They simultaneously recorded fMRI and electrical activity (single units, multi-unit activity, and local field potentials) from visual cortex while the monkeys were shown rotating checkerboard patterns (a stimulus that results in a strong visual response). The researchers also varied the contrast of the checkerboards (i.e., the difference between the light and dark patterns) to change the response (in prior studies, higher contrast was shown to produce a stronger neural response in visual cortex). The researchers found that, as expected, the visual stimulation resulted in changes to both the electrical and BOLD activity in visual cortex, and furthermore, that changing contrast altered both measures of activity. Interestingly, although all methods showed contrast-related changes, the BOLD activity changed to a lesser degree. In relating the different forms of electrical measurement to BOLD activity, the local field potentials were statistically the most strongly related. The take-home message was that BOLD activity was strongly related to, but not precisely identical to, electrical activity.

Many other studies have tried to further understand the relationship between electrical activity and the hemodynamic response. Generally speaking, there is good agreement between the two, but they are not perfectly related. So, in general it is a relatively safe assumption that fMRI data reflect underlying neural activity, with an awareness of some caveats. These findings highlight the importance of gathering converging evidence from multiple methods (for example, electrophysiology in addition to hemodynamic methods) to ensure our conclusions hold up. (See Box 2.2.)

blood oxygen level dependent (BOLD) fMRI; most of the time when not specified this is what researchers are using. Blood oxygen level dependent fMRI relies on the fact that the magnetic properties of oxygenated hemoglobin differ from those of deoxygenated hemoglobin. When regional blood flow changes in response to increased neural activity, the relative concentrations of oxygenated and deoxygenated hemoglobin change, which produces the BOLD signal. The spatial resolution of fMRI has gradually been improving over the past 20 years, from about 4 mm down to 2 mm; similarly, the speed at which an image

Box 2.2 Spatial scales of brain activity.

It is important to keep in mind the scale of brain activity measured by different approaches. For example, animal electrophysiology experiments might record from single neurons (single-unit data) or groups of neurons (multi-unit activity). Except for very rare instances where single-unit data is available in human neurosurgical patients, human functional brain imaging is limited to detecting changes of populations of neurons. That is, when a single neuron is active, it changes its electrical potential and corresponding magnetic field, and metabolic (and thus blood flow) demands – all of the methods we have discussed of measuring human brain activity. However, these changes are far too small to be detected with our current methods. Rather, the signals that we can detect reflect the coordinated activity of thousands and thousands of neurons. (Here "coordinated" simply means occurring about the same time, and typically at about the same place, in the brain.) This type of large-scale activity is often referred to as **population activity**.

The dependence of human functional brain imaging methods on coordinated population activity is a bit of a double-edged sword. On the one hand, it can make findings from human neuroscience difficult to directly relate to an enormous and well-developed history of studies in animals. The challenge is not only a technical one (comparing single-unit data to fMRI data, for example) but also a broader theoretical one: The types of questions that lend themselves to each class of measurements differ. For example, with access to single-neuron data, a researcher might be interested in the pattern of action potential firing (how "bursty" a neuron is); this level of detail is simply not available with noninvasive human methods, and thus not a question researchers tend to ask.

However, at the same time, there can also be *advantages* to measuring population-based brain activity. Hundreds of years of studies with people suffering brain damage (for example, due to a stroke) have cemented the idea that to at least a first approximation brain *regions* play important and dissociable roles in guiding behavior. That is, the coordinated activity of populations of neurons seems to underpin many complex behaviors. From this perspective, studying brain activity at the population level is a good match for behaviors we are often interested in understanding. A continuing challenge for all fields of neuroscience is to continue to better understand the mechanisms linking activity at these different scales.

of the brain can be acquired has also been improving, from 3–4 seconds per image to down to under 1 second, depending on scanning parameters. Though, it is worth considering the fact that the hemodynamic response is relatively slow (peaking about 5 or 6 seconds after neural activity), a fact that collecting data more rapidly does not change.

In addition to its ability to provide relatively good spatial localization, practical considerations have also helped fMRI to become, and remain, popular among researchers. For example, hospitals and medical centers typically have MRI scanners for clinical reasons, making them widely available (in contrast to other modalities, which are frequently only used for research). Magnetic resonance imaging is noninvasive and does not require any radiation. And, because an MRI scanner can provide many types of images (for example, a standard structural brain image, diffusion-weighted images, and functional images), researchers can collect converging types of information from a single machine during a single experiment.

Another method for measuring regional blood flow is optical brain imaging, most commonly **functional near-infrared spectroscopy (fNIRS)** (Figure 2.8). Light is directed into the head using one or more optical sources, and light exiting the head is measured using one or more detectors. The sources emit light of known wavelengths; some of this is absorbed by materials in the head, some of it diffuses, and some of it will travel through the head to exit again. Because different materials absorb light differently (depending, in part, on the wavelength), it is possible to reconstruct what the light passed through on its path between source and detector. Specifically, fNIRS and related methods focus on estimating oxygenated and deoxygenated hemoglobin – precisely the things that contribute to the BOLD signal in fMRI. Light emitted by optodes travels through the head in the shape of an arc (commonly described as a "banana"); thus, the deepest measurements are not directly under each optode, but at the peak of the arc. The spatial resolution of fNIRS thus depends on the number of optical sources and detectors, and how densely these are spaced.[13] The temporal resolution of fNIRS is on the order of 1–10 Hz (keeping in mind that, like fMRI, the underlying hemodynamic signal is relatively slow).

2.2.5 Noninvasive Brain Stimulation

Most of the methods reviewed in this chapter are concerned with *measuring* the structure or function of the brain. Another class of methods uncovers brain function by *altering* brain activity. If altering the activity of a particular brain region can change behavior – either by disrupting it or improving it – we have additional evidence supporting the link between brain and behavior.

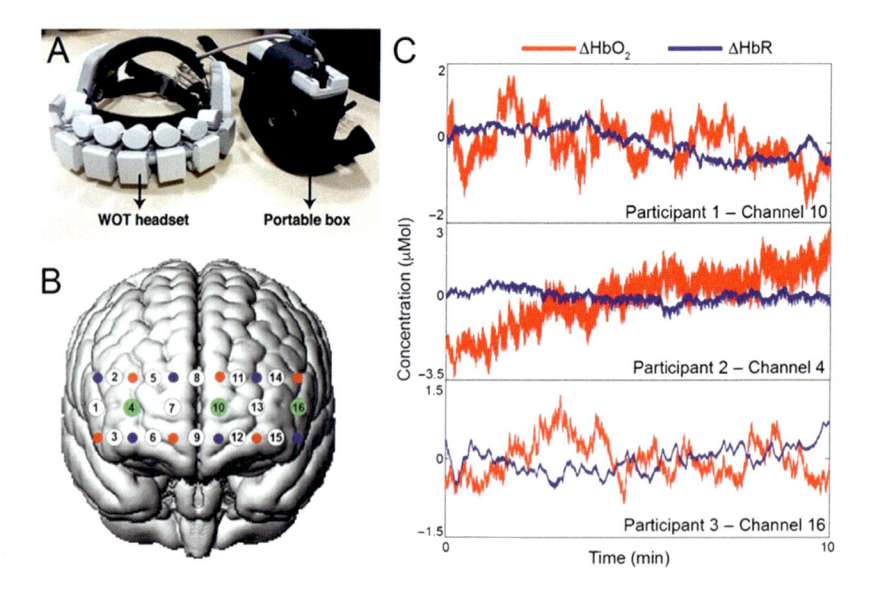

Figure 2.8 Functional near-infrared spectroscopy (fNIRS). (a) A Hitachi Wearable Optical Tomography (WOT) fNIRS device. (b) Sources (red dots) and detectors (blue dots), and channels (white dots) plotted over a model of the brain. (c) Raw signal for oxygenated hemoglobin (ΔHbO2, red) and dexoygenated hemoglobin (ΔHbR, blue) resting-state signals for one channel for each of three participants. From Pinti and colleagues (2019), CC-BY.

Perhaps the best-known method for noninvasive brain stimulation is **transcranial magnetic stimulation (TMS)**. TMS relies on the fact that a magnetic field can induce an electrical current. A magnetic coil is placed on the surface of the head; the magnetic field of the coil then affects electrical activity in the brain. The effects of TMS depend on the stimulation parameters (the strength, duration, and frequency of stimulation) and the brain region stimulated. Transcranial magnetic stimulation can be used to either excite or inhibit the activity of different brain regions. In many cases, TMS can be used to disrupt normal function, and is sometimes referred to as a "reversible lesion." Of course, this is not actually true – there is no damage or lesion caused – but conceptually, the link between a disrupted brain system and altered behavior complements measurements of brain activity.

Another approach to brain stimulation comes through **transcranial electric stimulation (tES)**, in which electrical current is used to stimulate the brain. To be noninvasive, this current is delivered to the scalp, and thus spreads considerably before impacting the brain. The voltages used are low enough to ensure safety. In tES, the electric current can be direct (**transcranial direct current stimulation; tDCS**) or alternating (**transcranial alternating current stimulation; tACS**). Different stimulation approaches can be used depending on the specific research question. Electric stimulation approaches can affect a broad range of language function and have also been used in the context of post-stroke rehabilitation.[14]

Noninvasive brain stimulation techniques face a challenge that electric current spreads through the scalp and brain, which is particularly relevant for tES. The part of the brain affected by stimulation can be estimated using current modeling, often in combination with a structural MRI scan of a participant.

2.3 Methodological Considerations

A deep dive into statistical considerations is beyond the scope of this book. At the same time, understanding the nuances and potential pitfalls of various approaches is essential for the field. In this section I briefly review a few key methodological points that may come in useful later.

Of course, no single study is perfect due to limitations in the experimental design, participants, and analysis method. The most solid findings are those that rely on **converging evidence** – that is, information from different approaches supporting a similar conclusion. For example, using fMRI we see that healthy adults engage Area X when performing a task; patients with damage to Area X have difficulty with this task; and training on this specific task alters the brain response in Area X. When these complementary sources of information seem to agree, particularly over and over, we can feel more confident in our conclusions. (See Box 2.3.)

One way to formalize "finding the same answer over and over" is through a **meta-analysis**, a formal comparison of the results of many studies. Meta-analyses are incredibly useful for the field, but also challenging to conduct.[15] When relating brain function to behavior, for example, it is rare that two different labs use completely identical experimental approaches. It can therefore be difficult to select studies that are similar enough to be combined, and if we are too selective in grouping studies, we may not have enough studies to provide an informative result. On the other hand, if we are not restrictive enough, we may get a statistical "answer" that is difficult to interpret (because of the variability in the studies we included).

One statistical error that is commonly encountered in both behavioral and brain imaging studies concerns the need to directly test whether two values are different using a statistical test (and not assume they are different based on intuition or visual inspection). For example, consider the pretend brain images in Figure 2.9. In condition A we see a large area of activity compared to a baseline condition, whereas in condition B we do not see any activity compared to baseline. We might thus be tempted to say something like, "There is more activity for condition A than for condition B." However, this is incorrect – in fact, we don't have any evidence comparing A and B.[16] Part of the issue is that most statistical tests incorporate not only the average values, but also the variability in the measurements. The average level may indeed be higher, but if there is a considerable amount of variability we may not be confident this result will hold up. The solution is simple: Directly compare conditions using a statistical test before moving on to interpret differences across conditions.

Condition A   Condition B

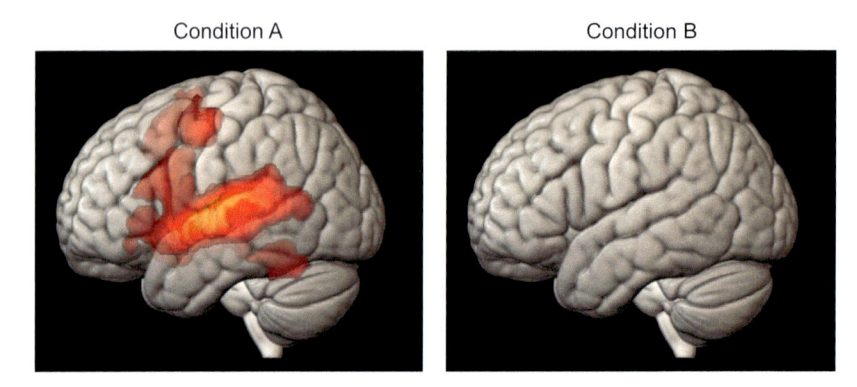

Figure 2.9 Although activity for different regions of the brain are shown for Condition A and Condition B, without a statistical test comparing them, we cannot say that the activity for conditions A and B is different. Available from https://osf.io/geqb6/ (CC-BY).

Box 2.3 Converging evidence regarding the neurobiology of language from patients with neurodegenerative disease.

Neurodegenerative diseases – the most well known of which is Alzheimer's disease – are conditions impairing brain function that worsen over time. Although the specific causes and mechanisms underlying these diseases are not fully understood, different conditions are associated with distinct patterns of brain damage, which result in specific behavioral changes. Alzheimer's disease, for example, is associated with damage to the hippocampus, a structure deep in the brain important for memory. As a result, memory difficulties are common in people with Alzheimer's disease.

Box 2.3 (cont.)

A family of diseases that have proven particularly revealing for language function fall under the umbrella of frontotemporal degeneration (FTD).[17] At the broadest level, patients with FTD can be classified as having a primary language impairment, or not. Those with a primary language impairment are diagnosed with primary progressive aphasia (PPA): *primary* because language impairments are a defining characteristic, and *progressive* because – unlike patients with post-stroke aphasia – the condition will continue to worsen.[18] Patients with PPA are grouped according to two specific subtypes. Those with nonfluent speech and production difficulties are termed nfvPPA (nonfluent variant PPA); others have fluent speech but difficulty remembering concepts and word meanings (semantic variant PPA, or svPPA).

Patients with FTD but *not* PPA often have difficulties with executive function (including decision-making and inhibition), as well as adhering to social conventions (for example, taking one's clothes off in public or using rude gestures, when these were not typical behaviors before FTD). This variant of FTD is often called behavioral variant FTD (bvFTD) (in earlier years, also sometimes called social/executive FTD because of the frequent difficulties with social comportment and executive function). However, people with bvFTD also exhibit language difficulties. These can be on a pragmatic level (for example, difficulty taking turns in a conversation) or a more subtle linguistic level (for example, executive difficulty interfering with understanding the theme of a story).[19]

Critically, these different subgroups of patients have different characteristic patterns of brain damage, illustrated in Figure 2.10. Patients with nfvPPA have damage to the left inferior frontal gyrus and surrounding regions (more on this in Chapter 4 and Chapter 8), patients with svPPA have damage to the left temporal lobe (see Chapter 7), and patients with bvFTD have damage to dorsolateral prefrontal cortex (typically not substantially involving the inferior frontal gyrus [IFG]).

Working to understand challenges faced by various populations – including people with neurodegenerative disease – is a two-way street. Better understanding the nature of the challenges caused by neurodegenerative processes can be useful in helping patients, caregivers, and health professionals manage care and set expectations. Specifically for patients with language difficulty, the type of language challenge and prognosis might affect the type of communication support needed.[20] At the same time, understanding the challenges faced by patients – particularly when the pattern of damage to their brain is also known – informs our basic understanding of how the brain supports complex behavior (which may, or may not, directly inform patient care). These complementary facets of clinical research are frequently what compels many clinician scientists to pursue research in addition to direct patient care.[21]

Box 2.3 (cont.)

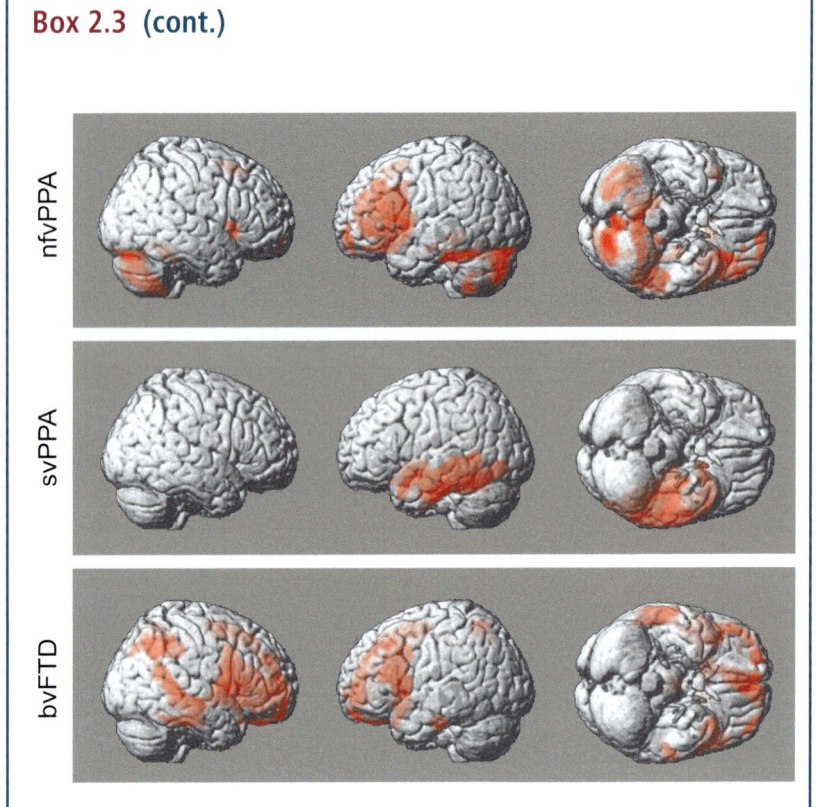

Figure 2.10 Distribution of brain damage in three subtypes of frontotemporal dementia:[22] nfvPPA – nonfluent variant of PPA; svPPA – semantic variant of PPA; bvFTD – behavioral variant of FTD. https://osf.io/geqb6/ (CC-BY).

2.4 Summary

- Neurons use a combination of electrical and chemical signaling to convey information. Neural activity is associated with signals relating to electrical activity, magnetic field changes, and changes in regional blood flow that can be detected with a variety of methodological approaches.
- Structural brain imaging approaches provide information on the shape and composition of the brain. The most common type of structural MRI is a so-called T1-weighted image, which distinguishes between different tissue

types (gray matter, white matter, cerebrospinal fluid). Diffusion-weighted imaging, including DTI, are more specific to white matter.

- Functional brain imaging approaches reflect activity in the brain over time that can be linked to a task (or to a period of rest). Common approaches that rely on electrical or magnetic properties of the brain include EEG, MEG, and ECoG; these have excellent temporal resolution but face challenges with spatial resolution. Measures that rely on blood flow – including fMRI, and fNIRS – have poorer temporal resolution due to the sluggish hemodynamic signal. Of these, functional MRI has the best spatial resolution.
- Noninvasive brain stimulation complements imaging techniques by allowing brain activity to be altered. Stimulation through the skull can be accomplished using either magnetic fields (TMS) or electric fields (tES). Because electrical signals travel, the part of the brain being stimulated can be estimated using models of electrical current.

Notes

1. Estimating the number of neurons in a brain is no small task. Azevedo and colleagues (2009) examined the brains of people who donated them to science when they died. The authors dissected the brain and used a process called the isotropic fractionator method to estimate the number of cells. In brief, the isotropic fractionator method uses chemicals and agitation to break down tissue into a suspension, after which the density of nuclei can be calculated under a microscope. Based on their findings, and the average size of a human brain, they estimated about 86 billion neurons (give or take a few billion). Their findings also suggest a proportion of neurons to non-neuronal cells similar to that found in nonhuman primates.

2. Perhaps the best-known early histologist documenting different cell types is Santiago Ramón y Cajal (1852–1934), a Spanish neuroscientist and histologist. His gorgeous drawings show intricate dendritic branching and overall morphology, or shape, of many types of neurons. He and Italian biologist Camillo Golgi (1843–1926) shared the Nobel Prize in Physiology or Medicine in 1906 "in recognition of their work on the structure of the nervous system."

3. I have dramatically oversimplified the exquisite mechanisms of how neurons go from rest to firing an action potential, because these dynamics are largely invisible to the methods used in human neuroscience. A comprehensive textbook on basic neuroscience, including action potentials, is *Principles of Neural Science* (Kandel et al., 2021).

4. The intricate link between neurons and the vascular system – *neurovascular coupling* – is reviewed by Iadecola (2017), who also provides an overview of the history of his field dating back to the nineteenth century. Perhaps the most intriguing

historical investigations come from Angelo Mosso (1880) and Roy and Sherrington (1890), who examined changes in brain volume related to blood flow (hinting at activity-related changes subsequently discovered). Sandrone and colleagues (2012, 2014) provide a detailed examination of the work of Mosso (1846–1910), an Italian physiologist who worked on "human circulation balance." Mosso hypothesized that mental activity could affect blood flow. To test this idea, he invented the plethysmograph, which could measure changes in cerebral blood flow using pulse variations in patients with skull defects (in other words, providing better access to the vascular system). Mosso's physiological recordings included balance (as in, human circulation balance), breathing, and pulse, and the recordings – for example, as reproduced in Sandrone and colleagues (2014) – look surprisingly modern. See also Drew (2022) for a discussion of why metabolic demands are unlikely to be the sole driving factor behind changes in blood flow.

5. In fact, the temporal resolution can refer to at least two things. The first is the sampling rate: how often data are collected. A definition based on sampling rate is the most straightforward way to think about temporal resolution and most commonly encountered. However, I don't always like this framing, because generally what we actually care about is the brain activity we are measuring (rather than the machine we happen to be using to measure it). So, a more useful perspective is to think about the temporal dynamics of the brain activity, and then decide whether we can capture this using a given approach. I sometimes call this the *effective* temporal resolution. Imagine that you have a snail gliding along from one wall of your room to the next and you would like to document its progress. You bring in an extra-high-frame video camera that captures 4,000 frames per second and film the snail. What is your temporal resolution? You might think 4,000 Hz (that is, 4,000 measurements per second), which is very good! But that doesn't actually help you measure the snail's progress any better than if you took one picture every second, because the snail moves so slowly. Your sampling rate is high, but you're not measuring the movement of the snail any more accurately. Applied to the brain, consider that a hemodynamic response that usually peaks about 5 seconds after a brain event, and returns to baseline about 10–12 seconds after the event. A typical fMRI sequence might capture one image of the brain every 2 seconds or so. If you increase this to every 1 second, or every 500 ms, are you going to learn a lot more about brain activity? If you could somehow sample the hemodynamic response every 1 ms (1,000 times per second, or 1,000 Hz), would you learn any more about brain activity? (Further complicating matters, different rates of sampling can be more sensitive not only to brain signals, but to noise signals . . . so you might actually get improved measurement because you are better able to identify, and ignore, artifacts, not because you are measuring the signal of interest any better.) My point in all of this is not so much that there is a right way or a wrong way to think about temporal resolution, but that it is important to consider both the brain imaging approach and the signal of interest when comparing temporal resolution. Understanding both of

these contributions goes some way toward understanding the advantages and disadvantages of different methods.

6. Allam Cormack and Godfrey Hounsfield were jointly awarded the 1979 Nobel Prize in Physiology or Medicine for "the development of computer-assisted tomography."

7. *Topography* refers to the study of surface features (think of a topographic map, which typically indicates terrain height using contour lines). *Tomography* refers to a three-dimensional reconstruction of an image using a series of two-dimensional slices or planes.

8. In 1973, Paul Lauterbur (1973) published "Image formation by induced local interactions: Examples employing nuclear magnetic resonance." He described how it was possible to use two magnetic fields to create an image of an object, and proposed the technique be called zeumatography (from the Greek ζευΥμα, "that which is used for joining"). To demonstrate feasibility, he showed two-dimensional images of two tubes of water. Although the term "zeumatography" didn't stick, nuclear magnetic resonance (NMR) imaging was nevertheless poised to usher in a revolution. Lauterbur and Peter Mansfield continued to develop these techniques and were awarded the 2003 Nobel Prize in Physiology or Medicine for "discoveries concerning magnetic resonance imaging."

9. One of the most famous examples in which researchers linked regional gray matter to behavior is informally referred to as the "London Taxi Cab study" (Maguire et al., 2000). The authors used structural MRI to look at gray matter in the hippocampus, a structure in the medial temporal lobe associated with memory and spatial navigation. They compared the volume of hippocampi in London taxi drivers with people who did not drive taxis. Critically, successfully driving a taxi in London (a city known for its complicated layout and large number of streets) requires drivers to remember a large amount of complex spatial information (and requires taxi drivers to pass an extensive test about navigating London's streets, called "The Knowledge"). The authors found that taxi drivers showed greater gray matter in the posterior hippocampus than controls, but less gray matter in the anterior hippocampus. These findings suggested that years of experience navigating a complex environment led to changes in the hippocampus, and more generally lent support for a relationship between gray matter and behavior.

10. The random movement of particles in a liquid or a gas is technically known as Brownian motion, named after Robert Brown (1773–1858), a Scottish botanist who discovered the phenomenon while viewing plant pollen in water (he was not viewing the pollen itself, but much smaller particles). For a more detailed discussion, see Pearle and colleagues (2010).

11. Yes, having multiple microphones will help, and, indeed, EEG has many electrodes ... but electrical activity spreads through the brain from potentially multiple sources at the same time, so, although having many electrodes can help, it does not completely solve the problem.

12. Michel and He (2019) provide a comprehensive overview of approaches to source localization, including dipole-based source localization and distributed source estimates.

13. An emerging flavor of fNIRS is high-density diffuse optical tomography (HD-DOT) (Eggebrecht et al., 2014). HD-DOT relies on closely spaced optodes that provide not only higher spatial resolution, but homogenous sensitivity over the field of view (White and Culver, 2010).

14. Price, McAdams, and colleagues (2015) conducted a meta-analysis to assess effects of tDCS on language processing, finding a significant effect across tasks including verbal fluency and novel word learning. Fridriksson and colleagues (2018) conducted a randomized clinical trial comparing the effects of anodal tDCS to sham stimulation in participants recovering from a stroke. Compared to sham, participants receiving tDCS showed a 70 percent improvement in picture-naming accuracy.

15. A particular hurdle for cognitive neuroscience has been the challenge of extracting data to include in a statistical analysis, given the nature of the results we usually care about. One common method has been manually identifying coordinates of peak activity in every included study, and using these peaks to crudely reconstruct 3D results maps (Laird et al., 2005). In recent years, automated methods for extracting data have radically changed the ease with which meta-analyses can be conducted, at a cost of some specificity about the studies that get included. Two examples are NeuroSynth (Yarkoni et al., 2011) and NeuroQuery (Dockès et al., 2020).

16. This error is so commonly made in cognitive neuroscience that it is sometimes referred to as the "imager's fallacy" (Henson, 2005).

17. Also sometimes referred to as frontotemporal lobar degeneration (FTLD). Historically, this family of syndromes was known as Pick's disease, after Arnold Pick (1851–1924), a Czech psychiatrist who is credited with the earliest observations of symptoms and pathology of FTD around the turn of the twentieth century. For more on FTD and local support resources, see the Association for Frontotemporal Degeneration (www.theaftd.org).

18. M.-Marsel Mesulam (2001) provides an overview of primary progressive aphasia and the primary subtypes, although certain aspects of our understanding have continued to evolve since that time.

19. Ash and colleagues (2006) took a clever approach to narrative production by asking people to describe the story of a wordless children's book (*Frog, Where Are You?* by Mercer Mayer). The stories told by healthy participants and those with FTD could be compared across a number of linguistic variables. One of the findings is that patients with social and executive problems (social/executive FTD) had trouble organizing the story. For example, failing to recognize the climax of the story when the boy (the protagonist, who has lost his frog early in the story) *finally* finds his frog.

20. As one example, Jamie Reilly and colleagues have been exploring whether extensive practice with a small set of words can prevent loss of word use in neurodegenerative disease (Flurie et al., 2020). The logic of these studies is that even if the disease progression cannot be slowed, the functional consequences of the disease for language may be minimized. Importantly, this treatment approach is informed by a basic understanding of the anatomical distribution of brain damage in

neurodegenerative disease, how this is likely to change over the course of the disease, and what parts of the brain support different types of language function.

21. A stellar example of this is found in the career of Murray Grossman (1952–2023), a mentor, collaborator, and friend. Murray earned his EdD (comparable to a PhD) in 1977 at the famed Boston VA Aphasia Research Center, followed by a postdoctoral fellowship at MIT. He obtained his medical degree from McGill University in 1985 and completed his residency at the University of Pennsylvania Department of Neurology, where he stayed. Throughout his career, Murray was deeply committed to patient care and understanding the neural basis of language. His lab was extraordinarily productive along many parallel fronts, including language, cognitive, histopathological, neuroimaging, and clinical investigations. Murray was a pioneer in not only understanding and treating neurodegenerative disease but also in patient advocacy, serving on the medical advisory council for the Association for Frontotemporal Degeneration and, in 2010, founding the Penn Frontotemporal Degeneration Center. I started working with Murray at the start of my PhD as part of a collaboration, followed by a postdoctoral fellowship in his lab. I continued to benefit from his advice and example for the rest of his life.

22. These are examples of brain damage in individual patients compared to healthy age-matched controls from Peelle and Grossman (2008). See also Gorno-Tempini and colleagues (2004) and Grossman and colleagues (2023).

Further Reading

Evans S, McGettigan C (2017) Comprehending auditory speech: previous and potential contributions of functional MRI. *Language, Cognition and Neuroscience* 32:829–846. https://doi.org/10.1080/23273798.2016.1272703.
    Introduction and overview of functional MRI in the context of speech and language processing.

Peelle JE (2017) Optical neuroimaging of spoken language. *Language, Cognition and Neuroscience* 32:847–854. https://doi.org/10.1080/23273798.2017.1290810.
    Introduction and overview of optical brain imaging in the context of speech and language processing.

Wilson SM (2017) Lesion-symptom mapping in the study of spoken language understanding. *Language, Cognition and Neuroscience* 32:891–899. https://doi.org/10.1080/23273798.2016.1248984.
    Introduction and overview of lesion-symptom mapping (using structural MRI) in the context of speech and language processing.

Wöstmann M, Fiedler L, Obleser J (2017) Tracking the signal, cracking the code: speech and speech comprehension in non-invasive human electrophysiology. *Language, Cognition and Neuroscience* 32:855–869. https://doi.org/10.1080/23273798.2016.1262051.
    Introduction and overview of EEG and MEG in the context of speech and language processing.

CHAPTER THREE

A Structural Foundation

Anatomical Considerations and Primary Brain Regions

Before getting into details of brain *function*, we'll need to first gain a working vocabulary of the brain and understand a few critical organizational principles and assumptions. I introduce these in the context of some key historical developments in language science. To some degree, the following historical threads are simply interesting (and you may well come across many of these ideas, and people, in other contexts). But perhaps more importantly, many ideas in modern cognitive neuroscience (including the neuroscience of language) flow directly out of this history. Being aware of the historical influences on modern thinking can help us better understand the reasons for some popular viewpoints, and – hopefully – also realize when a different framework might be warranted.[1] We will start by looking at the motivation and history behind language localization generally, before moving into specific terminology and anatomy related to human brain organization.

3.1 Why Do We Care about Localization?

Much of cognitive neuroscience has focused on understanding what parts of the brain support different kinds of tasks. The idea that cognitive functions can be specifically associated with one or more brain regions – which I refer to as **localization of function** – has a fascinating history with far-reaching effects throughout all of neuroscience (but perhaps especially human neuroscience).

If we agree that cognitive functions rely on specific brain areas, an important theoretical avenue is opened up for researchers, because anatomical location can now tell us something about how separable cognitive functions are. For example, let's say that I have a theory that knowledge about all objects is organized in a similar way in the brain, because most objects have features that need to be linked together. A dog has four legs, a tail, ears, and barks; a car has four tires, an engine, and drives; an apple is round, has seeds, and grows; and so on (more on word meanings is found in Chapter 7). I thus predict that similar cognitive processes support all of these different kinds of object knowledge.

Now imagine that I meet a patient who has had a stroke, and as a result has damage to part of their brain. If I find that they have difficulty understanding cars but not dogs, that suggests the part of their brain related to CAR was damaged and the part related to DOG was not (I use capital letters for concepts to indicate they are not just a word, but the entirety of the meaning associated with the concept). In other words, a different part of the brain was used for CAR than for DOG (which is why knowledge about one concept was preserved, and another impaired). Knowing that a different part of the brain is involved, I may rethink my hypothesis that CAR and DOG are treated the same by the brain. So, the difference in localization suggests at the very least a nonequivalence in how these types of information are treated, which then influences my cognitive theory about object knowledge. This type of reasoning would be impossible if cognitive functions weren't localized. It is the link between localization and cognitive theory that has so captivated researchers and kept brain "mapping" at the center of cognitive neuroscience for many decades.[2]

At this point, it is worth taking a deep breath and remembering that localization is not *equivalent* to function. Localization may tell us *about* function, but it is not the same thing. There is some nuance required to understand this distinction, but it is vitally important that we do so.[3]

Consider the previous example about how cars and dogs are represented in the brain, and the patient who has preserved knowledge about one but not the other. The patient's behavior tells us that CAR and DOG are not represented in the same anatomical location. But what about the *structure* of their storage? In other words, my theory was that objects have features that need to be linked together in some sort of hierarchy. For example, a DOG has fur, a tail, and four legs, and it is part of a larger group of MAMMALS which share additional features. Just because separate chunks of brain store information about cars and dogs doesn't tell me anything about the structure of the representation. It could be that, indeed, both CAR and DOG are stored in a hierarchical fashion (supporting my theory), but for whatever reason this happens to be implemented in two different parts of the brain. Alternatively, it could be that even if cars and dogs were stored in the *same* region of the brain, their storage is structured differently due to the specifics of how the brain is wired at the level of individual neurons. Some additional experiments, beyond simply observing a differential impairment in a person with brain damage, would need to occur for us to be confident about a difference between representations of CAR and DOG.

In practice, most cognitive neuroscientists indeed tend to view anatomical separation of two processes as indicating at some evidence for a different type of storage or processing, and I think this is generally a reasonable assumption. The critical (if subtle) point is that anatomical separation does not *actually* tell us about the structure of the representation – it's just a hint. I emphasize this point because a great deal of research, in language and other fields, has been focused on the anatomical localization of function, and it is a good exercise to consider to what degree these efforts have improved our understanding of the structure of representations and *how* they are processed.

3.2 A Brief Historical Overview of Localization of Language Function

Although language has played a starring role in developing ideas related to the localization of function, thinking about the brain and how it might be organized goes back well before the neuroscience of language takes center stage. To start with, the very importance of the brain to our body and mind is definitely not a modern idea. Perhaps the best-known early documentation is from the Edwin Smith Surgical Papyrus, written around 1600 BCE in Egypt[4] and named after the American Egyptologist who discovered it in 1862. The document describes a number of neurological cases and includes the first recorded use of the word "brain."[5] The Ancient Greeks also appreciated that the brain was a key organ for sensing and thinking. In *On the Sacred Disease*, Hippocrates (c. 470–360 BCE) wrote:

> Men ought to know that from nothing else but the brain come joys, delights, laughter and sports, and sorrows, griefs, despondency, and lamentations. And by this, in an especial manner, we acquire wisdom and knowledge, and see and hear, and know what are foul and what are fair, what are bad and what are good, what are sweet, and what unsavory; some we discriminate by habit, and some we perceive by their utility.

However, it was a long journey from appreciating the importance of the brain in a general sense to our contemporary understanding of how different functions are supported by different regions of the brain.[6] The modern story is most directly traced to **phrenology**: the study of human abilities using the shape of the skull.

3.2.1 Phrenology

Although phrenology came about in an environment in which many people were thinking about localization in the brain, Franz Joseph Gall (1758–1828) is generally considered the founder of phrenology.[7] In the 1790s Gall developed his system of phrenology,[8] and began offering lectures on it from his home in Vienna. Johann Spurzheim began attending Gall's lectures in 1800 and became a paid assistant in 1804. Gall and Spurzheim moved to Paris in 1807, where they jointly published papers outlining their approach – but parted ways in 1813. In the following decades, Spurzheim continued to lecture in Britain and elsewhere, inspiring George Combe, who took up the mantle of phrenology in Edinburgh (including founding the Edinburgh Phrenological Society).[9]

The basic tenets of phrenology included some version of the following:

1. The brain is the organ of the mind.
2. The mind is composed of multiple distinct, innate "faculties" (which today we might call a mental function or cognitive ability).
3. Each faculty must have a separate seat or "organ" in the brain (which today we might call a brain region).
4. Other things being equal, the size of an organ is a measure of its power.
5. Because the skull takes its shape from the brain, the surface of the skull can be read as an accurate index of mental aptitudes and tendencies.

In other words, measuring someone's skull will tell you about the underlying shape of their brain, and understanding the shape of their brain can tell you about different mental abilities.

The last stage of this – that the shape of the skull relates to the shape of the brain – is pure nonsense, and as a result, phrenology is routinely looked on with contempt by modern eyes. However, the preceding points are all present in modern cognitive neuroscience, where they are not looked on with contempt (at least, not by cognitive neuroscientists). The growing discussion regarding phrenology throughout the 1800s thus involved both the parts of phrenology related to skull measurement (which did not end up being useful), and also the underlying doctrine regarding functional localization in the brain (which is firmly cemented in modern cognitive neuroscience).

An example of a phrenological diagram is shown in Figure 3.1. Based on the examination of many skulls, and considering what they believed were core mental functions (or "faculties"), phrenologists divided the skull into separate, numbered regions (corresponding to brain regions below the skull).

The belief in regional specialization of brain areas, a key tenet of phrenology, was a watershed moment in the history of brain science and influenced generations of surgeons and scientists. However, phrenology was also routinely used to support racist beliefs. Because phrenologists (incorrectly) believed that the shape of a person's skull related to the shape of their brain, they associated head and skull shape with specific traits. This mode of thinking made it easy to use nonscientific and racist beliefs about skull shape to reinforce existing prejudices under a guise of "science." Although not primarily intended as a contribution to phrenology, a clear example of this philosophical stance is found in Samuel George Morton's 1839 book *Crania Americana*.[10] He included illustrations of many skulls he had collected, including of European Americans and Native Americans. The skulls were drawn using high-quality lithographic techniques

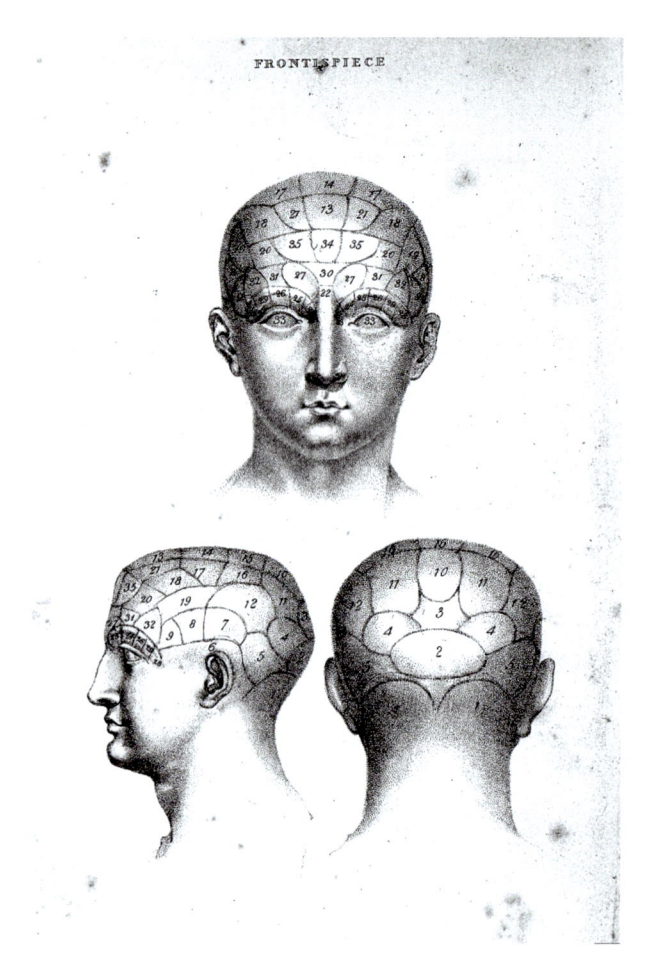

Figure 3.1 "Phrenology, or the doctrine of the mind: and of the relations between its manifestations and the body" (Spurzheim, 1825), illustrating some portions of the skull that would be interpreted by phrenologists as corresponding to certain mental faculties. Image public domain courtesy of the Wellcome Collection.

that were expensive, and relatively rare, adding to the mystique of the book. In his description of "the races of the human species," Morton relies on stereotype after stereotype of various people groups, backed in some cases by specific anecdotes, and in other cases by nothing. Phrenology is certainly not unique in being co-opted to support biased attitudes, but its complicity in perpetuating racism should not be overlooked.

3.2.2 Broca

At the same time that phrenology and its focus on functional localization was being discussed in many scientific circles, Pierre Paul Broca (1824–1880) was born in Sainte-Foy-la-Grande, Bordeaux, France. Broca, pictured in Figure 3.2, is a historical giant in the field of language science, and one of only a handful of nineteenth-century neurologists whose names you might recognize.[11] At school, Broca was a gifted pupil who was good at languages and mathematics, played the horn, and enjoyed writing (especially letters and creative satire).[12] He attended medical school in Paris and became a doctor of medicine in 1849. He was a prolific reader and writer, and a broad thinker whose work extended well beyond language science: His doctoral thesis demonstrated for the first time the spread of cancer through the veins, and 10 years later he wrote a 1,000-page work on "aneurysms and their treatment."

Broca met the first of his most famous patients, Monsieur Leborgne, in 1861. Leborgne was transported to the hospital because of a serious problem with his right leg. However, what caught Broca's attention was Leborgne's speech: Every time Broca asked a question, Leborgne responded "tan, tan" (leading

Figure 3.2 Portrait of Pierre Paul Broca (year unknown). Wellcome Collection. Attribution 4.0 International (CC-BY).

to Leborgne's nickname, "Tan"). Broca interviewed whoever he could about the patient's history, and learned that Leborgne had experienced epileptic attacks since he was young; around the age of 30, he lost his ability to speak and was admitted to the hospital, where he stayed for 20 years until his leg problem led him to cross paths with Broca. Broca's own examination suggested that despite his difficulties producing speech, Leborgne's speech *comprehension* was relatively good (including understanding Broca enough to be able to convey information about his sickness). Leborgne died shortly after Broca met him. Following standard hospital protocol, 24 hours after the patient's death Broca performed an autopsy and noted a significant lesion (that is, brain damage) in the left inferior frontal lobe. Broca had the brain preserved and displayed at the Dupuytren museum.[13]

The second of Broca's most famous patients was Monsieur Lelong, whom Broca also met in 1861. Lelong was 84 years old, and following a loss of consciousness developed a severe speech difficulty, which Broca termed "aphemia" (in modern terms, this would be described as **aphasia**: difficulty producing or understanding language). Lelong was only able to produce five words. At autopsy, like Leborgne, Lelong was found to have a lesion in a similar region of the left frontal lobe (in what we would now call the inferior frontal gyrus). (See Figure 3.3.) Lelong's brain was also preserved and remained in the Dupuytren museum until its closure.[14]

The similarity of the speech difficulty faced by Leborgne and Lelong, coupled with the similarity of the location of the damage to their frontal lobes, began to crystallize Broca's views regarding language in the brain, articulated in his 1865 work *Sur le siège de la faculté du langage articulé* (On the site of the faculty of articulated speech) (translated by Berker, Berker and Smith in 1986), where he affirms the special role the "third frontal convolution" plays in speech articulation (as well as a broader doctrine regarding cooperation between hemispheres and compensatory activity, which is often overlooked). This region of the brain is what is often termed "Broca's area." (Be sure to read Box 4.2 for a modern perspective on Broca's area.)

The ways that different regions of the brain, including Broca's area, contribute to language processing are the subject of much of this book. But for now, the critical point is broader and has to do with how scientists and neurologists viewed brain organization. Broca's discoveries about language and the third frontal convolution, and his adept communication of these findings through lectures and publications, came after decades of scientific discussion about phrenology and its weaknesses. The localization of a specific cognitive function – language – to a particular region of the brain, in multiple patients, seemed to provide clear evidence for at least some degree of functional localization in the brain. Broca's work thus played an important

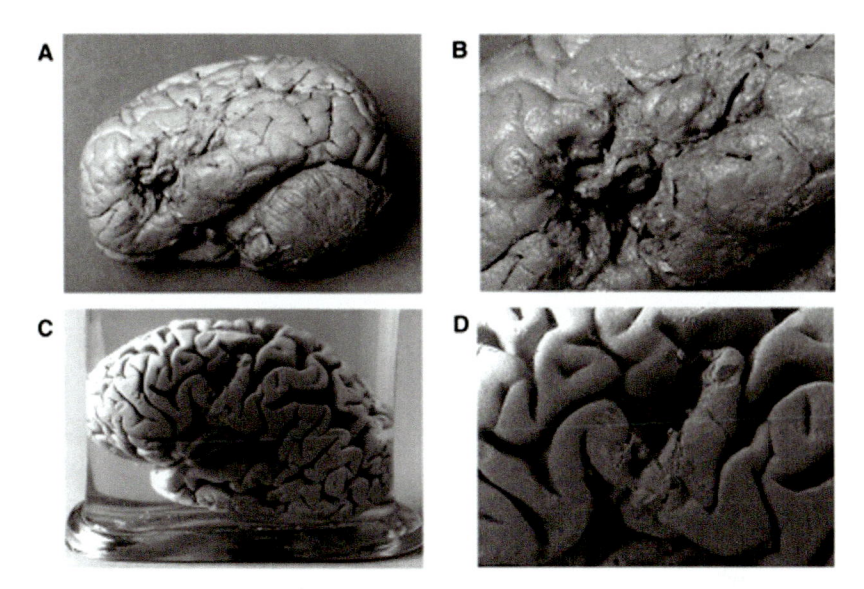

Figure 3.3 Brains of Broca's famous patients Leborgne and Lelong showing damage to the left inferior frontal gyrus (from Dronkers et al., 2007). (a) Lateral view of Leborgne's brain. (b) Close-up of the visible lesion in Leborgne's brain. (c) Lateral view of Lelong's brain. (d) Close-up of the visible lesion in Lelong's brain.

role in broader thinking about brain organization, while simultaneously helping to start serious discussions about how language, in particular, might be represented in the brain.[15]

3.2.3 Wernicke, Lichtheim, and the Move from Regions to Networks

Broca may be the best-known nineteenth-century language-oriented neurologist, but Carl Wernicke (1848–1905) is a close second. Wernicke, born in what was then Prussia (now in Poland), was aware of Broca's work, and became interested in how language was affected by damage to various regions of the brain. In 1874, he published *Der Aphasische Symptomencomplex* (The Aphasic Syndrome), in which he described sensory aphasia, the syndrome now commonly known as Wernicke's aphasia. Importantly, Wernicke distinguished sensory aphasia from the "motor" aphasia described by Broca. Wernicke identified damage to the posterior left temporal lobe (often called "Wernicke's area") as underlying the sensory syndrome. Wernicke's area since became well known for playing a crucial role in speech comprehension.

In addition to being an important discovery on its own, Wernicke's work took on special significance when viewed alongside that of Broca. Working independently, Broca and Wernicke had identified two distinct types of language difficulty, associated with damage to different parts of the brain. "Language" no longer seemed easily localized to a single region of the brain; instead, it seemed more likely supported by a *network* of regions.

Ludwig Lichtheim (1845–1928), following the work of Broca, Wernicke, and others, classified language disorders into several different aphasias (including Wernicke's aphasia). Wernicke then adopted Lichtheim's system, which became widely known as the **Wernicke-Lichtheim model** (Figure 3.4). The Wernicke-Lichtheim model lay the foundation for decades of neuropsychological investigation into language and provided a scaffold for classifying different aphasias. A key feature of the Wernicke-Lichtheim model was the **arcuate fasciculus**, a bundle of white matter tracts connecting the posterior temporal lobe to the frontal lobe. Its inclusion in the model was theoretically significant because it reflected an appreciation not only that brain regions were important but also of how they communicated (the arcuate fasciculus being partly responsible for bringing information between the temporal and frontal lobes). There was thus a move to think about a language network, comprised of multiple regions (Broca's area, Wernicke's area) and their connectivity (the arcuate fasciculus).

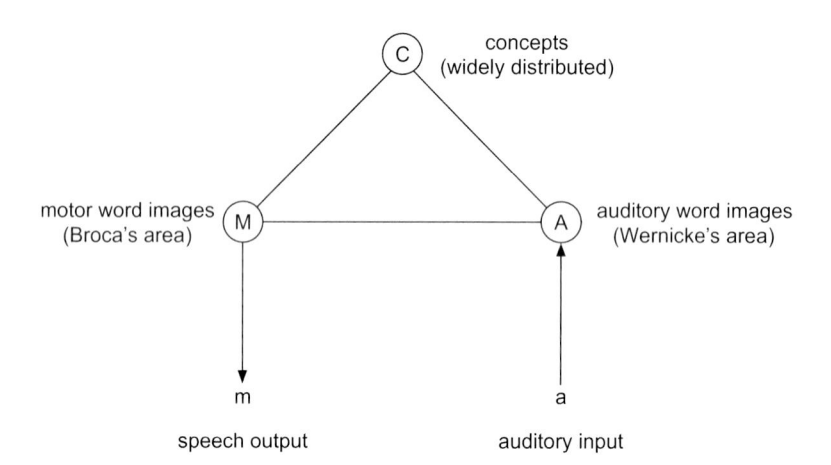

Figure 3.4 Reproduction of the Wernicke-Lichtheim model (sometimes referred to as the "house" model). Damage to regions and pathways is traditionally represented with slashes through them. https://osf.io/geqb6/ (CC-BY).

The move to think about connectivity accompanied thinking about what happens when connections are damaged – so-called disconnection syndromes. A prime example is found in **conduction aphasia**. People with conduction aphasia are generally able to express themselves fairly well and with reasonable fluency. However, they have difficulty repeating speech, classically associated with damage to the arcuate fasciculus that disrupts communication between Wernicke's area and Broca's area. In other words, comprehension is relatively spared (as Wernicke's area is not damaged), and fluent speech production is relatively spared (as Broca's area is not damaged). However, because the link between these systems is impaired, repetition (which relies on coordinating comprehension and production) is impaired.[16]

The twentieth century saw gradual adoption and expansion of these ideas. Particularly notable is the work of Norman Geschwind (1926–1984), who spent time at the famed Boston VA and Boston University before joining the department of neurology at the Harvard Medical School. Geschwind is often credited with coining the term "behavioral neurology," and for helping propel the understanding of aphasia forward.[17]

3.2.4 The Advent of Human Brain Imaging and the Modern Age of Localization

The latter part of the twentieth century saw tremendous advances in human brain imaging which had two critical impacts on the field. Linking language *difficulty* in patients to a location of brain damage (for example, due to a stroke) had long formed the backbone of theories relating language to the brain. With brain imaging, researchers no longer had to wait for a patient to die (and consent for an autopsy) to determine which parts of their brain were damaged – offering researchers more opportunities to study a variety of patients with language difficulty.[18] However, developing the ability to look at brain *function* was also momentous as it meant that researchers were no longer restricted to studying people with language difficulty: Language functions could, in principle, be localized in healthy people by observing which parts of their brains were more active while they performed language tasks compared to other tasks. As with other areas of cognitive neuroscience, the ability to observe regional brain activity led to a proliferation of new theories and expansion of the discussion regarding brain regions and networks supporting mental function. In the context of localization, modern cognitive neuroscience remains in this stage, with the strongest theories finding support from many different types of investigation. Although there continue to be new proposals for how to think about brain organization, and ever-improving techniques for capturing brain structure and function, theoretical viewpoints have nearly all come to rest solidly on the side of functional localization (though see Box 3.1 for some caveats).

Box 3.1 The problems with reverse inference and other limitations on localization of function.

In a typical cognitive neuroscience experiment, a researcher manipulates a variable and observes the result. For example, if I am interested in the brain regions supporting auditory processing, I might play a sound, and observe activity in the brain. I would then infer that the region of the brain I saw being active (auditory cortex) was related to processing the information I manipulated (here, sound).

In what is sometimes referred to as **reverse inference**, I would observe activity in auditory cortex, and then conclude that the brain was processing sound. The key distinction is that I am now drawing conclusions about cognitive function based *purely on anatomical location* of brain activity, not on an experimental manipulation. But, you might wonder, if cognitive functions are localized, why is this a problem?

Poldrack (2006) highlighted challenges of reverse inference for functional neuroimaging. One of the key difficulties concerns the fact that regions of the brain are not typically exclusive to a particular cognitive process (at least, given the current level at which most cognitive processes are defined).[19] So, for example, we might consider primary visual cortex as reflecting visual information processing. Visual cortex is also active during reading, and sometimes during auditory-only speech. Thus, the same brain region is involved in many tasks, making it impossible – based on activity in that region alone – to determine the task in which they were engaged.[20] Figure 3.5 illustrates the different ways experimental tasks might be mapped on to neuroimaging measurements.

One way to formalize this challenge is: If I show you someone who has activity in visual cortex, how likely are you to correctly guess what cognitive task they are engaged in? Poldrack (2006) took exactly such an approach. Using coordinates from published studies, he found that the location of brain activity provided only a modest amount of information regarding the specific task. These findings show that although cognitive functions are localized, there is not a one-to-one mapping between cognitive processes and brain regions. As a result, drawing conclusions about cognitive processes based purely on brain activity is probably ill-advised.

Box 3.1 (cont.)

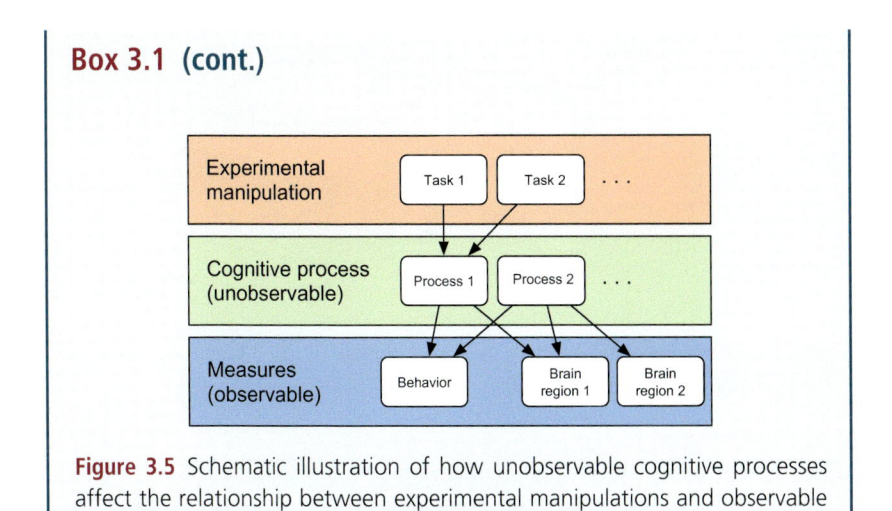

Figure 3.5 Schematic illustration of how unobservable cognitive processes affect the relationship between experimental manipulations and observable data (after Poldrack, 2006). https://osf.io/geqb6/ (CC-BY).

3.3 Introducing the Brain

Having seen something about how the methods and philosophy of anatomical localization have developed, we now turn to the brain itself. It is impossible to effectively discuss the neuroscience of language without having a working vocabulary for the brain. There are many different naming conventions for the brain, which sometimes get mixed together. Rather than provide a comprehensive treatise on neuroanatomy, my goal here is to introduce you to a working set of terms that commonly appear in the scientific literature and which will be used throughout the remainder of the book.

3.3.1 Major Subdivisions

A critical distinction concerns cortical and subcortical regions of the brain. The **cortex** consists of a "sheet" of gray matter, which in humans (and some other animals) is folded over in convolutions to increase the surface area. So, *cortical* regions of the brain refer to regions in cortex. ("Cortical" is sometimes used as a synonym for "brain," but this is incorrect, because there are parts of the brain that are not cortex!) When you look at a brain, most of what you see is cortex. *Subcortical* brain regions are parts of the brain below or underneath cortex, including portions of the brainstem, thalamus, and basal ganglia. As we will see in Chapter 5, a great deal of auditory processing occurs subcortically in auditory thalamic nuclei (a **nucleus** – of

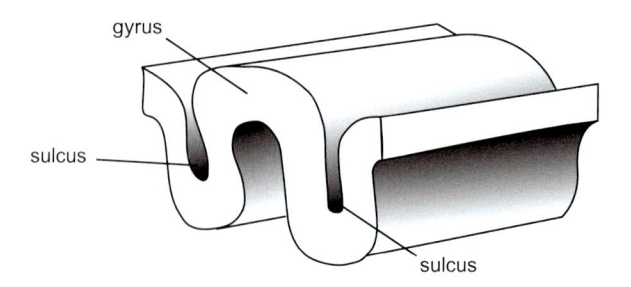

Figure 3.6 The folded cortical surface includes a number of gyri ("mountains") and sulci ("valleys"). https://osf.io/geqb6/ (CC-BY).

which nuclei is the plural – is a collection of brain cells that has a specific function). Generally subcortical structures are evolutionarily older and involved with more basic functions compared to cortical structures, which are evolutionarily more recent and support more complex processing (such as language).

When looking at the foldings on the cortical surface, it is useful to distinguish between the "mountains" and the "valleys" (Figure 3.6). The mountains (or bumps) are **gyri** (singular: gyrus), and the valleys (or crevices) are **sulci** (singular: sulcus). The major gyri and sulci of the brain are present in everyone (with some variability in their sizes and locations), making them useful landmarks for neuroanatomy.

3.3.2 Directions and Modifiers

A list of some important "modifiers," and common synonyms, is found in Figure 3.7. Anterior means toward the front, posterior toward the back; inferior toward the bottom, superior toward the top. Lateral is toward the side of the brain, and medial toward the middle. As you'll see later, these terms are seldom used in isolation but instead combined with other descriptors to offer some additional specificity. For example, "posterior lateral temporal lobe" and "anterior medial temporal lobe" both offer more precision than simply "temporal lobe."

These terms are used regardless of the orientation of the brain in the world: If I stand on my head, we consider the "top" of the brain to be in the same place, even if it is closer to the ground than the "bottom" of my brain. (Some of these terms – particularly rostral and caudal – are interpreted differently with regard to the spinal cord, or in animals who walk on all fours and whose brains thus have a different orientation with the rest of their body.)

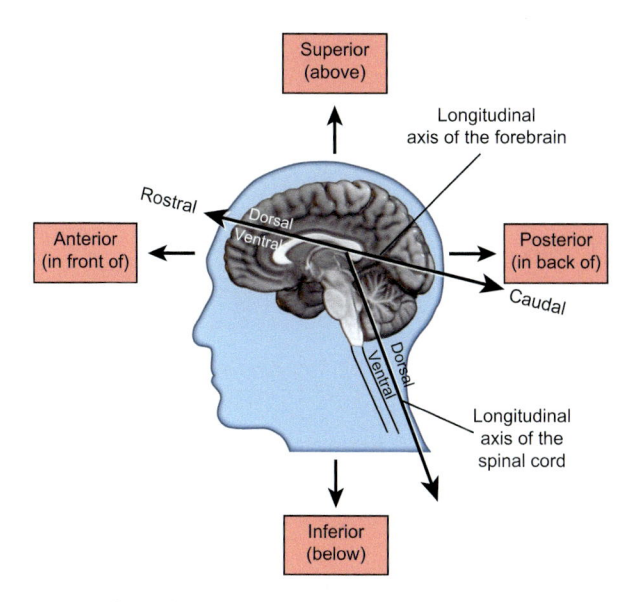

Figure 3.7 Common brain directions and modifiers. https://osf.io/geqb6/ (CC-BY).

3.3.3 Macroanatomical Landmarks

Features of the brain you can see with your naked eye, either on a real brain or an MRI scan, are **macroanatomical** features. Historically (and to some degree, continuing to the present day), macroanatomical features have been the most obvious divisions of a brain, and as a result they have featured heavily in the terminology and descriptions of brain regions.

The brain has two hemispheres, a left hemisphere and a right hemisphere (defined from the perspective of the person whose head the brain is in). The left and right hemisphere are similar but not mirror-reflection identical. The gap between the left and right hemisphere is the **longitudinal fissure**. Interestingly, most of the major anatomical features of the brain are present in both hemispheres.

Let's next examine the side, or lateral view, of the brain (Figure 3.8). With two macroanatomical landmarks – the **lateral sulcus** (also known as the Sylvian fissure) and the **central sulcus** – you can outline the four lobes of the brain, which is how I always orient myself. The lateral sulcus separates the temporal lobe from the rest of the brain; the central sulcus separates the frontal lobe from the parietal lobe. The occipital lobe is at the back of the brain ("occipital" coming from the Latin *ob*, meaning behind, and *caput*, head). The occipital lobe boundary is slightly trickier, generally being indicated by

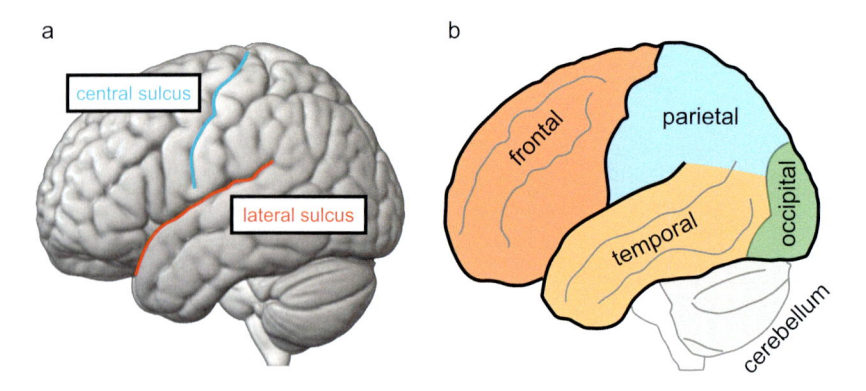

Figure 3.8 (a) Lateral view of the left hemisphere with the lateral sulcus and central sulcus highlighted. (b) The brain has four major subdivisions, called lobes: frontal, parietal, temporal, and occipital. The cerebellum sits below the back of the brain. https://osf.io/geqb6/ (CC-BY).

an imaginary line extending from the preoccipital notch (an indentation on the bottom of the temporal lobe) up to the parieto-occipital sulcus.[21]

The cerebellum is not a lobe, but an anatomically distinct structure hanging off the back of the brain, with characteristic tiny folds (distinct from the larger folds of the main cortical surface).

Three main gyri are visible on the lateral temporal lobe: the superior temporal gyrus (STG) (along the top), middle temporal gyrus (MTG), and inferior temporal gyrus (IFG) (Figure 3.9). Similarly, the frontal lobe has a superior frontal gyrus, middle frontal gyrus, and inferior frontal gyrus. Major divisions of the parietal lobe are the superior parietal lobule and inferior parietal lobule, separated by the intraparietal sulcus.

Turning to the middle of the brain (Figure 3.10) – that is, a midsagittal view – we can see the brainstem, with the thalamus at the top. The **corpus callosum** is prominent and consists of bundles of white matter tracts connecting the left and right hemisphere (and thus, is white). On top of the corpus callosum is the **cingulate gyrus**. Some of the other regions we first learned about from the lateral view are also visible from this midsagittal view, including the lobes of the brain and the cerebellum.

3.3.4 Microanatomical Divisions

In addition to major gyri and sulci, using the naked eye we can also distinguish between major tissue types (for example, gray matter vs. white matter). However, doing so tells us next to nothing about the cells making up these

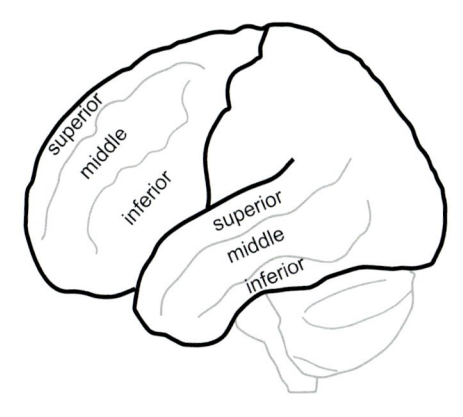

Figure 3.9 Major gyri of the temporal lobe (superior temporal gyrus, middle temporal gyrus, inferior temporal gyrus) and frontal lobe (superior frontal gyrus, middle frontal gyrus, inferior frontal gyrus). https://osf.io/geqb6/ (CC-BY).

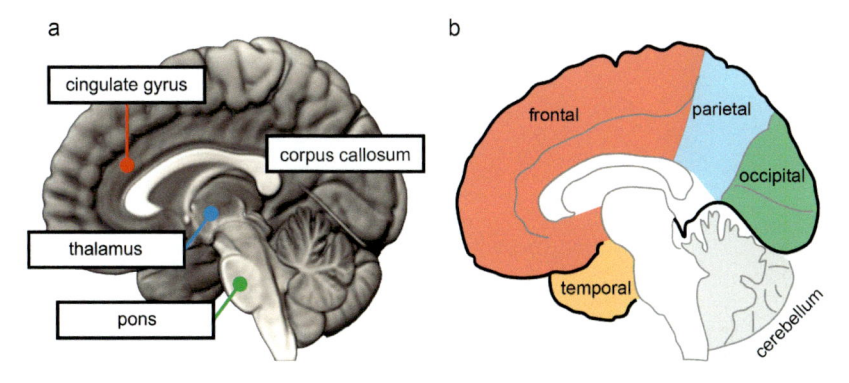

Figure 3.10 Midsagittal view of the right hemisphere. (a) Major features visible from this view. (b) Brain lobes, and the cerebellum, pictured from a midsagittal view. https://osf.io/geqb6/ (CC-BY).

tissues. For example, although we often refer to the entire cortex as "gray matter," it is made up of multiple layers, each of which has different types of cells. These cells differ in their functional properties and connectivity profiles, which contribute to the regional specialization of the brain. The cellular makeup of the brain is called **cytoarchitecture** (that is, "cellular architecture").

Before noninvasive brain imaging, cytoarchitecture was studied exclusively using histological staining techniques in postmortem brains. **Histological**

staining involves placing a chemical on the brain which is then absorbed by the brain tissue. Different cellular compositions absorb chemicals differently, and thus differences in staining can be interpreted as differentiating between cytoarchitectonic organization. Importantly, cytoarchitectonic maps show some degree of correspondence with macroanatomical features, but the relationship is not perfect.[22] The imperfect overlap of cytoarchitecture with macroanatomical features illustrates the fact that macroanatomy does not fully capture the nuances of brain structure.

The most well-known cytoarchitectonic map was published in 1909 by German neurologist Korbinian Brodmann (1868–1918). Using histological techniques, Brodmann divided the brain into 52 different areas (Figure 3.11). Many of these correspond relatively closely to clear sensory or cognitive functions. For example, Brodmann area 17 is at the back of the occipital lobe and corresponds to primary visual cortex; Brodmann area 4 is primary motor

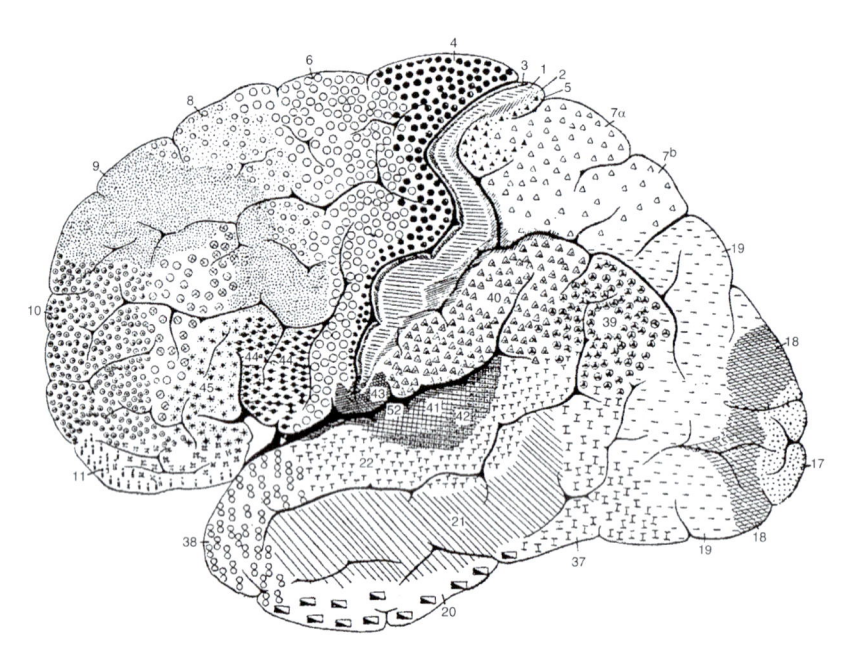

Figure 3.11 Brodmann's cytoarchitectonic map (1909). Based on visual inspection of histological staining, Brodmann colored in a brain figure to indicate boundaries between staining patterns – the shading on the brain is from his coloring, not the stain itself. He numbered these regions, giving rise to what are typically called Brodmann areas. Figure from Amunts (2021), used by permission.

cortex; and so on. You may come across references to Brodmann areas (often abbreviated "BA") in research articles.

One of the challenges with using cytoarchitectonic labels is that with current noninvasive technology it is not possible to achieve a high degree of accuracy labeling cytoarchitecture: That is, cytoarchitecture is difficult or impossible to observe based on typical structural MRI scans. Postmortem histology therefore remains the only way to get a clear picture of cytoarchitectonic organization in humans. This presents a challenge for cognitive neuroscientists, who typically want to characterize the brains of a relatively large number of people while those people are still alive (!). We thus have somewhat of a conundrum: On the one hand, we know that macroanatomical features do not perfectly convey the cellular composition of different brain regions; however, the only method for accurately measuring cytoarchitecture is an approach we can't use in living participants. One solution is to use probabilistic atlases that can provide information on likely cytoarchitecture based on findings in a separate group of people. However, in current practice most anatomical localization continues to be done with macroanatomical labels, with the understanding that doing so is imperfect. (See Box 3.2.)

3.3.5 MRI-Specific Terminology

Although, as discussed in Chapter 2, there are many methods used to study the human brain, the centrality of MRI to contemporary cognitive neuroscience makes knowledge of specific MRI-related terms particularly useful.

An MRI scan is a three-dimensional image of the brain, the basic units of which are called **voxels** (similar to how an image on a monitor or television screen is comprised of pixels). The size of a voxel conveys the degree of spatial detail that can be obtained. Currently, a typical voxel size for structural MRI is $1 \times 1 \times 1$ mm, for functional MRI $2 \times 2 \times 2$ mm.

Before MRI, to view different regions of the brain neuroanatomists would literally use a sharp blade to slice through a postmortem brain. Magnetic resonance imaging has maintained the same convention, but now using imaging to show different "slices" of the brain. As shown in Figure 3.12, the main planes are **axial** (also known as transverse, or horizontal), **coronal**, and **sagittal**.

A recurring challenge for cognitive neuroscientists is that although major landmarks in the brain are present in everyone, no two brains are identical. Comparing different brains, or looking for common activity in a group of people, requires a way to line up brains together (in imaging, referred to as **image registration**). A related, but different, challenge involves being able to communicate results across different labs. The most common solution to these

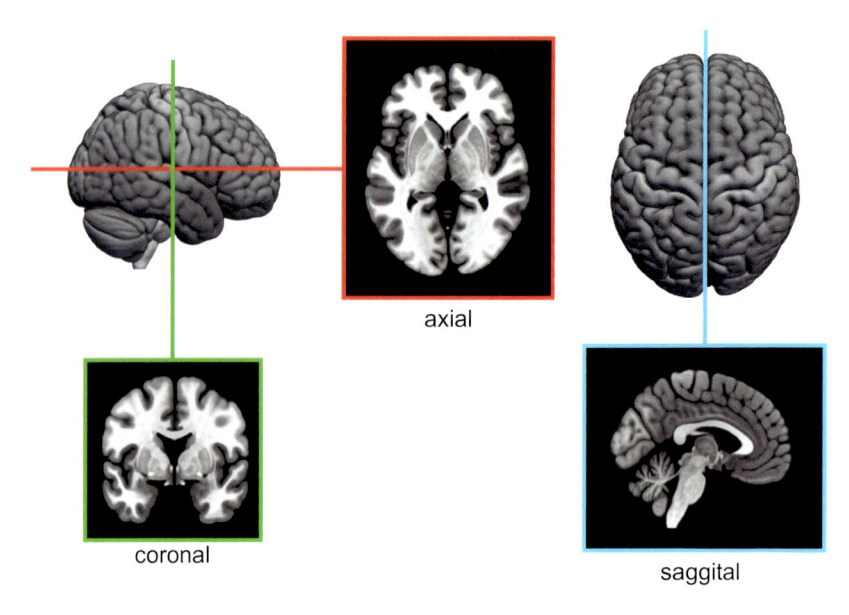

axial

coronal

saggital

Figure 3.12 The planes at which slices through the brain are typically taken: axial, coronal, and sagittal. https://osf.io/geqb6/ (CC-BY).

challenges is to use image processing algorithms to warp, or normalize, brains into a common space. In spatial normalization, the MRI images of individual participants are compared to a template or atlas, and then altered to be lined up with the template. These atlases are **stereotactic**, meaning that they are situated in a three-dimensional coordinate system.

The most common template brain was developed at the Montreal Neurological Institute,[23] and the space defined by this template is referred to as **MNI space**. Being three dimensional, every location in a brain can be described using an X, Y, and Z coordinate. When using a standard space, then, it is possible to use coordinates to compare across studies or to share data across labs. The origin ([0, 0, 0]) is the anterior commissure, a small white matter tract below the corpus callosum, and the units of the coordinates are millimeters.

3.4 Anatomical Connectivity

Although many brain regions are specialized for specific cognitive processes, there has long been an appreciation that connectivity between regions is also important. Modern cognitive neuroscience reflects an increasing focus on brain *networks* as opposed to brain *regions*, and analysis techniques are improving the ways in which coordinated activity can be quantified.[24] However, before considering functional connectivity (that is, regions of the brain showing coordinated activity), a foundation of understanding structural, or anatomical, connectivity is warranted.

Many of the major white matter pathways, or tracts, are visible to the naked eye and also identifiable using DTI (Figure 3.13). Finer-grained connections, though, are difficult to observe without specific techniques available only in animal studies. As a result, comparative anatomy (that is, using what we learn about anatomical connectivity in other animals to better understand the human brain) continues to play an important role in human neuroscience.

3.4.1 The Dorsal Stream, Ventral Stream, and Beyond

Vision neuroscience was famously shaped by Leslie Ungerlieder and Mortimer Mishkin's characterization in the 1980s of dorsal and ventral visual pathways. In this framework, the dorsal pathway is responsible for the spatial location of an object (that is, *where* an object is) and the ventral pathway for object identification (*what* an object is). The functional distinction proved useful in understanding not only vision but more generally how the brain might engage in some forms of parallel processing.

A similar dual-stream organization has been proposed for the auditory system, particularly as it relates to speech,[26] as shown in Figure 3.14. Primary auditory cortex, located on **Heschl's gyrus** (also called the transverse temporal gyrus) along the top of the temporal lobe, is the first area where auditory information enters the cortex. The **dorsal stream** for speech travels back from auditory cortex, up around through the parietal lobe, and into the dorsal portion of prefrontal cortex. The primary white matter pathway associated with the dorsal stream in humans is historically the arcuate fasciculus (a *fasciculus* referring to a bundle of fibers), which features prominently in the Wernicke-Lichtheim model classifying different types of aphasias.[27] The dorsal stream runs through inferior parietal cortex (potentially important for auditory sound localization – a "where" pathway for speech) and into premotor cortex. The connectivity between auditory and premotor regions suggests a role for the dorsal stream in sensory integration and feedback (covered in detail in Chapter 4).

The **ventral stream** travels forward along the temporal lobe, through the **uncinate fasciculus** into the frontal lobe. These regions of the temporal lobe are concerned with extracting meaning from speech: Listening to phonemes, words, concepts, and sentences all result in activity along various portions of the ventral stream, particularly along the temporal lobe.

Although the "division of labor" between the two streams is still debated, the existence of white matter pathways that correspond to these dorsal and ventral

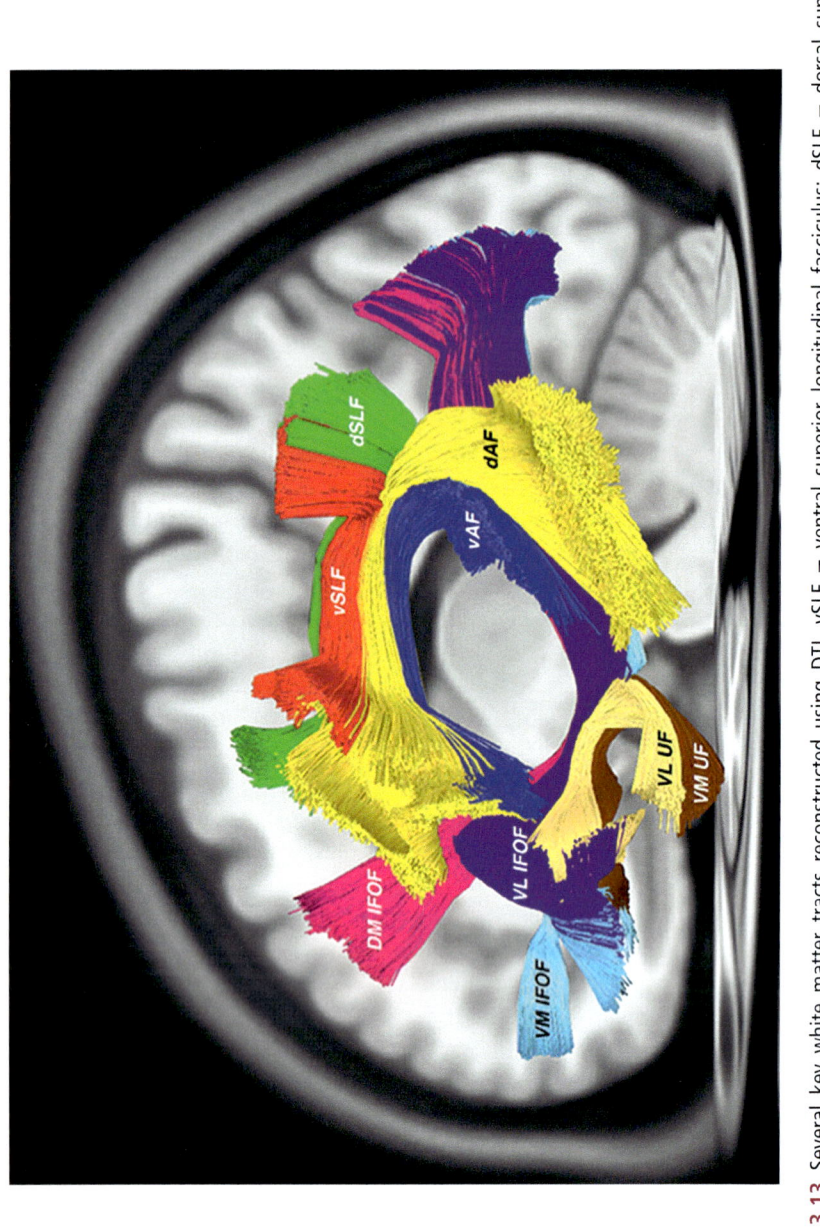

Figure 3.13 Several key white matter tracts reconstructed using DTI. vSLF = ventral superior longitudinal fasciculus; vAF = ventral arcuate fasciculus; dAF = dorsal arcuate fasciculus; DM IFOF = dorso-medial inferior frontal occipital fasciculus; VM IFOF = ventro-medial inferior frontal occipital fasciculus; VL UF = ventro-lateral uncinate fasciculus; VM UF = ventro-medial uncinate fasciculus (CC-BY from Panesar and Fernandez-Miranda, 2019).[25]

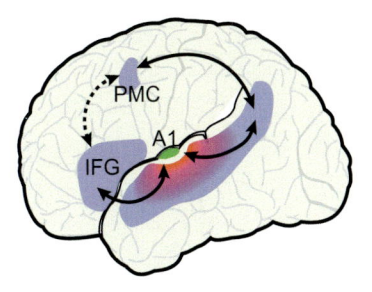

Figure 3.14 Schematic of a dual-stream model for speech (from Peelle et al., 2010). A1 = primary auditory cortex; IFG = inferior frontal gyrus; PMC = premotor cortex. https://osf.io/geqb6/ (CC-BY).

pathways is uncontroversial. However, our focus in this section is on anatomy, and it is important to note that a theory with (only) two streams fails to capture the complexity of the anatomical brain networks related to auditory processing (and thus, potentially, speech processing).

Some additional hints about the complexity of the connections between the temporal and frontal lobes can be found in animal studies. In order to determine the anatomical pathways connecting auditory cortex to the rest of the brain, scientists often use **tracers**: chemicals that are absorbed by neurons and which travel along axons. By placing tracer in one region, waiting, and then seeing where the tracer has spread, it is possible to map connectivity pathways in the brain. Tracers are measured in the brain postmortem, which – coupled with the invasive injection of the tracer in the first place – restricts this type of detailed anatomical investigation to nonhuman animals. Using these invasive approaches, it has been clearly demonstrated in multiple species that there are far more than two anatomical connections between auditory regions of the temporal lobe and various parts of frontal cortex (Figure 3.15).[28] Thus, although a focus on two parallel streams for speech processing has been useful for the field, it likely fails to capture the full complexity of the structural network supporting speech understanding.

Why should we care so much about connectivity between the frontal and temporal lobes? As noted previously, a common theme in language processing is the interplay of bottom-up and top-down processing. Although there are many ways such an arrangement might be instantiated in a biological system, a common view is that regions of temporal cortex (including auditory cortex and nearby regions) are primarily responsible for sensory-driven bottom-up processing, and regions of frontal cortex (for example, left inferior frontal gyrus) are responsible for top-down processing. Thus, frontotemporal connectivity has long been a key point of interest for language researchers.[29]

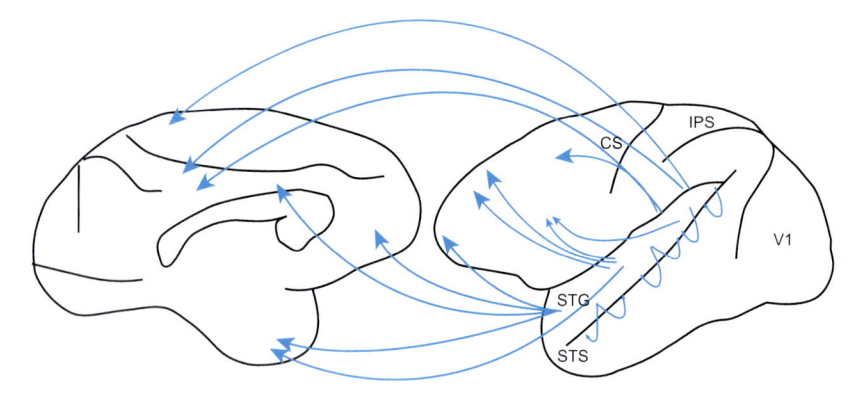

Figure 3.15 Schematic illustrating anatomical connectivity between the frontal and temporal lobe based on studies in monkeys (after Hackett, 2011). The left side of the figure shows a sagittal view of the left hemisphere (i.e., looking out from the middle); the right side of the figure shows a lateral view. CS = central sulcus; IPS = intraparietal sulcus; V1 = primary visual cortex; STG = superior temporal gyrus; STS = superior temporal sulcus.

Box 3.2 What is a brain region called?

Given a region of the brain, what is the best way to label it? It turns out this is a complicated question, and one to which there is no agreed-upon answer. One reason for the variety of labels is no doubt different traditions and perspectives that affect our current thinking, even without our being aware of this fact. However, another is that there are complementary ways to think about brain organization, and thus complementary terms and labels. Understanding the motivation and science behind each approach can go a long way toward reducing confusion. For example, when describing the location of your house, you might provide a house number, a latitude and longitude coordinate, or relationship to some landmark ("next to the house with the goat in the yard") – all of these are valid descriptions but relate to different properties of the house.

Macroanatomical labels refer to landmarks that can be identified by "eye" on a brain or structural MRI scan. **Microanatomical** labels refer to cellular structure and cannot typically be identified using MRI scans. Functional definitions might be made based on response to a specific kind of information – for example, the fusiform face area is typically identified by finding a region of the fusiform gyrus that shows a stronger response to faces than other objects. And some areas have historical labels – such as "Broca's area" – which are harder to objectively define. Thus, the same region of the brain could correctly be referred to by any of the following:

> ## Box 3.2 (cont.)
>
> - left inferior frontal gyrus, *pars triangularis*
> - Broca's area
> - MNI coordinate [−51, 26, 11] (for example, if this coordinate referred to the highest value of the cluster)
> - Brodmann area 45.
>
> Each of which highlights a different heuristic for localization. The choice of which label to use is not always straightforward, and you may come across a variety of terms used for the same brain region.

3.5 Summary

- Localization of function has a long history, tracing its modern roots to phrenologists of the nineteenth century, and to Broca's influential writings on the brain basis of language.
- Most brain regions can be described in several complementary ways which reflect macroanatomy, microanatomy (e.g., cytoarchitecture), functional significance, or tradition. Understanding how these naming systems relate to each other is critical for reading primary research articles.
- Although contemporary frameworks for speech focus on two primary connections from the temporal lobe to the frontal lobe, anatomical studies indicate many more pathways.

Notes

1. You may have heard some version of the following (probably apocryphal) story. A man was cooking a ham for a holiday meal. Just before putting it in the pan, he took out a knife and cut off the end of the ham. His daughter, who was helping prepare dinner, asked him why he did that. "I don't know," the man replied. "My dad always did the same thing." So the man went and asked his father about the ham. "I don't know, my dad always did the same thing," came the reply. So the man went and asked his grandfather why he cut off the end of the ham. The grandfather laughed. "The only pan we had in the house was a small one, and the hams we bought from the store never fit. So we had to cut off the end to fit the ham in the pan!"
2. The Organization for Human Brain Mapping (www.humanbrainmapping.org) (full disclosure: I am a member) traces its history back to a meeting in 1995; it was at this annual conference that many foundational issues related to human brain imaging were discussed and debated. The flagship journal for the society is *Human Brain Mapping*.

3. Uttal's 2001 book *The New Phrenology* takes head-on the issue of whether it is possible to localize cognitive function in the brain. This quote from the preface gives a sense of his perspective (pp. x–xi): "Much of this work on the localization of psychological functions in the brain seems to have plunged off the rock of scientific certainty into a lake of unknowns with an exuberance typical of a science suddenly provided a powerful new tool – or, perhaps, of a child given a new toy."

4. In fact, different dates are sometimes given for the document. Atta (1999) and others note that the papyrus may have been copied from an older manuscript (dating between 3000–2500 BCE) because of the word choices and the fact it included a commentary, which may explain the discrepancy. The seventeenth century BCE date seems the most common one for the manuscripts themselves, though I saw no objections to the notion that the content may indeed have been much older.

5. The translation of the Edwin Smith Surgical Papyrus by Breasted (1930) is worth at least a look (and you would be forgiven for skipping portions of the introduction). The document had 17 columns, spanning 377 lines, describing 48 cases throughout the body. Of these, 27 cases relate to the head, and at least one is hypothesized by Minagar and colleagues (2003) to be the earliest recorded case of aphasia. (The back of the document consists of recipes and incantations.) A shorter and more accessible overview is found in Atta (1999).

6. Prior to the early 1800s, speculation about how the brain related to the "mind" have little in common with modern understandings. Medieval thinkers conceived of different parts of the brain relating to different functions, of faculties, but these were grounded in views of the brain distinguishing between sense and intellect and focused on the ventricles (fluid-filled portions) of the brain under an incorrect conception of the brain as a pneumatic device.

7. Young (1990, p. 11) relates that a decade before Gall begin his medical studies in Vienna, Prochaska published a *Dissertation on the Functions of the Nervous System* (1784), in which he wrote: "But since the brain, as well as the cerebellum, is composed of many parts, variously figured, it is probably, that nature, which never works in vain, has destined those parts to various uses, so that the various faculties of the mind seem to require different portions of the cerebrum and cerebellum for their production." Thus, the environment was set for Gall to push this line of thinking in the direction that he did.

8. The term "phrenology" was given to the system by Dr. Thomas I. M. Forster in 1815.

9. The introduction to LaPointe's (2013) *Paul Broca and the Origins of Language in the Brain* includes a concise review of the phrenology movement, and how this set the stage for Broca, whom we meet again later in this book.

10. Poskett (2015) goes into detail about the transatlantic context and influence of *Crania Americana*, including pointing out the afterword written by noted Scottish phrenologist George Combe. As related by Poskett, Morton encouraged Combe to use his essay to explain "the principles of Phrenology, and their application to the heads of the American Race." The implications of cataloging and emphasizing racial differences in skull shape were apparent.

11. Broca is one of 72 names of scientists, engineers, and mathematicians inscribed on the Eiffel tower (the south-west side), which was completed in 1889. Depressingly,

though perhaps not surprisingly, that list contains no women. (Surely there is a more authoritative list of the names on the Eiffel tower, but I have only been able to find this documented on Wikipedia: https://en.wikipedia.org/wiki/List_of_the_72_names_on_the_Eiffel_Tower.)

12. These and other details are found in LaPointe's (2013) comprehensive account of Broca's life and career.

13. The Dupuytren museum was formed in 1835 following a bequest from Guillaume Dupuytren (1777–1835), French anatomist and military surgeon. (The museum closed in 2016, with its exhibitions moved to the Jussieu Campus of the Faculty of Medicine of Sorbonne University.) As summarized by Goldwyn (1969), Dupuytren was a noted surgeon with a broad range of interests. To name a few: he was the first to excise the mandible, one of the first to treat a brain abscess, and one of the first to remove the neck of the uterus for cancer; he also noted the effect of skin tension related to wounds. Personally, he saw enemies everywhere, and consistently focused on making sure others knew his worth. A favorite saying of Dupuytren's was "Nothing should be feared as much by a man as mediocrity" – which his ruthless work ethic and exacting standards suggest steered many of his decisions. Dupuytren died after an illness, the severity of which he concealed from his doctors. In his will, in addition to the bequest for a museum, he left funds for an "asylum" or home for 12 retired physicians, perhaps hoping to provide the rest that he himself found so elusive.

14. The fact that the brains of Leborgne and Lelong were preserved offered a unique opportunity for cognitive neuroscientist Nina Dronkers and colleagues (2007), who used modern MRI scanning to re-examine these two famous brains. The results from structural MRI scans were generally consistent with Broca's initial observations, but also revealed damage deeper that than Broca could have observed, as well as damage to white matter tracts (specifically the superior longitudinal fasciculus).

15. Although Broca is widely credited with promoting notions of language localization, he was not the first scientist to do so. A fascinating example comes from Gustave Dax, related by Finger and Roe (1999). Gustave's father, Marc Dax (1770–1837), wrote a memoir in 1836 in which he related cerebral dominance of language. Marc Dax was a doctor in Sommières, a small town in the south of France. He came across his first case of aphasia in 1800. Over the following years he noted a number of such cases, which led him to hypothesize that damage to the left hemisphere was more likely to result in language difficulty than damage to the right hemisphere. However, Marc Dax died in 1837, and his findings were not published until 1865 by Gustave. Thus, although Broca is the name most associated with cerebral dominance for language, Marc Dax came to similar conclusions 30 years prior. Further interesting discussion is found in Manning and Thomas-Anterion (2011).

16. Ardila (2010) provides some historical context about conduction aphasia, including raising the question of whether damage to the arcuate fasciculus is necessary for conduction aphasia to occur. Part of this question arises due to uncertainty regarding

the degree to which the arcuate fasciculus provides direct connections to Broca's area proper vs. nearby regions of premotor or motor cortex (Bernal & Ardila, 2009).

17. Kushner (2015) provides an overview of Geschwind's contributions to our understanding of language, informed in part by his going back to original sources, namely, Wernicke. After a move away from disconnection in the early part of the twentieth century, Geschwind argued for its importance (Geschwind, 1965a, 1965b).

18. An interim approach was the Wada test, covered in Box 6.3, which provided information about localization at the level of cerebral hemisphere.

19. Part of the solution to this challenge is to have a more specific framework for cognitive processes. Poldrack and colleagues (2011) introduced the Cognitive Atlas (www.cognitiveatlas.org), which attempts to provide a formal organization relating different experimental tasks, cognitive processes, and phenotypes.

20. Behrens and colleagues (2013) used coordinates from activity in published papers to determine that the pre-supplemental motor area (pre-SMA) was the most "popular" brain region. NeuroSynth (Yarkoni et al., 2011), introduced previously as a meta-analytic approach to functional brain imaging, provides a formal way of quantifying the discriminability of a region given the keywords it is associated with in published literature.

21. The anterior boundary of the occipital lobe is always challenging to identify. Flores (2002) goes into much detail, noting in part: "The preoccipital notch is an anatomical structure poorly defined by specialized neuroanatomy literature . . . Its location was quite variable, and it was average positioned 44 mm from the occipital pole."

22. Using a combination of structural MRI and human postmortem histological data, Fischl and colleagues (2008) examined the relationship between macroanatomical features (the folds in the cortex) and cytoarchitecture. They found relatively good, but imperfect, relationships between cortical folding and cytoarchitecture, with primary areas (such as visual cortex) showing relatively less variability than higher-level areas.

23. Now the Montreal Neurological Institute and Hospital, or The Neuro. It was created at Royal Victoria Hospital in 1933, obtaining its own building shortly thereafter. The first director was Wilder Penfield (1891–1976), a pioneer in neurosurgery and neurostimulation, who held the post from 1934 until his retirement in 1960.

24. Modern cognitive neuroscience certainly did not discover the importance of connectivity and network structure; indeed, as mentioned earlier, famed neurologist Carl Wernicke talked at length about the importance of connections between brain regions. However, early functional brain imaging papers focused primarily on localization, with network- and connectivity-based analyses coming later as improved analysis methods were introduced.

25. For a complementary perspective on frontal-temporal white matter tracts, see Mandonnet and colleagues (2018).

26. A dual-stream framework for speech perception was consistently championed by Hickok and Poeppel (2000, 2004, 2007), though these ideas also appear elsewhere (e.g., Rauschecker, 1998; Romanski et al., 1999; Scott, 2005).

27. Debate continues regarding the distinction between various branches of the superior longitudinal fasciculus, which in some views includes the arcuate fasciculus. See, for example, Mandonnet and colleagues (2018); Panesar and Fernandez-Miranda (2019); Catani and colleagues (2004).

28. Hackett (2011) provides a nice summary of numerous studies in monkeys and cats investigating anatomical connections of auditory cortex, illustrating a plethora of pathways within and between the temporal and frontal lobes.

29. In this context, it might also be surprising to realize just how multisensory the frontal lobe is. Animal tracing studies show a multitude of connections from regions of auditory cortex to various subdivisions of the frontal lobe, and electrophysiological recordings in the frontal lobe in fact show some neurons that respond to sound in similar ways to neurons in auditory cortex (Romanski and Goldman-Rakic, 2002). These findings suggest that the full picture of connectivity between the frontal and temporal lobes is decidedly more complex than most current models of auditory and speech processing reflect.

Further Reading

Brett M, Johnsrude IS, Owen AM (2002) The problem of functional localization in the human brain. *Nature Reviews Neuroscience* 3:243–249. https://doi.org/10.1038/nrn756.
Provides an overview for different levels of localization in human brain imaging, from the macroanatomical to the microanatomical level, and discusses some of the challenges faced in comparing brain activity from different people.

Dronkers NF, Plaisant O, Iba-Zizen MT, Cabanis EA (2007) Paul Broca's historic cases: high resolution MR imaging of the brains of Leborgne and Lelong. *Brain* 130:1432–1441. https://doi.org/10.1093/brain/awm042.
Summarizes modern investigations into the neuroanatomy of Broca's original patients using structural MRI, including a discussion of how modern imaging shapes interpretation of Broca's original findings.

Fischl B, Rajendran N, Busa E, Augustinack J, Hinds O, Thomas Yeo BT, Mohlberg H, Amunts K, Zilles K (2008) Cortical folding patterns and predicting cytoarchitecture. *Cerebral Cortex* 18:1973–1980. https://doi.org/10.1093/cercor/bhm225.
Discusses the relationship between sulci and gyri and cytoarchitectonic characteristics of human brains, an important part of the discussion on how we label brain areas.

Romanski LM, Tian B, Fritz J, Mishkin M, Goldman-Rakic PS, Rauschecker JP (1999) Dual streams of auditory afferents target multiple domains in the primate prefrontal cortex. *Nature Neuroscience* 2: 1131–1136. https://doi.org/10.1038/16056.
Provides an example illustrating the complexity of the brain regions supporting auditory processing: specifically, identifying auditory responses in prefrontal cortex of nonhuman primates.

CHAPTER FOUR

Speech Production

The Beginning of the Speech Chain

In ongoing conversation, speech production and speech understanding are continuous – there is no clear "starting" point because it's a back-and-forth interaction. But since we need to begin our overview somewhere, the actions of a talker seem a reasonable place to do so.

Fluent speaking involves the rapid engagement of numerous muscles, including those related to breathing, the vocal folds, larynx, and articulators (the lips, mouth, and tongue). In fact, it is commonly said that something in the neighborhood of 100 muscles are involved in talking! Thus, although most of us find talking relatively automatic, speech production is a prime example of an extraordinarily complex feat of coordination and control that spans cognitive and motor systems. In this chapter we will focus on the brain regions supporting speech planning, production, and monitoring.

A good place to start our thinking about speech production is to consider what a talker is doing, as illustrated in Figure 4.1: From among a large set of sounds they know how to make, they are selecting a subset that works together to form an utterance and providing motor regions of the brain sufficient information to produce these sounds. As the sounds are produced, the talker is monitoring feedback from both their body (somatosensory feedback) and their ears (auditory feedback) to gauge how closely their motor commands came to producing the intended target. (See Box 4.1.)

4.1 Speech Motor Planning and Execution

Brain regions associated with speech motor planning and execution are shown in Figure 4.3. Although we are focusing on motor action in the context of spoken language, many researchers view speech production within a larger context of motor control. As such, selecting and preparing speech movements shares a number of processes with other types of motor movement. A region near the midline of the brain is known as the supplemental motor area (SMA), which is involved in producing motor responses;[3] one key region associated with *preparing* motor responses is the pre-SMA, a region adjacent to SMA proper. Manipulating response selection demands during word production

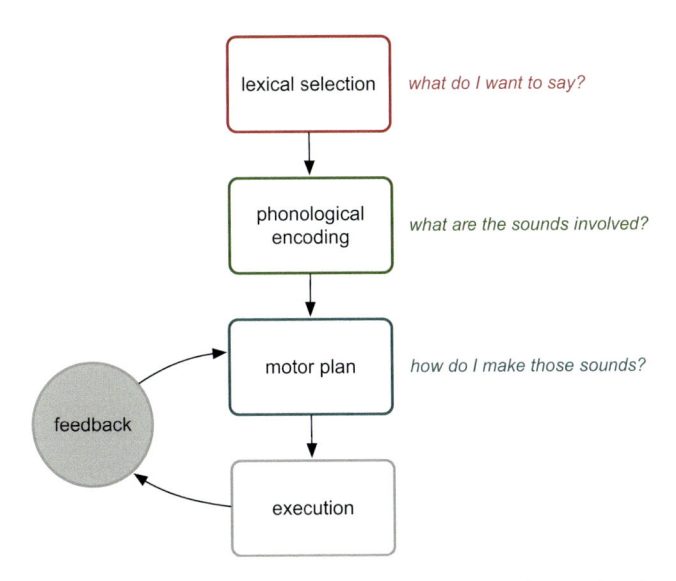

Figure 4.1 Simplified illustration showing stages of speech production (see for example Levelt, 1989; Levelt et al., 1999; Tremblay et al., 2016). When a talker has a meaning in mind (conceptual preparation), the specific words they use to convey the idea must be chosen (lexical selection). These words are then transformed into sound units to be produced (phonological encoding). Once the intended words are selected, they must be translated into a representation that can be produced by the talker. The final representation is often a sentence; talkers thus need to put together how different units – phonemes, syllables, words, phrases, and so on – are produced by the motor system. The phonological plan involves a set of syllables chosen from a talker's inventory of known speech sounds. From here, specific motor control of the speech production apparatus follows, along with monitoring of the output so that adjustments can be made if necessary. https://osf.io/geqb6/ (CC-BY).

affects activity in the pre-SMA, as well as the cingulate motor area (CMA; located just beneath the SMA along the cingulate sulcus) and ventral premotor cortex.[4] Pre-SMA also plays a role in selecting nonverbal gestures, consistent with a general role in motor response selection.[5]

The caudate nucleus of the basal ganglia has also been implicated in speech motor planning. The caudate nucleus is anatomically connected with the SMA and pre-SMA, allowing for response selection to be supported by cortico-striatal loops.

Many contemporary views assume that the planning stage involves internal models of what the motor result should be. These are often considered to be an **efference copy** of the plan sent to the motor system (a signal from the central

Box 4.1 Using real-time MRI to study speech production.

Simultaneous measurement of all of the body parts involved in speech production is a challenging task. Historically, approaches to studying speech production have involved focusing on the acoustic signatures of speech motor commands: tracking sensors attached to the lips, jaw, and tongue. Some studies have also used **electropalatography**, in which a plate of electric sensors is inserted in the mouth, much like a retainer. These sensors can be used to measure tongue-to-palate contact during speech production and quantify consistency and speech errors.[1] However, none of these approaches is able to simultaneously capture movement along the entire speech motor pathway.

In recent years, an innovative approach to studying the mechanisms underlying speech production is to use a special kind of structural MRI scan to image the speech production apparatus. As covered in Chapter 2, for structural brain imaging, we typically collect a detailed three-dimensional representation of the entire brain, which takes several minutes. While a structural brain image is being acquired, participants are instructed to hold still so that the image is not blurred. However, to capture the rapid movements involved in speech production, a different approach is used. Here, instead of a full three-dimensional image of the brain, a limited amount of data is acquired – in some cases, a detailed picture, but only in one sagittal plane (Figure 4.2). Because a much smaller image is acquired, it can be acquired much faster, effectively producing a movie of speech movements.[2] This approach is usually referred to as **real-time MRI**.

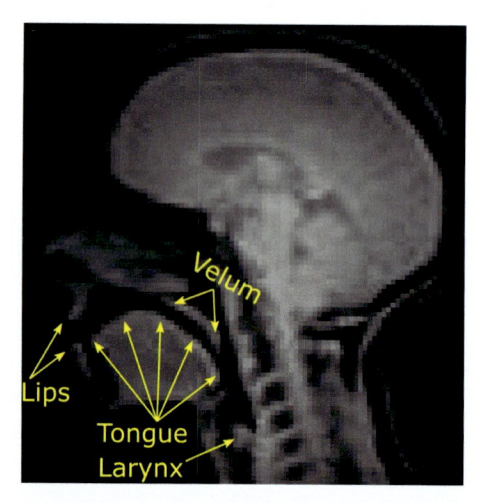

Figure 4.2 Example image from real-time MRI. The figure shows a labeled mid-sagittal slice from a single time point. Air and bone appear as dark, soft tissue (including the brain) show as lighter colors (from Belyk et al., 2023, CC-BY).

Box 4.1 (cont.)

Using real-time MRI in combination with image analysis algorithms, it is possible to get a detailed picture people make while talking. Combined with computer programs to label parts of the image, real-time MRI can be used to measure the complex movements of many parts of the speech production apparatus.

In one application of real-time MRI, Belyk and colleagues (2022) used real-time MRI to look at how talkers manipulated their voices to exaggerate certain characteristics (for example, to sound bigger – which may relate to social traits such as authority and dominance). By doing so they were able to look at individual differences in how well people were able to modulate their voices, which related to how well they were able to alter their vocal tract.

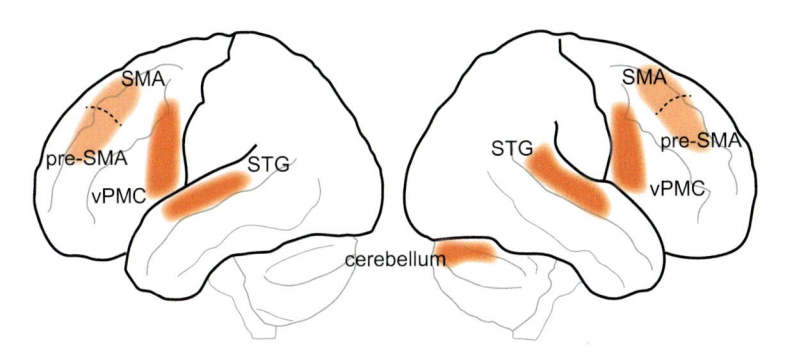

Figure 4.3 Brain regions associated with motor planning and execution, including superior temporal gyrus (STG), ventral premotor cortex (vPMC), SMA, pre-SMA, and the cerebellum. STG = superior temporal gyrus; vPMC = ventral premotor cortex; SMA = supplemental motor area. https://osf.io/geqb6/ (CC-BY).

nervous system to the periphery is an *efference*, and thus an *efference copy* is a copy of that information *not* sent to the periphery). The actual speech produced can thus be compared to the intended target, and adjustments can be made if needed (that is, if errors are detected).[6]

Executing motor movements for speech involves the exquisite coordination of a complex set of muscles related to breathing, articulation, and voicing. Timing is absolutely crucial: Mistimed sounds will be difficult for talkers to produce and difficult for listeners to comprehend.[7] The motor sequencing involved in this stage of planning appears to rely on nonprimary motor areas, including SMA, cerebellum, and basal ganglia.[8] Because syllables and words are never produced identically, movements must also be fine-tuned, including aspects related to movement range, direction, and velocity. Such adjustments may rely on regions including the cerebellum, SMA, and basal ganglia.

The final signals controlling speech muscles come primarily from ventral motor cortex, which controls the vocal tract. Upper motor neurons in the cortex are connected to lower motor neurons located in the brainstem and spinal cord via the pyramidal system. Primary motor cortex is also connected to a number of nonprimary motor regions, including SMA, CMA, and other parts of premotor cortex. These regions have connections to the spinal cord and thus might influence motor control, regardless of signals from primary motor cortex.[9] (See Box 4.2.)

Box 4.2 Where is "Broca's area," and what is its role in speech production?

Based on macroanatomy and cytoarchitecture, the inferior frontal gyrus has three major subdivisions (Figure 4.4): *pars opercularis*, *pars triangularis*, and *pars orbitalis*.[10] These correspond roughly to areas 44, 45, and 47 identified by Brodmann (see Section 3.3.4) and are often referred to by their Brodmann numbers. However, because we typically do not have access to histological staining in humans, in practice "Broca's area" is usually defined based on macroanatomical landmarks. And, its precise definition depends on who you ask, making comparisons across studies challenging.[11] Broca's original definition specified the "third frontal convolution," corresponding to Brodmann Area 44 (*pars opercularis*). However, in practice many researchers have extended the definition to include Brodmann Area 45 (*pars triangularis*).

Even relying on cytoarchitectonic differences is not foolproof, as cellular divisions vary from person to person.[12] More importantly though, a number of researchers over many decades have noted that patients with Broca's aphasia seldom have damage restricted to *pars opercularis* (or even that and *pars triangularis*). Beginning at least in the late 1970s, Mohr and colleagues (1978) summarize their findings the following way: "The speech disturbance resulting from infarction limited to the Broca area has been delineated; it differs from the speech disorder called Broca aphasia, which results from damage extending far outside the Broca area. Nor does Broca area infarction cause Broca aphasia."

Box 4.2 (cont.)

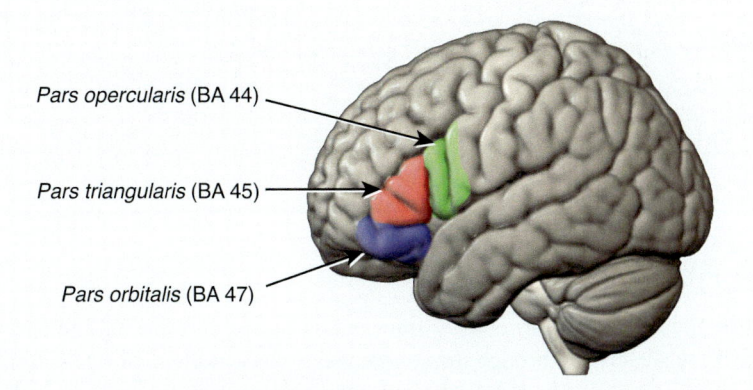

Pars opercularis (BA 44)

Pars triangularis (BA 45)

Pars orbitalis (BA 47)

Figure 4.4 Outlines of the macroanatomical subdivisions of the left inferior frontal gyrus – *pars opercularis, pars triangularis, pars orbitalis* – on a template brain. Traditional Brodmann Areas (BA) – relating to cytoarchitectonic differences – are given in parentheses. https://osf.io/geqb6/ (CC-BY).

Using the statistical technique of voxel-based lesion symptom mapping (VLSM),[13] Bates and colleagues (2003) were able to examine the relationship between post-stroke brain damage and language processing in more than 100 participants. They found the regions most closely associated with verbal fluency were the left insula and the left arcuate fasciculus and superior longitudinal fasciculus – *not* the traditional regions of Broca's area.

Thus, people with damage to traditionally defined "Broca's area" do not always present with Broca's aphasia. And in fact, modern brain imaging clearly supports the fact that Broca's original patients indeed had damage well beyond a limited definition of Broca's area.[14] It could be that, had Broca more clearly emphasized the extent of the damage in his original patients, we would have a different – and perhaps less focal – view of the brain regions supporting language. Indeed, modern studies continue to accumulate evidence supporting the involvement of regions beyond the third convolution in fluent language production. In addition, recent studies have also provided evidence that Broca's area may not always be active during speech production, contrary to long-held assumptions.[15] And surgical removal of classic Broca's area does not reliably result in Broca's aphasia.[16]

What are the implications of these findings? In the context of the anatomical circuits discussed throughout this book, hopefully they will serve as

Box 4.2 (cont.)

a reminder that details of the anatomical and functional definition of regions matter and can significantly affect our interpretations. Despite years of evidence suggesting a more complicated relationship between post-stroke damage to IFG and speech difficulty, many textbooks still gloss over these details, which is frustrating to language researchers. However, having read *this* textbook, you now know the truth!

4.2 Prosody

When speaking, we also convey information above and beyond the specific words we are saying through the sound of our voice: for example, the timing, loudness, and inflection.[17] Imagine saying the sentence "Look out the window" in the following situations:

- giving a lecture in a classroom
- speaking to a pet dog
- having a conversation with your friends when suddenly you realize there is a giant spider crawling up the side of your building.

It would be surprising if you said the sentence identically in all of these situations. Instead, you would use your voice to communicate the urgency (or lack thereof) in your command.

Prosody refers to the timing, loudness, and inflection of speech; because it can be conveyed without words, it is sometimes classified under nonverbal communication.[18] Prosody has many purposes. Grammatical functions include distinguishing word forms: for example, "obJECT" (to disagree with) versus "OBject" (an item), to convey compound words ("greenhouse" vs. "green house"), or to signal a question. Pragmatic use will help draw a listener's attention to a part of an utterance, including providing a clarification. (Sometimes, grammatical and pragmatic prosody are grouped under the heading of "linguistic" prosody.) Finally, emotional or affective prosody is used to convey attitude or emotion.

Aprosodia is an impairment processing prosody. Unlike lexical and semantic information, which seem to show some lateralization to the left (dominant) hemisphere, affective prosody in particular is differentially supported by right hemisphere regions. Evidence for right hemisphere contributions to affective prosody comes from people who have had a stroke resulting in damage to the right hemisphere. People with right hemisphere damage often have difficulty with both perceiving and producing prosodic cues.[19] For example, they may have difficulty conveying the correct tone for a question or a sarcastic comment.

The specific regions of the right hemisphere underlying prosody production are still not entirely clear: Many of the research studies did not have access to detailed information about the region of brain damage. Some candidate regions for prosody production involve inferior parietal cortex (consistent with a dorsal stream component to prosody production) and right inferior frontal gyrus (i.e., a right hemisphere homolog to "Broca's area").[20] However, as yet a firm consensus has not been reached. (See Box 4.3.)

Box 4.3 Using speech errors as a window into production mechanisms.

A behavioral method with a long history in speech production research involves analyzing speech production errors. Table 4.1 shows several examples of sentence production errors (from Garrett, 1975), many of which you may have encountered in your own life (as either the producer, or receiver, of similar errors).[21]

One of the most useful pieces of information gleaned from speech errors relates to the degree to which listeners plan ahead when producing a sentence.[22] For example, sometimes a part of a sentence that belongs *later* in the sentence is (mistakenly) produced early on – for example, "Jike

Table 4.1 Examples of errors made during sentence production.

Type of error	Example sentence	Explanation
Addition	"I don't see any many paddocks around here."	intended either *any* or *many* but not both
Deletion	"I'll just get up and mutter __intelligibly."	intended *unintelligibly*
Substitution	"At low speeds it's too light."	intended *heavy*
Complex addition	"The exPosner experiment that … "	intended *Posner*
Complex deletion	"That would be __having like Harry."	intended *behaving*
Shift	"That's so she'll be ready in case she decide__ to hits it."	intended *decides to hit it*
Exchange	"Fancy getting your model renosed."	intended *nose remodeled*
Fusion	"At the end of today's lection … "	intended *lecture* or *lesson*
Double whammy	"He's a laving runiac."	intended *raving lunatic* or *maniac*

Box 4.3 (cont.)

and Mill" (instead of *Mike and Jill*). In this case, the speaker clearly has planned more than one word ahead, and somehow the elements of the plan have gotten switched. The units that get switched can be phonemes, morphemes, or whole words.

Speech errors have also proved influential in helping researchers decide the type of sound that can be considered a speech "unit" in the first place. One reasonable assumption is that units stay together when they are rearranged, and thus by keeping track of the sounds that are incorrect, omitted, or exchanged, we learn something about how speech units are sequenced for production.

4.3 Sensory-Motor Feedback

One of the processes central to speech production is to know, as a talker, whether our speech is correct. In other words, given the complex coordination of multiple motor systems required for fluent speech production – is the output what we intended? Thankfully, we have sensory input from our body that is informative on this matter. In the context of speech, **sensory-motor feedback** refers to the process whereby our sensing of speech sounds can affect how our motor systems produce speech. This sensory information can either be somatosensory (that is, our perception of our muscle action and body position) or auditory (we hear the speech that we produce). If the result isn't what we intended, we can adjust our production (for example, the velocity or timing of certain muscles).

An exaggerated instance of sensory-motor feedback can be seen when a talker's speech production is artificially perturbed. One way to accomplish this is to disrupt the mechanisms involved in speech production – for example, by exerting pressure on the lips or tongue using an external mechanism. In these cases talkers adjust their motor systems to compensate for the perturbation so that the produced utterance matches what was intended.[23] The brain regions responding to physical perturbations during talking include a distributed network of motor-related regions, including regions of ventral premotor cortex and portions of the inferior frontal gyrus.[24] An additional area implicated in sensory-motor feedback is the posterior part of the Sylvian fissure at the parieto-temporal boundary (area Spt).[25]

A complementary way to introduce perturbation in the link between motor plans and expected sound is to artificially alter what a talker hears while speaking. For example, using a microphone to record a talker and play a digitally altered version of their speech back to them using headphones.[26] Under such circumstances, talkers adjust their speaking to maintain the target acoustic representation.[27] The phenomenon is also seen when people talk in the midst of significant background noise: The **Lombard effect** (or Lombard reflex) refers to how talkers adjust their speaking in noise to maintain intelligibility.[28] Many of the brain regions identified in response for physical perturbations are also present for altered auditory feedback, including ventral premotor cortex, inferior frontal gyrus, and posterior STG.[29]

4.4 Challenges in Speech Production

In the context of the complicated systems described for producing fluent speech, perhaps it is not surprising that disruptions to any part of this system can cause difficulties producing fluent speech. In this section we briefly cover three conditions associated with speech production difficulty.

4.4.1 Dysarthria

Dysarthria refers to difficulty with the motor execution of speech due to weakness or problems with control of muscles used to produce speech. Dysarthria is different from other speech disorders in that many speech subsystems can be affected (e.g., respiratory support, voice quality, resonance of speech, and clarity of articulation). These deficits often result in reduced speech intelligibility and can make it challenging for people with dysarthria to communicate effectively. Adults who have developed speech and language normally can acquire dysarthria following damage to the brain or nervous system, including as a result of a stroke or neurodegenerative disease (such as Parkinson's disease or amyotrophic lateral sclerosis). Damage to regions including the basal ganglia or motor neurons can interfere with speech sound production.

A common cause of dysarthria in children is **cerebral palsy**, a neurodevelopmental condition associated with difficulties in motor, sensory, and cognitive domains. Cerebral palsy is the most common cause of motor disability in children, and is often caused by neurological damage before, during, or soon after birth (including in-utero stroke or anoxia/ trauma). The constellation of challenges faced by children with cerebral palsy manifest in a wide variety of ways: Some children are nonverbal, some have speech disorders (commonly dysarthria), and some have unimpaired speech.[30] In cases of speech production difficulty, **alternative and augmentative communication (AAC)** strategies may be developed in consultation with a speech language pathologist to facilitate communication.[31]

4.4.2 Apraxia of speech

Apraxia is a motor disorder characterized by difficulty carrying out movements. Specific types of apraxia are classified according to the ability or body part(s) affected. **Apraxia of speech** is characterized by difficulty planning and programming speech motor output. Speech rate is slow, speech sounds are prolonged, and pauses between words are frequent. Acquired apraxia of speech frequently occurs with Broca's aphasia and is typically associated with damage to the left hemisphere (e.g., following a stroke) (see Box 4.4). Historically, the distinction between apraxia of speech and Broca's aphasia was a topic of debate: Even though theoretically apraxia of speech can occur without language impairment, in practice, it is rare to have apraxia of speech in the absence of aphasia.

Characteristics of prosody can help distinguish apraxia of speech from other motor speech difficulties. In addition to the slow speech rate, syllables are often stressed equally and may be produced one at a time. The fluency of speech is often diminished, with talkers having a halting rhythm or pausing to find the correct articulatory position.

The brain regions in which damage leads to apraxia of speech have been subject to debate over the years. There is increasing agreement that the regions associated with apraxia of speech are near to, but not identical to, those associated with Broca's aphasia. Regions associated with apraxia of speech include the insula, inferior frontal gyrus, and arcuate fasciculus.[32]

4.4.3 Stuttering

People who stutter typically produce utterances that include periods of fluent speaking disrupted by temporary interruptions, or dysfluencies. The person knows what they want to say but has difficulty moving forward in the speech sequence. Dysfluencies in people who stutter share some characteristics in common with dysfluencies in people who do not stutter: For example, they most often occur at the beginnings of words or sentences, and are exacerbated by stress and fatigue. However, the degree of dysfluency is significantly more pronounced in people who stutter. Developmental stuttering usually starts in early childhood, and affects approximately 1 in 20 children between the ages of 2 and 4 years. Most of these cases resolve, but for approximately 1 percent of individuals stuttering continues to adulthood. The variety of behaviors, and variability in the locations of brain differences, in people who stutter compared to those who do not suggests a complex set of causes, including regions related to both motor function and sensory-motor feedback.[33]

Box 4.4 Living with aphasia.

Mary, a teacher, had just been appointed as principal of her school and was leading an active life when she had a stroke. She was 47 years old.

Immediately following her stroke, Mary was not able to speak. She spent three weeks in the hospital before she woke up. She tried to talk, but nothing came out. She also had difficulty with spatial awareness and motor control of the right side of her body related to her stroke. However, she understood what others were saying. She could shake her head "yes" or "no," and for the first few weeks the doctors encouraged people to communicate with Mary by asking her questions that could be answered this way. Eventually she was transferred to a rehabilitation hospital that had a program for stroke survivors. After nine weeks of rehabilitation, Mary was able to say a new word: "Tailgate!" (which she attributes to her time at football games in her college days).

One of the hardest parts of Mary's journey was in the rehab hospital shortly after her stroke when she was told she might never be able to speak normally again. She was devastated, realizing she might lose her job and the activities she enjoyed. But she was also motivated and determined to do all she could to regain as much language function as possible. She took advantage of every possible opportunity for rehabilitation or speech therapy.

Looking back on that time Mary remembers her drive to regain her language. "I worked so hard. My leg and my arm on my right side had weakness. But I wanted to learn to talk again!" When her teacher friends came to visit, she had them bring games they would play with their students. In part through this constant practice, Mary started to regain some of her language function. "I learned the alphabet from the beginning again, I learned how to write with my left hand ... it was a long journey but it paid off."

After many months of diligent work, a year of shadowing, and an additional year of nearly full-time rehab, Mary returned to work as an English Language (ELL) teacher in her old school. Many times the students would need some extra time to come up with the right words during their lessons; this was a point of connection for them with Mary, who also sometimes needed some extra time to come out with the right words. "In English as a second language, time is very key. I always gave them a minute to think. And while they were thinking of their answer, I was formulating in my head what I was going to say to them."

One of Mary's frustrations is that because she may need more time to express her thoughts, people sometimes think she might have diminished cognitive ability. She is very clear: Her mind is as sharp as ever, but it is sometimes just difficult to get the right words out. If there is one thing Mary

Box 4.4 (cont.)

wished people would understand, it is the importance of being patient. "Patience is the most important thing. All people with aphasia need patience. All of the processes have to go in my brain and then out my mouth, where other people might just speak."

Mary was always an assertive person, and this personality trait has been useful. She finds that informing people about her condition is often helpful. "Every time I introduce myself to someone I'm working with I tell them: I have aphasia. It is a communication disorder. It might take me some time to get my thoughts across, but my thoughts are in my head."

After ten years of English Language teaching, Mary retired three years ago. She stays busy volunteering for research studies, book clubs, writing classes, and public engagement opportunities (including speaking with professors who are writing textbooks!).

One of the brain systems implicated in developmental stuttering is the basal ganglia. The **basal ganglia** are a collection of nuclei located deep in the brain and are often associated with movement and motor control (basal ganglia function is disrupted in Parkinson's disease, for example, in which many of the defining symptoms relate to motor function).[34] The basal ganglia are critical for the production of the neurotransmitter dopamine, and also have reciprocal connections with many regions of cortex, including the SMA. The pathway relating basal ganglia to stuttering may thus include alterations in dopamine production.[35]

Although there is no "cure" for stuttering, numerous therapeutic approaches and strategies exist that are designed to improve fluency. One remarkable facet of stuttering is that it is usually absent when people sing, despite a number of shared aspects of vocal motor control that are shared between talking and singing.

4.5 Summary

- Speech production relies on coordinating a large number of muscles related to breathing, voicing, and articulation. Much of the research on speech production is situated in the context of either psycholinguistics or motor control.
- Primary regions involved in speech motor planning and execution include pre-SMA, ventral premotor cortex, the CMA, and the cerebellum.

- Sensory-motor feedback plays a critical role in maintaining production accuracy, and comes from both somatosensory and auditory sources. Regions of posterior STG play an important role in auditory feedback.
- Challenges to speech production can arise from disruptions to any stage of motor production, and include dysarthria, apraxia of speech, and stuttering.

Notes

1. As one example, McMillan and Corley (2010) used electropalatography to look at how competition between phonemes affected consistency of production. They had participants produce pseudoword tongue-twisters (for example, "kef def def kef") compared to simple, noncompeting versions ("kef kef kef kef"). Competition resulted in increased variability in production, suggesting that competition during planning stages carries through to articulation (which wouldn't have to be the case).
2. Carey and McGettigan (2017) provide a detailed description of real-time fMRI for studying the vocal tract, as well as how to incorporate this data into brain imaging studies of speech production.
3. The SMA was a term coined in the 1950s by the famous neurosurgeon Wilder Penfield and colleagues (e.g., Penfield and Welch, 1951). It's *supplemental* because it lies outside primary motor cortex proper but contributes significantly to motor representations (Penfield and colleagues found stimulating this area affected motor responses).

   Although the SMA and pre-SMA are frequently discussed in the context of speech *production*, Lima and colleagues (2016) review the role of the supplemental motor area in auditory *perception* (as well as a nice description of the anatomy and distinctions between SMA and pre-SMA). Interestingly, the frontal aslant tract connects SMA and pre-SMA with the inferior frontal gyrus (*pars opercularis*), providing a pathway linking SMA and pre-SMA to regions associated with speech understanding.
4. Tremblay and Gracco (2006), for example, conducted an fMRI experiment in which they had participants either read a word written on the screen, or generate a word from a semantic category presented on the screen. The logic was that generating a word from a semantic category involved the same internal selection processes present to naturalistic word production (when a talker must internally select a word before speaking it), in contrast to reading (in which no selection is necessary). Compared to reading aloud, they found word generation associated with increased responses in pre-SMA and ventral premotor cortex, consistent with important roles for these regions in response selection.
5. Trembly and Gracco (2009) used repetitive TMS to interfere with processing in the pre-SMA as participants were asked to produce a word or an oral gesture (a whistle, a raspberry, or a kiss). Items could be specified (low response selection demands) or

chosen from alternatives (i.e., volitional; high response selection demands). Trials with TMS applied showed longer response times when response was volitional compared to when it was specified, with no significant difference between words and gestures. These results suggest a role for motor plan selection in the pre-SMA.

6. The DIVA model (Guenther, 1995; Guenther et al., 2006) proposes computational and neuroanatomical details for the phonetic encoding and articulation stages of speech production (see review by Kearney and Guenther, 2019). Among other aspects, the DIVA model includes both auditory and somatosensory targets that are compared to feedback from auditory and somatosensory systems. Relatedly, Hickok (2012) outlines a framework for hierarchical state feedback control, drawing on work in other domains of motor planning, in which internal models are generated and evaluated against outputs to correct errors. One possibility for the neural instantiation of these involve sensory targets in auditory cortex and motor targets in ventral premotor cortex (for example, IFG/BA 44 as well as BA 6). See also Gracco and Lofqvist (1994), who emphasize the rapid online adjustments talkers can make to perturbations of production.

7. A nice example of coordinated timing is found in Gracco (1988), who measured face and muscle movements as participants repeated "sapapple" (which I recommend trying because it's fun to say). The timing of peak velocities of the lips and jaw were closely related, indicating coordinated control.

8. In one fMRI study, Bohland and Guenther (2006) had participants repeat three-syllable pseudowords that varied in both syllable complexity and sequence complexity. For example, a simple syllable was a consonant-vowel (CV) item, like "ta"; a complex syllable would be a CC(C)V item, like "stra" (which requires more coordination of articulators than simple syllables do). A simple sequence involved repeating the same syllable three times ("ta, ta, ta" or "stra, stra, stra"), whereas a complex sequence used three unique items ("ka, ru, li" or "kla, stri, splu"). They found that sequence complexity was associated with increased activity SMA, premotor cortex, cerebellum, and insula; several of these regions also show effects if syllable complexity, as well as interactions between sequence complexity and syllable complexity.

Peeva and colleagues (2010) used an fMRI repetition suppression paradigm to investigate motor planning at different levels of speech processing: phonemes, syllables, and supra-syllabic sequences. *Repetition suppression* studies take advantage of the fact that the brain typically shows a smaller response to a repeated stimulus than to a novel stimulus. You can thus use brain responses to infer how different the brain thinks two items are. In Peeva and colleagues (2010), participants read pseudowords with two syllables that could vary from trial to trial in how they differed in order to test multiple levels of motor planning. The authors found several regions responding to phonemic information, including the left pallidum, left SMA, left posterior STG, and left superior cerebellum. Syllabic information was associated with left ventral premotor cortex, and supra-syllabic information with the right superior cerebellum.

9. When the CMA is electrically stimulated in monkeys, vocalizations are triggered (von Cramon and Jürgens, 1983).

10. Although perhaps not the most straightforward names, these Latin descriptions based on macroanatomical observations have persisted into the modern literature. The most posterior part of the IFG abuts the frontal operculum, hence *pars opercularis* (opercular part). The IFG typically has a triangular portion (*pars triangularis*). And the most anterior and ventral portion (corresponding to Brodmann Area 47) is near the orbital cavity (eyes), hence *pars orbitalis*.

11. Keller and colleagues (2009) provide a nice overview of the naming and definition of Broca's area, as well as how terminology relates to behavior: "The posterior region of the left frontal convolution is Broca's area because this is the area to which Paul Broca attributed the seat of speech expression, but it is not the area alone that accounted for the language disturbances in Broca's patients."

12. Amunts and colleagues (1999) examined cytoarchitectonic markers for Brodmann Areas 44 and 45 in 10 human brains. They found, first, that the cytoarchitectonic subdivisions did not cleanly map on to macroanatomical features (i.e., gyral and sulcal boundaries). Furthermore, they found notable differences in the shape and size of these areas across the 10 brains. (In this sample, left hemisphere regions were always larger than right hemisphere homologs, although the lateralization – or lack thereof – of these regions remains an area of discussion.) Also of interest, the authors note: "The present study has demonstrated the presence of parcellations within areas 44 and 45. Thus, neither area seems to be completely homogeneous cytoarchitectonically."

13. In VLSM, brain damage is labeled on structural images for each participant. These binary maps can then be statistically related to a behavior of interest (for example, verbal fluency). The analysis thus provides a statistical map showing the voxels which, across the group, are most strongly related to behavior. The technique works, in part, because of the variability in lesion location across people, providing a sort of "natural experiment" on the specific regions of brain damage and behavior.

14. This is the same study from Dronkers and colleagues (2007) mentioned in Chapter 1. The authors used structural MRI to scan the brains of Broca's original patients and found gray matter damage that extended beyond classic Broca's area, as well as damage to white matter tracts. Dronkers (2023) summarized these findings as that Leborgne's primary lesion was more anterior than BA 44, and Lelong's lesion also included the combined arcuate fasciculus/superior longitudinal fasciculus complex.

15. Using intracranial recordings in humans, Flinker and colleagues (2015) find evidence that Broca's area is not active *during* word production but appears to play a role in coordinating a cascade of activity between temporal and motor areas. These findings do not, of course, suggest that Broca's area is not important for speech production, but raise questions about the best way to characterize its involvement (for example, planning and coordination rather than execution).

16. Andrews and colleagues (2023) studied 289 neurosurgical patients, of whom 19 had postoperative Broca's aphasia. Using VLSM (Bates et al., 2003), the authors identified regions of the brain associated with Broca's aphasia. These included an area covering ventral premotor cortex and corresponding regions on the post central gyrus (somatosensory cortex) – *not* portions of the inferior frontal gyrus (i.e., Brodmann Areas 44 and 45).

17. Cutler and Isard (1980) poetically describe prosody in the following way (p. 245): "Prosody is the sauce of the sentence – it adds to, enhances or subtly changes the flavour of the original. And like a good sauce, the realization of a sentence's prosodic structure is a blend of different ingredients none of which can be separately identified in the final product." (Although it should be noted, many researchers have in fact attempted to dissociate different aspects of prosody, despite the challenges of doing so.)

18. Some cartoon characters – such as the teacher in the old Charlie Brown cartoons – are depicted as talking without using words. You might experience the same thing if you try to communicate without opening your mouth or using a single word. (In fact, some patients with aphasia have a severely restricted vocabulary, and can only say one word – but they can say it with prosody helping to communicate their intended meaning.)

19. Weintraub and colleagues (1981) tested nine people with right hemisphere damage following a stroke on both perception and production tasks. Perception tasks included being able to distinguish compound words based on stress (greenhouse vs. green house) and distinguish between short sentences spoken with either the same or different prosody. Production tasks involved repeating question or statement intonation contours and producing sentences with specific stress patterns. In all tasks, patients with right hemisphere damage performed more poorly than neurologically healthy participants. See also systematic reviews and meta-analyses by Durfee and colleagues (2021) and Stockbridge and colleagues (2022).

20. Wright and colleagues (2018) studied four patients with right hemisphere brain damage (three following a stroke, one resulting from frontotemporal degeneration). Participants with brain damage were selected because they had difficulty with at least one type of affective prosody (for example, identifying emotions from sentences). The goal was to dissociate impairments to perceptual, cognitive, or motor contributions to affective prosody. Indeed, the authors found different participants had selective difficulty with several components, supporting an architecture of hierarchical levels to prosody processing – largely supported by the right hemisphere – that may mirror other aspects of speech processing.

21. Garrett (1975) describes a corpus of 3,400 speech errors that he and Stefanie Shattuck collected over three and a half years from their own interactions and as reported by colleagues and students.

22. Stefanie Shattuck-Hufnagel (2015) provides a nice review of prosodic frames during sentence production, including compelling evidence that listeners plan ahead during this process.

23. In a study that exemplifies the perturbation approach, Abbs and Gracco (1984) connected participants to a machine that could apply force to the lower lip. Participants were asked to say either "aba" or "sapapple." Muscle signals (EMG) were recorded for relevant muscles of the lips and face. They found compensatory reactions in the lower lip during perturbation, not reflected in the upper lip, demonstrating rapid awareness of somatosensory signals and the independence of control of various speech muscles (i.e., the upper and lower lips).

24. Golfinopoulos and colleagues (2011) conducted an fMRI study in which they used a small inflatable balloon (actually, the finger of a glove) to perturb participants' jaw movements while they talked. Compared to the non-perturbed speech condition, perturbed speech was associated with increased activity in bilateral somatosensory regions, including anterior supramarginal gyrus, as well as smaller regions of IFG and the cerebellum. The authors interpret these findings as reflecting a network of regions that monitor motor output for errors in order to adjust motor commands.

25. Hickok and colleagues (2009) conducted an fMRI study in which they presented Jabberwocky sentences (that is, sentences with valid syntax but in which the content words were replaced by pseudowords). In one condition participants listened to the sentence; in another they listened for three seconds, and covertly rehearsed what they heard. Area Spt was activated by both perception and production of speech, and multivoxel pattern analysis showed that activity in Spt could distinguish between perception and production trials. See also Buchsbaum and colleagues (2001).

26. You may notice that people tend to talk differently if they are listening to music over headphones, particularly if the music is on the loud side. This is because the acoustic environment of the talker (which includes whatever is coming over their headphones) does not match the acoustic environment of the listener. The talker adjusts their speaking to sound more "normal" to their own ears, despite the interference of the headphones, whereas the listener does not have any interference. As a result, the adjusted speech sounds odd!

27. Houde and Jordan (1998) used a digital signal processing to shift frequency information – specifically, the first three formants (F1, F2, F3) – in real time during speech production. They found that all participants in the experiment adjusted their speaking to compensate for the shifts in order to maintain the intended acoustic signal. See also Villacorta and colleagues (2007) for another example of formant shifting.

28. Credit for documenting this phenomenon typically goes to French otolaryngologist Étienne Lombard (1869–1920) (see Lane and Tranel, 1971, for a review). Lombard used a device made by Austrian otologist Robert Bárány (who would go on to win a Nobel prize in 1914) that provided noise to one ear only, allowing examination of

the other ear. Lombard noticed that when he asked people using the device to speak, they elevated their voices, which returned to normal when the device was switched off. He presented his findings in 1909 to the Academy of Sciences.

29. Chang and colleagues (2013) used human intercranial recordings to study brain activity while participants heard pitch-shifted versions of their speech. They found evidence for complementary profiles of suppression (that is, reduced responses to altered speech during speaking relative to listening) and enhancement (increased responses to altered speech during production relative to listening alone). The authors interpret these findings as being consistent with complementary processes that both relate to compensatory behavior during speech production.

30. The heterogeneity in people with cerebral palsy is significant. One nice example of this is found in Nordberg and colleagues (2013), who looked at 129 children born with cerebral palsy. They found speech disorders in 21 percent of the children, and 32 percent were nonverbal – however, the remaining 47 percent had no speech disorders.

31. Alternative and augmentative communication (AAC) approaches involve strategies, aids, and techniques to enable communication in people with severe speech and language impairment. Some conditions that may benefit from AAC support include cerebral palsy, traumatic brain injury, multiple sclerosis, Alzheimer's disease, and stroke. AAC devices are often categorized as being technology-based or not technology-based. Technology-based options often include speech generating devices – that is, a device that produces synthetic or digitized speech to convey a message. Low-tech solutions can include grids of words or pictures a person can point to.

32. Dronkers (1996) examined patients who had strokes who differed in their articulation difficulties. She identified a region of the insula that was damaged in all of the patients with articulation difficulty, and summarizes (p, 159): "All patients with articulatory planning deficits had lesions that included a discrete region of the left precentral gyrus of the insula, a cortical area beneath the frontal and temporal lobes. This area was completely spared in all patients without these articulation deficits. Thus this area seems to be specialized for the motor planning of speech." Subsequent studies provide additional support for this point. For example, Chenausky and colleagues (2020) examined 52 patients with chronic aphasia, of whom 47 also had apraxia of speech. Using videos of speech production tasks, they quantified individual levels of apraxia of speech and found these scores related to brain damage in the insula and arcuate fasciculus. However, Hillis and colleagues (2004) suggest that the involvement of the insula may be due to its vulnerability to damage, and instead implicate the left inferior frontal gyrus in speech articulation. Given the complexity and interdependency of the processes supporting speech articulation, perhaps the lack of clear agreement should not be surprising.

33. SheikhBahaei and colleagues (2023) suggest that stuttering might be best viewed as a spectrum, with causes and behaviors existing along a continuum – a stuttering

spectrum disorder (SSD). In their words (p. 5): "If our hypothesis proved to be correct, SSD could refer to a broad range of conditions characterized by challenges with speech communication (i.e., stuttering phenotype) . . . Under SSD framework, each person with stuttering has a distinct set of strengths and challenges, and individuals who stutter are empowered to have a freedom of choice to pursue their own personalized treatment course."

Bradshaw and colleagues (2021) investigate the role of sensory-motor feedback in stuttering. Major hypotheses reviewed include a speech motor skills account (people who stutter are on the lower end of a motor skill continuum), unstable or insufficiently activated internal models, overreliance on feedback control, an impaired left hemisphere basal ganglia motor loop, and disrupted auditory prediction or feedback monitoring. Broadly, the authors conclude that people who stutter seem impaired in their use of auditory feedback during speech production.

34. The basal ganglia consist of the striatum (which is further divided into the putamen, caudate nucleus, and ventral striatum), globus pallidus (further divided into an external and internal part), substantia nigra, and subthalamic nucleus. Utter and Basso (2008) provide one of many comprehensive reviews on the complicated circuits and function of the basal ganglia, and how some conditions associated with basal ganglia dysfunction can be helped through the use of deep brain stimulation.

35. Alm (2004) reviews the role of the basal ganglia in stuttering and discusses the hypothesis that dysfunction in the basal ganglia impairs timing cues during speech production, leading to stuttering. Giraud and colleagues (2008) also report a correlation between activity in the basal ganglia and severity of stuttering. Importantly, activity in the caudate nucleus (part of the basal ganglia) was normalized following therapy. Watkins and colleagues (2008) also identify differences in brain activity in the basal ganglia in people who stutter compared to people who do not. They also identify regions of ventral premotor cortex that show differences in both white matter integrity (that is, fractional anisotropy) and activity in people who stutter and those who do not.

Further Reading

Andrews JP, Cahn N, Speidel BA, Chung JE, Levy DF, Wilson SM, Berger MS, Chang EF (2023) Dissociation of Broca's area from Broca's aphasia in patients undergoing neurosurgical resections. *Journal of Neurosurgery* 138:847–857. https://doi.org/10.3171/2022.6.JNS2297.

Reviews a group of neurosurgical patients, of whom a subset developed Broca's aphasia after surgery, to identify brain regions associated with speech production difficulty.

Bohland JW, Guenther FH (2006) An fMRI investigation of syllable sequence production. *NeuroImage* 32:821–841. https://doi.org/10.1016/j.neuroimage.2006.04.173.

An fMRI study of speech production in which both syllable complexity and sequence complexity were manipulated, allowing identification of speech production regions responding to increased speech motor planning.

Castellucci GA, Kovach CK, Howard MA, Greenlee JDW, Long MA (2022) A speech planning network for interactive language use. *Nature* 602:117–122. https://doi.org/10.1038/s41586-021-04270-z.
Uses an interactive communication paradigm to study brain activity during conversation with intercranial electrocorticography, highlighting regions of the frontal lobe associated with speech planning that lie outside the normal speech production network.

Stark BC, Basilakos A, Hickok G, Rorden C, Bonilha L, Fridriksson J (2019) Neural organization of speech production: a lesion-based study of error patterns in connected speech. *Cortex* 117:228–246. https://doi.org/10.1016/j.cortex.2019.02.029.
An analysis of speech production errors in connected speech in a group of participants following a left hemisphere stroke to identify regions associated with different types of speech errors.

CHAPTER FIVE

Auditory Processing

Getting Sound from the Ear to the Brain

If you are wondering what business a chapter on the auditory system has in a book about language, you're not alone: Many discussions of the neurobiology of language largely skip over sensory processing. However, doing so overlooks some of the most remarkable feats listeners accomplish during conversation, as well as some of the most common challenges to communication. If you remember the speech chain (Figure 1.1), ignoring the auditory system assumes that language magically passes from talker to listener (or, even if you allow for speech production, then magically from the mouth of the talker to the brain of the listener). The truth is very different. In this chapter, we will trace how the sound waves produced by a talker end up represented in auditory cortex of a listener, and cover some (but certainly not all) of the complexities supporting this journey. We will also look at how problems with hearing can affect speech and language processing. These aspects are absolutely required to understand spoken communication in the real world, which necessarily involves sensory processing. And, they help us better appreciate the environmental constraints and pressures – on both a momentary and evolutionary time scale – that influence how our brains process spoken language.

5.1 The Ear

Although in everyday conversation we talk about "the" ear, anatomically the ear is divided into outer, middle, and inner portions, each with its own function.

The **outer ear** starts with the pinna – what you see on the side of your head. The pinna functions to "collect" sound and channel it toward the middle ear. The shape of the pinna and ear canal also provide additional cues used in **sound localization** (that is, the fact that most people can tell the difference between a sound in front of them and a sound behind them, or off to the side) and boost sound frequencies that are most important in human communication (2–4 kHz). The ear canal leads from the pinna toward the middle ear, and terminates at the **tympanic membrane** (also known as the ear drum).

The **middle ear** consists of the tympanic membrane and the **ossicles**, the three smallest bones in the human body: the incus, malleus, and stapes. The ossicles act together to transfer energy from the tympanic membrane to the oval window using a lever-based mechanism. Because the tympanic membrane has a much larger surface area than the oval window, this process also results in a significant increase in the force generated, mechanically amplifying the auditory input. When the ossicles can't move freely, the middle ear amplification mechanism doesn't work particularly well, which can happen because of a mismatch in air pressure (the reason you might have trouble hearing when taking an airplane trip) or due to an infection. The stapes then transfers energy to the inner ear by pressing on the oval window, and the inner ear.

The **inner ear** contains the fluid-filled **cochlea**, which is the sensory organ for hearing. "Cochlea" is Greek for "snail," because the cochlea can look like a snail's shell. The adult cochlea is about the size of a pea; when uncurled, it is about 30 mm long. The cochlea contains the Organ of Corti, where the magic of sound transduction occurs. (The inner ear also contains vestibular canals which provide the foundation for balance and motion sensitivity – but we are ignoring those here.[1])

Spanning the Organ of Corti are **hair cells**, so named because they have protrusions (stereocilia) sticking out that look like hairs (Figure 5.1). There are two families of hair cells. **Inner hair cells** are responsible for turning

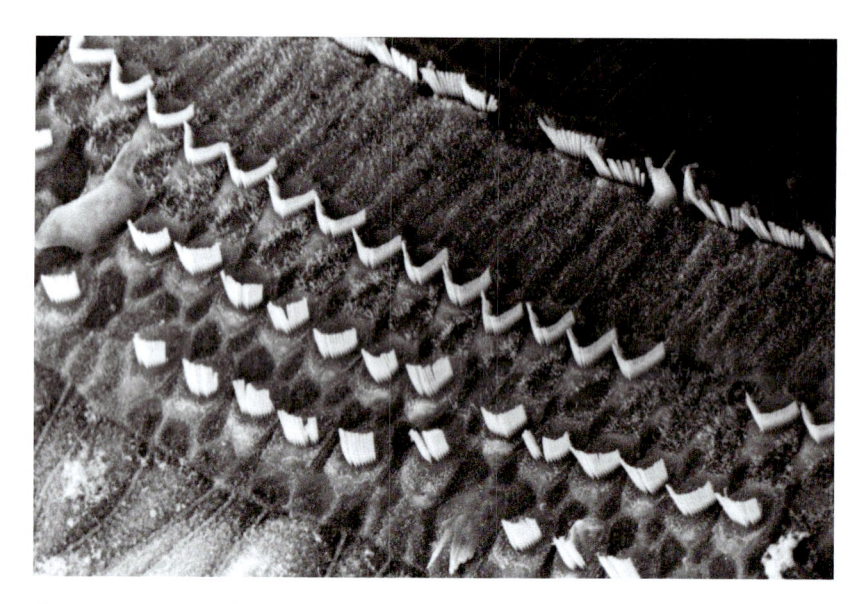

Figure 5.1 Scanning electron micrograph of hair cells along the Organ of Corti in the guinea pig cochlea. Prof. Andrew Forge. Attribution 4.0 International (CC-BY 4.0). Source: Wellcome Collection. https://wellcomecollection.org/works/rruhwss6.

mechanical energy into a nerve impulse.[2] **Outer hair cells** act as little amplifiers, and thus assist in the generation of neural signals (by amplifying the incoming signal, boosting quiet sounds) rather than directly stimulating the auditory nerve.

When the middle ear presses on the oval window, it causes fluid in the cochlea to move and displace the Organ of Corti. Critically, the basilar membrane (underlying the Organ of Corti) varies in stiffness over its length due to changes in thickness and width. As a result, different frequencies of waves in the fluid will maximally displace different areas of the basilar membrane, and thus the Organ of Corti and the hair cells along it. This arrangement is central to **tonotopy**: the ordered arrangement of brain responses according to tone or frequency, and a key organizing principle of the auditory system. Tonotopic organization starts in the cochlea, where hair cells with similar frequency sensitivities are located near each other, and are laid out along the basilar membrane from high at the base, to low at the apex. Thus, damage to a location of the cochlea will result in a corresponding loss of hearing sensitivity in a particular frequency range. (See Box 5.1.)

The inner hair cells synapse onto the auditory spiral ganglia, which form the auditory nerve and transmit information to the cochlear nuclei, the first auditory regions in the brainstem.

Box 5.1 Measuring hearing using the audiogram.

The most common clinical measure of hearing sensitivity is the pure-tone audiogram (which you may have experienced in school or at a doctor's office, even if you have never been to an audiologist).[3] Tones of different frequencies are played over headphones, and listeners are instructed to indicate if they hear a tone. The tester varies the loudness of the tones; for each frequency, the tester determines the softest level at which a listener reliably hears a tone. This threshold is then noted and another frequency tested. Because hearing can differ between ears, the procedure is performed separately on the left and right ears.

A cartoon of a standard audiogram is shown in Figure 5.2. The loudness of sounds is typically measured in decibels (dB).[4] For hearing thresholds, the decibel scale is typically adjusted so that "normal" hearing is 0 dB (which would be specified 0 dB HL, where "HL" specifies "hearing level"). Thus, a value of –5 dB HL means a person has better hearing than normal (a quieter tone is reliably heard), and a threshold of +5 dB HL means a person has slightly worse hearing than normal (a sound would have to be 5 dB louder than "normal" for them to hear it reliably).

Box 5.1 (cont.)

Although useful, it is important to note that the traditional audiogram only captures a small part of what the auditory system does. There are numerous aspects of auditory processing – including many that contribute to speech – that are not reflected, including binaural integration (combining sounds across two ears), spatial localization, temporal processing, frequency discrimination, and others. As a result, it is possible for someone to have a completely normal audiogram, but still report difficulty understanding speech, particularly in noise.

Nevertheless, audiograms can provide a significant amount of information about the integrity of the auditory system. In particular, if a loss of sensitivity is apparent on the audiogram, it may indicate a problem with hearing that will affect speech understanding. Figure 5.3 shows example audiograms for problems that can be identified using the audiogram.

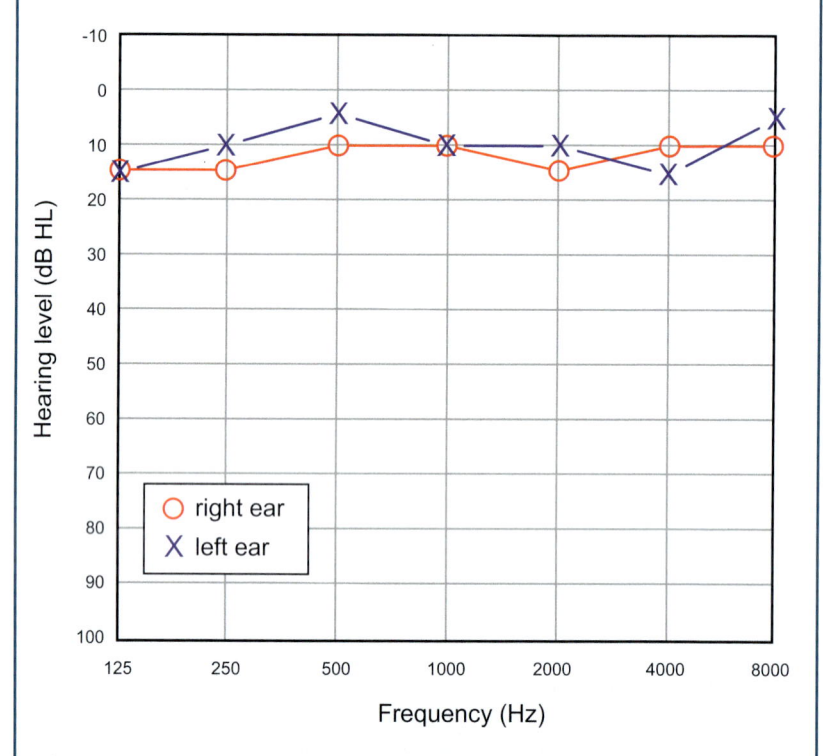

Figure 5.2 A standard audiogram. For each frequency tested, the thresholds of the left and right ears are plotted. By convention, positive values go *down* because a higher threshold (more positive value) corresponds to poorer hearing.[5] https://osf.io/geqb6/ (CC-BY).

Box 5.1 (cont.)

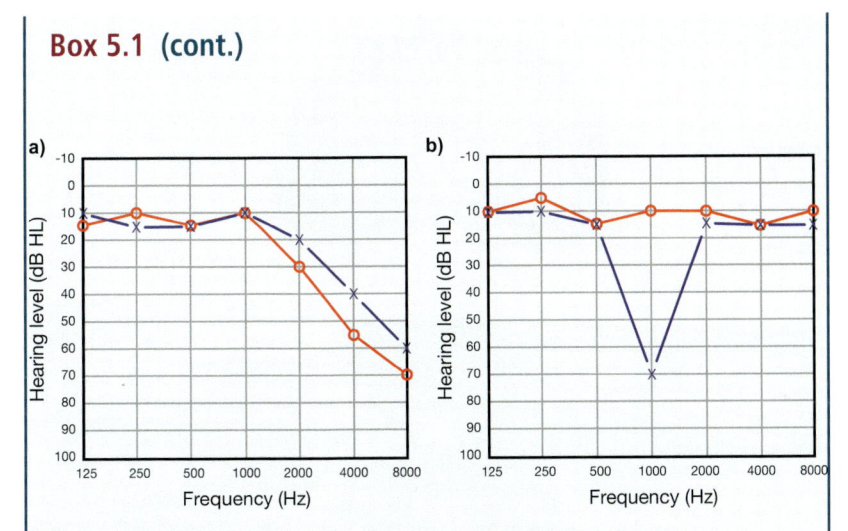

Figure 5.3 Characteristic audiograms associated with hearing difficulty. (a) Sloping high-frequency declines typical of age-related hearing loss (presbycusis). (b) A notch-shaped dip in hearing may reflect acoustic trauma (noise-induced hearing loss), as occurs following repeated exposure to a loud sound at a particular frequency: Hair cells corresponding to that frequency (but not others) are selectively damaged, leading to poor hearing sensitivity in that range. Noise-induced hearing loss can be present in one ear or both ears, depending on the nature of the exposure. https://osf.io/geqb6/ (CC-BY).

5.2 Subcortical Auditory Processing

Located in the middle of the brain, the brainstem contains distinct populations of cells, or nuclei, that respond to specific types of information (Figure 5.4).[6] A key part of the auditory system is found in the **brainstem**, comprised of the midbrain, pons, and medulla oblongata.

After the cochlea, the auditory nerve innervates the **cochlear nuclei (CN)** in the medulla, and on to the inferior colliculus. The **inferior colliculus (IC)** has three subdivisions: a central nucleus, a lateral nucleus, and a dorsal nucleus. The central nucleus receives inputs organized both tonotopically and periodotopically[7] and receives inputs from contralateral and ipsilateral auditory pathways, as well as descending cortical inputs.[8]

The **medial geniculate body (MGB)**, part of the thalamus, is the primary provider of input for auditory cortex.[9] The MGB is divided into dorsal, ventral,

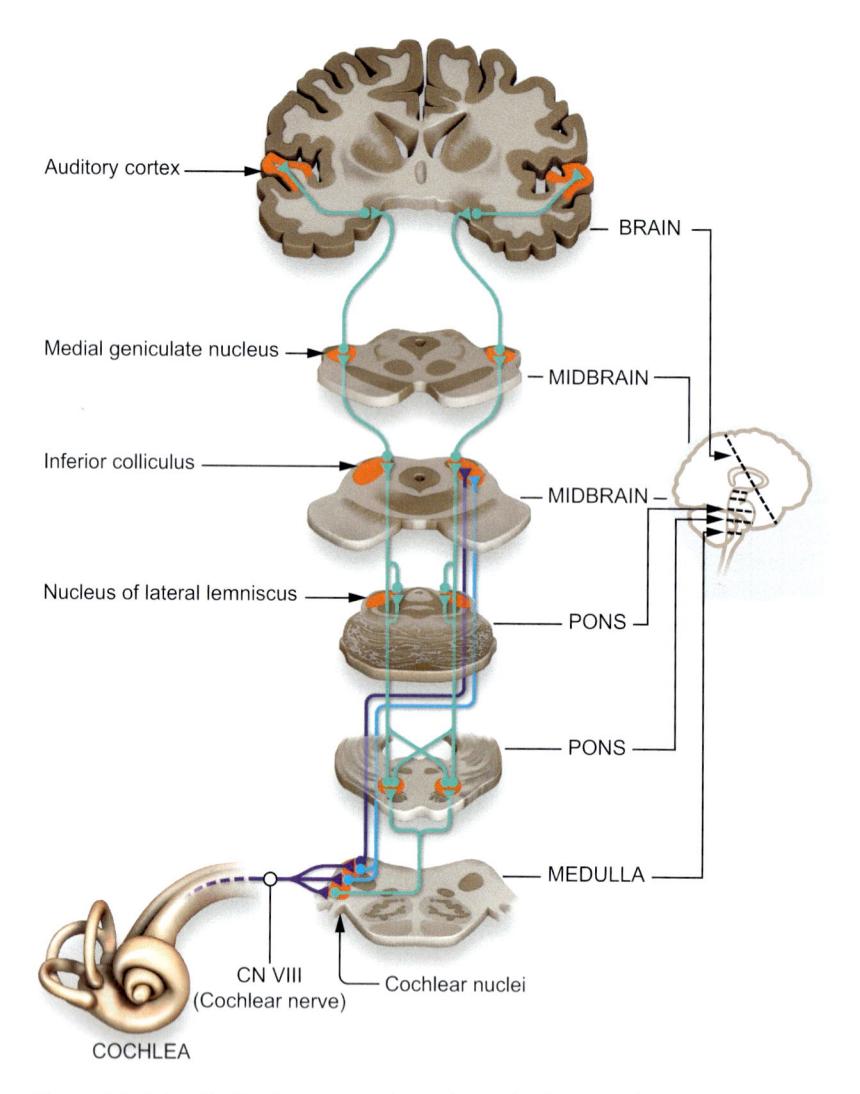

Figure 5.4 Subcortical auditory processing pathways leading to auditory cortex (Peelle and Wingfield, 2016; available via CC-BY-4.0 license from https://osf.io/u2gxc).

and medial parts, each of which have their own functional properties and anatomical connectivity profiles. From the MGB, information passes on to primary auditory cortex along the top part of the temporal lobe.

Importantly, electrical activity in the human brainstem can be measured from electrodes placed on the head and neck. Thus, EEG can be used to measure brainstem responses, and diagnose problems with auditory processing.

One of the most common brainstem responses is the **auditory brainstem response (ABR)**. The ABR reflects evoked auditory responses related to stimulus onset, and is often observed around 5–10 ms after a stimulus (in contrast to cortical responses, which begin closer to 50 ms after a stimulus). Clicks or tone bursts are most often used to elicit ABRs. Typically, thousands of repetitions are required to obtain a robust measurement; because the ABR is an obligatory response driven by simple acoustic information (i.e., the start of a sound), repeating stimuli is not a problem.

Another popular signature of subcortical auditory processing is the **frequency following response (FFR)** (Figure 5.5).[10] The FFR reflects sustained fluctuations that are matched in timing and amplitude to an auditory stimulus, and differs in response properties from the ABR.[11] Speech sounds – such as a consonant-vowel combination (e.g., "da") – are typically used to generate FFRs. A key feature of the FFR is the phase locking to an auditory stimulus, thought to reflect general auditory ability of encoding periodic auditory information. Like ABRs, thousands of trials are typically required to obtain a clear FFR response.

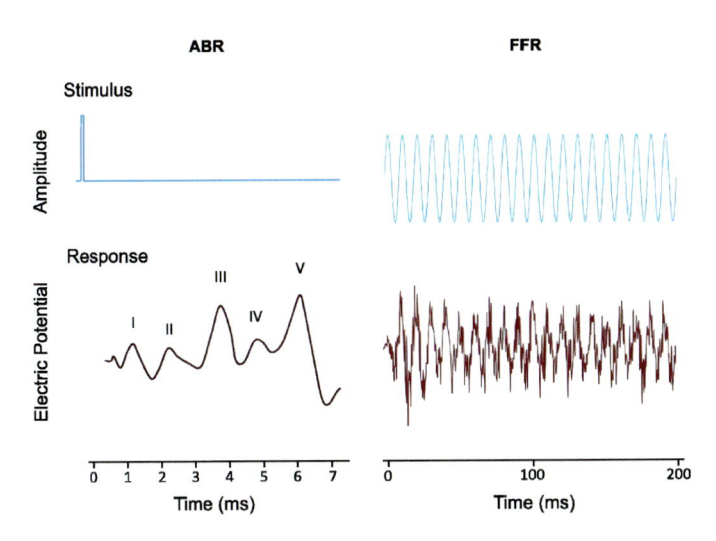

Figure 5.5 An illustration of typical stimuli and recorded waveforms (response) for two electrophysiological measures of auditory neural coding: the ABR and the FFR. From Plack and colleagues (2016), CC-BY.

Frequency following responses and ABRs are generated by neurons in the cochlear nucleus and IC.[12] They thus require input from the peripheral auditory system (the cochlea and auditory nerve) and functioning subcortical nuclei. These subcortical responses differ in the acoustic features that most strongly drive them, with ABRs responding more strongly to sound onsets and FFRs more tuned to sustained sounds (in this context, "sustained" can refer to tens of milliseconds, such as a vowel). Both ABRs and FFRs are generally considered to occur in the absence of attention and can be measured while a listener is sleeping or watching a silent movie.

Periodicity refers to the regular amplitude fluctuations in a sound wave that provide frequency information (think of a sine wave; see also the speech signal in Figure 5.5). Frequency following responses are often used as a measure of how accurately the auditory system can encode periodic information, a sort of summary measure of how well the auditory system is functioning between the cochlea and subcortical nuclei.

Frequency following responses in particular have been shown to reflect a wide array of listener experiences, suggesting they are reflecting more than "just" a faithful encoding of acoustic information. For example, speakers of Mandarin – a tonal language that requires precise discrimination of tone contours – display FFRs that are more closely aligned to Mandarin tones than do speakers of English (a non-tonal language).[13] Frequency following responses also reflect musical experience, with experienced musicians showing stronger pitch representation than those with less musical experience. For musicians in particular, this type of enhanced FFR has been linked to better understanding of speech in noise due to more finely tuned auditory representations.[14]

One mechanism likely underlying this type of plasticity in subcortical auditory processing lies in the projections from cortex to subcortical nuclei. **Corticofugal pathways** provide connections from auditory cortical regions to the auditory brainstem – efferent pathways that allow the cortex to modulate brainstem responses.[15] Although these pathways are consistent with complex and complementary bidirectional communication along the auditory pathway, the precise function played by these connections is still being worked out. Thus, although ABRs and FFRs reflect subcortical responses, there is also good evidence they reflect cortical inputs.[16]

In summary, the mammalian auditory system includes several stages of processing before information reaches auditory cortex, organized around circuits that pass information bidirectionally (that is, feed-forward and feedback). The complex contributions of these subcortical regions, and how they interact with cortical processing, are still being unraveled.[17]

5.3 Auditory Cortex

Like the rest of the auditory system we have encountered so far, primary auditory cortex is arranged tonotopically. In humans, primary auditory cortex is located on Heschl's gyrus,[18] also known as the transverse temporal gyrus, along the top of the temporal lobe[19] (Figure 5.6).

In the context of speech processing, auditory cortex has traditionally occupied somewhat of a strange position, due in part to the fact that many auditory researchers spend most of their time studying either cortical *or* subcortical regions *or* the auditory periphery, but not all of these. Thus, for researchers who focus on the cortex, auditory cortex is often the first brain region considered and performs the "simplest" types of operations. However, from the perspective of researchers considering peripheral or subcortical auditory processing, auditory

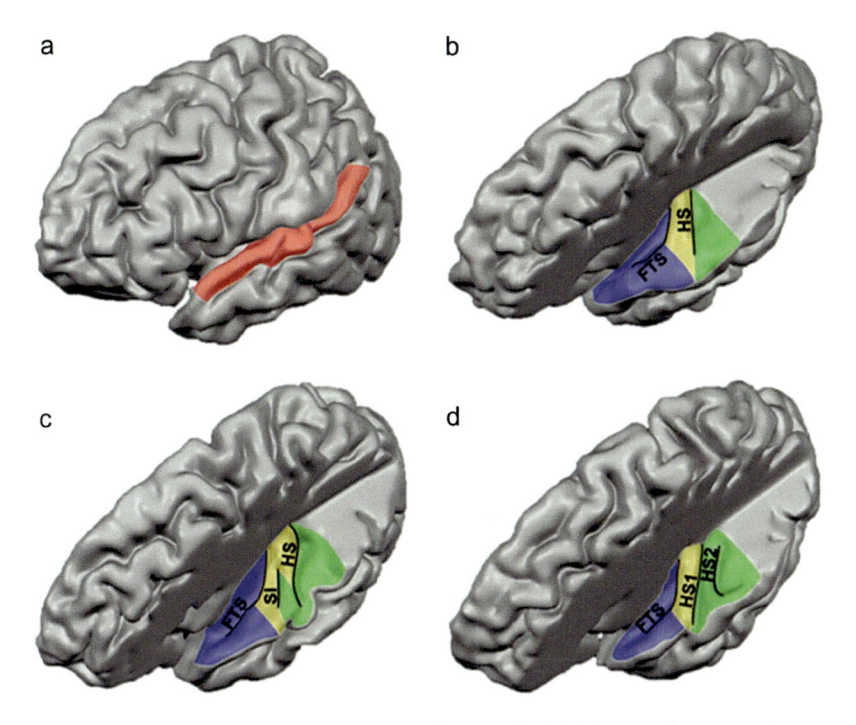

Figure 5.6 Anatomy of the superior temporal plane. (a) The left superior temporal gyrus (highlighted in red). Remaining panels show examples of brains with a single (b), partially divided (c), and fully divided (d) Heschl's gyri, with a large portion of the parietal removed to aid visualization. HS = Heschl's sulcus; FTS = first transverse sulcus. Reproduced from Moerel and colleagues (2014), CC-BY.

cortex is receiving the outputs of several complex operations occurring in subcortex, and thus responsible for quite advanced computations. As we'll see, both of these perspectives are valid.

The most detailed understanding of primary auditory cortex comes from electrophysiological recordings in animals, including nonhuman primates. Years of research has led to general acceptance of three major subdivisions: the core, belt, and parabelt (Figure 5.7).[20] The *core* of auditory cortex in fact contains multiple tonotopic fields that process information in parallel.[21] Surrounding the core are the belt and then parabelt regions. The *belt* contains cells that lack cellular and histological characteristics of core auditory cortex and does not receive the dense connections from the medial geniculate body. The *parabelt*, lying along the lateral surface of the superior temporal gyrus, is not strongly connected to the core area but has strong connections with the belt. The parabelt also has connections with regions outside auditory cortex, including medial temporal cortex, prefrontal cortex, and parietal cortex.

It is important to note that the specific subdivisions – not only their boundaries, but even the number and arrangement of subdivisions – is not uncontroversial, and different authors approach the task from various perspectives. Challenges in defining subdivisions stem from the need to rely on multiple

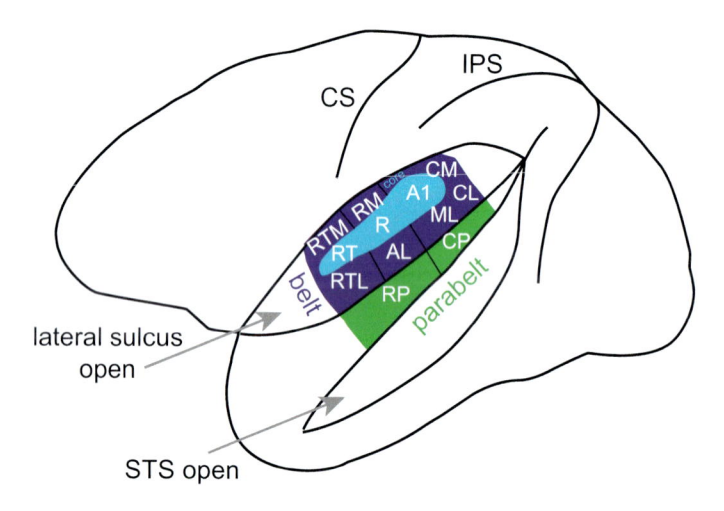

Figure 5.7 Schematic of auditory cortex subdivisions in nonhuman primate (after Kaas et al., 1999). The auditory core, belt, and parabelt contain multiple subdivisions, identified based on a combination of cytoarchitectonic and functional properties. https://osf.io/geqb6/ (CC-BY).

modalities of data and a necessary amount of subjectivity in determining what constitutes a "subdivision." For our purposes, the critical point is to acknowledge the remarkably dense, complex, and hierarchical architecture of auditory cortex, and consider what implications such an arrangement might have for auditory processing (for example, of speech).

In humans, postmortem studies – although rare – have also identified cytoarchitectonic subdivisions in auditory cortex.[22] More commonly, fMRI has been able to demonstrate a tonotopic organization in auditory cortex. Perhaps because the spatial resolution of fMRI is rather coarse compared to the type of invasive electrophysiology used in animal studies, clear distinctions between core, belt, and parabelt regions have remained elusive. However, numerous studies have identified a low-high-low-frequency gradient across Heschl's gyrus.[23] In fMRI studies of auditory processing, activity is often seen in regions outside of Heschl's gyrus, even for simple sounds like noise or tones. These are sometimes referred to as "secondary" auditory cortex to distinguish from primary auditory cortex, although the macroanatomical boundary for secondary auditory cortex is not well defined (in animal studies, histology and electrophysiology help identify auditory regions).[24]

Although auditory cortex responds to speech sounds, it may not respond particularly differently to speech compared to various nonspeech sounds. Furthermore, activity in auditory cortex does not vary substantially with whether or not speech is intelligible.[25] Thus, processing in primary auditory cortex does not seem to typically reflect higher-level computations related specifically to language processing (some of which are covered in Chapter 6). However, this is not to say that auditory cortex does not show any specialization: There is a long history of findings showing asymmetrical processing such that the left auditory cortex and surrounding regions preferentially respond to temporal complexity, and the right auditory cortex to spectral complexity.[26]

5.3.1 Multisensory Processing in Auditory Cortex

A key feature of auditory cortex, often overlooked, is that its responses are not *only* driven by auditory input. In fact, auditory cortex receives inputs from other senses, which can shape auditory processing. Anatomically, there are a number of potential routes for nonauditory information to reach auditory cortex.[27] Subcortical pathways to the auditory cortex include connections from several areas of the thalamus, including the medial geniculate nucleus (associated with visual processing) and ventral posterior complex (associated with somatosensory processing). Cortical origins of multisensory input may be travel through feedback projections from the temporal cortex, intraparietal sulcus, and prefrontal cortex.[28] Thus, calling this region of the brain "auditory" cortex is somewhat of a misnomer, and does a disservice to the multisensory processing that occurs.[29]

5.4 Auditory Processing beyond Auditory Cortex

Although auditory cortex is the primary cortical region involved in processing auditory information, it is not the only one: Other parts of the brain have auditory-responsive neurons. Regions of the superior temporal gyrus (STG), for example, show responses to acoustic as well as phonetic features.[30]

Given the importance of the frontal lobe to many aspects of speech and language processing, one of the most provocative findings in this context involves neurons in frontal cortex that respond to auditory information – in some cases, neurons in the frontal lobe of nonhuman primates respond to auditory stimuli within tens of milliseconds.[31] Prefrontal cortex receives projections from auditory cortex,[32] providing a potential mechanism for these rapid responses.

The functional significance of these auditory regions is best understood in the context of popular dual-stream frameworks for auditory processing (Section 3.4). Although still a matter of investigation, direct auditory input to the frontal lobe may circumvent a strict serial processing pathway and facilitate certain behaviors (e.g., multisensory processing, attention to salient sounds, and so on). Perhaps most importantly, these findings convey a complexity of sensory processing that defies simple delineation between brain regions.

5.5 Hearing Impairment

Hearing impairment affects millions of people around the world: over 1.5 billion people today, projected to rise to 2.5 billion by 2050.[33] The toll of hearing impairment includes cognitive challenge, strained social interactions, and economic burdens (related to healthcare costs, lost educational opportunities, and loss of productivity). Difficulty with hearing can be present from birth, occur with normal aging, or as a result of acoustic trauma or other medical conditions. There are many kinds of hearing loss, and here we will just cover some of the more common forms.

5.5.1 Conductive Hearing Loss

If the travel of sound through the outer or middle ear is impeded, hearing is poorer, particularly for quiet sounds. This hearing loss is referred to as

conductive hearing loss because it involves disruption to the conduction of information from the outer ear to the inner ear. Conductive hearing loss can be caused by problems with the tympanic membrane (eardrum), the middle ear, or the ossicles. These problems can arise from congenital malformation of these structures, damage acquired through illness or trauma, or fluid in the middle ear. As noted earlier, the middle ear acts to mechanically amplify sound from the tympanic membrane to the inner ear through the movement of the ossicles; dysfunction of middle ear function results in "turning down the amplifier" and thus less acoustic energy reaching the inner ear. (Many of us experience consequences of middle ear dysfunction when changing altitude, as on an airplane: The pressure mismatch between the environmental air pressure and middle ear pressure reduces the effectiveness of the middle ear amplification, making it difficult to hear.)

5.5.2 Sensorineural Hearing Loss

Sensorineural hearing loss occurs due to dysfunction of the cochlea, typically the hair cells responsible for both amplifying sound (outer hair cells) and those involved in translating sound-induced vibrations to a neural signal (inner hair cells). Sensorineural hearing loss is the most common kind of age-related hearing loss, also known as **presbycusis** (Box 5.1, Figure 5.3).[34] As such, people with high-frequency hearing loss might have difficulty perceiving the ticking hand of a watch or the high-frequency acoustic energy that marks the "s" at the end of some words. For reasons that are still not fully understood, age-related hearing loss preferentially affects hearing at higher frequencies. Fortunately, the progression of hearing loss from higher frequencies to lower frequencies means that hearing in the range most critical for understanding speech – up to 4,000 Hz or so – tends to be relatively preserved, though as hearing loss progresses speech understanding will be affected. Sex differences in age-related hearing loss are commonly reported, with males more likely to show the effects of hearing loss than females.[35]

As the name suggests, **noise-induced hearing loss** results from exposure to loud noise. A "loud" noise is associated with significant changes in air pressure, which displaces the basilar membrane more than sounds in the normal range. The resulting increase in mechanical force on the hair cells can damage the stereocilia, reducing their ability to function correctly.

An important aspect of noise-induced hearing loss is that damage to the cochlea depends on both the loudness of a sound being heard, and how long a listener is exposed to the sound. In other words, a single exposure to a very loud sound (like an explosion) can be damaging, but so can a couple of hours of exposure to a moderately loud sound (such as an engine or concert).

One cause of noise-induced hearing loss comes from repeated exposure in industrial and work settings.[36] Many machines produce sounds above the recommended range and require hearing protection to be worn. Recreational activities such as playing in a music group, using leaf blowers, woodworking, or using shop tools can also exceed safe levels of loudness.

In recent decades, increasing awareness about the dangers of noise exposure and regulations regarding hearing protection in the workplace have reduced (though not eliminated) workplace causes of noise-induced hearing loss. However, new concerns are being raised about exposure outside the workplace, particularly through listening through headphones that are too loud.[37]

What is the best way to protect your hearing? A good first step is recognizing which sounds are likely to be too loud to hear safely. You can wear earplugs or other protective devices, or move away from the noise (which diminishes its impact). It is especially important to protect the ears of those who can't do so themselves (e.g., children). (See Box 5.2.)

Box 5.2 Hearing loss and dementia.

Over the past decade increasing interest has been paid to a possible link between hearing loss and cognitive decline, particularly in older adults. A key piece of evidence comes from epidemiological, or population-based, studies. These studies typically collect data from a relatively large number of people, but because so many people are in the study, the amount and quality of data collected on each person can be somewhat limited.

Nevertheless, several epidemiological studies have shown a statistically significant correlation between age-related hearing loss and cognitive ability. Some studies examine the relationship between hearing loss and how likely a person is to receive a dementia diagnosis; others look at cognitive functioning in healthy older adults. And, in at least one study, the relationship between hearing and dementia extends into middle age.[38]

Although the basic finding has been replicated in multiple groups of people, the underlying causes of this relationship are unclear, and many possible pathways exist.[39] One possibility is that a reduction in auditory stimulation (due to hearing loss) reduces activity in auditory cortex. Although changes in auditory activity on its own might not directly impact cognitive functioning, auditory regions of the brain are connected to other regions, and even a small change in auditory function might therefore, in principle, disrupt a wide range of brain networks, including those involved in general cognitive function.[40] Evidence for this type of relationship might come from longitudinal studies of adults measuring both hearing ability and

> ## Box 5.2 (cont.)
>
> brain activity, which would enable us to determine whether loss of hearing
> sensitivity leads to changes in brain activity supporting general cognition.
> Unfortunately, these types of studies are difficult to run and to date direct
> evidence is lacking.
>
> Another avenue through which hearing loss might affect cognitive function
> relates to social engagement. People with hearing loss are sometimes more
> reluctant to engage in social situations associated with background noise,
> such as going to a restaurant, bar, or coffee shop: The background noise in
> such situations can make understanding what someone is saying difficult or
> impossible. The resulting reduction in social engagement, however, might
> lead to reductions in physical activity, social support, or happiness, which
> might then affect cognitive function.

5.6 Cochlear Implants

In some cases of severe hearing loss, the hair cells of the cochlea are damaged, but the auditory nerve is intact. In other words, the hair cells cannot adequately stimulate the auditory nerve, and so a person cannot hear. However, if the auditory nerve *could* be stimulated, it would function adequately. In these cases, listeners are sometimes considered candidates for a cochlear implant.[41]

Cochlear implants (Figure 5.8) are neuroprosthetic devices that can electrically stimulate the auditory nerve, bypassing the hair cells of the cochlea.[42] A cochlear implant consists of an external microphone (similar to that found on a hearing aid) and a transmitter coil that sits outside the scalp. Under the scalp is a surgically implanted receiver, and a wire leading to electrodes that wrap around the inside of the cochlea. When the microphone detects sound, the implant electrically stimulates the auditory nerve.[43]

The number of electrodes that a cochlear implant has relates to the complexity of the acoustic stimulus it can convey to the auditory nerve. Because the cochlea is tonotopically arranged, the spatial location of the electrodes determines which frequencies are perceived when an electrode is activated. Early cochlear implants had only a single electrode. Due to technological advances, the number of electrodes increased steadily, and modern cochlear implants often have 16 or 22 electrodes, and can therefore convey about 16 or 22 independent channels of frequency information to the auditory nerve.[44] These electrodes are attempting to replace the function of thousands and thousands of hair cells, which as you might guess, is simply not possible. The result is that the signal provided by a cochlear implant has less acoustic detail than what would be provided by normal hearing.

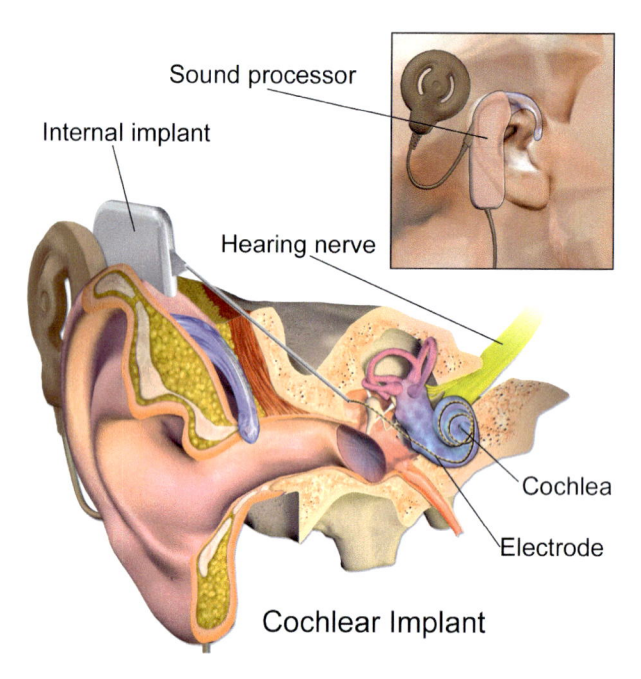

Cochlear Implant

Figure 5.8 Schematic of a cochlear implant. The external sound processor includes a microphone to detect sound in the environment (similar to a traditional hearing aid). The signal is passed to a receiver coil embedded in the skull, which passes the signal to a tiny, coated wire coiled in the cochlea. The electrodes on this implant provide tonotopically arranged electrical stimulation along the cochlea. From Blausen.com staff (2014).

Specifically, although temporal information (the timing and rhythm of speech) is relatively well preserved, the spectral information (difference in information at different frequencies) suffers. Understanding speech with a cochlear implant is therefore more effortful, even in quiet, and many listeners with cochlear implants have difficulties recognizing spoken words compared to listeners with normal hearing. Music, which is often more acoustically complex than speech, is also difficult to fully perceive through a cochlear implant.[45] (See Box 5.3.)

A significant challenge in deaf children born to hearing parents (who do not know a sign language) is providing sufficient language exposure to support normal acquisition – relying exclusively on auditory speech delivered through a cochlear implant may not be sufficient. Fortunately, recent evidence shows that even parents who are just learning sign language can provide enough exposure for a deaf child to maintain a normal trajectory of language acquisition. (For more on sign language, see Section 9.4.)

Box 5.3 Listening with a cochlear implant.

Rahmeh is a third-year undergraduate university student studying speech language pathology and audiology. She was born with significant hearing loss due to an enlarged vestibular aqueduct. She started wearing hearing aids, but found these were not adequate to compensate for her hearing loss. Rahmeh received her first cochlear implant when she was three years old, and her second when she was nine. Rahmeh has some vague memories of being in the hospital for her first surgery but has clearer memories of what it was like after her second implant was activated. "It was really weird – sound was coming in all at once. I almost felt dizzy. Even though I was in a quiet room, and relatively there wasn't a lot of sound coming in, it was still sound I hadn't heard before. But then it got better and I started speech therapy, which helped."

Growing up, Rahmeh went to a lot of speech therapy, and had a lot of support from her family, who worked with her at home. Since coming to university, Rahmeh has found that professors have generally been accommodating. However, one class activity that Rahmeh finds particularly challenging is group work – she does well in group situations with limited background noise, but, when many groups are talking together during class, understanding what other group members are saying can be a real challenge.

Rahmeh enjoys baking, something she's done with her family since she was young (peanut butter cookies are a favorite recipe). She is also an avid podcast listener, which helps her pass the time on her train commute to campus – she is especially fond of thriller and crime podcasts. Her cochlear implant connects to her phone with Bluetooth, allowing her to turn up the volume on her podcasts without amplifying the noise from the train – a helpful feature! She finds podcasts with poor audio quality still present challenges.

Although Rahmeh thinks about her hearing a lot, it's not the main thing that defines her. She wants people to know she's just a normal person. Still, she appreciates when her friends help her out in noisy environments, especially when they do it without her needing to ask. "I prefer to go out with people who already know about my implants, so that way if I don't hear something or notice something, they'll tell me. If there's an announcement made or a friend says something important. My family is very helpful with this!"

One thing Rahmeh has thought about over the years is the degree to which she feels a sense of belonging in either the Deaf community or hearing community. In many ways, she doesn't feel completely a part of either community – but is also at peace with this feeling. Rahmeh understands that getting a cochlear implant may not be the choice everyone makes. But she's glad she has them and appreciates her connection to the sounds around her.

5.7 Summary

- Inner hair cells in the cochlea of the inner ear are the sensory receptors for hearing. They are arranged in a tonotopic fashion, an organization that is preserved through many stages of auditory processing.
- A series of nuclei in the brainstem process auditory information on its way to the cortex. Neural signatures of auditory brainstem processing can be seen using EEG in the ABR and FFR.
- Auditory cortex contains a number of subdivisions characterized by different cytoarchitechtonic properties, functional responses, and patterns of anatomical connectivity.
- Hearing loss affects millions of people worldwide, and can have profound effects on productivity, cognition, and well-being.

Notes

1. Day and Fitzpatrick (2005) summarize the vestibular system poetically:

   Small, beautifully formed and locked in the skull, the vestibular organs continuously bombard the brain with messages. The messages are quite unlike any others. They tell of accelerations, how the head is rotating and translating and its orientation in space. The messages never stop and cannot be turned off. Even when we are completely motionless, they signal the relentless pull of gravity. Perhaps because of their constant monologue, the vestibular sensation is different to the other senses. There is no overt, readily recognizable, localisable, conscious sensation from these organs. They provide a silent sense.

   The otolith organs and semicircular canals sense different types of acceleration: Two otolith organs (the utricle and the saccule) sense linear acceleration, whereas three semicircular canals sense rotational movement. One of the most important functions of the vestibular system is knowing which way is "up" – of paramount significance for most animals. The vestibular system is also intimately tied to eye movements and helping us maintain a stable percept of space, even as our bodies and heads move around in it. See Angelaki and Cullen (2008) for a comprehensive review of the vestibular function.

2. Inner hair cells contain mechanically gated ion channels that lead to changes in their activity. As the hair cells are displaced, a small chain, made out of protein, is stretched, and pulls open a gate, allowing ions to enter the cells. The bigger the fluid movement in the cochlea, the bigger deflection, and the larger ion influx to the hair cell.

3. As reviewed by Vogel and colleagues (2007), the history of the audiogram goes back nearly 150 years. Arthur Hartmann developed an "auditory chart" in 1885 to document how well people could hear a tuning fork of different pitches that looks similar to a modern audiogram. However, it was Max Wien's "sensitivity curve" – first presented in 1903 – that is typically credited with giving rise to the modern

audiogram. Vogel and colleagues also include a timeline of events important for hearing, including a note that in 377 BCE Hippocrates reported observing hearing loss in a patient following skull trauma. For another detailed overview of the history of the audiogram, see Jerger (2013).

4. The history of the decibel is also fascinating. As related by Jerger (2013, p. 150):

> Prior to 1923 the unit for expressing telephone transmission efficiency was the "mile of standard cable," but in that year the Bell system adopted a new concept, the "Transmission Unit" or TU, defined as 1/10 log P/Po, where P and Po are pressure levels in the ratio of 10:1. A year later Bell scientists decided that a more workable unit should be defined as 10 transmission units or, simply log P/Po. They proposed to name this new unit the bel, after Alexander Graham Bell, founder of Bell Laboratories, and to introduce the concept of 1/10th of a bel, the decibel. In effect they traded "transmission unit" for "decibel." This decibel notation was readily adopted by Harvey Fletcher to supplant the sensation unit on the intensity scale of the audiogram. Years later the International Union of Pure and Applied Physics evolved the rule that the first letters of physical units named after persons should be capitalized. Since the bel was named after an actual person, Alexander Graham Bell, it became the Bel, and decibel became dB.

5. Jerger (2013) explains that Edmund Prince Fowler (1872–1966), a renowned otologist who practiced in New York City in the first half of the 20th century, is responsible for this practice. To help clinicians answer a patient who asks "how much hearing do I have left?," Fowler suggested plotting hearing sensitivity as a percentage of "normal" hearing: that is, 100 percent (good hearing) would be toward the top of the chart, with hearing loss being reflected in values below 100 percent. Although the label for audiograms eventually shifted to dB HL rather than "percent normal hearing," the convention of having normal hearing at the top of the audiogram never changed.

6. A comprehensive overview of subcortical auditory processing, ABRs, and FFRs is found in Chandrasekaran and colleagues (2022).

7. **Periodicity** refers to the frequency at which a sound is modulated in time: For example, different neural populations are maximally sensitive to different temporal modulations. Just as tonotopic arrangement refers to responses being physically organized by the frequency of the auditory information, periodotopic arrangement indicates arrangement by preferred periodicity. Combining spectral (frequency) and temporal modulations can result in sensitivity to a large variety of natural sounds.

8. Casseday and colleagues (2002) provide a thorough overview of the inferior colliculus. Among other points, they highlight connections to the motor system, making the inferior colliculus well positioned to help coordinate action based on incoming acoustic information.

9. An overview of the medial geniculate body and its role in speech processing is found in Bartlett (2013).

10. Coffey and colleagues (2019) provide an accessible introduction and perspective on the FFR. Among other points, they raise the possibility that the FFR reflects the combined activity of multiple groups of neurons – that is, in EEG parlance, multiple *generators* – which may differentially contribute to the measured signal depending

on the specific task, and picked up with varying degrees of sensitivity by different neuroscience methods (for example, EEG vs. MEG). They frame the implications of this possibility for interpreting the FFR in the following way (p. 7):

> It is our view that the FFR should be thought of as an aggregate measure of the response of the auditory system, reflecting its cumulative prior history. Specific auditory brain centres may contribute differently to a measured response, but those centres function jointly, and in the context of broader neural networks. This gives us the "functional view" of the FFR – we see it as a measure of how well the entire brain is coding sound features much more than as a reflection of activity within any single nucleus, because the nuclei are embedded in complex functional networks.

11. Bidelman (2015) used 64-channel recordings of ABRs and FFRs, concluding that FFRs could not be easily explained by overlapping ABRs – that is, they are likely generated by different populations of neurons.

12. Marsh and colleagues (1970) found that severing the auditory nerve made the FFR disappear (demonstrating that the source needed to be above the auditory nerve; i.e., not in the cochlea), and that cooling the cochlear nucleus (a method of neural inactivation) reduced the response.

13. Krishnan and colleagues (2005) presented listeners with four instances of the Mandarin syllable /yi/. Depending on the tone contour, /yi/ can mean "clothing," "chair," "aunt," or "easy," recording FFRs to repeated presentations in listeners for whom either English or Mandarin was their first language. They found a greater pitch strength and more robust tracking of pitch contour in speakers of Mandarin (a tonal language) relative to a nontonal language (English). They conclude that "experience-driven adaptive neural mechanisms are involved subcortically that sharpen response properties of neurons tuned for processing pitch contours that are of special relevance to a particular language." For another compelling demonstration of FFRs affected by language experience, see Xie and colleagues (2017).

14. Kraus and Chandrasekaran (2010) review a large number of reported effects of musical experience and training on brain structure and function. They summarize the literature on musical experience and the auditory system this way:

> The effect of music training on brain plasticity is not just a "volume-knob effect" – not every feature of the auditory signal improves to the same extent – but leads to the fine-tuning of auditory signals that are salient (with "sound to meaning" significance) … Musicians, compared with nonmusicians, more effectively represent the most meaningful, information-bearing elements in sounds – for example, the segment of a baby's cry that signals emotional meaning, the upper note of a musical chord or the portion of the Mandarin Chinese pitch contour that corresponds to a note along the diatonic musical scale.

15. Winer (2006) provides a comprehensive review of auditory corticofugal systems and pens a convincing argument for massive descending projections. For example, each subdivision of the medial geniculate body receives input from at least four subdivisions of auditory cortex. Many of these connections are tonotopically organized.

16. Chandrasekaran and colleagues (2014) review multiple lines of evidence consistent with experience-dependent plasticity being reflected in brainstem responses.

For example, experience with language and music – both complex processes that rely in part on auditory perceptual learning – are reflected in evoked brainstem activity.

17. As summarized by Chandrasekaran and colleagues (2022): "[T]here is a critical need to use a systems neuroscience approach to go beyond the traditional characterization of the subcortex as 'lower' sensory/perceptual structures. Understanding subcortical function within a larger cortical-subcortical circuit is critical for a holistic understanding of the neurobiology of speech perception."

18. The gyrus is named after Austrian anatomist Richard L. Heschl (1824–81). He published "Über Die Vordere Quere Schläfenwindung Des Menschlichen Großhirns," translated as "On the anterior transverse temporal gyrus of the human cerebrum." Heynckes, Gulban, and De Martino (2022) provide an English translation of the publication along with context provided by modern cognitive neuroscience, and some editorial clarifications: "German, especially around that time period, tends to be composed of very long sentences. Therefore, we have chosen to change this stylistic element in order to increase the fluidity of the text."

19. Most people have one Heschl's gyrus, but some people have two. This distinction doesn't appear to matter very much for auditory processing (although researchers are still investigating this question), but it can make trying to compare brain responses across people – or, as is commonly done, averaging brain responses across people – rather challenging!

20. Kaas and colleagues (1999) provide a review of the anatomy and response profiles of the core, belt, and parabelt regions, focusing on invasive studies in nonhuman primates. Hackett and colleagues (1998) show different anatomical subdivisions of auditory cortex using staining techniques. Core, belt, and parabelt regions show different connectivity profiles: "Injections confined to the parabelt region labeled few neurons in the core, but large numbers in parts of the belt, the parabelt, and adjacent portions of the temporal lobe." Human auditory subdivisions are reviewed by Moerel and colleagues (2014). Although some similar organization principles are found in both human and monkey studies, a strict homology has proved elusive.

21. Rauschecker and colleagues (1997) mapped tonotopic subdivisions of core auditory cortex in four rhesus monkeys. They then inactivated (aspirated) A1, and measured responses in the other areas: a rostral area (R) and what they describe as a caudal medial area (CM). They found responses in R unchanged, suggesting parallel inputs from MGB to A1 and R, with reduced responses in CM suggesting it received information in parallel from A1.

22. Sweet and colleagues (2005) examined postmortem human brains applying comparable criteria as used in studies with nonhuman primates. Using staining techniques, they identified human core, belt, and parabelt regions that were generally comparable to those identified in nonhuman primates. The auditory core was centered on Heschl's gyrus (particularly the crest); the lateral belt was located primarily along the banks of Heschl's sulcus; the parabelt located mostly on the

planum temporale (posterior to Heschl's gyrus), although it could also extend to Heschl's gyrus.

23. A nice review of human fMRI studies looking at tonotopic mapping is found in Saenz and Langers (2014). Although fMRI does not provide the detailed spatial resolution available from histological studies, it is nevertheless able to review basic organizational principles such as tonotopy (and possibly periodotopy).

24. Interestingly, patterns of myelin – so-called *myeloarchitecture* – can help identify some brain regions. Myeloarchitecture analysis is appealing because it can be done in living participants using standard MRI sequences. Fred Dick and colleagues (2012) used quantitative T1-weighted MRI scanning to assess myelination, and found regions of high myelination corresponding to Heschl's gyrus and functionally defined auditory cortex. Furthermore, a listener's attention can modulate responses in auditory regions, suggesting a mechanism for frequency-based auditory attention (Dick et al., 2017).

25. In an fMRI study, Davis and Johnsrude (2003) varied speech intelligibility and conducted a correlation analysis to identify brain regions in which the level of activity was related to the degree of speech intelligibility. Auditory cortex (i.e., Heschl's gyrus) was not identified.

26. In a now-classic PET study, Zatorre and Belin (2001) played tones for participants. In one condition, the tone spacing remained constant but the speed of tone presentation was varied (temporal complexity); in another, the speed stayed constant but the number of tones was varied (spectral complexity). The authors found evidence suggesting stronger left hemisphere responses for temporal processing, and stronger right hemisphere responses for spectral processing. It is notable that these asymmetries are observed in and near auditory cortex, although – as pointed out by Zatorre (2022) – they may reflect top-down influences, in addition to biases in "basic" auditory processing. Differences in sensitivity to different frequencies of oscillation also play heavily into the asymmetric sampling in time theory (Poeppel, 2003).

27. Some subcortical pathways to auditory cortex are covered by Schroeder and colleagues (2003). Characterizing connections to auditory cortex (and elsewhere) relies in part on the fact that different layers of cortex reflect inputs related to feed-forward and feedback, meaning that electrophysiological recordings that can distinguish laminar activity profiles can also give clues as to the direction of information flow.

28. Hackett and colleagues (1998) report connections of auditory cortex in macaque monkeys. Pandya and Vignolo (1969) studied connections of the parietal lobe. These and other studies paint a picture of rich multisensory connectivity between auditory cortex and other regions of the brain, supporting multisensory processing. Lewis and Van Essen (2000) focus on multisensory connections in parietal cortex but find some involvement of auditory regions (though more through belt and secondary, as opposed to core, regions).

29. Schroeder and Foxe (2005) review several studies showing multisensory effects in auditory cortex, as well as cortical and subcortical pathways that may underlie these observations. They emphasize that multisensory interactions in "early" sensory cortex likely reflect a combination of bottom-up and top-down processes, enabling a rich repertoire of integrative processes.

30. Leonard, Gwilliams, and colleagues (2023) report single-unit recordings from human STG in response to spoken sentences, including responses that differ as a function of cortical depth. These responses reflect features including speech onset, amplitude envelope, and pitch.

31. Romanski and Goldman-Rakic (2002) presented sounds to two monkeys while recording from prefrontal cortex, and found that of the 400 neurons they examined, 70 showed auditory responses – about 18 percent. These neurons showed a variety of response profiles and preferred stimulus categories, with vocalizations resulting in the most reliable responses.

32. Romanski and colleagues (1999) found projections from both belt and parabelt regions of auditory cortex to prefrontal cortex of the rhesus monkey. In addition to identifying connections between auditory cortex and prefrontal cortex, they found a systematic organization along a rostral-caudal gradient.

33. The World Health Organization (2021a, 2021b) sponsored a comprehensive review of hearing health, which also makes the following point regarding global hearing healthcare (2021b, p. 8):

> Perhaps the most glaring gap in health system capacity is in human resources. Among low-income countries, for example, approximately 78% have fewer than one ear, nose and throat specialist per million population; 93% have fewer than one audiologist per million; only 17% have one or more speech therapist per million; and 50% have one or more teacher for the deaf per million.

34. Dutch physiologist Hendrik Zwaardemaker (1857–1930) is often credited with the first quantification of high-frequency hearing loss in older adults in his 1891 manuscript. Interestingly, Zwaardemaker's primary research focus was on smell, and he invented an olfactometer (apparatus for presenting odors). He also discovered certain pleasant odors that blocked people's awareness of unpleasant ones – termed Zwaardemaker pairs.

35. Morrell and colleagues (1996) present comprehensive profiles of hearing sensitivity (pure-tone thresholds) stratified by sex and age. The reasons for sex differences in age-related hearing loss are still not fully understood. Shuster and colleagues (2019) discuss the possibility that hormone differences may underpin at least some of the reported sex differences in hearing.

36. In fact, dangers of noise exposure are not limited to humans: Schneider and colleagues (2019) report noise-induced hearing loss in three working dogs (all presumed due to firearm noise).

37. Portnuff and colleagues (2011) report that portable music players (of the day) were capable of producing harmfully loud music. In a large sample, Vogel and colleagues

(2010) report that about half of the adolescents surveyed exceeded safety standards for occupational noise exposure.

38. Using data from the Baltimore Longitudinal Study of Aging (n=639), Lin and colleagues (2011) found a significant relationship between hearing status (no hearing loss, mild hearing loss, moderate hearing loss, severe hearing loss) and dementia (see also Lin et al., 2013). Golub and colleagues (2019) showed that subclinical hearing loss – that is, variations in hearing that do not meet standard definitions for hearing loss – *also* relate to cognitive decline. These findings suggest a continuous relationship between hearing loss and cognitive function, and further support the importance of hearing preservation as a possible way to maintain cognitive function throughout the lifespan.

39. Discussions on the relationship between hearing loss and cognition can be found in Lin and Albert (2014), Powell and colleagues (2021), and Wayne and Johnsrude (2015). All discuss the multiple potential pathways that might connect hearing loss to cognitive decline. Wayne and Johnsrude also emphasize the relatively small effect sizes present in many epidemiological studies, which may affect how we weigh the results.

40. As covered in more detail in Chapter 10, some brain networks are active across a broad range of cognitive tasks. Many of these networks are involved in things like paying attention to the current task, maintaining task goals, and monitoring performance for errors (potentially helping to re-engage in the task following an error). The multiple-demand network (Duncan, 2010) is one way to describe these regions. Critically, (1) the multiple-demand network seems to be engaged when listening is effortful (as is the case in hearing loss), and (2) the multiple-demand network supports flexible problem solving (sometimes called fluid intelligence).

41. Vickers and colleagues (2016) conducted a survey to examine criteria for cochlear implant candidacy across 17 countries. Although there was general agreement on many areas, clinicians also reported variability in the funding model, tests used for assessment, and exclusion criteria. It is also important to note that guidelines for candidacy for both children and adults continue to evolve as we learn more about who stands to benefit from a cochlear implant.

42. A prothesis is an artificial device designed to replace or assist an impaired function. For example, a prosthetic limb might help someone who was missing a leg to walk more easily. A neuroprosthetic device is simply a prosthetic device in the context of nervous system function. The cochlear implant is widely considered a clear example of a successful neuroprosthetic device in that it can allow hearing and speech understanding in otherwise deaf individuals by replacing the function of damaged inner hair cells in the cochlea. Similar attempts in other areas – such as replacing function of a damaged retina to restore vision – have so far met with less success and are not widely used, although of course this may change in the future.

43. The first cochlear implant was implanted in 1961 by American physician William House (1923–2012), an otologist, and brothers John Doyle (a neurosurgeon) and

Jim Doyle (an electronics engineer). The fascinating history of the cochlear implant is summarized by Henkel (2013), which includes the following tidbit: "In the 1790s, Alessandro Volta, who developed the electric battery, placed metal probes into his own ears and connected them to a 50-volt circuit. Upon switching on the flow of current, he experienced a jolt but, more importantly for auditory science, he also heard a noise, which he noted was akin to the sound of boiling soup." (It should go without saying that no one should try this at home!)

44. In fact, the electrodes are not necessarily conveying *independent* information, due in part to the fact that electrical current travels through the cochlea. Because electrical current from the electrodes spreads, the specific frequency-selective regions stimulating the auditory nerve that any electrode stimulates are broad, and it is impossible to obtain a very focal stimulation (for example, corresponding to a single tone – which can be heard with normal hearing). Thus, improving the performance of cochlear implants is not a simple matter of including *more* electrodes; improvements in electrical stimulation are also needed, and the electrical current spread plays a critical role in determining the limits of cochlear implant function.

45. Limb and Roy (2014) review a number of challenges to traditional music perception experienced by listeners with a cochlear implant.

Further Reading

Kaas JH, Hackett TA, Tramo MJ (1999) Auditory processing in primate cerebral cortex. *Current Opinion in Neurobiology* 9:164–170. https://doi.org/10.1016/S0959-4388(99)80022-1.
Overview of the organization of the primate auditory cortex, including subdivisions based on cytoarchitectonic and functional features.

Kraus N, Chandrasekaran B (2010) Music training for the development of auditory skills. *Nature Reviews Neuroscience* 11:599–605. https://doi.org/10.1038/nrn2882.
Review article outlining the relationship between music training and auditory processing, with a focus on electrophysiological responses from the brainstem.

Musacchia G, Sams M, Skoe E, Kraus N (2007) Musicians have enhanced subcortical auditory and audiovisual processing of speech and music. *Proceedings of the National Academy of Science* 104:15894–15898. https://doi.org/10.1073/pnas.0701498104.
Study examining electrophysiological brainstem responses to speech in musicians and nonmusicians.

Powell DS, Oh ES, Lin FR, Deal JA (2021) Hearing impairment and cognition in an aging world. *Journal for the Association for Research in Otolaryngology* 22:387–403. https://doi.org/10.1007/s10162-021-00799-y.
Summary of research on the association between hearing loss and dementia and possible mechanisms mediating this relationship.

CHAPTER SIX

Speech Sounds

Phonemes and Word Forms

Linguists have long made a distinction between phonemes and word forms, categories which have persisted into modern-day cognitive neuroscience. A **phoneme** refers to a basic unit of speech, such as a consonant or a vowel.[1] You can think of them as the individual speech sounds that are combined to form words. For example, the phonemes "b," "a," and "t" are combined to form the word "bat." Phonemes are language-specific and reflect **phonotactics**, or the "rules" governing which sounds are permitted to occur together in a language. Thus, as a speaker of English, if I hear "b" it will convey some degree of linguistic meaning (I recognize it as a "valid" speech sound).

A **word form** refers to the acoustic sound of a word. I am purposefully specifying word *forms* and not just "words" to distinguish between the acoustic part of a word (the word form) and a richer representation that would also include a word's meaning (covered in Chapter 7). So, the word form "bat" includes three phonemes ("b," "a," and "t"). Word-level information is also referred to as **lexical** information, with the totality of the words a person knows being their **lexicon** (or sometimes "mental lexicon," to distinguish the words a person knows from all of the possible words in a language). This chapter concerns the processing of phonemes and auditory word forms in the brain. Because words are necessarily comprised of phonemes, separating the brain responses to words and phonemes is not always straightforward: That is, looking at the brain's response to words *requires* looking at a response to phonemes. However, with the help of some clever experiments, responses to the two can be distinguished.

6.1 Sublexical Speech Information: Phonemes and Syllables

Spectral information refers to information distributed across different frequency ranges (i.e., information in the frequency domain); **temporal information** refers to information contained in the time domain. Phonemes are acoustically complex in that they vary in both spectral and temporal information. They are recognizable as speech, but – because they are not words – do not convey lexical or conceptual information. Phonemes are important because they help demonstrate what listeners can (or can't) perceive as a speech category, and reflect some portion of learned linguistic experience (that is, different languages have different sets of phonemes). In the context of word processing, phonemes are sometimes used as a "simple" speech condition, allowing researchers to study acoustically complex, language-appropriate processing in the absence of lexical information. Syllables can be formed by combining phonemes, and may or may not form words. For example, the real word "bat" is a single syllable, but so is "ba." Phonemes and nonword syllables make up **sublexical** information in speech: that is, speech units that do not rise to the level of a word.

A common way of assessing regions of the brain that respond to sublexical information is to compare processing for phonemes or syllables to that seen for a control condition, such as a tone (also called a "pure" tone, because it consists of a simple sine wave). Consider the spectrograms shown in Figure 6.1. A pure tone consists of a single frequency that stays constant over time. By contrast, a syllable such as "ba" includes energy at multiple frequencies that changes over time. Phonemes and syllables are thus acoustically relatively complex compared to many other types of auditory sounds that might be used in experiments.

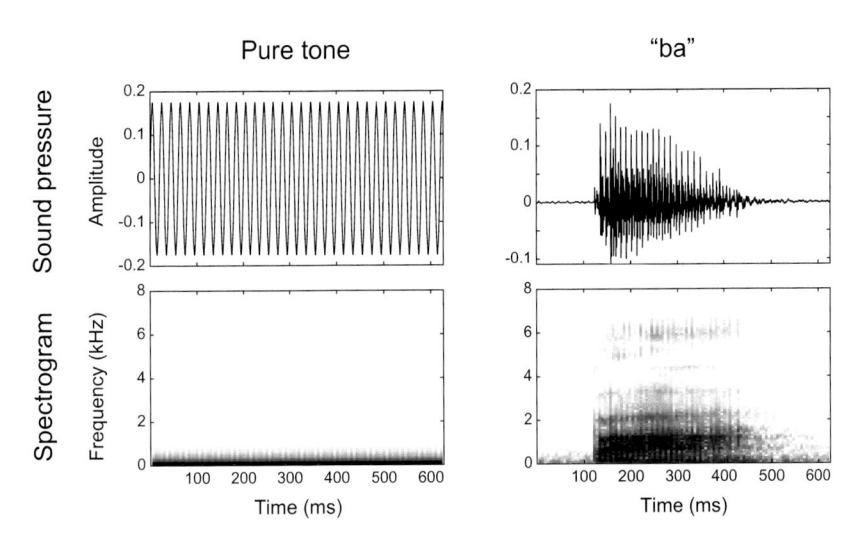

Figure 6.1 Example plots of a pure tone compared to speech sounds. A spectrogram shows, at each time, how much energy is in different frequency bands. *Left:* Amplitude and spectrogram of a 50 Hz pure tone (sine wave). *Right:* Amplitude and spectrogram of the syllable "ba," which is acoustically more complex than the tone. https://osf.io/geqb6/ (CC-BY).

Perhaps more importantly, though, phonemes (and syllables) are recognizable to listeners as building blocks of speech: That is, they are not simply generic auditory stimuli but reflect our experience with language. It is for this reason we typically talk about phonemes and syllables as being linguistic, rather than acoustic, units. The role of experience and learning in phoneme representation was demonstrated in a series of experiments with infants beginning in the 1980s. A number of studies made use of a **conditioned head turn procedure** that takes advantage of infants' tendency to look at what is most novel or interesting in the environment.[2] The infants sit on a parent's lap and watch a researcher silently manipulate toys to their right, while a loudspeaker on their left plays speech sounds continuously. For example, the sounds might be a series of vowels. The infants are trained to turn their head toward the speaker when they detect a change in the sound. When they correctly respond, something rewarding might happen – for example, a toy bear playing a drum might appear. Once the infants understand that they should look to the left when they hear a change in the sound, researchers can manipulate the sounds that are played and record the infants' responses. For example, they might play vowels from a different language or a different person.

A consistent finding is that over the first year of their lives, children learn behaviorally relevant speech sounds, and lose sensitivity to contrasts unimportant in their everyday language. For example, children who were native speakers of English during their first year of life could detect a speech contrast present in Hindi but not English.[3] In this case, the fact that the difference between the speech sounds was not relevant for English phonemes meant that the infants stopped distinguishing between them. These findings highlight the role of experience and learning in listeners' representation of phonemes that may help distinguish them from other auditory stimuli.

Where in the brain does sublexical processing take place? You may recall that the superior temporal sulcus sits between the superior temporal gyrus and middle temporal gyrus. Illustrated in Figure 6.2, the posterior part of the superior temporal sulcus (pSTS) appears to be particularly important for phoneme processing, and typically shows greater activity for phonemes than other types of acoustic stimuli, including tones and temporally reversed phonemes.[4] (Reversed speech is historically a favorite control stimulus because it contains the same overall levels of temporal and spectral variability as forward speech, but does not correspond to speech sounds a listener would have learned; see Box 6.1.)

As we have seen, a key distinction between phonemes and nonphonemes is that phonemes convey meaningful distinctions in the language of a listener. A complementary approach to studying phoneme perception, then, is to study how native speakers of two languages respond to the same acoustic stimuli. In

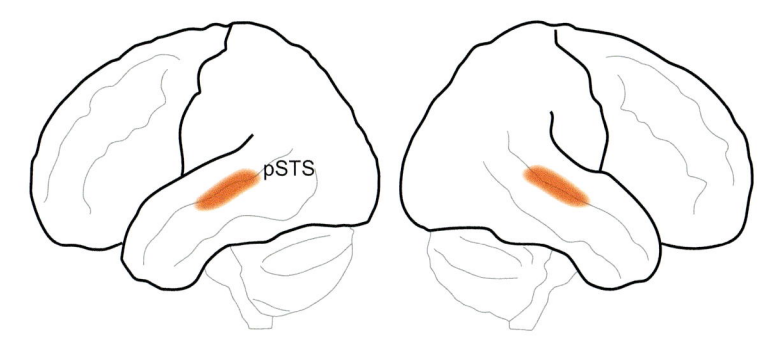

Figure 6.2 Illustration of bilateral posterior superior temporal sulcus (pSTS), important for sublexical speech processing. https://osf.io/geqb6/ (CC-BY).

Box 6.1 The importance of control conditions.

For historical and technical reasons, many experimental designs rely on explicit comparisons between stimuli of interest (say, phonemes, words, or sentences) and some control condition. A *control condition* is typically chosen to possess many, but not all, of the characteristics of the thing experimenters *actually* want to study. More formally the use of subtracting activity during a control condition to a condition of interest is referred to as **cognitive subtraction**, which before neuroimaging took the stage has a long history in behavioral science (for example, of reaction times).[7]

Let's say we want to understand how the brain processes words. We compare brain activity measured when people are listening to words to that seen when they are staring at an X on a computer screen, and find many regions of the temporal lobe are more active for words than looking at an X on the screen. Although this tells us *something* about how words are processed, it's not very specific. Words convey acoustic, lexical, syntactic, and conceptual information – which of these types of information is associated with each area we see being active? A more precise brain map of word processing can be obtained by choosing a stimulus that is more closely matched to spoken words. At a minimum, researchers frequently try to control for some type of auditory processing, so that effects seen with speech stimuli are not "only" due to auditory stimulation. Controlling for nonspeech sounds helps us be more confident that the activity seen for words is related to speech or language. (Of course, sometimes researchers are not interested in speech or language, in which case other control conditions would be more appropriate.)

Box 6.1 (cont.)

A selection of some potential control conditions used in the speech literature is shown in Table 6.1. Each has advantages and disadvantages, and none
is perfect – researchers need to decide what seems to best isolate the specific
computations of interest for a given study. However, as readers of research
articles, it is also useful to understand the considerations and compromises
that have to be made in selecting a control condition.

Broadband noise involves some type of random amplitude fluctuations in
all frequencies. (The "band" refers to the frequencies represented: "broadband" has many frequencies, "narrowband" is limited to a few frequencies.)
Because the fluctuations are random, there is no pitch, or systematic variations in timing information – this type of noise is what we often think of as
"static" on TV or radio (which younger readers may have heard about in
stories). By convention, broadband noise is described using colors to indicate
the spectral content (that is, the frequencies that are emphasized). White
noise has a flat frequency spectrum (all frequencies are equally represented);
pink noise has less power in higher frequencies than lower frequencies. Some
studies use "speech-shaped noise," with noise filtered to have the same long-
term average spectrum as speech (that is, frequencies corresponding to the
human voice). All of these types of noise stimulate the auditory system, but
they do not contain pitch or timing information, which are key acoustic
features of speech.

Pure tones are sine waves that oscillate at a specific frequency; the signal for
a 1,000 Hz tone, for example, completes 1,000 cycles every second. For
frequencies in the range of human hearing (generally about 50 Hz through
20,0000 Hz),[8] this provides pitch information. However, a standard pure tone
is a single pitch and does not change over time; thus, there is relatively low
spectral and temporal complexity.

Table 6.1 List of some popular control conditions for speech.

Stimulus	Temporal complexity?	Spectral complexity?	Lexical information?
Broadband noise	no	no	no
Modulated noise	yes	no	no
1-channel vocoded speech	yes	no	no
Reversed speech	yes	yes	no

Box 6.1 (cont.)

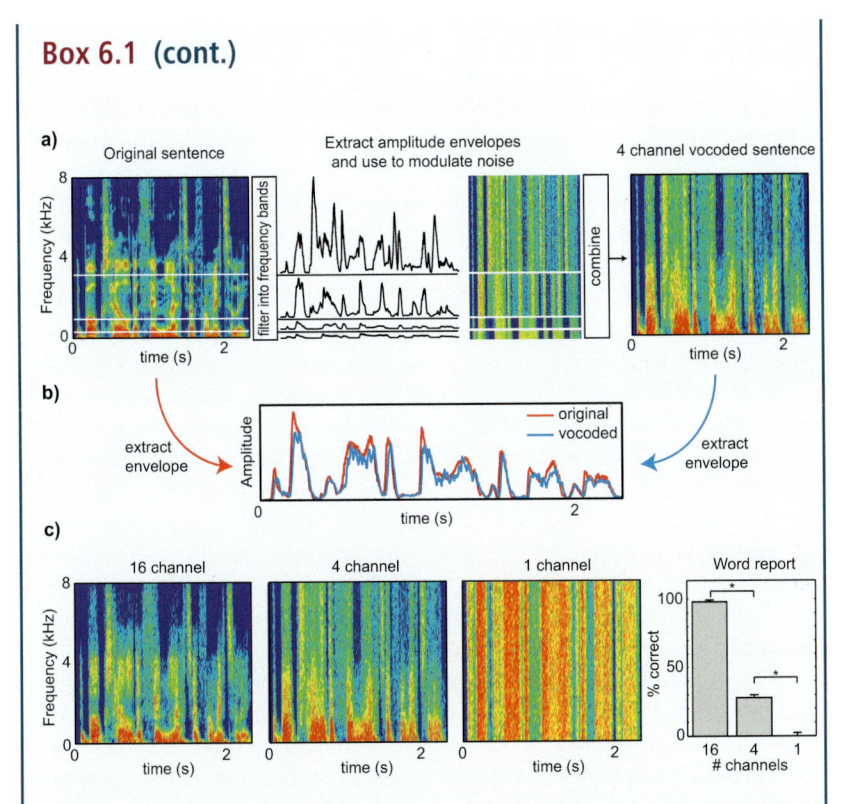

Figure 6.3 Illustration of noise vocoding. (a) The frequency range of a stimulus is divided into a number of frequency channels (in this case, 4), usually logarithmically spaced to approximate cochlear processing. For each channel, the original sound is filtered to retain information in the given frequency range, and the amplitude modulation profile (envelope) is extracted, typically by rectification and filtering (e.g., Shannon et al., 1995) or using a Hilbert transform (e.g., Smith et al., 2002). Each amplitude envelope is used to modulate white noise filtered into the same frequency band. The amplitude-modulated white noise is then combined to form a vocoded stimulus that has significantly reduced spectral detail compared to the original speech. The more channels included in the vocoder, the more spectral detail results leading to more intelligible speech. (b) The overall amplitude envelope of a clear and vocoded sentence is nearly identical. Thus, although vocoded speech can differ markedly in intelligibility from clear speech, it retains the low-frequency amplitude modulations critical for perceiving speech rhythm. (c) Examples of the same sentence vocoded with 16 channels, 4 channels, or 1 channel. Fewer channels result in less spectral detail, as well as lower intelligibility. Figure and caption reproduced from Peelle and Davis (2012) under a CC-BY license.

Box 6.1 (cont.)

Noise vocoding (Figure 6.3) is a type of digital signal processing that removes spectral detail from the speech signal.[9] The frequency spectrum is broken up into a number of bands, or channels. Within each channel, the spectral information is averaged (technically, the envelope is extracted and used to modulate broadband noise). Thus, using a greater number of channels provides more spectral detail, and a smaller number of channels provides less spectral detail, allowing intelligibility to be manipulated. Using a single channel to vocode speech results in speech that is unintelligible but that retains the overall rhythm – that is, the overall amplitude envelope – of the original. Particularly for multisyllabic words and sentences, the preservation of rhythmic energy is an important consideration. The rhythmic modulation provides some temporal complexity, but the spectral complexity is diminished (depending on the number of channels, often considerably).

It is worth noting that despite the importance of comparison conditions for understanding brain activity, the criticisms of cognitive subtraction continue.[10] In the spirit of converging evidence (see Section 2.3), the most robust conclusions can be drawn when evidence from multiple methods supports a hypothesis.

A final method for creating a control condition is to temporally reverse a speech signal (this is easy in most sound editors): Thus, if in the original speech the pitch starts low and goes up, in the temporally reversed version the pitch would start high and become lower. Reversed speech thus captures several key features of normal speech, including the spectral and temporal complexity (in fact, the spectral and temporal complexity are completely matched with the original). However, reversed speech also presents some challenges. Many times researchers would prefer a control condition not to contain any recognizable speech sounds (i.e., phonemes). Although temporally reversing speech indeed reduces intelligibility, many sounds (such as long vowels) are still recognizable. Secondly, reversing the speech signal changes the temporal properties of the speech in ways that are unlikely to occur naturally, which may induce additional processing by the listeners (in other words, listeners may treat reversed speech as "unusual utterance by a human that I should try to understand" instead of "unintelligible noise that I should ignore"). The degree to which these details matter is still an open question.

these cases, the pSTS also seems to reflect language-relevant acoustic change.[5] Intracranial recordings have provided nicely converging evidence for the role of the pSTS in phonological representation. In particular, activity can be recorded while people listen to words or sentences; activity along the superior temporal sulcus corresponds to different classes of phonemes.[6]

Thus, data from both fMRI and intracranial recordings points to the pSTS as playing a key role in phoneme representation. Anatomically, pSTS lies outside, but nearby, primary auditory cortex, which makes sense given that distinguishing phonemes requires both detailed acoustic analysis and additional experience-dependent representations.

6.2 Words

Hearing a word activates the word form (i.e., you recognize the word as a *word*) as well as associated information (the part of speech, the meaning associated with the word, and so on). Some of the earliest functional imaging experiments with positron emission tomography (PET) involved listening to spoken words.[11] These studies routinely showed word-related activity in both left and right superior temporal gyrus. Critically, the activity includes not only primary auditory cortex (Heschl's gyrus) but extends through other regions of the superior temporal gyrus, superior temporal sulcus, and middle temporal gyrus. Notably, there is a greater extent of activation seen for words than for phonemes – perhaps most obviously into middle temporal gyrus.

Of course, seeing auditory regions of the brain responding to spoken words should not be surprising; after all, listeners are processing a complex acoustic stimulus (which happens to be speech). What would be potentially more informative for understanding speech processing is to see where the response to words differs from other types of auditory stimuli. The logic behind this comparison is that a wide variety of sounds – speech, but also natural sounds, background noise, and so on – will require auditory processing. In order to isolate the processes *specific* to speech, we want to remove the activity associated with listening to auditory nonspeech sounds. Indeed, listening to words shows greater activity than listening to a variety of control sounds.[12] These increases in activity are seen to some degree in primary auditory cortex, but also in surrounding regions such as the superior temporal sulcus and middle temporal gyrus. The increase in the magnitude and extent of brain activity for words compared to control conditions is consistent with additional cognitive processes required for words but also reveals how much of the brain activity observed during listening is attributable to nonlanguage factors. Thus, using control conditions is very important for obtaining more accurate maps of brain regions responding to speech (although it can be challenging to select the most appropriate control condition, as discussed in Box 6.1).

Depending on the specific control stimuli used, though, it can be challenging to understand what aspects of words relate to different types of linguistic processing. For example, compared to noise or tones, words differ in the following ways:

1. They are acoustically complex in both temporal and spectral domains.
2. Words have lexical status (that is, listeners recognize them as a word).
3. Words have a grammatical status (noun, verb, adverb, etc.).
4. They have a meaning (that is, an associated concept).

Although some sounds do a reasonable job controlling for speech acoustics, it can be difficult to disentangle other aspects. A complementary approach to the use of control conditions and cognitive subtraction involves more sophisticated modeling of speech responses, which has several advantages. We noted earlier that because words contain phonemes it can be difficult to disentangle brain activity related to these two levels of processing.[13] And, as you may already have thought of, for most of us daily conversations do not simply involve isolated words. Moreover, many of the experiments on word processing have used lists of unrelated words – doing so provides a larger hemodynamic response (which is thus more detectable) but is not closely aligned with our everyday communication experiences.

In response to these challenges, researchers have begun to measure responses to single words in the context of connected speech in a way that relies on detailed modeling of speech content to disentangle responses to different levels of acoustic and linguistic information. Because of the rapid nature of the speech signal, much of this work has used techniques with high temporal resolution (EEG, MEG, and ECoG), which make it easier to relate brain responses to the rapidly varying acoustic signal.

Consider the analysis approach illustrated in Figure 6.4. Given a speech signal, we can transcribe the phonemes it contains and estimate when each begins (although this process is not necessarily trivial!); we can do the same for words. We can also use the speech signal itself (that is, the audio recording) to measure the loudness of the acoustic stimulation over time. Using these markers, the brain responses to connected speech – for example, in a short story or podcast – can be understood as the sum of responses to loudness (i.e., the amplitude envelope), phonemes, words, and various attributes of these features (such as how predictable they are). The evoked responses to features estimated this way are sometimes termed the **temporal response function (TRF)**.

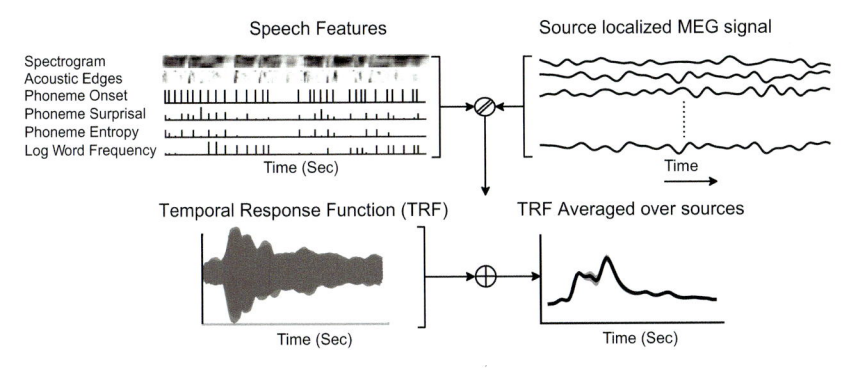

Figure 6.4 Illustration of TRF analysis from Tezcan and colleagues (2023), CC-BY. *Top:* Given an auditory stimulus (such as a story), acoustic and linguistic features can be identified. These might be based directly on the acoustic signal (for example, examining the acoustic amplitude envelope to identify rapid changes, or "acoustic edges"); or they might be based on analyzing the linguistic content of the signal to identify phonemes, words, and associated psycholinguistic properties. These features can then be related to the recorded data (typically, EEG or MEG data). *Bottom:* Using statistical analysis (i.e., linear regression), the features in the brain data corresponding to these events can be captured and expressed as a TRF. The TRF can thus be interpreted as reflecting brain activity associated with a particular speech feature or event. In Tezcan and colleagues (2023), the authors showed that understanding a language being spoken increases the strength of the responses to phonemes.

Papers using these approaches have generally found good agreement with less naturalistic approaches: for example, acoustic information in auditory cortex and nearby areas of the superior temporal gyrus, compared to lexical information in superior and middle temporal gyri.[14]

6.3 Lexical Competition

Contemporary views of spoken word recognition are largely grounded in an **activation-competition framework**. The idea is that every word you know has some baseline level of activation (here, "activation" does not refer necessarily to brain activity but rather to a more abstract notion of activity within a computational network); as you hear an acoustic sound, words that are similar to that sound increase in activation, until at some point there is (hopefully) sufficient evidence to decide which word has been heard. Critically, words with similar sounds will be active under similar conditions, and thus "compete" to be chosen. Words that share acoustic features with a target word are called "competitors" or "phonological neighbors."[18] (See Box 6.2.)

Box 6.2 Predictive coding in spoken word recognition.

Like other areas of sensory processing, understanding spoken language appears to rely both on incoming information and our expectations about what it will be. However, the mechanisms through which our prior expectations and sensory detail are combined remain incompletely understood. One appealing theory is structured around **predictive coding**, a more general perspective on neural processing.[15] Most varieties of predictive coding assume that the brain has evolved to efficiently process and predict the stimuli commonly encountered in our daily experience. If something that we expect to occur actually occurs, little additional information is obtained (given that we already anticipated the outcome). However, *unexpected* events provide a great deal of new information and are important to bring to awareness. **Prediction error** is conceptualized as the difference between the predicted input and the actual input.

To investigate predictive coding in the context of speech perception, Blank and Davis (2016) conducted an fMRI study of spoken word processing in which they experimentally manipulated prior knowledge using explicit cues. Participants heard words that were perceptually degraded using noise vocoding, which was done using either 4 channels (low sensory detail) or 12 channels (higher sensory detail). Paired with each word was written text that varied in its relation to the spoken word: (1) matching written text + spoken words ("SING" + sing); (2) neutral written text ("XXXX") + spoken words (e.g., fork); and (3) written-only text ("PASS"). They then used representational similarity analysis[16] – a type of multivariate pattern analysis – to investigate the impact of prior knowledge on word representations.

They focused on representations in pSTS, which are associated with syllable and phonological representations (rather than strictly acoustic ones). They compared the patterns of activity in pSTS across the different conditions in the data, and as would be predicted by competing frameworks for sharpened signals or prediction error. Specifically, they hypothesized that when the written information matches the acoustic signal, it would *increase* the information content but *decrease* the prediction error.

As shown in Figure 6.5, the fMRI results in pSTS are generally consistent with a prediction error interpretation. That is, for speech following neutral cues, increased sensory detail (moving from 4 channels to 12 channels) resulted in more information (indicated by increased multivariate similarity). However, for speech that was *predicted* based on prior information, increasing sensory detail led to *reduced* information – because the more detailed sensory information was expected, there was no need to encode it. Some other work implicates regions of left inferior frontal cortex in helping drive these predictions, but a consensus has yet to be reached.[17]

Box 6.2 (cont.)

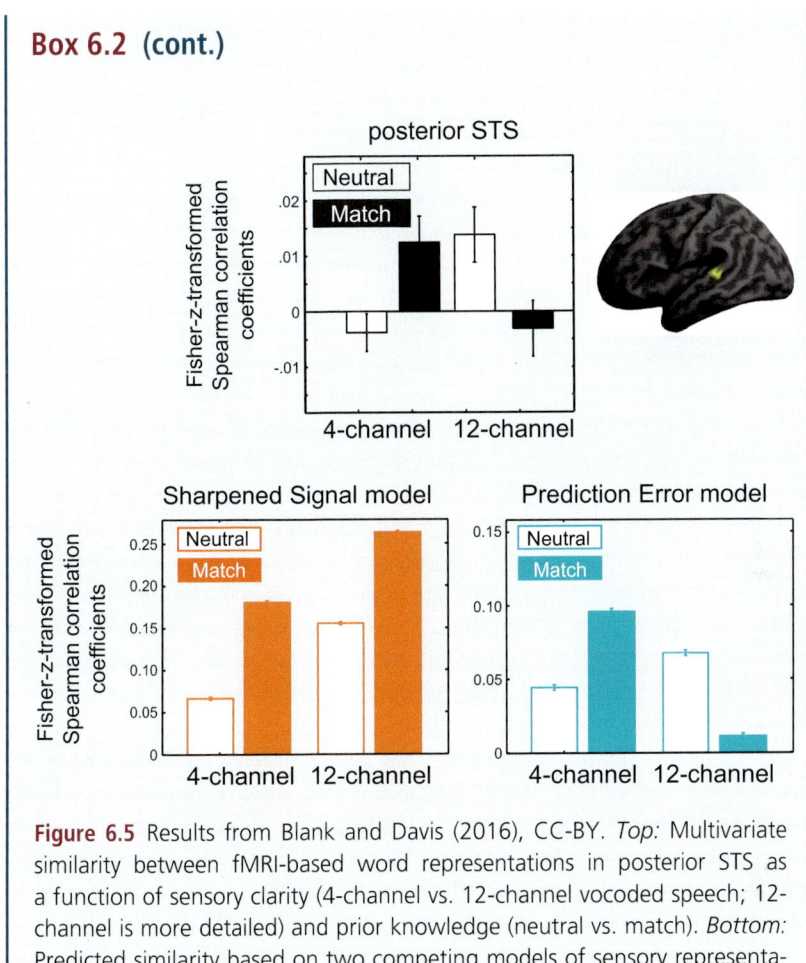

Figure 6.5 Results from Blank and Davis (2016), CC-BY. *Top:* Multivariate similarity between fMRI-based word representations in posterior STS as a function of sensory clarity (4-channel vs. 12-channel vocoded speech; 12-channel is more detailed) and prior knowledge (neutral vs. match). *Bottom:* Predicted similarity based on two competing models of sensory representation. In the sharpened signal model, increasing information always results in greater similarity of activity, regardless of whether the information comes from prior knowledge or sensory detail. In the prediction error model, improved prior knowledge results in less activity for a detailed signal (because the result is expected, hence, low prediction error).

Consider a word like "cat," which shares sounds with a large number of other words (cap, can, kit, etc.). To correctly recognize "cat," a listener needs not only to activate the correct word (cat), but also select it from among the list of alternatives, a process which may require inhibiting the nonmatching words. Contrast this process with a word such as "cathedral," which has few competitors, and would thus be easier to select (and has no competitors to inhibit). Words with many competitors are thus frequently more effortful to understand in quiet, and result in more errors in the presence of background noise.[19]

Most studies of lexical competition use phonetic dictionaries to compute how many words are similar to a target word, using this information to estimate the number of competitors (sometimes including other factors, such as how frequently words occur). To test for effects of lexical competition, then, researchers compare responses for "high-competition" words to "low-competition words" (or make predictions on the time during the word at which it could be recognized).

It is also possible to *experimentally manipulate* lexical competition by teaching people new words.[20] Although much of our word learning occurs during childhood, we continue to learn new words throughout our lives (for example, readers of a certain age had to learn "internet," "wi-fi," and "Twitter"). A relevant point is that although sometimes we learn a word and its meaning at the same time, we can also learn an acoustic form is a word without associating it with a concept. Sometimes we hear a word in passing (or read it in a book) not knowing what it means, but we would recognize it if we were to hear it again. In these cases we have learned something about its lexical status (that is, that it's a word) but not to what it might refer.

To manipulate lexical competition, we would want to either remove competitors from a target word's neighborhood (that is, force people to forget these words – a difficult task!), or add words to a target word's neighborhood (a much easier task). Consider again the word "cathedral" – a word with few competitors and thus relatively easy to recognize. If we create a competitor such as "cathedruke," it would increase the competition. We could then examine how people responded to "cathedral" before and after learning a competitor, keeping the stimulus ("cathedral") identical, but manipulating lexical competition. Adding competitors affects activity in left STG/MTG, consistent with its role in lexical representation.[21]

In activation-competition models of spoken word recognition, the correct target word must be selected from among a group of competitors; or, the activation of the competitors needs to be inhibited so that the correct target "wins" the competition. Processes of selection and inhibition may require additional cognitive processing, which we could expect to be higher in words with more competitors. Consistent with this, some fMRI studies have reported increased activity in frontal cortex (e.g., IFG) when people listen to words associated with increased competition.[22]

6.4 Acoustic Context

In everyday situations, words typically do not occur in isolation but are heard in an acoustic context – that is, a specific talker, speaking at a particular rate, saying a particular sentence. Although sentence processing is covered in more detail in Chapter 8, here we consider what effect the broader *acoustic* context has on speech perception.

One important speech cue is **voice onset time (VOT)**. Voice onset time refers to the time between the beginning of a stop consonant (like "b" or "p") and when the vocal folds begin to vibrate ("voicing" refers to the vibration of vocal folds). Voice onset time is a primary cue for distinguishing many speech sounds. For example, to determine whether someone says a "b" or a "p" typically relies on appreciating differences in VOT; the movement of the lips and other articulators – and thus other acoustic features of the items – are very similar (Figure 6.6).

A simple model relating VOT to speech sounds might involve determining a region of VOTs that are likely to indicate "b," and a longer range likely to indicate "p." The logic might be that as listeners with a great deal of experience

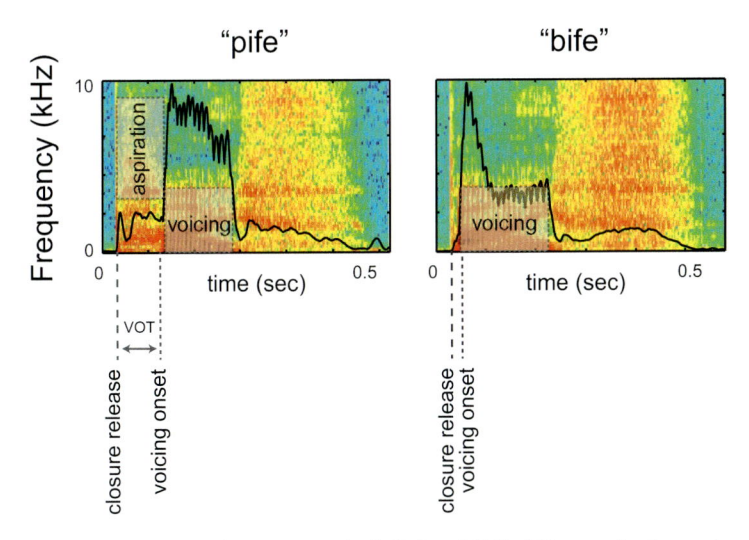

Figure 6.6 Spectrograms of two nonwords, "pife" and "bife." The amplitude envelope for each is overlaid in black. The *closure release* refers to when the mouth opens after a stop consonant, and *voice onset* to when the vocal folds start vibrating. Of note, the VOT – the delay between closure release and the onset of voicing – differs between the two items (there is a longer VOT for "pife" than for "bife"). Figure reproduced from Peelle and Davis (2012) under a CC-BY license.

hearing both "b" and "p," we (unconsciously) build up a sense of these distributions, allowing us to rapidly distinguish "b" from "p" in conversational speech.

However, a challenge for this simple model is that talkers vary quite a bit in how rapidly they speak. Is a VOT of 200 ms a short VOT, or a long VOT? Similarly, is a closure interval of 100 ms a short or long closure? The answer is that listeners make use of the contextual speech rate to interpret individual speech cues. What counts as a "long" VOT in someone who is a fast talker might well be the same duration as a "short" VOT in a slower talker.

The use of contextual speech rate can be studied by presenting listeners with sentences containing words that could have multiple interpretations.[23] For example, "Actually, the tiger that the man had to chase was _____," in which the last word could be heard as "rapid" or "rabid." Sentences were presented at five speaking rates with the talker saying the word "rabid." The word "rabid" was edited to vary in closure interval, producing a continuum from "rabid" to "rapid" based solely on this cue. Finally, the examples were played in the context of the different speech rates. If closure interval were perceived in absolute terms, then the speaking rate of the carrier sentence should have no effect on whether participants perceived a "b" or "p." However, speaking rate *does* impact listeners' perception, indicating that the relevant speech cues are interpreted in the context of the current talking rate.

Another elegant demonstration of the effects of speech rate on perception comes from the relationship of speech to a function word (Dilley and Pitt, 2010; Figure 6.7). In this case, the researchers were not looking for speech *identity* ("b" vs. "p") but *presence*. In other words, whether listeners perceived a word at all. Critically, the sentence was valid with or without the word. For example, in the sentence "Fred wanted a summer (or) lake house," the sentence makes sense with or without the word "or." The authors had people write down each sentence they heard, which were then scored for whether the target words (in this case, "or") were present. The critical manipulation is that the target word and its immediate context – here, "summer or l–" – could be manipulated independently of the rest of the sentence. Thus, by speeding the target portion, or slowing the rest of the sentence, the authors were able to change the contextual speech rate without changing the acoustics of the target word itself. They found that when the target word was presented more rapidly than the context – either through speeding the target or slowing the context – it was less likely to be perceived. In other words, listeners showed they were expecting a particular rate of speech based on the surrounding context and did not perceive words that occurred faster-than-expected.[24]

Surrounding speech is not the only context that can affect how we understand speech: Nonspeech sounds can also change our perception. In fact, hearing

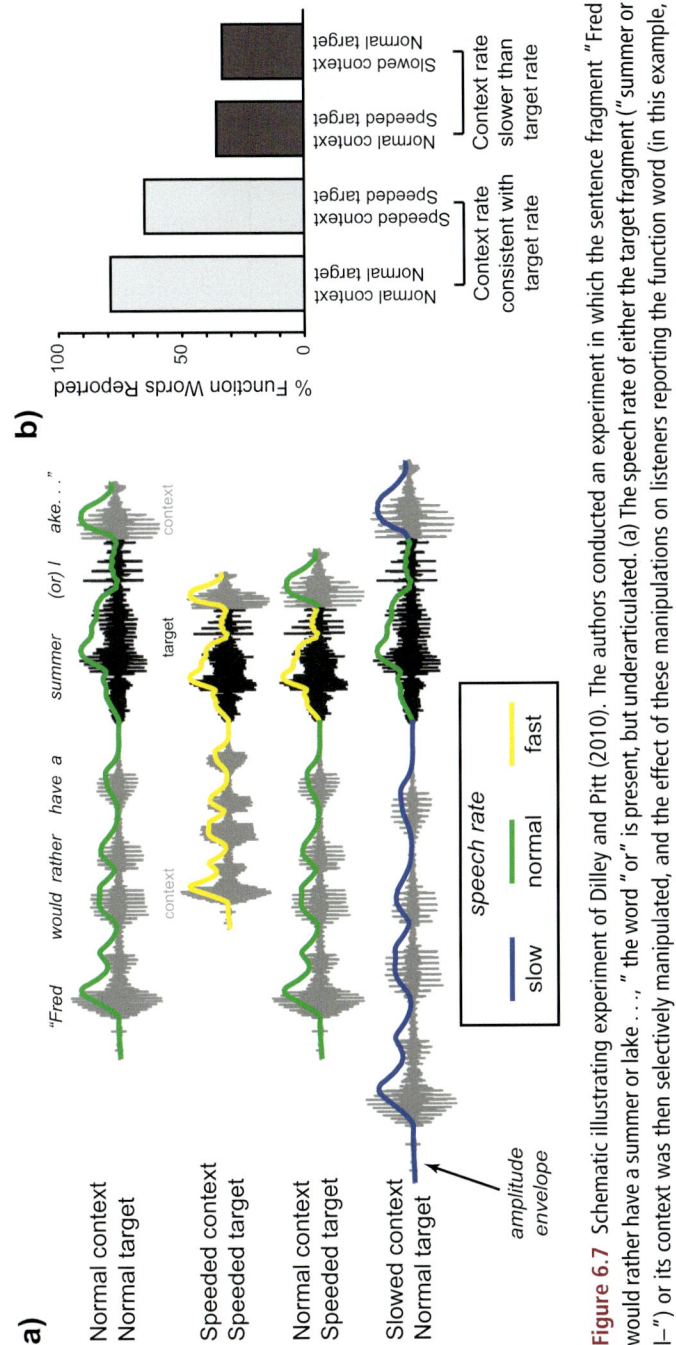

Figure 6.7 Schematic illustrating experiment of Dilley and Pitt (2010). The authors conducted an experiment in which the sentence fragment "Fred would rather have a summer or lake . . ." the word "or" is present, but underarticulated. (a) The speech rate of either the target fragment ("summer or l–") or its context was then selectively manipulated, and the effect of these manipulations on listeners reporting the function word (in this example, "or") was measured. These conditions are shown along the left side of the figure, along with the acoustic amplitude envelope for each stimulus (colored lines). (b) The authors found that when the speech rate of the context and target word matched, word report for the function word was relatively high; by contrast, when the context was slower than the target word, fewer function words were reported. This result shows how listeners make use of contextual speech rate to guide lexical segmentation during speech comprehension. Figure from Peelle and Davis (2012) under a CC-BY license.

nonspeech sounds – like tones – can affect how we process speech. For example, when deciding whether a speech token is "ga" or "da," hearing a series of tones that are relatively lower in frequency biases listeners toward "da" compared to tones that are relatively higher in frequency.[25] Because the acoustic token stays the same – only the context is changed – these findings indicate that auditory experience affects how speech is processed.

Importantly, these and other similar demonstrations highlight the fact that in many types of real-world communication words are processed in relation to the context in which they are heard. The neural bases for these context effects remains an area of active study. With respect to speech rate, one possibility – covered in more detail in Chapter 8 – is that ongoing brain oscillations entrain, or lock in to, ongoing speech and provide a neural indicator of speech rate. However, compelling experimental evidence supporting this view is currently lacking.

6.5 Lateralization of Phoneme and Word Processing

As you will recall, hemispheric lateralization references the degree to which a cognitive process depends more heavily on one hemisphere. Speech and language processing have long featured centrally in this discussion. As noted in Chapter 3, patients with Wernicke's aphasia provided early and compelling evidence for the importance of the left hemisphere in word recognition: These patients have damage to portions of posterior left temporal cortex, and difficulty understanding spoken words. However, several pieces of evidence suggest that phoneme and word recognition is not carried out entirely in the left hemisphere:[26] The picture is somewhat complicated.

One line of evidence comes from patients undergoing a Wada procedure (Box 6.3), which effectively renders one hemisphere unconscious. If the left hemisphere were necessary for word recognition, then surely putting the left hemisphere to sleep would lead to an inability to understand words. However, that is not the case: Patients with only a functioning right hemisphere are indeed able to recognize spoken words (although arguably not as well as with a functioning left hemisphere).[27] A complementary line of evidence comes from functional brain imaging studies, which routinely show activity in both the left and right hemisphere during phoneme and word processing that distinguishes speech from nonspeech acoustic noise.[28]

On balance, then, it seems safe to rule out the possibility that phonemes and words are processed *exclusively* by the left hemisphere. At the same time, current evidence also seems to leave open the possibility that the left and right hemispheres may indeed be more specialized for some types of information than for others.

Box 6.3 The Wada test.

Although the exact degree to which different language functions are lateralized is still debated, there is good agreement that nearly everyone has a dominant hemisphere for language. For most people, this is the left hemisphere (although a greater proportion of left-handed people show right hemisphere dominance). More than just a question of theoretical interest, the dominant language hemisphere assumes tremendous practical importance in the context of brain surgery: If a surgeon is going to remove part of the brain, they would like to avoid severely interrupting language function!

Early in his storied career, Juhn Wada (1924–2023) (Figure 6.8) was a young neurologist in Japan who was interested in treatments for epilepsy.[29] He had an interest in helping to inactivate (that is, put "to sleep") one of the brain's hemispheres to prevent convulsions during treatment. Sodium amytal is a short-acting barbiturate, and Wada proposed injecting it into one of the carotid arteries. (Because of the way blood is supplied to the brain, injecting sodium amytal into one of the carotid arteries would only affect one hemisphere.) A patient with epilepsy that was otherwise untreatable provided an unplanned opportunity to test Wada's theory. Wada tried the sodium amytal injection, and the patient's seizures stopped. But, as Wada (2008) writes, "In spite of this immediate success, the gravity of witnessing the profound hemiplegia and mute state rendered me speechless, and chills coursed up and down my spine while we awaited the patient's recovery of motor and then much-delayed speech function." In other words, the effect of the sodium amytal injection on language function was an unplanned side effect of the treatment for seizures. (The patient's language function eventually returned to normal.)

Wada published his findings in 1949, and the application of using sodium amytal to study language lateralization was not far behind. Surgeons were in dire need of a method to ascertain language dominance to avoid severe language complications following surgery, and Wada's test was a near-perfect solution (it would be another 40 years until functional brain imaging for language localization was a practical option). In 1955 Wada introduced the test to the famed Montreal Neurological Institute, which helped spur its adoption worldwide. (Wada himself spent time at the Montreal Neurological Institute before moving to the University of British Columbia, where he spent the rest of his career.[30])

The Wada test gained widespread popularity because of its effectiveness, and because of the lack of other viable options. However, the Wada procedure is not without risk, and there is widespread hope that as functional brain imaging approaches become both more accurate and more widely available, the need for the Wada procedure will decrease.

Box 6.3 (cont.)

Figure 6.8 Dr. Juhn Wada in 1956. University of British Columbia Archives (UBC 5.1/3162).

6.6 Summary

- Phonemes are the building blocks of speech and reflect language-specific rules. Phonemes are processed bilaterally in the posterior STS.
- Word forms are also processed bilaterally in the posterior STG and MTG. The degree to which the left and right hemisphere contribute to word understanding is still an open question.
- Lexical competition, in which listeners need to select a target word from among a set of similar-sounding words, underlies many theories of spoken word recognition.
- Listeners make use of both context, prior knowledge, and sensory detail to make sense of what they are hearing.
- The degree to which regions of inferior frontal cortex contribute to spoken word recognition, particularly with relation to resolving lexical competition or incorporating prior knowledge, is the subject of ongoing study.

Notes

1. As elsewhere, this section focuses on spoken language. However, it is also important to know that other forms of language have comparable structural components. For example, in sign languages, basic building blocks consist of handshapes, locations on the body, and movements (Brentari, 2019).

2. Werker and colleagues (1997) review the conditioned head turn procedure, tracing its history to approaches for testing hearing in children ("peep shows," Dix and Hallpike, 1947) before entering infant language research in the 1980s. (The diagrams in the Dix and Hallpike article are both detailed and entertaining!) Golinkoff and colleagues (2013) also review preferential looking in studying language acquisition. They list some of the challenges of studying language in children (p. 317): "First, young children do not understand the conventions artists use to indicate action ... Second, distinctions between who is doing what to whom in events – what sentences are about – may only be incompletely captured in static two-dimensional displays, making it difficult to study children's comprehension of relational terms like verbs."

3. Werker and Tees (1984) studied Hindi and Salish contrasts in children between the ages of 6 to 12 months, and found that infants' sensitivity to speech sounds changed: Infants whose primary language was English were initially (6–8 months) sensitive to Hindi and Salish contrasts, but by a year were not. In a conceptually similar study, Kuhl and colleagues (1992) also studied the role of experience in infants' categorical perception. The researchers used a clever crossover design in which infants from two countries, the United States and Sweden, listened to either American English or Swedish vowels. They found that infants showed stronger evidence for categorical perception in their native language, relative to a different language. Specifically, infants were less sensitive to vowel deviations from a prototype, termed the magnet effect. You might be tempted to assume that experience and expertise with a language would enable a listener to be more sensitive to acoustic changes. In the context of speech perception, however, it is the ability to perceive speech sounds categorically that is critical. And, as shown by this study, infants develop language-specific sensitivity by 6 months of age. (It was important to show these effects in multiple languages to show that there wasn't anything special about the syllables in one language – or the specific way that the researchers produced them – that might be driving the effect. If the sounds are identical but infants with different amounts of experience respond differently, we can attribute the differences in behavior to their language exposure.)

4. Liebenthal and colleagues (2005) conducted an fMRI study to identify regions of a listener's brain that respond to phonemes. They played speech sounds containing a consonant-vowel (CV) pair, along a continuum from /ba/ to /da/. Responses to these phoneme sounds were compared to responses to nonphoneme sounds. The nonphonemes were created by spectrally inverting the first formants of the phonemic continuum – doing so keeps the overall spectral complexity of the items, but

changes them enough that listeners do not hear them as phonemes. In the scanner, participants performed a discrimination task in which they heard three stimuli, and pressed a button to indicate whether the third token matched either the first or the second. The researchers found greater activity for the phoneme condition than the nonphoneme condition along the left superior temporal sulcus.

5. Jaquemot and colleagues (2003) played speech sounds for listeners, some of whom were native speakers of French, and others of whom were native speakers of Japanese. The items presented a phonological change (that is, a change based on phoneme information) for one language, but not the other. The neural response to phonological change could then be compared to that for acoustic change, a comparison that identified the left superior temporal gyrus (neighboring the superior temporal sulcus).

6. In an elegant example, Mesgarani and colleagues (2014) used ECoG to study the representations of phonemes in the left temporal lobe. Participants heard a series of sentences that were coded for their phonetic content so that responses to each phoneme could be statistically extracted. The researchers identified electrodes – and by extension, regions of the superior temporal sulcus – that responded to specific classes of phonemes. And, importantly, the activity related to phonemes could be separated along similar dimensions as those shown in behavioral studies.

Identifying small patches of brains in awake humans that respond to specific phonemes is an extraordinary accomplishment. However, it is also interesting to think about what theoretical advances occurred. In the absence of functional brain imaging, we knew that humans perceive speech categorically and can distinguish speech sounds in their native language. Where would this information be encoded if not the brain? And, given the acoustic nature of speech, auditory regions also seem like extremely likely (though, to be fair, not certain) locations where learned acoustic representations might be found, although the activity observed in the temporal lobe might also reflect top-down inputs from other regions, including frontal cortex.

7. Hermann von Helmholtz (1821–94) was a German physicist and physician. He was a polymath who contributed to an enormous variety of disciplines. One of these areas concerned human perception, in which he studied properties such as loudness of sound and brightness of light to understand the relationship between physical properties in the world and our perceptual experiences. Helmholtz was also interested in nerve conduction and in 1849, as an associate professor at the University of Königsberg, he measured the speed of conduction in the nerve of a frog.

Franciscus (Franz) Cornelius Donders (1818–89) was a Dutch ophthalmologist who – although well known in ophthalmology – spent much of his time studying biology and cognition (another polymath!). As related by Ulrich and colleagues (1999), Donders was inspired by Helmholtz's experiments on the speed of nerve conduction, and wondered whether similar measurement principles might be applied to human cognitive processing. He introduced what is now often called the *subtraction method* for measuring the speed of cognitive processes based on reaction times (Donders, 1868). One of the assumptions of Donders' approach is that a mental process can be added or omitted without affecting the duration of the other processes – the idea of *pure insertion*. Although there have been many objections to cognitive subtraction (and particularly the notion of pure insertion) over the last 150 years, it has remained firmly entrenched in cognitive science (and cognitive neuroscience).

8. The range of human hearing varies from person to person. In addition, beginning even in middle age, the hair cells responsible for amplifying high-frequency noises typically stop functioning, leading to high-frequency hearing loss. Thus, with advancing age, fewer of us are able to hear up to 20,000 Hz! This fact is capitalized on by some businesses that play high-frequency noise to annoy youngsters they don't want hanging around (while not annoying their older customers). Furthermore, there is some evidence that loss of hearing in these very high frequencies may be an early indicator of hearing difficulty at lower frequencies.

9. Noise vocoding was originally introduced by Shannon and colleagues (1995) as a simulation for speech as might be heard through a cochlear implant. The use of the term "channels" to refer to frequency bands comes out of this motivation, as cochlear implants have channels used for electrical stimulation. Although it is likely that the actual percept of speech through a cochlear implant is not identical to that provided by noise vocoded speech, the types of information that are transmitted – specifically, a reduction of spectral detail and preservation of temporal information – are comparable.

10. Friston and colleagues (1996) provide a cogent critique of cognitive subtraction in the context of human neuroimaging. In their words (p. 98):

> Pure insertion is implicit in cognitive subtraction. The idea is that as a new cognitive (A) component is added to a task, the implementation of the preexisting components (e.g., B) remains unaffected. If this were not the case the difference between tasks that did, and did not, include component B would depend on the presence of component A. In other words pure insertion requires that one cognitive component does not affect the effect of another. In factorial designs pure insertion is another way of saying that the interaction terms are negligible. The fact that interactions can be measured, using functional imaging ... means that the validity of pure insertion can now be addressed empirically. In this paper we use a simple factorial design to demonstrate that the physiological brain does not conform to pure insertion.

The critique remains applicable despite nearly 30 years of studies in cognitive neuroscience. The critical point being that interactions (as opposed to main effects) may hold important clues to cognitive function.

11. In one of the earliest functional imaging studies of language, Petersen and colleagues (1988) used PET to measure cerebral blood flow while participants listened to words only, repeated words, or generated uses for words (for example, upon hearing "cake" a response might be "eat"). They found that listening to words

activated left and right superior temporal gyrus. In another foundational PET study, Price and colleagues (1992) varied the rate of word presentation, and reported a dissociation between primary auditory areas (in which activity varied with presentation rate) and posterior temporal regions (corresponding roughly to Wernicke's area) where it did not.

12. Binder and colleagues (2000) provide a nice example of this approach. They used fMRI to study responses to words, compared to the following control conditions: temporally reversed words, pseudowords, noise, and pure tones. These control conditions each capture some aspect of the full speech signal but not all of it. For example, broadband noise does not have pitch information (but is nevertheless an acoustic stimulus); temporally reversed words contain complex spectral and temporal information, but no lexical information. Using this approach, Binder and colleagues found increased responses in bilateral superior temporal gyrus, superior temporal sulcus, and middle temporal gyrus for speech compared to various control conditions.

13. Indeed, another, broader issue is whether the speech categories generally agreed upon by linguists and speech scientists – such as phonemes, syllables, and words – map clearly on to levels of neural processing. In other words, our existing models of language have led us to attempt to identify phonemes and words as separate processes. However, it might be that a different set of starting assumptions would lead to different findings. As noted previously, Poeppel (2012) discusses, among other things, the challenges of mapping cognitive constructs to neuroscientific ones.

14. Brodbeck and colleagues (2018) provide a prime example of this approach. They played participants portions of an audiobook and measured brain activity using MEG. They constructed predictors based on word onset time, acoustic amplitude envelope, phoneme onset, cohort (number of lexical competitors). They found robust bilateral responses to acoustic information in superior temporal gyrus, a suggestion of acoustic and phoneme onset responses in the right hemisphere, and surprisal and cohort entropy measures closer to superior temporal sulcus and middle temporal gyrus more in the left hemisphere.

15. Friston (2005) places predictive coding in the context of free energy in complex systems in a Bayesian perspective – specifically, an empirical Bayesian framework in which priors are learned from the data (in other words, our past experience with the world shapes how we process future stimuli).

16. Kriegeskorte, Mur, and Bandettini (2008) introduced representational similarity analysis (RSA) as a way of abstracting relationships into high-dimensional spaces. For fMRI data, distances between items are frequently operationalized as the difference between patterns of voxels (i.e., a multivariate representation). For example, in a region with 1,000 voxels, we could think of stimuli in a 1,000-dimensional space, with each dimension represented by activity at a particular voxel. Multivariate analyses that take into account the *pattern* of activity over voxels are fundamentally distinct from traditional univariate analyses that look at

the level of activation. Kriegeskorte and colleagues (2008) elegantly demonstrated the utility of RSA by using it to compare visual object processing in monkeys (recorded using electrophysiology) and humans (using fMRI).

17. Sohoglu and colleagues (2012) conducted a combined MEG+EEG study that, similar to Blank and Davis (2016), presented participants with written words that could match an acoustically degraded spoken word, or not. Sohoglu and colleagues found that activity in both left IFG and pSTG differentiated between matching and mismatching prior knowledge; however, the timing of the effect suggested a top-down role of IFG on STG.

18. Activation-competition models differ in how they frame spoken word recognition. An early influential perspective was championed by William Marslen-Wilson (Marslen-Wilson, 1975, 1987; Marslen-Wilson and Tyler, 1980), who focused on the online nature of speech recognition (here "online" in a traditional psychological sense, meaning "in real time"). That is, listeners' ability to perceive words as they unfold, and adjust their perceptual systems in real time as new information becomes available. From this perspective a word's competitors change over time: Hearing "ca" would activate all words starting with "ca"; after hearing "cap . . . " words like "cat" and "can" would no longer be competitors, but "captain" would be. A word like "hat" would never be activated, because the very first sound of the word is never heard. By contrast, in the neighborhood activation model (Luce and Pisoni, 1998), competitors are characterized at the word level, which allows for competition between rhyming words ("hat" and "cat" would be competitors). The distinctions between these (and other) frameworks for lexical competition have significant implications for understanding how listeners process spoken language.

19. Longer response times for words with more competitors are consistent with this idea, as are increases in pupil response (McLaughlin et al., 2022) – as the task-evoked pupil response can be used as an index of cognitive effort (Van Engen and McLaughlin, 2018).

I have a classroom demonstration that illustrates the concept of lexical competition surprisingly well. I play words with few neighbors, and many neighbors, in different levels of background noise, and ask students to both write down the word they think they heard, and rate how difficult it was on a scale of 1–5. Unfailingly, words with many competitors are recognized less accurately and rated more difficult to understand, even though the noise levels don't differ between the easy and hard words. For example, when I play the word "push" in noise, I get the responses "push" or "bush." When I play the word "fill" (with more neighbors) I get more responses (fill, fell, film, pill, quill . . .). One important outcome is the sheer *number* of errors that listeners make is greater for words with many competitors. But it is also important to note the specific errors made are not random words but *similar* sounding words (i.e., competitors). For example, for the word "push" no one guesses "cathedral"; they guess "bush." This point may seem obvious, but it illustrates the power of activation-competition frameworks in explaining everyday listening experiences.

20. Gaskell and Dumay (2003) investigated the effect of word learning on lexical competition; Dumay and Gaskell (2007) demonstrated the importance of sleep for word learning; Davis and Gaskell (2009) present a framework for word learning that incorporates these data. It turns out sleep is important for this effect to work. Across many types of task – not just word learning – our memories change as we sleep. This process, known as *memory consolidation*, is sometimes associated with a change in the brain regions representing a particular memory.

21. Gagnepain and colleagues (2012) provided an elegant example of manipulating lexical competition by teaching participants new words in the context of an MEG study. They and colleagues taught participants several novel words that differed from already-known words. For example, "mushroom" is a real word (with few competitors); participants were taught the new word "mushrood." Related to the above point, participants were trained using a phoneme monitoring task to ensure attention during exposure to the novel words, but no meaning was associated with the novel words. Brain activity in response to the new words was then tested on Day 1 (after word learning, before consolidation) and Day 2 (after sleep, and thus consolidation). They found that after consolidation, newly learned words ("mushrood") indeed showed different patterns of activity in the left superior temporal gyrus, extending to middle temporal gyrus.

22. Zhuang and colleagues (2011) found high-competition words associated with increased activity in both left and right IFG. In a later study (Zhuang et al., 2014), they found further evidence dissociating effects of competition (ventral IFG, *pars orbitalis*) and selection (IFG, *pars triangularis*).

23. Joanne Miller and others in the 1980s tackled these and related questions (see also Port, 1979). The specific example here is from Miller and Grosjean (1981).

24. There are a number of specific details of this study that are probably required for the demonstration to work. First, as noted, the sentence has to make sense both with and without the target word – otherwise, listeners will be biased toward the interpretation that makes sense. In the sentences used by Dilley and Pitt (2010), the target words were both function words, short, and underarticulated (creating some acoustic ambiguity). It is unlikely that this same paradigm would be effective at making just any word disappear, but the specific stimuli chosen by the researchers nicely illustrate the effect of contextual speech rate on word processing.

    A real-world example of this issue can be found in Baese-Berk and colleagues (2016), who report an analysis of how listeners perceive Neil Armstrong's famous quote from the moon landing. Armstrong has said that he said, "one small step for a man," rather than "one small step for man." They conclude (p. 9): "These results suggest that Neil Armstrong's statement could have been a 'perfect storm' of conditions making the listener more likely to perceive *for* rather than his intended *for a*."

25. Lori Holt and colleagues have done a great deal of elegant work in this area. In Holt (2005), participants heard about two seconds of varying tones before a speech sound. This acoustic history could vary in its average frequency (high frequency vs. low frequency) and its variance (how much tones varied around the average frequency). Participants then heard a speech sound and asked whether it was /ga/ or /da/, a distinction that relies in part on spectral contrasts in speech formants. Provocatively, the content of the acoustic history – that is, recent spectral experience – affected how likely participants were to report hearing "ga." Idemaru and Holt (2011) explored a complementary aspect of this effect using dimension-based statistical learning. They manipulated the correlation between two speech features, VOT and fundamental frequency (F0), during an exposure phase in which the cues could be consistent or inconsistent with normal properties of English. Participants were then given targets to classify; when these targets were ambiguous, listeners' performance varied depending on their prior exposure. These results show how listeners adapt their perceptual categories to reflect recent acoustic experience.

26. Greg Hickok and David Poeppel made this point (among others) throughout a series of influential review articles (2000, 2001, 2007).

27. Wada and Rasmussen (1960) reported results from the Wada procedure in 20 patients. Their focus was on identifying language hemispheric dominance to aid in presurgical planning. They asked patients to count aloud before administering the sodium amytal. Following injection and inactivation of the dominant (that is, typically the left) hemisphere, counting stopped ("In each instance counting was arrested within a second or two after completion of the injection, and the patients were unable to resume counting on command."). However, patients *were* able to follow verbal commands to wriggle their fingers and toes, indicating some level of intact speech understanding. Whether this level of speech understanding shows equivalent processing in the two hemispheres is open to interpretation.

  Hickok and colleagues (2008) used a four-alternative forced-choice (4AFC) procedure to assess word comprehension in people undergoing a Wada procedure. Participants were shown four pictures and asked to point to one of them (for example, "Point to the bear"). In addition to the target ("bear"), there was a phonological distractor ("pear"), a semantic distractor ("moose"), and an unrelated distractor. Accuracy was generally high regardless of anesthesia hemisphere. Patients made more errors overall for left anesthesia (26.3 percent errors) than for right (4.3 percent errors). Most of these errors were semantic in nature. However, patients still made more phonemic errors under left anesthesia (7.5 percent) than right anesthesia (.06 percent). See also Breese and Hillis (2004), in which patients with left hemisphere damage following a stroke made relatively few word identification errors in a four-alternative forced-choice task. Taken together, these findings certainly support some level of word understanding in the right hemisphere but do not necessarily provide strong evidence for *equal* processing in the left and right hemisphere.

28. A few examples are found in Price and colleagues (1992), one of the first PET studies of spoken word recognition; Binder and colleagues (2000); and Rogers and colleagues (2020). Further evidence comes from electrophysiological studies that explicitly model features related to linguistic units such as phonemes, words, and predictability (Brodbeck et al., 2018). However, it is also important to realize that simply observing *activity* in the left and right hemisphere is not the same as a statistical comparison, and most studies do not properly compare activity. Thus, it is very possible that in some studies the left hemisphere is contributing more than the right hemisphere. Perhaps more interestingly, increasingly sophisticated analysis methods – using computational models and multivariate statistics – are poised to help better identify the specific types of information each hemisphere may be specialized for.

29. This information is summarized from Wada (1997, 2008), where he reflects on the history of what is now known as the Wada test, and the brutal wartime conditions in which he worked as a medical student and young physician.

30. Wada was an active clinician and established the UBC Hospital's First EEG and Seizure Investigation Unit and Epilepsy Surgery Program. He was honored by both Canada and Japan for his dedication to medicine, including being inducted as an Officer of the Order of Canada (OC) in 1992, conferral to the Order of the Sacred Treasure from the Emperor and Empress of Japan in 1996, and the awarding of the Queen Elizabeth II Diamond Jubilee Medal in 2012. He remained active in the University of British Columbia following his retirement until his death in 2023. As noted by Yatham (2023): "For many who had the pleasure of his friendship and collegiality over the years, Dr. Wada will be remembered not only as a brilliant scientist but also a man of genuine kindness, integrity and humility."

Further Reading

Binder JR, Frost JA, Hammeke TA, Bellgowan PS, Springer JA, Kaufman JN, Possing ET (2000) Human temporal lobe activation by speech and nonspeech sounds. *Cerebral Cortex* 10:512–528. https://doi.org/10.1093/cercor/10.5.512.
   An early fMRI study looking at responses to spoken words and several control conditions in order to isolate responses related to acoustic and language aspects of speech.

Brodbeck C, Hong LE, Simon JZ (2018) Rapid transformation from auditory to linguistic representations of continuous speech. *Current Biology* 28:3976–3983.e5. https://doi.org/10.1016/j.cub.2018.10.042.
   Using MEG to examine human brain responses to short stories, the authors disentangle responses to acoustic and linguistic features of the speech.

Liebenthal E, Binder JR. Spitzer SM, Possing ET, Medler DA (2005) Neural substrates of phonemic perception. *Cerebral Cortex* 15:1621–1631. https://doi.org/10.1093/cer cor/bhi040.
In a study using fMRI, responses to phonemes were examined relative to complex nonphoneme sounds.

Mesgarani N, Cheung C, Johnson K, Chang EF (2014) Phonetic feature encoding in human superior temporal gyrus. *Science* 343:1006–1010. https://doi.org/10.1126/science.1245994.
Using intercranial electrocorticography, responses to continuous speech were used to identify specific responses to phonetic features.

CHAPTER SEVEN

Word Meanings and Concept Representations

In the preceding chapters, we followed the acoustic signal from the mouth of a talker to the ear and brain of the listener, to where words were recognized. But as listeners, simply recognizing the word *form* is not usually what we are interested in – we want to know the *meaning* of a word.

Semantic memory refers to knowledge about the world – people, places, facts, and concepts – that we accumulate throughout our lives. Our focus in the current chapter will be on the meaning of words – that is, concepts – and how these meanings are represented in the brain. It is important to emphasize that although some of our knowledge about concepts is verbal, not all of it is. For example, if I ask you to define the word "apple," you might tell me that an apple is a small, round fruit that grows on a tree. However, if you pause for a moment to think, you may also be able to feel how heavy an apple is in your hand, remember the smoothness of its skin, or taste its sweetness. You remember these aspects of apple-ness, even if they don't always appear in a dictionary definition. This knowledge thus contributes to your concept of APPLE, which is associated with the word form "apple." (You may remember that I use all capital letters to refer to concepts.)

Thinking back to our look at localization of cognitive processes, perhaps it occurred to you that deciding the level at which functions are localized presents somewhat of a challenge. For example, we might agree the "meaning of a word" is a useful thing for the brain to represent. But how do we know whether there is a single "word meaning" region (just as there is a primary region for vision,[1] a primary region for hearing, and so on), or whether different kinds of words each get their own region?

In some ways, what might be most interesting to know regarding how semantic memory is organized in the brain is whether different concepts are stored in the same way. But what does "the same way" mean? One solution is to invoke what we know about localization of function, and consider concepts supported by the same region(s) of the brain to be stored in the "same way." Or perhaps more accurately, we might reasonably conclude that concepts stored in *different* regions are *not* stored the same way.[2] In this chapter we will look at various ways cognitive neuroscientists have tested these ideas in the domain of semantic memory, and the primary brain regions that have been identified.

7.1 Categorical Semantic Representation

As we've seen in other areas, one approach to testing localization of function comes from patients with focal brain damage (most often due to stroke). In the context of semantic memory, one of the most interesting observations following brain damage has been seen in patients who show a deficit in a select category of concepts – what is known as a *category-specific* deficit.[3] From a broad perspective, it may not matter terribly much what specific category is impaired: Simply showing that *any* category can be selectively impaired tells us something important about how concepts are represented in the brain more generally. However, if we are interested in understanding semantic representations on a deeper level, then the specific types of information impaired or preserved become critical.

If we are interested in identifying a category-specific impairment, we must first identify a category of concepts to test. Of course, there are many ways to think about all of the different concepts we know about, and thus many different sorts of categories we might identify. One distinction made in the research literature is between natural objects (such as animals and plants) and manufactured objects (that is, objects made by humans, such as tools or vehicles). To explore whether semantic memory differs based on category, Warrington and Shallice (1984) tested two patients who had damage to their temporal lobes as a result of herpes simplex encephalitis.[4] In one task, patients were given words and asked to define them – the words could be either inanimate objects (some human-made, some not) or living things. Examples of inanimate objects were an umbrella, a wheelbarrow, and a towel; for living things, a parrot, a duck, and an ostrich. Accuracy for identification and naming responses from the two patients, J. B. R. and S. B. Y.,[5] are shown in Figure 7.1. It is clear both that these patients have some difficulty with understanding concepts; most adults with comparable levels of education would have near-perfect accuracy at identifying and describing these objects, but J. B. R. and S. B. Y. performed relatively poorly. In particular, both patients showed a great deal more difficulty with living things than with inanimate objects.[6] The qualitative differences in detail the patients provided for inanimate objects and living things were equally striking. For example, when asked to define a tent, J. B. R. responded, "temporary outhouse, living home"; a briefcase as a "small case used by students to carry papers." By contrast, his responses to living things lacked detail: A daffodil was a "plant" (a correct superordinate answer); an ostrich was "unusual." These findings led the authors to conclude that concepts are represented by complementary semantic systems – that is, not all concepts are represented the same way.

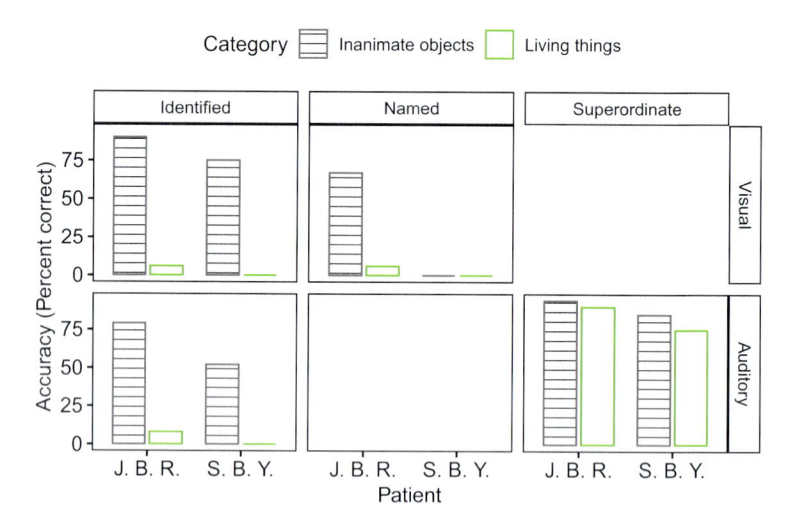

Figure 7.1 Behavioral results table for patients J. B. R. and S. B. Y. showing percentage of correct responses for visual and auditory items (based on data in Warrington and Shallice, 1984). Patients were first asked to name or identify by describing each picture (the visual condition), after which they were asked to define each picture name spoken to them by a researcher (the auditory condition). Correct superordinate responses are those that match the correct higher-order category; For example, for "daffodil," most people would call this a "flower," but "plant" would be a correct superordinate response. https://osf.io/geqb6/ (CC-BY).

Another important distinction in semantic memory is often drawn between concrete and abstract concepts. A **concrete concept** is one that we can experience with our senses (we can see, hear, touch, taste, or smell it); objects all fall into this category (for example, APPLE, CHAIR, or CAT). By contrast, **abstract concepts** refer to things that cannot be directly experienced with our senses (for example, JUSTICE, TRUTH, or PRIDE).[7] Interestingly, patients J. B. R. and S. B. Y. also showed differential impairments on concrete relative to abstract concepts. For example, S. B. Y. defined the relatively abstract concept "debate" as "Discussion between people, open discussions between groups," but had difficulty with concrete concepts (ink: "Food – you put on top of food you are eating – a liquid"; cabbage: "Use for eating, material it's usually made from an animal"). A challenge for the anatomical locus of these effects is the poor knowledge regarding which regions of the brain were damaged in neuropsychological studies from the twentieth century: Even when brain scans were available, the quality was relatively poor and detailed assessments impossible.

Functional brain imaging studies have also suggested differences in how different categories of concepts are stored. One area in which categorical representation has been extensively studied is visual objects. Visual objects are a category we are well practiced in, and visual objects can be categorized fairly easily (for example, as natural vs. manufactured). Functional imaging studies have reliably found differences in areas of strongest activation for a number of categories – perhaps most notably for faces and houses (see also Box 7.1).[8]

Box 7.1 The interface of high-level vision and memory.

The hippocampus is a deep structure situated in the medial temporal lobe, damage to which is associated with profound disruptions to episodic memory.[9] Even a cursory look through the memory literature over the past 50 years will quickly convince you that the hippocampus[10] plays an important role in storing our past experience.

Interestingly, several medial temporal lobe structures – including the hippocampus, perirhinal cortex, and entorhinal cortex – have also been implicated in high-level vision.[11] In the realm of vision, object recognition is often thought of as a hierarchical process whereby simple features (for example, lines) are progressively combined into more and more complicated shapes (for example, a tree). By "high-level" vision I mean our ability not only to recognize objects but to recognize objects of different sizes, orientations, and lighting conditions than we have seen before. (And in fact, to correctly categorize objects we have never seen. If I were to show you a picture of the chair in my basement where I'm writing this paragraph, you would recognize it as a "chair," even though you have never seen it before.)

Somewhat frustratingly, historically perception and memory have largely been studied independently (for example, "perception" and "memory" typically have different chapters in textbooks and different groups of researchers working on them). But upon closer examination, perhaps they should be viewed as part of the same continuum. We use our senses to perceive the world around us; memory is what allows us to travel back in time and retrieve elements of this experience. When I see a chair and recognize it as a chair (that is, a perceptual experience), I can only do so because of my past experience with chairs and ability to make use of that experience (a process requiring memory). The ability to form a visual category of CHAIR and extrapolate these properties to new instances sounds a lot like examples of concept representation we have covered under the heading of "semantic memory."

Box 7.1 (cont.)

One example of category specificity from the vision literature comes from human face processing. There is good reason to think that faces may occupy a special place in our representations: Faces convey identity and emotion, providing important information about safety, security, and relationships that would be useful from an evolutionary perspective. Using fMRI, Nancy Kanwisher and colleagues (1997) showed that a region of the inferior temporal lobe – which they named the **fusiform face area (FFA)** – responded more strongly to human faces than any other picture they showed it, including objects, houses, and hands. They concluded that the study "demonstrates the existence of a region in the fusiform gyrus that is not only responsive to face stimuli . . . but is *selectively* activated by faces compared with various control stimuli" (p. 4310). Although not directly linked to memory in that context, one can see bridges between category specificity in visual object processing and examples of categorial semantic representations discussed previously.

A more explicit link between the medial temporal lobe and memory was made by Morgan Barense and colleagues (2012), who focused on the perirhinal cortex (a region of the medial temporal lobe just next to the hippocampus). They used a task in which they presented pairs of abstract shapes to participants. The shape pairs varied in how similar they were, creating low-interference and high-interference conditions. They found that patients with damage to perirhinal cortex were more affected by perceptual interference than were patients with damage to the hippocampus. The authors interpret these findings as suggesting a role for perirhinal cortex in object conjunctions – that is, how different features of a visual object combine to form a whole. More broadly, the findings emphasize the link between perception and memory, and that some forms of "memory" difficulty may instead reflect impoverished perceptual representations.

One interpretation of these findings might be that the authors have identified "modules" – regions of the brain that selectively respond to a particular category of object (a view that would be broadly consistent with category-specific impairments observed in some patients). However, although it is true that some regions have *preferred* categories – a category for which they show a stronger response than the others – these same regions also often respond to *non-preferred* categories. For example, a region that shows the strongest response to houses might also respond to faces and chairs (just not as strongly as to houses). Such distributed representations are somewhat at odds with the strict localization of function championed by phrenologists as described in Chapter 3.[12]

Finally, although the focus in this section has been on evidence for category-specific representations, it is an interesting exercise to consider *why* certain categories may be represented differently in the brain. When comparing natural objects to those made by humans, for example, it is apparent that human-made objects are historically more recent, and thus evolutionarily distinct. In addition, many human-made objects (at least, those used in research studies) have very specific intended purposes. For example, a jug, jar, or vase are intended to hold liquid, even if their specific visual attributes are different. As tools have been developed and refined over human history, they become more functionally differentiated – the toolbox of a modern carpenter is a different thing altogether than what would be available to the earliest humans. It may be the function, rather than the form, of these items which determines their representation.[13]

7.2 Distributed Semantic Representation

If I ask you to define an apple, you might say it is a round, edible fruit that grows on a tree; it can come in various colors but is most often red, green, or yellow; and so on.[14] These are reasonable parts of a dictionary definition of an apple. But, as we've already discussed, your knowledge about the concept APPLE goes beyond this. Now let's think about *how* you know all of these things about an apple.

It's true, you may have read about apples in books or heard about them from a family member. But you probably also learned quite a lot about apples by experiencing them yourself. If you have looked at, held, and tasted a lot of apples over your lifetime, you are somewhat of an apple expert, and your knowledge about apples is informed by your experience with them. (Of course, if for some reason you don't like apples, you can just substitute any other food you like in this example.)

Now consider what this experience-based learning might mean for concept representation. Your senses depend on different brain systems. For example, to appreciate the color of an apple, you rely on your visual system (and perhaps specifically color representations, which have a specialized brain region: V4). The sweet taste of an apple relies on your gustatory (taste) system, the smell on your olfactory (smell) system, and so on. Your total experience with an apple is made up of a large number of sensory-specific inputs which occurred during your many interactions with apples. Because of the nature of sensory and motor representations in the brain, these inputs are necessarily distributed – that is, they occur in different parts of the brain, rather than a single region.

In this context, an influential family of theories about object concepts is that they, too, have a distributed organization in the brain, mirroring the inputs we have experienced throughout our lives. So, if your experience with an apple is visual, gustatory, and olfactory, your representation of the concept APPLE would rely to some degree on visual cortex, gustatory cortex, and olfactory cortex.

Considering all of the object concepts (nouns) we might encounter in our lives, you can imagine they vary in the degree to which they rely on modality-specific information. APPLE may rely on many senses (even sound, for the sound made by a crunchy bite, or what happens if you drop an apple on the ground). By contrast, a concept like THUNDER is almost solely auditory; TREE strongly visual (and low auditory, low gustatory); and so on. Thus, in order to test the hypothesis that concepts are represented in part by modality-specific regions of the brain, we could present words that vary in their modality-specific information to patients who have damage to parts of the brain important for that modality and see whether they are impaired. Indeed, this appears to be the case: As shown in Figure 7.2, patients who have damage to modality-specific parts of the brain show impairments on concepts associated with those modalities.[15]

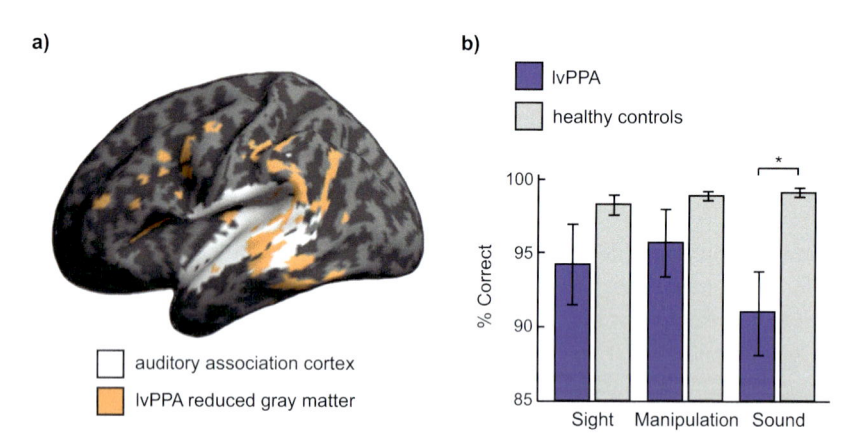

Figure 7.2 Results from Bonner and Grossman (2012). (a) Overlap of brain damage in people with lvPPA (orange) and auditory association cortex (white, defined using an auditory task in a separate group of fMRI participants). People with lvPPA had damage to auditory association cortex. (b) Accuracy results for a lexical decision task on three categories of words (sight, manipulation, sound), for controls and people with logopenic variant primary progressive aphasia (lvPPA), and performed differentially poorly on concepts related to sound (compared to concepts related more strongly to sight or manipulation) – suggesting that auditory regions helped support the representation of sound-related concepts.

As we have seen, evidence for distributed representations of concepts comes from classic category-specific impairments to semantic memory, and studies testing representations of specific types of concepts (for example, those relying heavily on one type of sensory information). However, there are also good reasons to think the story doesn't end here.

7.3 Unified Semantic Representation

Despite the evidence we have reviewed so far in favor of distributed semantic representations, there are also theoretical reasons to think about *unified* semantic representations (that is, a single representation of a concept that is not distributed across multiple brain regions). For example, it is all well and good that you have a distributed representation of APPLE that relies in part on sensory and motor regions. But what ties them together? If your visual cortex represents the color red and your gustatory cortex represents an apple's sweetness, that still does not make an APPLE unless the information from these senses can somehow be tied together. The challenge of connecting information that is anatomically segregated in the brain is sometimes referred to as the **binding problem**, and it has been a key consideration in distributed theories of semantic memory. A straightforward solution is to propose that some brain regions either represent concepts in their entirety (thus, no need for binding), or serve as central nodes that connect the bits of information stored in distributed sensory and motor cortices. In either case, some sort of central representation (or point for connection) is needed.

Another argument in favor of a unified semantic representation – or at least, a reason to accommodate concepts that is not purely based on sensory and motor features – relates to abstract concepts. We can quickly see how APPLE relates to our physical experiences with apples. But what about a word like HONESTY? We know what these words mean, but it is not based on the same kind of sensory or motor experience. Similarly, other forms of semantic memory – for example, that Paris is the capital of France – also are not grounded in physical experience. We return to abstract concepts later in the chapter, but for now it is enough to realize that abstract concepts may not fit neatly into a distributed sensory-motor representation, suggesting the need for some type of additional representation.

In fact, although these and other theoretical arguments might push us to consider non-distributed (i.e., unified) semantic representations, some of the most compelling evidence comes from observing patients who have severe difficulty understanding concepts.

7.3.1 The Semantic Variant of Primary Progressive Aphasia

A revolutionary window into semantic memory was opened by studying patients with **semantic variant primary progressive aphasia** (svPPA), formerly widely known as semantic dementia (see Box 7.2). Patients with svPPA show a profound loss of concept knowledge across a wide variety of concepts, modalities, and tasks.

Box 7.2 Frontotemporal degeneration and the syndrome formerly known as semantic dementia.

The syndrome known for many years as semantic dementia was described in the early 1900s by Arnold Pick.[16] However, the modern renewal of interest in semantic dementia was spurred by Elizabeth Warrington's pioneering work in the 1970s. In 1975 Warrington published an article titled "Selective impairment of semantic memory" in which she described three patients who had difficulty with word meanings and recognizing objects (among other problems). For example, when given a picture of an object and asked to identify it, they were unable to do so correctly. In Warrington's summary she explains (p. 642) "these patients could recognize a flower, but not which particular flower; they could differentiate between fruit and vegetables but had great difficulty in identifying which particular one." Warrington ran a large number of experiments probing pictures and words (with both auditory and visual presentation); in nearly every case, patients had difficulty understanding concepts.

A particularly telling task was to ask patients to define a list of words (similar to that used by Warrington and Shallice, 1984). One patient – A. B. – demonstrated a stark contrast between definitions of concrete and abstract words. His definitions of some abstract words were not only correct, but fairly precise (p. 646):

Supplication	Making a serious request for help.
Vocation	What one's job is.
Tame	An animal not behaving wildly.

By contrast, he was unable to define many concrete words:

Hay	"I've forgotten."
Poster	"No idea."
Cabbage	"Eat it" (no further information on questioning).
Geese	"An animal but I've forgotten precisely."

Thus, despite an overall impairment on most concepts, these patients also illustrated a selective impairment of concrete concepts.[17] Importantly, the patients identified by Warrington had relatively intact cognitive functioning in other areas, pointing toward a specific difficulty with semantic memory.

Box 7.2 (cont.)

Interestingly, Warrington's 1975 paper came shortly after memory researcher Endel Tulving outlined a formal distinction between different types of memory systems. In Tulving's proposal, **episodic memory** (a term he introduced) concerns information about distinct events, or episodes. These events have specific details, for example about the time and place. If I ask you to remember your most recent birthday party, you may be able to picture where you were, who you were with, what activities occurred, the kind of cake you ate (at least, I hope you had cake!), and so on. These details are specific to an event, and the event information (time, place, and context) is essential to the memory. In contrast, as we have discussed, **semantic memory** concerns knowledge about the world (including language and the meaning of words), not depending on specific episodes. If I ask you to define the word "cake," you could do so without linking it to any specific instance of cake eating. Both categories of information are clearly examples of *memory* in that they permit us to access information not currently available to our senses. However, the types of information stored have a number of qualitative differences. The distinctions outlined by Tulving have largely persisted into current thinking about subdivisions of memory.[18] Thus, Warrington's report of three patients with semantic difficulty was momentous because it renewed interest in a particular patient population, but also because it coincided with a shift in how researchers conceived of memory in the first place.

Over the next 20 years, the syndrome in which patients exhibited profound semantic impairment with relatively intact other forms of cognition became known as **semantic dementia**. Current consensus standards now refer to this syndrome as semantic variant primary progressive **aphasia** (svPPA), a subtype of frontotemporal degeneration (FTD). Throughout the book I stick to the current naming conventions, but it is also worth knowing the historical background.

Why change the widely used name of a syndrome, you might be wondering? In part, there was a concerted effort among clinicians and researchers to help standardize the criteria for diagnosis for all variants of frontotemporal degeneration, and standardizing naming conventions can help with this. Another reason is that "dementia," although historically a common term, can have negative connotations, and as a result some naming conventions have taken to avoiding the term where possible.[19]

One especially telling experiment involves patients drawing pictures of animals. If you have five minutes, you can do this with a friend. Each of you draw a bird, a fish, and an elephant (or any other animal of your choosing).

Then have the other guess which drawing corresponds to which item (see Figure 7.3). Although the drawings may not be detailed, chances are you will correctly identify each of the animals drawn.

Given the poor quality of the drawings – and that these black-and-white printed drawings in no way look like *actual* animals – how are you able to correctly identify them? A primary reason is that each drawing captures one or more characteristic features of the animal. A **characteristic feature** is a quality of a concept that helps distinguish it from other similar items. For example, many mammals walk on four legs, and so walking on four legs is not particularly distinguishing. However, very few animals have trunks, so a trunk on an elephant carries a disproportionate amount of information about what animal it is. Most people are actually remarkably good at intuitively identifying characteristic features (as seen in the drawing example above, or perhaps a game of Pictionary).

When asked to draw animals, patients with svPPA frequently omit characteristic features: Animals tend to blur together. Thus, both a duck and a rhinoceros might be drawn with four legs and no horns (because many animals have four legs, and few animals have horns).[20] The lack of distinctiveness mirrors the lack of detailed conceptual information. Importantly, the lack of these object features in drawings from patients with svPPA is not a *drawing* problem, but a *conceptual* problem (as you saw in Figure 7.3, drawings do not have to be particularly detailed to include characteristic features). The core behavioral symptoms of patients with svPPA are well suited to teaching us about the nature of semantic memory, and potentially areas of the brain that support its storage.

Brain damage in svPPA starts in the left (i.e., dominant) hemisphere at the anterior pole of the temporal lobe (Figure 7.4). Because svPPA is a progressive disease, the damage worsens over time, working back along the inferior and lateral portions of the temporal lobe, and brain damage eventually often moves to encompass the right (i.e., nondominant) temporal pole as well.

The anatomical location of damage in svPPA and the associated profound loss of concept knowledge suggests that the regions damaged in svPPA – in particular, the left temporal pole – play a critical role in semantic memory.[21]

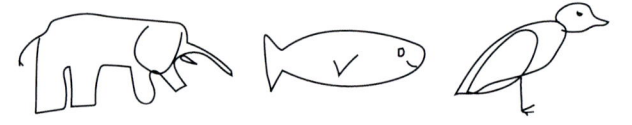

Figure 7.3 Drawings of an elephant, a fish, and a bird, done hastily by a professor working on a textbook. Although the drawings are lacking in detail, most people are able to correctly label each drawing with the correct animal. https://osf.io/geqb6/ (CC-BY).

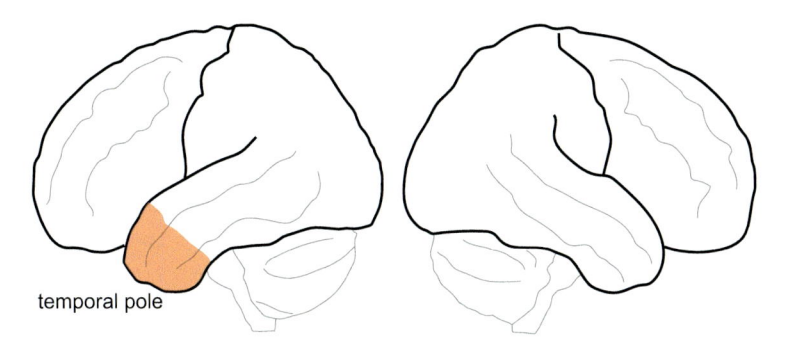

temporal pole

Figure 7.4 Brain damage in svPPA is most severe in the left temporal pole. As the disease progresses, it often progresses to the right temporal pole. https://osf.io/geqb6/ (CC-BY).

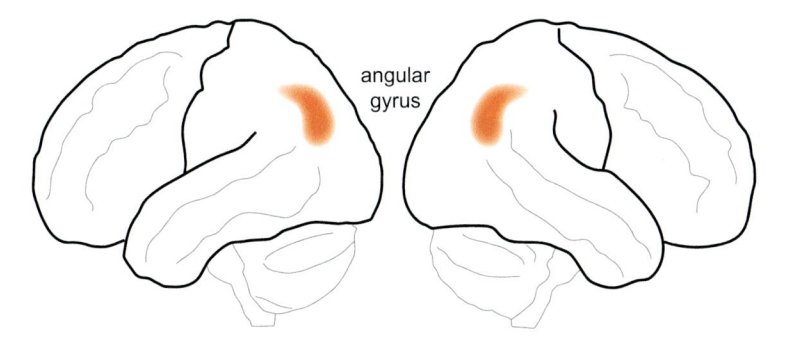

angular gyrus

Figure 7.5 The angular gyrus, located in the inferior parietal lobe, sits at the extension of the middle temporal gyrus. https://osf.io/geqb6/ (CC-BY).

7.3.2 The Angular Gyrus as a Site of Multimodal Integration

A complementary proposal for solving the binding problem in semantic memory developed through many years of anatomical and functional brain imaging studies, and focuses on the angular gyrus.[22] (See Figure 7.5.) The angular gyrus is the extension of the middle temporal gyrus into the inferior parietal lobe,[23] and one of several "heteromodal convergence zones" in the brain – regions that are anatomically connected to parts of cortex specialized for different sensory modalities but receive little direct sensory input. This anatomical connectivity provides a straightforward mechanism for linking disparate kinds of information.

Activity in the angular gyrus is also observed in many types of language studies (most of which involve semantic memory), including sentence processing and combinatorial word pairs (discussed in greater detail in Chapter 8).[24]

Despite the compelling support for the role of the angular gyrus in concept representation from anatomical connectivity and functional brain imaging, data from patient studies has been less persuasive. In particular, damage to the angular gyrus rarely results in significant impairments to semantic memory. Although this puzzle is far from being fully solved, one possible explanation might be in the degree to which concept representations in the angular gyrus are lateralized. In functional imaging studies of language, activity in the angular gyrus is frequently bilateral (both the left and right angular gyrus are involved). However, as you might recall from earlier chapters, patients with brain damage from a stroke nearly always have damage restricted to a single hemisphere because of how blood is supplied to the brain. Therefore, most patients with brain damage to the angular gyrus have it in just a single hemisphere. It could be that in these cases, the undamaged angular gyrus is sufficient for maintaining concept representations and thus behavioral impairments are difficult to observe.

7.4 The Challenge of Abstract Concepts

Although we have touched on abstract concepts briefly, it's now time to consider them in somewhat more detail. In exploring how concrete concepts might be represented across different sensory and motor modalities, we have focused on how concepts might be organized based on the type of information on which they rely. Historically, a parallel framework for abstract concepts has been harder to identify: Abstract concepts are not grounded in sensory and motor representations, so the space of possible organizing principles is large.

Early approaches to abstract concepts (including dual coding theory; Box 7.3) hypothesized qualitatively different types of representations for abstract and concrete concepts. Indeed, even assigning the dichotomous label of "concrete" or "abstract" suggests categorical differences between them. When comparing responses to concrete and abstract words in fMRI, numerous studies report differences between abstract and concrete words. A common finding is more activity for concrete words than abstract words in regions of posterior temporal cortex, inferior temporal cortex, and angular gyrus, and more activity for abstract words than concrete words in left frontal cortex (Figure 7.6).[25]

In contrast to this categorical view of abstract versus concrete concepts, more recently, researchers have taken a continuous approach to abstract concepts based on differing representational architectures.[26] For example, you might find it intuitive that physical objects can vary in size, and thus you could categorize the concepts PEBBLE, ROCK, and BOULDER along a "size" dimension. But perhaps abstract concepts can also be captured in some sort of magnitude. For example, IRRITATED, ANGRY, and FURIOUS express different degrees of particular emotional dimensions. Rather than a clear abstract versus

Box 7.3 Dual coding theory.

Dual coding theory (DCT) features prominently in the history of how researchers have thought about concrete versus abstract concepts. Developed by Allan Paivio,[27] DCT was initially informed largely by behavioral studies showing a "concreteness advantage" or "concreteness effect" – namely, that in many experimental paradigms, concrete words are processed faster or more accurately than abstract words. The core proposal of DCT is that *all* concepts are supported by verbal knowledge; concrete concepts are *additionally* supported by nonverbal representations (including "imagery," relating to sensory and motor representations discussed in the main text). Because concrete concepts are coded twice – that is, the "dual code" of DCT – they are processed more easily (for example, more accurately or more rapidly, depending on the task). The verbal and nonverbal systems are presumed to be independent, such that one system can be engaged without the other – but when both are active, the effects on behavior can be additive.

An example study is found in Paivio (1963).[28] Participants were presented with adjective-noun pairs; the nouns could be relatively concrete (e.g., wooden-box, bright-star) or abstract (e.g., wooden-heap; bright-idea). Children (fourth and fifth graders) were given lists of paired associates to learn. They were then tested by hearing a stimulus (e.g., "wooden") and writing the response (e.g., "heap"). Paivio found that accuracy for the abstract nouns was about 20 percent poorer than for the concrete nouns. Although in the 1963 article Paivio notes that "the concept of mediating imagery ... may be unnecessary," the basic finding of superior performance for concrete concepts spurred the development of DCT, in which imagery would play a starring role. Further studies by Paivio and others focused directly on the "imageability" of specific items, and found that imageability was a strong predictor of which items were correctly recalled in memory studies.[29]

The influence of DCT was profound, and served to emphasize the possibility that different forms of information are required to support concrete and abstract concepts. Furthermore, many of the fundamental questions about sensory and verbal representations raised during the development persist to the present day.

concrete distinction, perhaps abstract and concrete words are actually structured along continuous dimensions. One way to test this is to have people rate words along a number of relevant dimensions and use those ratings to determine a high-dimensional semantic space (see also Box 7.4). Doing so can provide more continuous measures of "concreteness" versus "abstractness" than simply assigning each word to a dichotomous category.

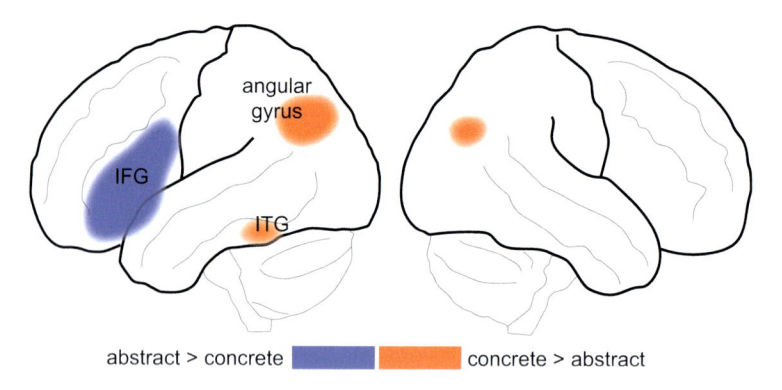

abstract > concrete   concrete > abstract

Figure 7.6 Illustration of differences in activity between abstract and concrete words. IFG = inferior frontal gyrus; ITG = inferior temporal gyrus. https://osf.io/geqb6/ (CC-BY).

7.5 Putting It All Together in a "Hub-and-Spoke" Framework

At first look, both theoretical considerations and evidence from experiments seem to suggest contradictory principles underpinning concept representations in the brain. On the one hand, our knowledge about many concepts comes from sensory and motor experience, and some patients are selectively impaired on certain categories of concepts – suggesting a distributed representation of concepts. On the other hand, patients with svPPA show broad impairment across many categories, and it seems clear that even in a distributed view, information about a concept needs to be tied together somehow. How do we reconcile these two rich lines of evidence?

One approach involves conceptualizing multiple semantic systems developed for different kinds of knowledge. Under a "multiple semantics" view, distributed sensory information could be primarily used to support concrete concepts, whereas amodal and verbal knowledge could be engaged for non-sensory concepts. Although historically some argued for this type of bifurcated system, modern theories tend to favor a unified semantic system.

An alternate solution to the challenges laid out above is to view semantic memory being arranged in a "hub-and-spoke" framework.[30] That is, if semantic memory is a wheel, the *spokes* describe modality-specific, distributed knowledge gained from sensory and motor experience. The *hub* is needed to tie these pieces of distributed knowledge together. Such an arrangement is shown in Figure 7.7.

It is also useful to consider that we do not always need to retrieve all of the information we know about every concept every time we hear a word. If you hear me say the word "dog," you will quickly understand I am referring to a domesticated animal with four legs, and you might even picture a "typical" dog (such as a golden retriever). But now if I ask you to see if you can remember what a wet dog smells like after playing in the rain, or how dog hair feels when you pet it, can you? These are part of your representation of DOG but aren't necessarily activated automatically. (Of course, if you don't have much experience with dogs, you might be able to think of a different example.) The point is that for some tasks we only need a relatively superficial understanding of a concept, and for others a deeper understanding. It may be that distributed representations are more important for detailed semantic representations and can be engaged differently by various kinds of tasks.[31]

Importantly, there may also be multiple hubs that serve these functions. Thus, we don't need to argue over whether "the" hub in semantic memory is situated in the anterior portion of the temporal lobe (i.e., the region damaged in patients with svPPA) or the angular gyrus: Current evidence supports both playing important roles (as shown in Figure 7.7). And indeed, there are other multimodal regions that may also function as hubs. What may be more useful going forward is determining more specifically what types of functions are supported by these regions to enable concept representation. There have been some recent attempts to move our understanding in this direction. For example, as illustrated in Figure 7.8, Reilly and colleagues (including me) (2016) propose a hierarchy of semantic hubs. Specifically, lower-order hubs – like the angular gyrus – are concerned primarily with simple feature and concept combinations. By contrast, higher-order hubs – potentially including the anterior temporal lobe – support symbolic transformations. These multiple kinds of hubs support different kinds of semantic processing and may be engaged differently depending on the task at hand.

7.6 Summary

- Representations for word meanings need to account for both sensory and motor information associated with our experiences and verbal knowledge *not* rooted in those experiences.
- Evidence for distributed semantic representations comes from people with category-specific semantic memory impairments and controlled studies of concepts that rely on different types of sensory and motor information.

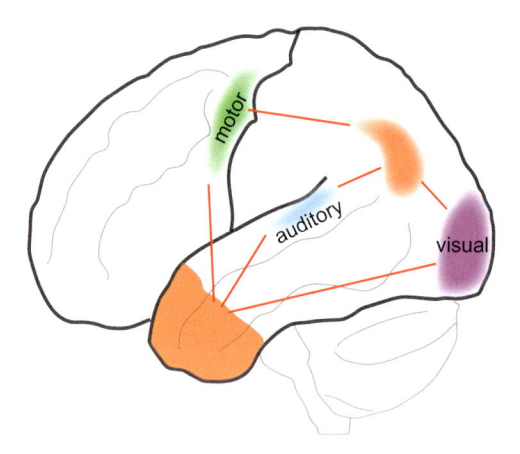

Figure 7.7 A version of a hub-and-spoke framework for semantic memory (see Patterson et al., 2007; Reilly et al., 2016). Here, the temporal pole and angular gyrus are shown as multimodal hubs, with sensory-motor representations in visual, auditory, and motor cortex. The relative engagement of these regions may depend on the specific demands of the current task. https://osf.io/geqb6/ (CC-BY).

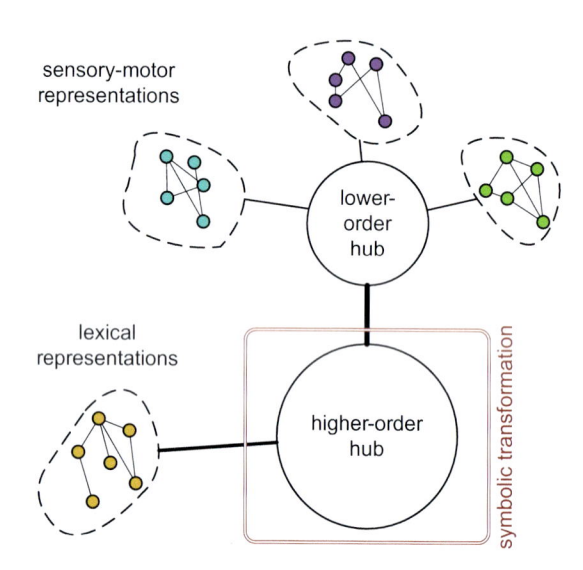

Figure 7.8 As part of the Dynamic Multilevel Reactivation Framework, Reilly and colleagues (2016) propose lower-order hubs supporting feature combinations, and higher-order hubs supporting symbolic transformations: a progression from sensory → heteromodal → amodal processing. https://osf.io/geqb6/ (CC-BY).

Box 7.4 High-dimensional semantic spaces.

Many researchers think about concepts as existing in a kind of "semantic space" – that is, closely related concepts are nearby in space, and distantly related concepts are far away, with the dimensions of the space reflecting different types of meaning. A simple example is shown in Figure 7.9, where I have plotted out two dogs and two tools in a made-up space. In Figure 7.9a, these objects are plotted on the dimensions of warmth and animacy. Dogs are high on both of these scales and tools are low. Thus, the dogs are near each other and the tools are near each other – reflecting the relative similarity of the concepts to each other. In Figure 7.9b, I have added a third dimension of size, which now also separates the dogs and tools a bit more. Hopefully, you can imagine other potential features that might get added to this space (color, weight, and so on); similarly, you might imagine where a new item would fit in this space (what about an ant? a chainsaw? etc.).

For this simple example, I made up the space (and the values for each object) – which does not seem very scientific. How do we construct real semantic spaces?

One popular method is based on the principle of **lexical co-occurrence**, or how often words occur near each other (for practical reasons, typically in written text). An early and influential demonstration of this approach was latent semantic analysis (LSA), introduced by Landauer and Dumais (1997).

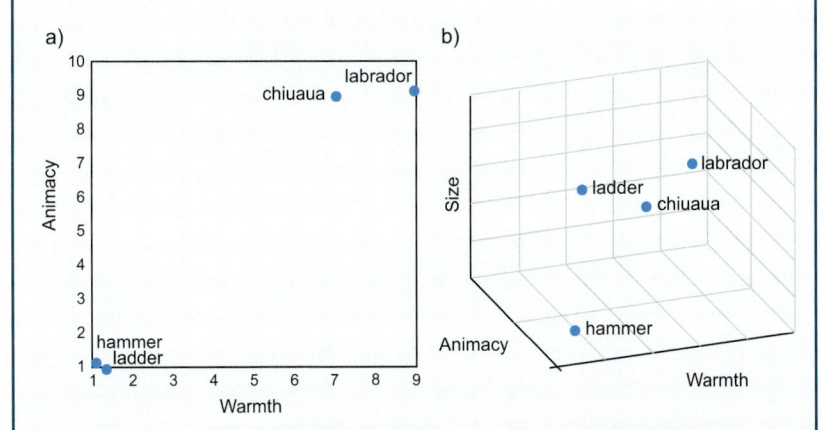

Figure 7.9 Cartoon of semantic spaces. (a) A two-dimensional semantic space with the dimensions of warmth and animacy. (b) A three-dimensional semantic space with the dimensions of warmth, animacy, and size. https://osf.io/geqb6/ (CC-BY).

Box 7.4 (cont.)

The basic approach is to analyze a corpus of language and keep track of words that occur near each other ("near" could be within one word, or three words, or however the researchers want to define it). Let's say you have a list of 10,000 words. For each of the 10,000 words, you then count up how often it is near the other 9,999 words, providing a vector with 10,000 entries. Each word then can be represented by those 10,000 numbers, which situates it in a 10,000 dimensional (!) space. A simple illustration with only five words is shown in Figure 7.10.

A key feature of the lexical co-occurrence approach is that words themselves that never appear near each other can still be close to each other in semantic space. This is because if each word has 10,000 dimensions describing it, *most* of those dimensions could be very similar between two words, even if the words themselves don't occur near each other in text. Thus "kitten" and "lion" might reasonably be near each other in semantic space – even if they never occur together they may share similar associations (paws, tail, fur, purr, pounce, etc.).

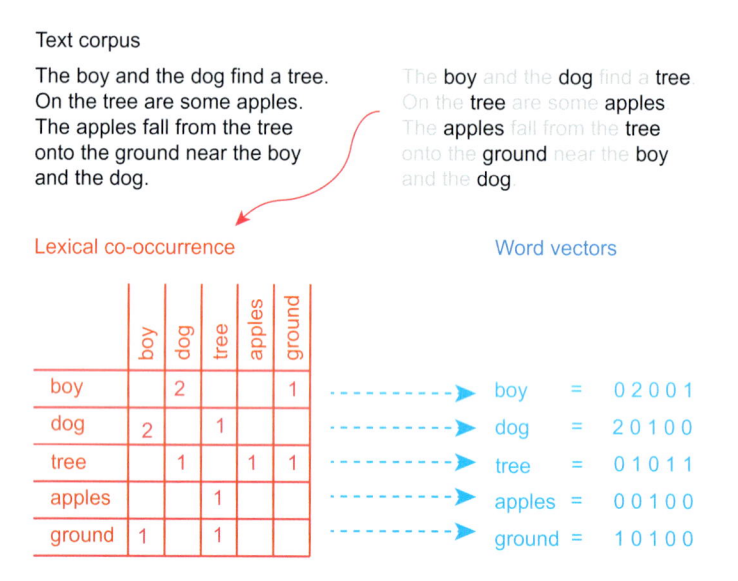

Figure 7.10 Simplified example of lexical co-occurrence for nouns. Given a corpus of text, the number of times each content word appears with each other content word is tallied into a lexical co-occurrence matrix. https://osf.io/geqb6/ (CC-BY).

Box 7.4 (cont.)

A major challenge to the lexical co-occurrence approach is that 10,000 dimensions is rather unwieldy to work with. In addition, each of those dimensions is not truly independent of all of the other ones – there is redundancy in the dimensions, which makes it less useful. One solution is to reduce those 10,000 dimensions to a smaller number of dimensions that preserves most of the variability (items near each other in the 10,000-dimensional space should also be near each other in the lower-dimensional space). A typical number of dimensions might be in the hundreds – still impossible to visualize, but easier to work with and interpret.

When defining a semantic space using word co-occurrence, a central question centers on which words to use. The corpus (that is, the set of words) chosen will have a significant impact on how the space is defined. In the landmark work from Landauer and Dumais, they used 6 million words from Grolier's *Academic American Encyclopedia* – which they describe as "a work intended for young students." A different choice of corpus – for example, all of the articles on Wikipedia, every web page indexed by Google, subtitles for movies produced during certain years, and so on – may result in different spaces.

A complementary approach to lexical co-occurrence involves asking people to rate words along specific dimensions. In one example of this approach, Binder and colleagues (2016) developed a list of 65 attributes on which to rate concepts, based on findings from neuroscience and neuropsychological literature.[32] For example, "color," "taste," "landmark," "human," and "fearful." Using an online experiment, they collected data in 16,373 sessions from 1,743 unique participants who answered questions such as: "does this item have a characteristic or defining color?" (nouns), "is this item associated with a color or change in color?" (verbs), or "does this item describe a color?" (adjective). Using these ratings, concepts can be arranged in a high-dimensional space that captures a number of distinctions present elsewhere in the literature.

- Evidence for unified semantic representations comes from people with svPPA, who have damage to the left temporal pole and impoverished representations of concepts. Additional evidence from functional brain imaging implicates the angular gyrus in many types of semantic memory.
- A hub-and-spoke arrangement – in which one or more heteromodal hubs help connect sensory and motor representations together – may offer a framework to account for the totality of the data.

Notes

1. I have taken some liberty in oversimplifying a "primary" region for vision to make a general point. There is certainly an area known as "primary visual cortex," which is the first region of the cortex through which visual information passes. However, there are a large number of regions that participate in vision, generally organized hierarchically with dense feedback projections. As noted briefly in Chapter 3, the dense interconnectivity and hierarchical organization of brain regions challenge a simple, strict one-to-one mapping between cognitive function and brain area.

2. The distinction may seem trivial but is actually critical, especially for human neuroscience. The reason is that the level of detail available regarding neural computation is relatively coarse: Most of our understanding about functional localization comes from patients with brain damage (which tends to cover a relatively broad area) or fMRI (which measures a signal related to the population activity of hundreds of thousands of neurons). So, even if two concepts both rely on the "same" brain region, they could easily reflect quite different neural connections and processing, and be – from a computational perspective – entirely different. However, if two concepts rely on *different* brain regions, we can be fairly confident that they are not stored identically in the brain.

3. Much more on semantic categories can be found in Capitani and colleagues (2003), who reference the Organised Unitary Content Hypothesis (OUCH) (Caramazza et al., 1990) and related theories. In their description of OUCH (p. 214):

   In this account, conceptual space is lumpy, in that objects that share many properties tend to be represented together. For instance, the semantic representations of things that are made of a certain kind of stuff, have similar shapes, or are capable of self-generated movement might cluster together. If it is assumed that brain damage can selectively affect lumpy areas of conceptual space, either because these conceptual clusters are neurally contiguous and thus susceptible to selective damage, or because damage to a given property will propagate to highly correlated properties, then it is possible for specific categories of objects to be damaged (relatively) independently of one another ... The crucial aspect to all OUCH-type theories is that the organising principle of conceptual knowledge in the brain is not semantic (e.g., animate vs. inanimate), but the degree to which properties of objects tend to co-occur in the world.

4. Encephalitis refers to a swelling of the brain, here caused by the body's reaction to the herpes simplex virus. In severe cases, long-lasting brain damage can occur. (In fact, Warrington and Shallice actually tested four patients, but two had significant difficulty with speech production and only completed one test. J. B. R. and S. B. Y., by contrast, "had fluent spontaneous speech with normal articulation, phrase length and syntax.")

5. There is a long history in the neuropsychological literature of providing a patient's initials in case reports. Doing so offers some anonymity to patients while allowing readers to have a reference for patients (which would be useful, for example, if a patient contributes to multiple studies, which happens relatively often for patients with rare conditions).

6. An interesting detail about the errors that the patients make with living things is that while some of the answers are incorrect, others reflect a different level of organization. For example, a duck is technically an animal (the response given by S. B. Y.), but most people would call it a bird. "Animal" is a broader category than "bird," called a *superordinate* category. Superordinate errors are particularly interesting because they indicate that a person has *some* knowledge about an object – S. B. Y. did not call a duck a "tool" or a "vehicle" or a "fruit" – but that they lack information about the specific category to which an item belongs (or perhaps, a lack of the characteristic features of objects in a category).

7. A more modern approach involves defining abstract concepts by what they *are* rather than what they *are not*; from this perspective, we might say that abstract concepts have meanings grounded in affective and social knowledge, interoception, verbal definitions, and linguistic associations. Much more on this and other aspects of semantic memory can be found in Reilly and colleagues (2024).

8. In one fMRI study, Ishai and colleagues (1999) presented pictures of objects to participants and examined the responses in posterior ventral temporal cortex (i.e., the ventral visual pathway). Participants saw houses, faces, chairs, and scrambled pictures – that is, pictures that are visually rearranged so they are not recognizable as objects, but which keep many of the same features (like pixel darkness) as the object stimuli. They found regions of ventral cortex that responded most strongly to each category: That is, regions that appeared sensitive to the category of the picture being presented. It is also interesting to consider the many dimensions on which these pictures differ: They differ not only in the category of object but in the level of detail of the pictures presented, size and spatial scale of the objects, and so on (later studies would go on to examine many of these issues in more detail). Importantly, although regions showed a *preference* for some categories, activity was not *exclusive* to a category. Thus, the authors viewed their results as against a strictly divided visual system, and instead in line with a distributed system: Different categories rely more or less on parts of the visual system depending on the type of information they require.

9. In contrast to semantic memory, *episodic memory* refers to memory tied to a specific episode – the time, place, and context are critical components of the representation. A groundbreaking advance in our understanding of human memory came from patient H. M., who in 1953 had much of his medial temporal lobes surgically removed to treat severe epilepsy. Although his seizures improved, the operation resulted in severe disruptions to his memory. In particular, H. M. showed severe anterograde amnesia – that is, the ability to make new memories (Scoville and Milner, 1957). However, other cognitive abilities – including language and some forms of procedural learning – were preserved (for an example, see Corkin, 1965; Milner et al., 1968). H. M. is one of the most famous neurological patients in the research literature, and he participated in countless research studies between 1957 and his death in 2008, at which time his name was revealed to be Henry Molaison.

10. So named because when dissected from the rest of the brain it resembles a seahorse – *hippocampus* is Greek for seahorse. For the similarity to be obvious though it is important to view the hippocampus from the correct angle. (Incidentally, it was while searching for pictures of seahorses to include in a lecture on memory that I discovered that male seahorses are the ones who give birth. Females deposit their eggs into a pouch on the front of the males, where the eggs are fertilized and develop.)

11. One of my favorite diagrams is a famous "wiring diagram" of the visual system from Felleman and Van Essen (1991), constructed primarily using data about anatomical connections between regions. At the apex of the diagram – the region that all other visual regions, in one way or another, connect with – is the hippocampus.

12. Devlin and colleagues (2002) provide an alternate perspective on functional brain imaging evidence for category specificity. They used a lexical decision task (low task demands) and a semantic categorization task (high task demands) while participants processed concepts belonging to four categories: animals, fruits, tools, and vehicles. They found broad activation in the temporal and frontal lobes during semantic tasks, including left inferior frontal gyrus and left anterior lateral temporal cortex. However, they did not observe any category-based differences in the overall magnitude of the response (that is, in their mass univariate analysis). They discuss a view in which category-specific semantic deficits do not necessarily come out of category-based organization at the level of brain regions. Rather, in a distributed system, damaging a single node might differentially affect one category more than another. The categories are represented differently (as in, they differentially rely on different nodes in a distributed network), but not in a simple category-to-structure mapping as might be envisioned by a phrenologist.

13. Warrington and Shallice (1984) highlight this distinction between "functional significance" (what an object is used for) and "sensory features."

14. I learned a great deal about apples from Michael Pollan's delightful *The Botany of Desire: A Plant's-Eye View of the World*, in which he examines four plants whose "success" has been helped by human interest: tulips, cannabis, apples, and potatoes. Among many other interesting facts, I had not realized that apple seeds are genetically diverse (planting the seed you got from a Red Delicious apple may or may not give you a tree with fruit resembling a Red Delicious apple; to be sure, you have to graft it), and that Johnny Appleseed (John Chapman) was a shrewd businessperson who helped supply fermented cider for settlers (which was often safer to drink than was water).

15. Bonner and Grossman (2012) presented written items, one at a time, and asked people to rate whether each item was a real word or not. (This type of task is called a lexical decision task because participants decide whether an item is a real word – that is, in their mental lexicon.) Although knowing that an item is a word does not technically require accessing the concept to which it refers, the assumption is that at least some degree of concept retrieval happens automatically. The words presented varied in their sensory and motor features, determined through a separate rating study. Participants included neurologically healthy adults, and a group of patients with the logopenic variant of

progressive aphasia. Critically, patients with logopenic variant progressive aphasia often have damage to the temporal lobe encompassing regions of auditory cortex but not to regions of cortex primarily associated to vision or motor processing. Thus, if concepts are represented according to sensory information, we might expect patients with logopenic variant progressive aphasia to have more difficulty with auditory-centered concepts like THUNDER. Indeed, that was precisely what the authors observed: Patients with logopenic progressive aphasia made more errors on auditory concepts than on concepts that relied more heavily on visual or motor properties. Even more compelling was the finding that individual differences in gray matter volume also predicted the degree of difficulty: Patients with more atrophy in auditory regions made more errors than those with less atrophy. A critical point here is that all of the words were presented the same way, as written words: The findings relate to the type of information contributing to the concept, not the modality of testing.

16. Arnold Pick (1851–1924) was a Czech psychiatrist perhaps best known for identifying Pick's disease – now known as behavioral variant frontotemporal dementia – and the Pick bodies present in the condition. According to Todman (2009), he was a meticulous clinician, and described cases of focal brain atrophy that challenged the prevailing notion at the time that brain atrophy was always diffuse.

17. As covered elsewhere (for example Box 7.3) in many tasks, concrete concepts show an advantage over abstract concepts (for example, decisions about these words may occur more rapidly). The *reversal of the concreteness effect* refers to the observation in svPPA that concrete objects are processed *worse* than abstract ones. Although still controversial, many reports support the basic finding (for more on this issue, see Bonner and colleagues, 2009, who suggest that degraded knowledge about visual features in patients with svPPA may contribute to this effect).

18. Tulving's chapter begins:

> One of the unmistakable characteristics of an immature science is the looseness of definition and use of its major concepts. In experimental psychology, a discipline less than a hundred years old, we can measure our progress by the number and generality of empirical facts and the power and scope of our theories, and we can assess the lack of progress by the degree of ambiguity of our most popular terms. (Tulving, 1972, pp. 381–382)

Tulving attributes the first use of "semantic" memory to Quliian's 1966 doctoral dissertation (which I have no reason to doubt). In the context of our other thinking about localization, it is also interesting to read Tulving say (regarding semantic vs. episodic memory):

> I will refer to both kinds of memory as two stores, or two systems, but I do this primarily for the convenience of communication, rather than as an expression of any profound belief about structural or functional separation of the two. Nothing very much is lost at this stage of our deliberations if the reality of the separation between episodic and semantic memory lies solely in the experimenter's and the theorist's, and not the subject's mind. (Tulving, 1972, p. 384)

In the context of this quote, it is perhaps particularly interesting that several decades of cognitive neuroscience indeed support different brain systems supporting episodic and semantic memory.

19. For more on the history of svPPA, Hodges and Patterson (2007) provide an excellent overview (including the references to Arnold Pick's early work in the area). Bonner and colleagues (2010) discuss classification of primary progressive aphasia variants, and Grossman (2018) offers a comprehensive look at the defining characteristics of these patient populations in terms of language function.

20. Bozeat and colleagues (2003) studied drawing in patients with svPPA. They found that when patients immediately copied a drawing, errors were relatively few (though still present); with a delay, errors increased. Many of these related to characteristic or distinctive features.

21. A term commonly used in the scientific literature to describe the region damaged in svPPA is the "anterior temporal lobe" (e.g., Hodges and Patterson, 2007). Although correct – the damage is in the anterior portion of the temporal lobe – the lack of specificity has caused some confusion. In other contexts, "anterior temporal lobe" may actually refer to the "anterior *lateral* temporal lobe," such as the anterior portion of the middle temporal gyrus, which is distinct from the temporal pole. Inferior temporal cortex is also distinct, and – provocatively – contains regions in perirhinal cortex, fusiform gyrus, and hippocampus that are related to high-level visual object recognition and memory. From one theoretical standpoint, these details of terminology may not matter and do not influence what we learn from the knowledge and behavior of patients with svPPA (regardless of the anatomy, there is still evidence for a unified form of semantic representation). However, the distinctions are critical when trying to understand an anatomically constrained framework for semantic memory and to relate brain regions across studies.

22. Binder and colleagues (2009) performed a meta-analysis of 120 functional brain imaging studies to identify regions consistently involved in semantic processing. The angular gyrus came out as one of the strongest regions. Of note, because of signal dropout present in common fMRI sequences, portions of the temporal pole implicated in svPPA often have poor, or no, signal in fMRI. Thus, the absence of fMRI results in portions of the anterior temporal lobe does not mean that brain activity in this region is not contributing to semantic representation. Other studies, with fMRI sequences specifically designed to minimize signal dropout, provide a less biased picture.

23. The medial boundary of the angular gyrus is the intraparietal sulcus, which separates it from the superior parietal lobule. Probabilistic maps of the inferior parietal lobe based on cytoarchitectonic features, including the angular gyrus, were provided by Caspers and colleagues (2006). In their parcellation, the angular gyrus corresponds to regions PGa and PGb; in Brodmann's map, approximately BA 39.

24. Humphries and colleagues (2007) presented lists of words and pseudowords to participants. The sentences could be semantically congruent (e.g., "the man on vacation lost a bag and a wallet"), semantically random ("the freeway on a pie watched a house and a window"), or made up of pseudowords (e.g., "the solims on a sonting grilloted a yome and a sovir"). Stimuli also included semantically congruent word lists (e.g., "on vacation lost then a and bag wallet man then a"), semantically

random words lists ("a ball the a the spilled librarian in sign through fire"), and pseudoword word lists (e.g., "rooned the sif into lilf the and the foig aurene to"). The authors found significant divergence in the task-related brain activity in the angular gyrus: The semantically congruent sentences showed the strongest response (a classic event-related hemodynamic response), followed by conditions with real words (but not a cohesive structure), followed by pseudowords. This pattern is broadly consistent with a role for the angular gyrus in word meaning (perhaps specifically related to combining meanings, given the difference between sentences and word lists).

25. Binder and colleagues (2005) report the general pattern of greater posterior and inferior temporal cortex activity for concrete words than abstract words, and greater activity in left frontal cortex for abstract words than concrete words, a pattern largely confirmed by meta-analyses (Bucur and Papagno, 2021; Wang et al., 2010).

26. Crutch and Warrington (2005) introduce a proposal for differing representations between abstract and concrete concepts, suggesting that abstract concepts rely more on associative connections than do concrete concepts. The paper is also of interest because Elizabeth Warrington – who helped raise awareness of semantic memory deficits in her influential 1975 work – is one of the authors. Crutch and Warrington (2005) studied a patient with semantic refractory access dysphasia, A. Z., who had more difficulty with associated abstract words than synonymous abstract words, while concrete words showed the opposite pattern. Because the primary manipulation centered on the *associations* between words – associative versus synonymous – the differences in performance were attributed to how these relationships structured semantic memory. In other words, the relationships between concepts seem different for abstract and concrete concepts, suggesting a different type of organizing principle.

27. Allan Urho Paivio (1925–2016) was born in Thunder Bay, Ontario, Canada. As a young adult he was passionate about exercise and had a successful career as a bodybuilder, winning the title of "Mr. Canada" in 1948. He earned his PhD from McGill University in 1959 and taught at the University of Western Ontario from 1963 until his retirement.

28. An informative retrospective is provided by Paivio (1991), in which the author traces nearly 30 years of development of DCT. At the outset Paivio notes that "DCT rests on the assumption that the representational substrate is multimodal and relatively concrete" (p. 256) and "the representational units of the two systems are assumed to be modality-specific perceptual-motor analogues" (p. 258). These points are particularly relevant when considering how focus on abstract concepts – for example, the work of Crutch and Warrington – can inform our understanding.

29. A provocative line of research from Westbury and colleagues (2013) investigates the relationship of imageability ratings to contextual and emotional associations for a word. They find that, at least in response times from a lexical decision task, effects often attributed to imageability can be explained by other factors.

30. A hub-and-spoke framework centered on findings from svPPA is elegantly laid out by Patterson and colleagues (2007). The authors focus on results from patients with svPPA, and thus the anterior temporal lobe is featured as the primary hub; subsequent work has also suggested involvement of regions of the anterior fusiform gyrus (Binney et al., 2012).

31. Selective reactivation of relevant concepts was a key feature of convergence zones, which are one of the earliest modern proposals for a hybrid semantic network. For a summary of this work and extension in the dynamic multilevel reactivation framework – which I like to pronounce "durmf," but don't tell the authors of the paper – see Reilly and colleagues (2016) (one of the authors of that paper argued for a more pronounceable acronym but was ultimately overruled).

32. Some of the many additional approaches to defining feature spaces are seen in McRae and colleagues (1997) and Troche and colleagues (2014).

Further Reading

Binder JR, Desai RH, Graves WW, Conant LL (2009) Where is the semantic system? A critical review and meta-analysis of 120 functional neuroimaging studies. *Cerebral Cortex* 19:2767–2796. https://doi.org/10.1093/cercor/bhp055.
  By combining data from many functional imaging studies, this paper provides a map of brain regions statistically associated with semantic memory.

Gage N, Hickok G (2005) Multiregional cell assemblies, temporal binding and the representation of conceptual knowledge in cortex: a modern theory by a "classical" neurologist, Carl Wernicke. *Cortex* 41: 823–832. https://doi.org/10.1016/S0010-9452(08)70301-0.
  The paper presents translations and commentary on writings of well-known neurologist Carl Wernicke's writings about semantic memory.

Patterson K, Nestor PJ, Rogers TT (2007) Where do you know what you know? The representation of semantic knowledge in the human brain. *Nature Reviews Neuroscience* 8:976–987. https://doi.org/10.1038/nrn2277.
  Review of semantic memory, including a proposal to reconcile evidence favoring modality-preferential and domain-neutral semantic knowledge in a "hub-and-spoke" framework.

Tong J, Binder JR, Humphries C, Mazurchuk S, Conant LL, Fernandino L (2022) A distributed network for multimodal experiential representation of concepts. *The Journal of Neuroscience* 42:7121–7130. https://doi.org/10.1523/JNEUROSCI.1243-21.2022.
  Using fMRI and representational similarity analysis examines the relationship of items based on a large number of sensory, motor, affective, and other experiential dimensions.

CHAPTER EIGHT

Combining Meaning across Words

In everyday conversation we frequently hear words in a linguistic context – that is, along with other words (as in a sentence or conversation). And, in fact, the surrounding context can fundamentally change how a word is processed. These changes range from minor (a word that is expected based on what has been heard previously will be processed more quickly and accurately than an unexpected word) to entirely different meanings being conveyed (for example, based on the syntax of the sentence: who did what to whom). In this chapter we will explore several examples of how we combine meaning across words and the brain systems that support this process.

8.1 Compositional Semantics

Before we get to sentences, we can start by looking at how *two* words are combined and shape meaning, a process often referred to as **compositional semantics** (contrasted to **lexical** semantics, which deals with single words). For example, you have a representation of the color GREEN, and of the fruit APPLE. But your concept of a GREEN APPLE is probably not as simple as just somehow adding these two concepts together; "green apple" evokes a specific meaning that comes from a deeper understanding of the concept (if you try, perhaps you can remember the tart taste of a Granny Smith). Indeed, not just *any* concepts can be combined – you understand the word "plaid" and the word "apple" but a "plaid apple" does not make much sense. One approach to understanding compositional semantics, then, has focused on pairs of words as a stepping stone to longer utterances.[1] The goal is not on understanding how the meanings of individual words are represented but on how these single word concepts are combined into a new concept.

Two regions of the brain have emerged as leading contenders in supporting the combination of meaning across words. Interestingly, these regions show some correspondence to some identified as underpinning semantic memory more generally (see Chapter 7). The first is the lateral portion of the left anterior temporal lobe (Figure 8.1). Anatomically, the lateral anterior temporal lobe sits beyond (that is, anterior to) regions involved in sound and single word

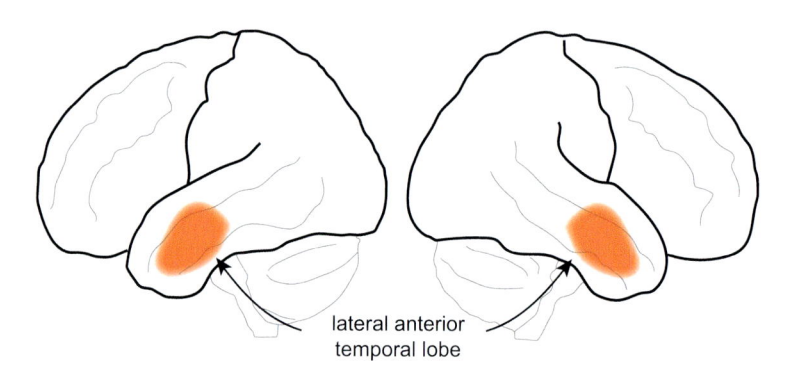

Figure 8.1 The lateral anterior temporal lobe. https://osf.io/geqb6/ (CC-BY).

processing (namely, posterior STG, STS, and MTG). From a computational standpoint, this makes the lateral anterior temporal lobe well positioned to work on the outputs of those regions. In other words, if the STG and MTG are concerned with mapping sounds onto words, the lateral anterior temporal lobe can work on putting these words together.

A common type of word combination comes from adjective-noun pairs. For example, you recognize the word "boat," and the color "red," but understanding a "red boat" requires these concepts be combined into a unified idea. This type of word combination is associated with a signal in the left anterior temporal lobe about 250 ms after stimulus onset.[2]

A second region implicated in combinatorial semantics is the angular gyrus. As we saw in Chapter 7, the angular gyrus (Figure 8.2a) has been implicated in semantic memory in a general sense. The question is whether it may also contribute specifically to combinatorial semantics.

One way to study composition – exemplified by the "red boat" studies (Box 8.1) – is to come up with two categories of word pairs: combinatorial and non-combinatorial. A second approach is more graded, and instead views how easily words can be combined along a continuum. For example, you might ask people to rate how easily word pairs could be combined. You might imagine that "red apple" or "green apple" might be rated as "high combination," "brown apple" a medium combination (possible, but not immediately obvious), and a "plaid apple" an unlikely combination. It is then possible to assess how people process differing levels of semantic combination while keeping many of the characteristics of the target noun (e.g., "apple") constant. In healthy adults, fMRI shows that high-combination word pairs are associated with increased activity in the angular gyrus[3] compared to low-combination pairs.[4]

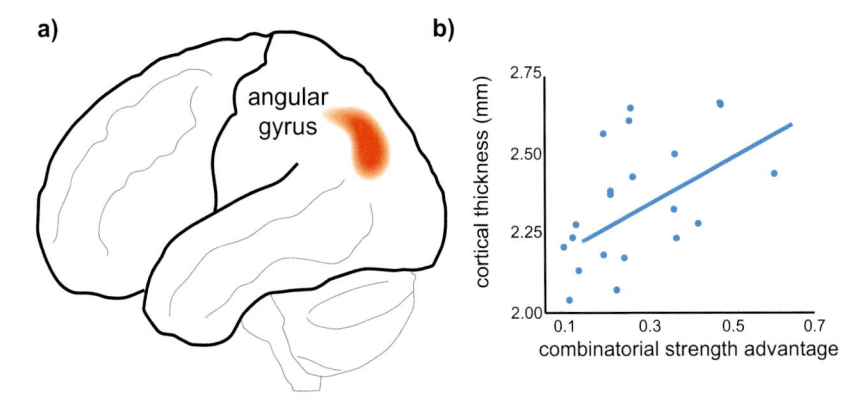

Figure 8.2 (a) The left angular gyrus. (b) Results from structural MRI analysis in Price, Bonner and colleagues (2015) showing that individual differences in cortical thickness in the angular gyrus correlate with behavioral performance on a combinatorial judgment task. https://osf.io/geqb6/ (CC-BY).

Box 8.1 The red boat studies.

In a series of elegant studies over several years, Liina Pylkkänen and colleagues have used MEG to study the neural basis of semantic composition.[6] As explained by Bemis and Pylkäanen (2011, p. 2801):

Human language derives its unbounded expressive capacity from an ability to take simple, familiar building blocks (such as words) and combine them effortlessly into more complex representations, regardless of whether or not the result is familiar. Such productive "composition" is present in the comprehension of even minimal linguistic expressions. For example, the phrase "blue flamingo" conjures a coherent and meaningful mental representation despite a listener's presumed unfamiliarity with such an object.

A recurring challenge for understanding different aspects of language processing in the brain comes out of the fact that in everyday speech, different levels of linguistic processing co-occur – that is, spoken sentences have acoustic, syntactic, and semantic effects on our comprehension, making it difficult to isolate effects of any stage (such as composition).

   To overcome these challenges, Pylkkänen and colleagues devised a word pair paradigm in which they presented composition-inducing word pairs ("red boat") that could be combined and word pairs that are not as easily combined ("red, blue"). For example, Bemis and Pylkkänen (2011) presented stimulus

Box 8.1 (cont.)

pairs, one at a time (Figure 8.3). In the two-word tasks, the words could either lend themselves to competition ("red, boat") or not ("cup, boat"); responses to the second item were analyzed. In the single word task, the first item was a letter string (e.g., "xkq"). Following the two words a picture was shown, and participants pressed a button to indicate whether or not it matched the preceding word. Because target stimuli (e.g., "boat") were matched across condition, the design allowed the authors to isolate neural processes related to two-word composition relative to the other conditions. This paradigm identified a change in ventromedial prefrontal cortex (vmPFC) around 400 ms after word onset, and in left lateral anterior temporal lobe around 225–250 ms after word onset. These results therefore suggest relatively early (~250 ms) responses related to semantic composition in the lateral anterior temporal lobe.

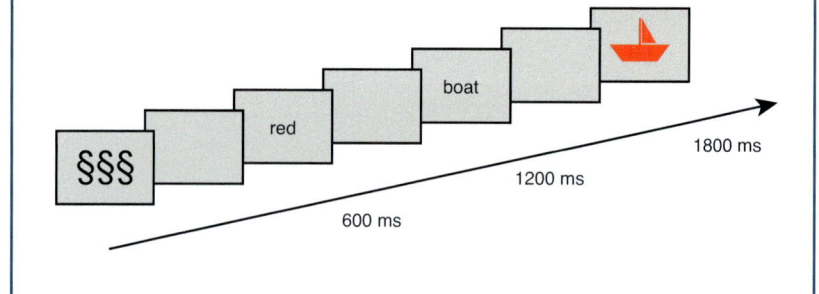

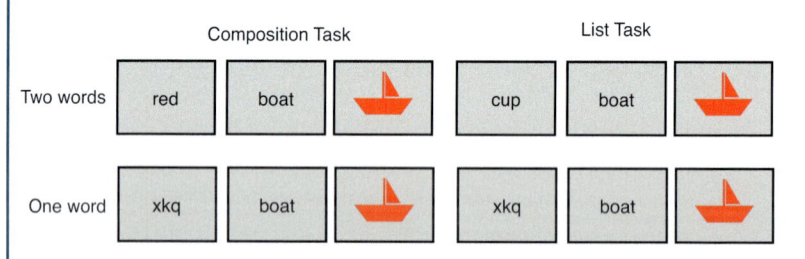

Figure 8.3 Schematic of the "red boat" task from Bemis and Pylkkänen (2011). On each trial, two text strings are presented; these can be two words (the "Two words" condition) or a letter string and a word (the "One word" condition). Following the text a picture appears. In the composition task, participants indicate whether the picture reflects both of the following words (in the example shown, a red boat does, whereas a blue boat would not). In the list task, participants respond if the picture matches either of the prior words. The authors used MEG to measure responses to the critical word ("boat") that are matched across conditions but differ in compositionality. https://osf.io/geqb6/ (CC-BY).

Furthermore, patients with atrophy to the left angular gyrus perform more poorly on tasks judging how well two words combine – that is, people with better-preserved gray matter in the angular gyrus performed more accurately on a combinatorial judgment task (Figure 8.2b). And disrupting processing in the left angular gyrus of healthy adults using tDCS results in modulations in combinatorial processing.[5]

Together, these studies suggest that at least two regions – the left anterior temporal lobe, and the angular gyrus – play important roles in combinatorial semantics. How these regions work together continues to be an open question for the field.

8.2 Sentence Processing

Even simple sentences differ substantially from individual words in the demands they place on listeners. This includes the fact that the co-occurrence and arrangement of words can affect their meaning, and also the fact that connected speech introduces acoustic and temporal properties not present in single words.[7]

One way of studying processes related to sentence comprehension is to compare activity seen in response to a meaningful sentence with that in response to a list of words. These two stimuli can thus be matched in the overall length and number of words but differ in the degree to which the words are processed as a sentence. Perhaps not surprisingly given what we discussed in Chapter 6, listening to lists of words is associated with bilateral activity in the STG, STS, and MTG.[8] When words are connected in a sentence, there is additional activity seen along the bilateral middle and superior temporal gyri, and (sometimes) in the left angular gyrus for congruent sentences.[9] Activity during sentences is also frequently seen in the left IFG – often *pars orbitalis* (the ventral portion of IFG).

In addition to comparison with non-sentence conditions (like a word list), another way to identify regions associated with sentence processing is to vary the intelligibility of what is being heard, while holding as much of the other acoustic attributes as possible the same between control conditions and speech. Noise vocoded speech (which we discussed in Box 6.1) is an appealing choice for this because it is possible to create a gradation of intelligibility, from unintelligible all the way to fully intelligible, by varying the number of channels used in the vocoding process (as you might recall, using more channels results in a more detailed spectral representation and higher intelligibility compared to using fewer channels). Intelligibility can also be varied by using different levels of background noise. The challenge provided by background noise is usually expressed as the signal-to-noise ratio (SNR), in decibels: an SNR of +10 dB indicates the signal (here, speech) is 10 dB louder than the noise. An SNR of −5 dB indicates the signal is 5 dB *quieter* than the noise. The more noise present relative to the speech – that is, the lower the SNR – the more difficult speech is to perceive.

As illustrated in Figure 8.4, intelligible sentences are associated with responses along the bilateral STG/MTG, left lateral temporal cortex, left IFG, and left inferior temporal gyrus (see Box 8.2).[10] Consider how these responses differ to those seen in response to single words (Figure 6.3): while the response to single words is frequently bilateral, responses to sentences begin to show a left hemisphere dominance,[11] particularly for regions more removed from auditory cortex.

When considering regions of the brain that respond to intelligible speech, it is important to remember that they do not respond in exactly the same way, either because of acoustic characteristics of the speech or the temporal profile of the response.[12] It seems that regions related to sentence processing are arranged hierarchically, with regions in and around auditory cortex being more concerned with acoustic details (such as whether speech is challenging because of background noise or some other reason), and regions further away more concerned with abstracted levels of representation (like "intelligibility"). Such a hierarchical organization is compatible with the dual- or multi-stream organization outlined in Chapter 3.

The findings reviewed in this section are consistent with additional cognitive processing needed to deal with the linguistic demands of sentences relative to word lists. However, they do not allow us to identify *which* specific processes are engaged: For example, as speech goes from being unintelligible to

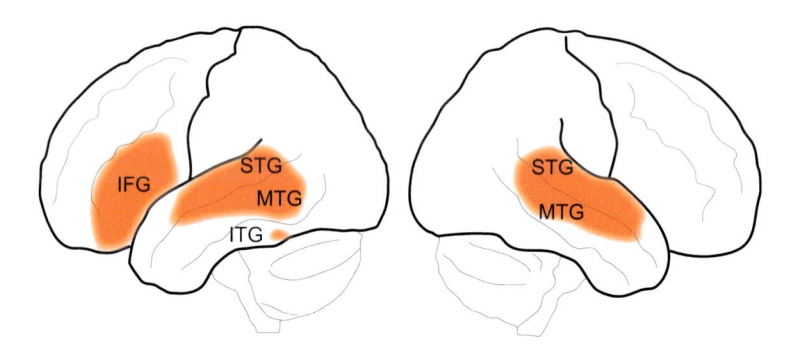

Figure 8.4 Brain regions associated with intelligible sentences include bilateral superior temporal gyrus (STG) and middle temporal gyrus (MTG), left inferior temporal gyrus (ITG), and left inferior frontal gyrus (IFG). https://osf.io/geqb6/ (CC-BY).

intelligible, many types of additional information are available, including individual words being recognized, semantic information, and syntactic information, not to mention other aspects of speech such as the tone, pitch, and rhythm of what is being said.[13] To draw specific conclusions about the processes involved, we need a manipulation that operates at a more specific level. These studies make up the remainder of the chapter.

8.3 Semantic Ambiguity

When trying to communicate an idea to someone, we choose specific words to convey our intended meaning. However, the number of existing words in any language is limited, and we might have to pick a word with a weaker meaning than we would like. Furthermore, in speech, words that sound the same (homophones) can actually convey more than one meaning, even if you might spell them differently. These words, on their own, are therefore ambiguous, and listeners have to determine the right meaning (the same thing happens as you read this paragraph, although spelling can help distinguish meaning in some cases in a way that can't occur with spoken language).

A surprising number of word forms can relate to more than one meaning. For example, "bark" can refer to either the sound a dog makes or the covering on a tree; "bank" can refer to the institution holding money in a safe way or to the side of a river. Other words have different "senses" of meaning: I can twist a rope, or twist the truth, and although these senses are related they are also distinct. Perhaps as many as 80 percent of words in English are considered to have multiple meanings.[14] And spoken language – without the benefit of spelling – also has to contend with word pairs like pair versus pear, bear versus bare, red versus read, and so on.

With that background, it never ceases to amaze me that in everyday conversation we are seldom confused by these semantic ambiguities. For example, if I tell you that "Jack was scared by the loud bark," most (if not all) of the readers of this book would assume a dog had barked (because, although not impossible, it is rare for tree bark to be described as "loud"). In fact, if you go back to the first paragraph in this section, you can count no fewer than 18 ambiguous words[15] – which I suspect you didn't notice at the time!

One reason we are not typically aware of ambiguous words is that the surrounding context usually helps us to understand the intended meaning – that is, to disambiguate them (**semantic disambiguation** referring to the process of identifying a meaning for an ambiguous word). In the sentence "Jamie deposited his money in the bank," people quickly understand that Jamie was probably more likely to give his money to a financial institution than to bury it beside a river. A key question for researchers interested in sentence processing is the degree to which semantic disambiguation is automatic or requires cognitive resources above and beyond those required for understanding nonambiguous words.

What happens when we hear a word with more than one meaning? First, all possible meanings of the word are activated[16] – with the important caveat that the degree to which this happens probably depends on the preceding context. If you hear "I saw the aunt (ant) in the back yard," AUNT and ANT would both be active (assuming you are operating in a dialect where "aunt" and "ant" are pronounced similarly!). However, if you heard "At the family gathering I saw my uncle hug my aunt (ant)," presumably the meaning that is closer to a family relative (as opposed to an insect) would be more likely, and thus more active. See Box 8.2 for more on how context and experience can affect the meaning of ambiguous words.

When more than one meaning is active, a single meaning must be selected to understand what has been said. Doing so requires inhibition of the incorrect meanings or a selection process to determine the most likely meaning. How do our brains accomplish this feat? Perhaps not surprisingly, both behavioral and neural evidence points to the fact that semantic disambiguation is not completely automatic. When listening to sentences containing ambiguous words, extra activity is seen in regions of both the left temporal and frontal lobe (Figure 8.5), suggesting that our brains need to do additional work when ambiguous words are heard to integrate the words with their surrounding context.[17]

An additional point of interest: Once an ambiguous word is disambiguated, the chosen meaning remains more active (in a psychological sense, at least)

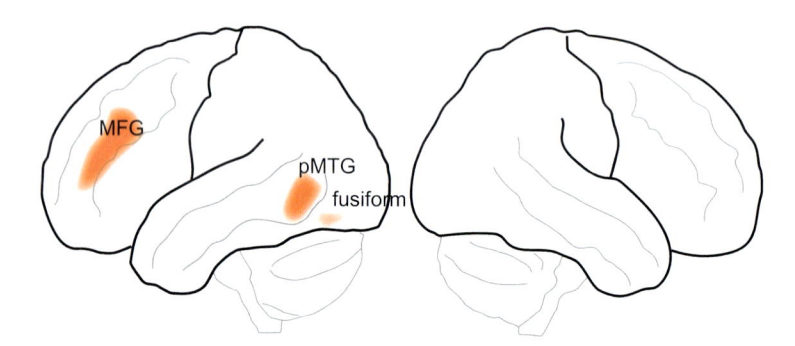

Figure 8.5 Brain regions responding more strongly to sentences with highly ambiguous words compared to sentences without, including left middle frontal gyrus (MFG), posterior middle temporal gyrus (pMTG), and fusiform gyrus. https://osf.io/geqb6/ (CC-BY).

Box 8.2 Experience affects word meaning.

You might wonder whether our daily experiences influence how we process words with multiple meanings. For example, you might imagine that someone who works in a financial institution and someone who works as a river guide have different assumptions about the meaning of the word "bank." Jenni Rodd and colleagues (2016) examined the role of experience on word meaning in a pair of elegant experiments. In the first study, they partnered with BBC Radio 4 and a program called *The Human Zoo* to conduct part of the experiment on live radio (allowing them to collect usable data from 1,800 participants!). Listeners to the program heard familiar radio presenters read scripts provided by the researchers, each of which contained a number of fully disambiguated ambiguous words. For example: "Mark hopes to become a professional tennis player. He practices on *court* at his *club* with his *coach* most days" (target ambiguous words italicized). Listeners were then asked to complete an online word association task sometime in the next week in which they were given a word and asked to generate a related word. The association task allowed researchers to assess both the degree to which listening to the program affected semantic priming, and how the delay between the radio program and task influenced this effect. They found that listeners showed an increase in related responses (that is, evidence of priming) on the first day after the program, but not on subsequent days; furthermore, within the first day, the priming effect decreased logarithmically over time (Figure 8.6).

In a second and complementary study, the authors looked at how word meanings vary based on life experience by studying people who were recreational rowers. Words such as "square," "crab," and "feather" have meanings apart from rowing that are generally known, but they also convey specific aspects of rowing that are presumably more salient for people who row.[19] Participants were given a word association task in which being presented with one word they were asked to generate a related word. The critical comparison was for words that had special meaning for rowers (which were a small proportion of all of the words presented, so that participants wouldn't be biased). In this case, people who rowed recently generated more rowing-related words than people who had not rowed recently – with this effect increasing with the amount of rowing experience a person had.

These findings suggest that short-term priming effects may help listeners understand ambiguous words in context – that is, once a word has been disambiguated, that meaning stays active (as would probably be useful in everyday conversation) but decays over time. Furthermore, although it is often convenient to think about "the" meaning of a word, in reality, our individual experiences affect what words mean.

> ## Box 8.2 (cont.)
>
>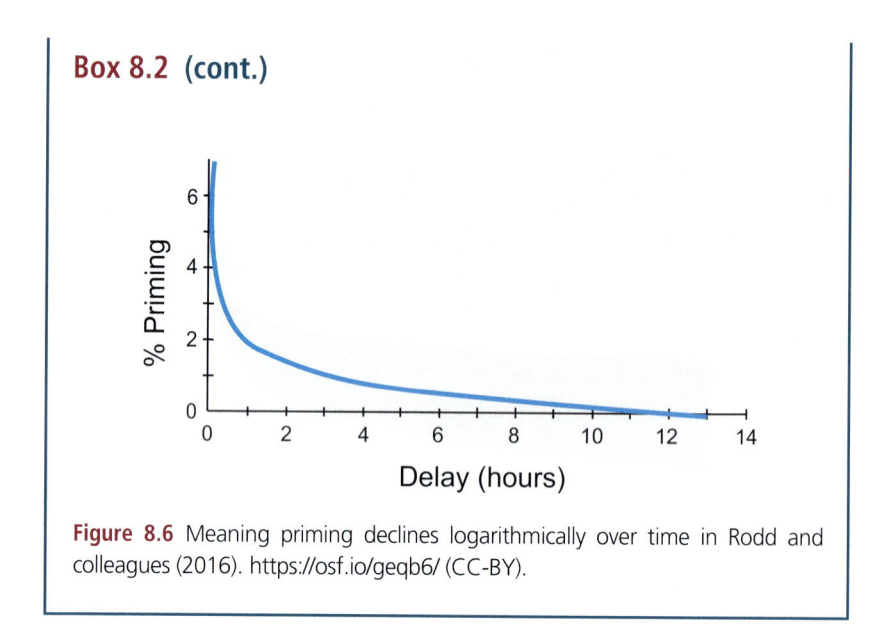
>
> **Figure 8.6** Meaning priming declines logarithmically over time in Rodd and colleagues (2016). https://osf.io/geqb6/ (CC-BY).

than the unchosen meaning(s). For example, if you understand "bark" to mean the sound a dog makes, when asked to provide a "related" word 10 minutes later, you are more likely to produce a dog-related word than a tree-related word. This is a perfect illustration of a **semantic priming** experimental paradigm. (Priming, generally, refers to past experience unconsciously influencing future behavior; semantic priming refers to when the information is semantic.[18])

8.4 Syntactic Complexity

Syntax refers to the rules that govern how words are combined, and commonly comes up in the context of sentence processing.[20] For example, in the sentence, "The child bit the dog," it is easy for you to understand who was doing the biting and who was being bitten, despite the unusual (though not impossible, in my experience) situation described. In many situations you might not *need* syntax to figure out what's going on: If you hear "child," "dog," and some form of "bite" you might hazard a reasonable guess as to the meaning of a sentence.[21] However, in this case, you might guess wrong, and the syntax is providing an unambiguous interpretation.

The brain regions supporting syntactic processing have been of great interest to researchers for decades, in part because the evolutionary development of syntactic processing has been proposed as a key turning point in human communication.[22] Among other facets, the degree to which syntactic processing is modular – that is, acts automatically – or might depend on other cognitive resources and (relatedly) the degree to which syntactic processing is preserved in adult aging[23] have featured prominently.

A particularly convenient way to examine the effects of syntax involves using identical words in a sentence that are arranged in different orders. For example, if you have a simple sentence:

Professors are nice.

Then you know that the subject of the sentence – professors – have an attribute (they are nice). You can then add what is known as an "embedded clause" to the sentence (here, "with long flowing hair").

Professors *with long flowing hair* are nice.

The meaning of the main sentence has not changed – professors are still nice – but now we have some additional detail.

Now consider a different type of embedded clause that introduces an object of the sentence:

Professors *that help students* are nice.

Again, professors are still nice, but now we also know they help students. Professors remain the subject of the sentence, and thus we refer to the embedded clause as a subject-relative embedded clause, because the subject of the sentence (professors) is also performing the action in the embedded clause (being nice).

For our last example, let's simply rearrange the words in the embedded clause:

Professors *that students help* are nice.

The six words in the sentence are the same as before, but now the embedded clause has a different meaning, because students are the ones performing an action. We refer to these as object-relative embedded clauses. Because the subject of the embedded clause is not the same as the subject of the main clause, these are typically considered more complex,[24] and thus more difficult: In behavioral studies, sentences with object-relative clauses result in longer reaction times than those with subject-relative clauses.[25]

Although there are, of course, many different ways to construct a sentence (and many ways to alter the complexity of construction), what is so compelling about these examples is that the six words are the same, but the meaning changes.[26] As listeners, we must somehow integrate or combine a set of words to arrive at the correct meaning.

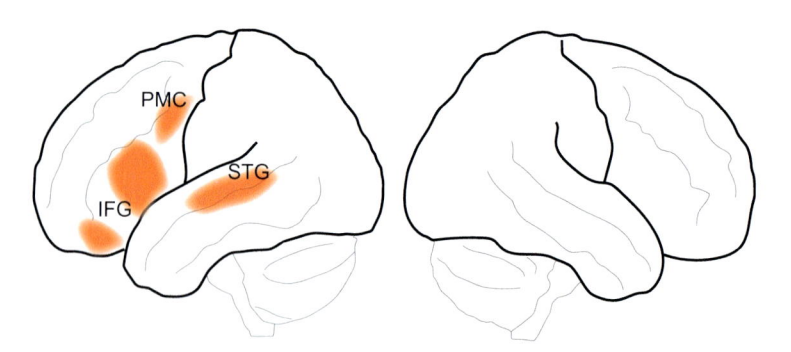

Figure 8.7 Regions of the brain associated with understanding syntactically complex sentences, including portions of left inferior frontal gyrus (IFG), premotor cortex (PMC), and superior temporal gyrus (STG). https://osf.io/geqb6/ (CC-BY).

Comparing syntactically complex sentences of the constructions described earlier, a common finding is that object-relative sentences are associated with increased activity in left IFG relative to subject-relative sentences, with other areas – including ventral IFG and posterior temporal cortex – also sometimes involved (Figure 8.7).

Another way to study syntactic processing is to present participants with sentences that contain grammatical errors. The logic of this is that regions of the brain that are involved in understanding the rules of syntax will be engaged when those rules are broken. When comparing ungrammatical sentences (i.e., sentences containing syntactic errors) to grammatical ones, activity is often seen in the left pSTG and left IFG.[27]

Ultimately, it may be that "syntactic" processing is too broad of a term – the specific regions involved may depend on the type of syntactic processing (complexity, grammaticality) and the task required of participants. However, across all of these, left inferior frontal cortex appears to play a central role (see also Box 8.3).

8.5 Brain Oscillations and Connected Speech

One of the most provocative areas of speech research over the past 20 years has centered on understanding how brain oscillations might relate to speech processing. Brain oscillations refer to periodic (that is, regular) fluctuations in the excitability of neurons over time. In human studies, oscillations are typically recorded from EEG, MEG, and ECoG, and thus reflect the synchronized activity of a large population of neurons. Because the electrical state of a neuron helps determine whether the neuron will fire an action potential, the

Box 8.3 What nfvPPA can tell us about syntactic processing.

You may recall that one of the subtypes of primary progressive aphasia is "nonfluent" – nfvPPA. Patients with nfvPPA have damage to their left IFG, and share many behaviors in common with patients with nonfluent post-stroke aphasia, especially difficulty producing fluent speech and word-finding errors.

Another aspect of language in patients with nfvPPA is their ability to process syntactically complex speech.[28] Grossman and colleagues (2005) used a word-detection paradigm to study sentence processing in patients with frontotemporal dementia. Compared to questions after a sentence (for example, to test comprehension), word-detection paradigms occur *during* the sentence and are thus sometimes referred to as "online" measures. On each trial, a target word was presented on its own, and after a short break, a sentence was played. Participants were instructed to press a button as soon as they heard the target word in the sentence. Unbeknownst to the participants, some of the sentences contained a grammatical error. Errors were divided between subject-verb pluralization agreement violations (for example, "The child were sad when it was time to leave"), determiner-noun agreement violations ("These flower would look beautiful in a small vase"), and quantifier agreement violations ("The duck all ran toward the boy carrying the bread"). Half of the violations came directly before the target word, and half after the violation (about four syllables). As seen in Figure 8.8, response times for target words were differentially impaired in patients with nfvPPA when the target words were distant from the grammatical violation.

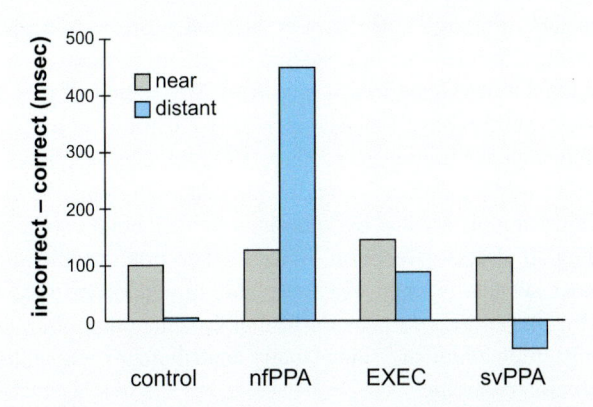

Figure 8.8 Results for the word monitoring task in Grossman and colleagues (2005). Average response time differences between incorrect and correct sentence are plotted for grammatical violations when the target word was near to the violation or far (about four syllables away). Patients with nfvPPA showed the largest difference from controls, selectively for the far condition. https://osf.io/geqb6/ (CC-BY).

> **Box 8.3 (cont.)**
>
> The use of violations to study grammatical processing can be tricky. If someone has difficulty processing syntactic information, you might assume they should be *more* affected by violations – but instead, what you might find is actually an insensitivity to grammatical violations (if I don't process syntax well, I may not react when syntactic rules are violated). In Grossman and colleagues (2005), they interpret the findings as indicating slowed (and, one might infer, disrupted) grammatical processing in patients with nfvPPA, which they posit is due to damage in left inferior frontal cortex.[29]

electrical bias introduced by ongoing oscillations can affect neural processing – in particular, making it more likely that a neuron will fire an action potential if inputs arrive during a "high excitability" phase, and lower if the identical input arrives at a "low excitability" phase (see Box 8.4).

Studies of oscillatory auditory activity in human listeners have largely relied on noninvasive recordings from EEG and MEG. A variety of analysis approaches have shown that the phase of ongoing activity in, and near, auditory cortex relates to the acoustic signature of spoken sentences.[30] These studies typically refer to brain activity that is entrained,[31] or phase locked, to the speech signal. Entrained oscillatory activity has been proposed to underlie the process of chunking a continuous auditory signal into words and phonemes, and to reflect syntactic as well as acoustic features of the speech signal.

The degree to which entrained oscillations reflect acoustic or linguistic information is critically important to our theoretical understanding of their function. In fact, although early studies focused primarily on phase-locked brain responses to the acoustic information in speech, subsequent studies have shown additional brain signatures of linguistic information (Figure 8.9).[32]

The previous studies have focused on what we learn from measuring brain oscillations in response to speech, and broadly agree that the phase of ongoing oscillations in auditory cortex relates to understanding speech. One way to provide further support for this hypothesis is to alter brain oscillations to see whether doing so affects perception. Indeed, when brain oscillations are synchronized with speech, listeners are better able to understand speech in noise (Figure 8.10). These findings provide further evidence that brain oscillations are not simply epiphenomenal[33] but actually contribute to computations underlying speech understanding.

The role of ongoing oscillatory activity remains an active area of study, and neural oscillations still have the potential to explain a number of fascinating phenomena in speech perception.[35] However, there are also reasons to think that

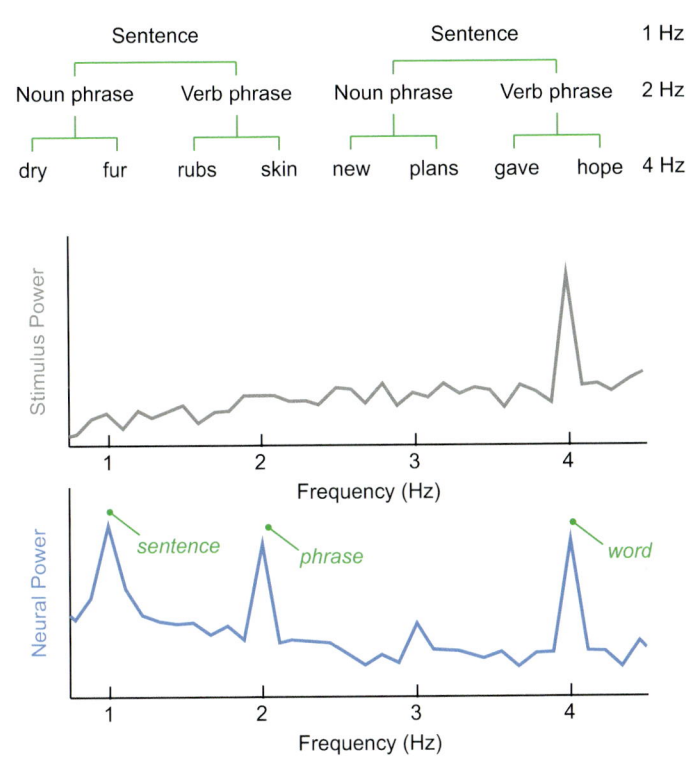

Figure 8.9 Schematic of experimental design and results from Ding and colleagues (2016). *Top:* Stimuli were constructed to convey linguistic information at three different frequencies (1, 2, 4 Hz), corresponding to sentence, phrase, and word level of presentation. *Bottom:* The stimulus power of the acoustic signal is strongest at 4 Hz; however, brain responses recorded with MEG additionally show peaks at 2 Hz and 1 Hz, suggesting phase-locked brain responses that are not driven primarily by the strength of the acoustic signal. https://osf.io/geqb6/ (CC-BY).

neural oscillations may have a modulatory, rather than foundational, impact on speech processing. First, as listeners, we are able to understand speech that is not rhythmic: This might be individual words (for which there is no ongoing acoustic signal to affect brain oscillations) or speech spoken in a nonrhythmic way (in an extreme case, for example, by a talker with dysarthria[36]). A second point is that when comparing intelligible speech to other types of auditory processing, the increase in phase locking is usually modest: If phase-locked oscillations were *foundational* for understanding, we might expect a more substantial difference between speech and nonspeech sounds.

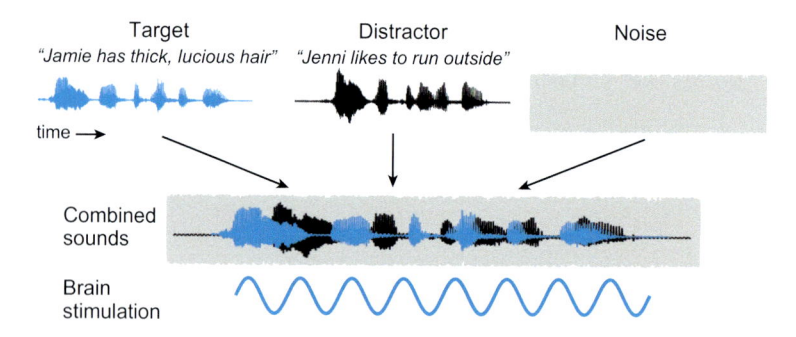

Figure 8.10 One method of brain stimulation is tACS (transcranial alternating current stimulation), which allows researchers to pulse weak electrical current to the brain through the skull. A challenge is that spoken language is not typically periodic (that is, perfectly regular). Riecke and colleagues (2018) cleverly constructed a large set of sentences that could be spoken with a regular rhythm. And, importantly, these sentences could therefore be spoken with alternating phases (the words of one sentence could be heard *between* words in another sentence). The researchers then played two sentences for participants, one of which was the target sentence, and one a distractor, and rhythmically stimulated the brain at different timings. They found that listeners performed better with rhythmic brain stimulation tuned to the target sentence.[34] https://osf.io/geqb6/ (CC-BY).

8.6 Summary

- Compositional semantics – that is, combining words to form a new meaning – may be supported by the lateral anterior temporal lobe and the angular gyrus.
- Compared to words, understanding well-formed sentences involves regions of both left temporal cortex (posterior STG and MTG) and frontal cortex (left IFG).
- The brain regions supporting sentence processing can be further modulated by demands from semantic ambiguity (associated with increased activity in left IFG, left pMTG, and left pITG) and syntactic complexity (associated with increased activity in left STG and left IFG).
- Ongoing oscillations in the 3–8 Hz range in and around auditory cortex may play a role in understanding spoken sentences, although the specific function of these oscillations is still a matter of active research.

Box 8.4 Brain Oscillations and Sensory Perception

Over the past two decades the potential role of neural oscillations in speech perception has been a provocative and expanding field of study.[37] Basic electrophysiological research in animals has taught us an incredible amount regarding the influence of cortical oscillations on perception. In general, there is strong evidence that fluctuations in a neuron's membrane potential can impact the processing of new inputs.[38] This is easy to understand if we think about it from the perspective of an individual neuron. As we saw in Chapter 2, each neuron has a membrane potential that reflects the sum of all of its excitatory and inhibitory inputs; when this membrane potential reaches a certain threshold, an action potential fires. If you picture a systematic fluctuation of the membrane potential, there are some points where the membrane potential is nearer to threshold, and some points where it is further away (Figure 8.11). Identical excitatory inputs arriving at a high-excitability phase will have an easier time bringing the membrane potential to threshold.

Of course, it is frequently not possible to measure fluctuations of membrane potential in individual neurons. However, we *can* measure fluctuations in populations of neurons. These are reflected in the local field potential (LFP) in invasive recordings, and in EEG and MEG signals recorded outside the brain. If a population of neurons is fluctuating in its excitability, we can also infer that individual neurons are doing the same thing.

Oscillations – particularly in auditory cortex – have been hypothesized to facilitate processing of speech information, perhaps through helping users identify words and/or "chunk" the incoming acoustic input into manageable segments.[39] They are modulated by attention: if listening to two talkers, auditory oscillations are more strongly phase locked to the attended talker.[40]

It is worth considering that the effect of oscillatory activity on perception typically only affects processing over a relatively narrow window of near-threshold stimuli. For example, if a very bright light flashes, you will notice it, regardless of the oscillatory phase of primary visual cortex. Conversely, a very faint light may not be visible, despite arriving precisely at a high-excitability phase of oscillation. Oscillatory activity can clearly affect sensory processing, but it does not dominate our perception.

The ability of oscillations to enhance processing is one reason the idea of rhythmic entrainment is so compelling. Indeed, the phase of auditory oscillations appears to reset so that the oscillations can lock on to rhythmic stimuli in a way that optimizes detection. If you can imagine hearing a metronome, or the beep of an open refrigerator – any regular sound – the first beep is unexpected (and arrives at some random phase of auditory excitability). But after a couple of beeps, auditory oscillations become synchronized with the sound, increasing the efficiency with which it is processed.

Box 8.4 (cont.)

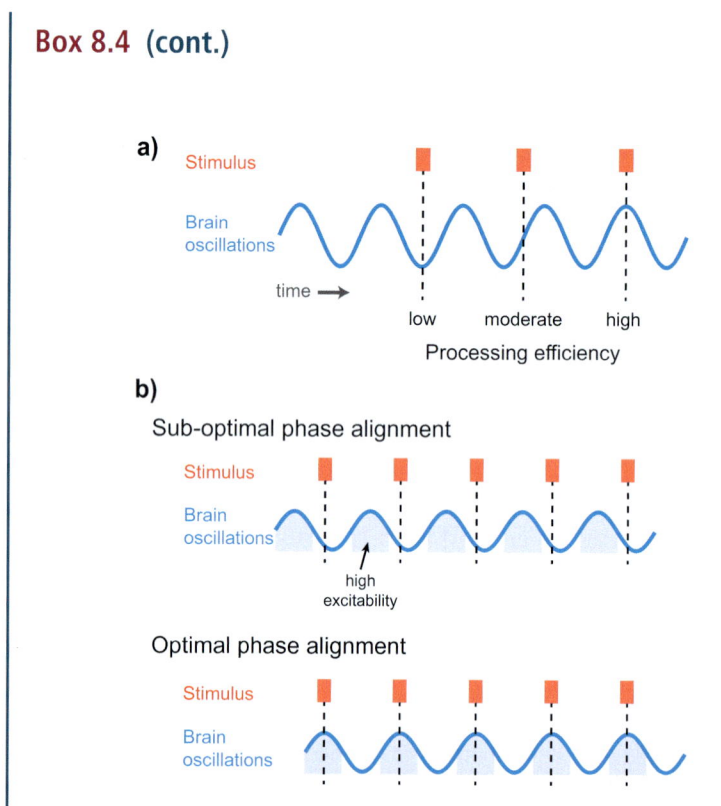

Figure 8.11 (a) Ongoing oscillatory activity determines how efficiently sensory stimuli drive perceptual processes, depending on the phase of oscillation at which they arrive. Information arriving at a low-excitability phase is processed relatively less efficiently, whereas that arriving at a high-excitability phase is processed more efficiently. (b) If sensory information exhibits temporal regularity, overall processing efficiency can be increased by shifting the phase of ongoing neural oscillations to line up with the phase of the stimuli. *Top:* Repeated stimuli arriving at sub-optimal phases of neural oscillations. *Bottom:* By shifting the phase of the brain oscillations, stimuli now arrive at a phase during which neurons are in a relatively excitable state and are thus processed more efficiently (i.e., lead to greater numbers of informative spikes). Reproduced from Peelle and Davis (2012), CC-BY.

Notes

1. "Stepping stone" is actually a good example of this!
2. A classic example of this effect is seen in Bemis and Pylkkänen (2011).
3. It is worth revisiting the fact that portions of the temporal pole are susceptible to signal dropout during fMRI, meaning that sensitivity in this region is reduced (or nonexistent) – a problem which does not affect MEG. This methodological consideration is always important to remember when noting a lack of anterior temporal lobe activity in fMRI studies.
4. Price and colleagues (2015) created 112 word pairs varying in combinatorial strength based on ratings from research participants. Interestingly, the plausibility ratings from in-lab participants were strongly correlated with how often the word pairs occurred in written text. The word pairs were presented in an fMRI experiment that identified a significant relationship between combinatorial strength and activity in the angular gyrus, followed by the patient study using the same stimuli. Patients were adults with neurodegenerative disease; the anatomical distribution of the disease varied, and some patients were more affected in the angular gyrus than others. The gray matter volume in angular gyrus was significantly related to patients' accuracy on the plausibility task.
5. In a follow up to the fMRI study mentioned earlier (Price et al., 2015), Price and colleagues (2016) used transcranial direct current stimulation (tDCS) to electrically stimulate the angular gyrus. Using anodal stimulation thought to enhance processing in a region, they presented word pairs that varied in how easy they were to combine. Participants were faster to judge combinations when stimulated, but the effect did not show up in a letter string judgment task, suggesting it was specific to semantic processing (or at least not a general disruption to all tasks). The effect of tDCS varied with combinatorial strength of the word pairs, offering additional evidence it was specifically related to combinatorial processing.
6. A nice overview of this series of studies, which span a number of years, is provided by Pylkkänen (2019).
7. Co-articulation refers to how speech sounds are made when adjacent to each other. As discussed in Chapter 4, speakers have a strong tendency to be efficient in their production, and typically only produce enough acoustic difference to remain intelligible. Because speech is so rapid, talkers tend to anticipate upcoming sounds, affecting the production of current sounds. Listeners, however, are typically able to accommodate these acoustic variations.
8. Binder and colleagues (2000) compared the presentation of word lists to pseudowords, temporally reversed word lists (which preserve acoustic complexity, but do not convey lexical information), tones, and noise bursts. All of these stimuli robustly activated bilateral temporal cortex; lists of real words showed greater activity in posterior STS and STG.
9. Humphries and colleagues (2007) presented listeners with word lists, pseudoword lists, and sentences. The stimuli could also vary in their congruence (i.e., whether

the words were semantically related to each other or not). They found increased activity for sentences relative to other conditions in left IFG. Left posterior STG/MTG showed largest responses for congruent items, and the angular gyrus uniquely showed increased activity following a congruent sentence. Although using written sentences, Pallier and colleagues (2011) identify many of these same regions as responding to changes in constituent size – that is, conceptually similar in that activity relates to the structure of the sentence rather than just a list of unrelated words.

10. An early and influential PET study on sentence processing was conducted by Sophie Scott and colleagues (2000). The authors presented sentences in four conditions: regular speech, spectrally rotated speech (which is unintelligible), vocoded speech, and spectrally rotated noise vocoded speech (which is unintelligible). A key contrast involved intelligible speech (normal, and vocoded) > unintelligible. The authors identified a region of the left anterior lateral temporal lobe that responded similarly to both kinds of intelligible speech, even though the acoustic properties were quite different. Furthermore, regions of the right temporal lobe seemed more tuned to acoustic features (discriminating between regular speech and vocoded speech).

    Further work using fMRI – including Davis & Johnsrude (2003), Narain and colleagues (2003), Evans and colleagues (2014), and others – continued to accumulate evidence for a left-lateralized response to intelligible sentences.

11. As addressed previously, most people seem to have preferential processing for language in the left hemisphere. So here, and elsewhere, "left hemisphere" preference can be read "dominant hemisphere" preference – the assumption is that of people with right hemisphere dominance for language, the situation is similar (but in a different hemisphere).

12. In an important fMRI study Davis and Johnsrude (2003) varied intelligibility using three different methods: noise vocoding, background noise, and segmented speech (in which noise is inserted at regular intervals). Critically, within each method they created a continuum of intelligibility. This allowed them to look for correlations with intelligibility that were similar across acoustic manipulation, as well as those that *differed* across acoustic manipulation. They referred to these as *form independent* and *form dependent* processing. Among the frontotemporal regions responding to intelligible speech, regions nearer to auditory cortex showed responses that depended on the acoustic form of the stimulus, whereas regions further away – including in the frontal lobe – responded similarly, with responses driven by intelligibility. These results are consistent with an anatomically scaffolded hierarchical arrangement of speech processing, with increasing abstraction as information moves away from sensory cortex (reviewed in Peelle, 2010). For more on time course analyses, see Davis and colleagues (2011).

13. Some years ago, I found myself reviewing a string of research papers that made competing claims about where the brain processes "speech." In fact, I did not find

the claims so much contradictory as simply relying on different definitions of "speech" – which in the literature is used to mean anything from isolated phonemes to complete stories. I wrote a paper (Peelle, 2012) attempting to highlight the link between type of linguistic demand and brain regions involved in order to reduce this type of miscommunication. The point being that we always need to consider what specific processing is being required of listeners depending on what they are hearing and the task in order to interpret what we find in the brain. If I argue that "speech processing depends on Area X" (but by "speech" I mean *sentence processing*) and you might say "no speech processing does not depend on Area X" (and you mean *word* processing) we could both be right.

14. This statistic is from the analysis reported by Rodd and colleagues (2002). For a more thorough, and still accessible, introduction to semantic ambiguity, see Rodd (2020), which also helpfully introduces different *types* of ambiguity (p. 411):

> The most salient form of lexical ambiguity is found in homonyms such as *trunk* that have multiple unrelated meanings (e.g., the trunk of a car/tree/elephant). This form of ambiguity is relatively rare and is present for about only 7% of relatively frequent word forms (Rodd, Gaskell, & Marslen-Wilson, 2002). In contrast, more that 80% of word forms are polysemous – they can refer to more than one related word sense (Rodd et al., 2002). For example, the verb *run* is highly polysemous; it has a multitude of different interpretations that are appropriate within different sentence contexts (e.g., the athlete/river/program/paint/manager/dye/train/candidate runs). Successful word-meaning access occurs when an appropriate interpretation (i.e., the interpretation that was intended by the speaker/writer) is selected from the range of familiar possibilities.

15. have (halve), pick, weak (week), would (wood), more (moor), speech, one (won), can, might (mite), spell, their (they're), own, right (write), read (reed), can, help, some (sum), cases.

16. In behavioral work, David Swinney (1979) used a priming paradigm to argue that when an ambiguous word is heard, all meanings of the word are activated (even those that conflict with the surrounding context). The results were used to argue for a level of automaticity in lexical access.

17. Rodd and colleagues (2005) constructed sentences containing high-ambiguity words ("The *shell* was fired from the *tank*") and sentences not containing high-ambiguity words ("There was beer and cider on the shelf"). Recordings of these sentences were played for participants in an fMRI study and activity for high-ambiguity sentences was compared to that for low-ambiguity sentences. Regions responding to semantic ambiguity included left posterior MTG, left IFG, and left ITG. Because other characteristics of the sentences were well matched, these increased responses can be attributed to semantic disambiguation. Rodd and colleagues (2012) further investigate differing responses to ambiguous words whose disambiguating information occurs before versus after the word.

18. The concept of semantic priming goes back at least to William James (1842–1910), American philosopher and academic who offered the first psychology course in the United States (the building currently housing the Department of Psychology at

Harvard University is William James Hall). James trained as a physician and taught anatomy at Harvard University, but never practiced medicine. Among his writing was *The Principles of Psychology* (1890), in which he wrote on semantic priming: "Each word is *doubly* awakened; once from without the lips of the talker, but already before that from within by the premonitory processes irradiating from the previous words."

19. "Square" means to turn the blade so it is perpendicular to the water's surface and is the opposite of "feather" (turn the blade so it is parallel with the water). A "crab" (or to catch a crab) occurs when the rower is unable to remove the oar from the water at the right time and it acts as a brake.

20. My mother was always scandalized that I never had grammar instruction in school. When I finally got to graduate school and began studying language, she was thrilled when I was able to identify the subject, verb, and object of a sentence. (I exaggerate but only slightly!)

21. In many situations, our past experience with the dominant meanings of words indeed lines up with the syntactic structure. People thus might develop two (unconscious) strategies: one strategy that relies on relationships between individual word concepts and a different one that involves a careful analysis of the syntax. Fernanda Ferreira and colleagues (2002) propose that in many situations we fall back on strategies that are "good enough" to get the right answer most of the time without doing a detailed syntactic analysis.

22. Angela Friederici (2018) focuses on BA 44 and its anatomical connection to posterior temporal cortex as a core component of processing hierarchical structure. BA 44 and posterior temporal cortex differ in humans compared to nonhuman primates, and also in adult humans compared to children, mirroring differences in syntax and sequence abilities. (The entire special issue from which this article comes – "The evolution of language as a neurobiological system" – is worth reading, and given a nice overview by Petkov and Marslen-Wilson, 2018.)

23. In some functional imaging studies (including Peelle et al., 2010), age differences in syntactic processing are reported. However, these studies also often include a metalinguistic task (for example, in Peelle et al., 2010, we asked people to indicate whether a man or a woman was performing the action in the sentence). It could be that age differences attributed to "syntax" are, instead, age differences related to the specific task participants are doing. Davis and colleagues (2014) looked at age differences in processing syntactically ambiguous sentences with and without an explicit task, and found age differences in prefrontal cortex – but only when an explicit task was present. Campbell and colleagues (2016) similarly found that, when no explicit task was present, processing of syntactically ambiguous sentences remained stable throughout the adult lifespan. In the aging literature this is sometimes framed as online processing as the sentence is being processed, which is preserved, versus offline processing – what we *do* with comprehension – which may show age effects (see for example Waters and Caplan, 2001).

24. Object-relative center-embedded clauses are also less common, which may also play a role in how easy they are to process.

25. A nice example of this is actually found in the very first scientific paper I helped with: Wingfield and colleagues (2003). In that paper we had short six-word sentences with subject-relative ("Boys that help girls are nice") or object-relative ("Boys that girls help are nice") center-embedded clauses. Each sentence had people with gendered descriptions (aunts/uncles, kings/queens, etc.), and participants were asked to press a button indicating the gender of the character "performing the action" in each sentence – effectively asking listeners to identify the subject of the center-embedded clause. We also manipulated speech rate (faster speech is typically harder). We found that object-relative sentences produced longer reaction times than subject-relative sentences, even after excluding error responses, suggesting that they required more cognitive processing.

26. We do not need to include embedded clauses to understand the importance of word order: Consider who you would think is at fault if you overheard your children say either "Jasmine pushed Ricky" compared to "Ricky pushed Jasmine." Obviously, we interpret these sentences differently, because specific rules govern the use of verbs in English, and we have learned these rules through years of experience.

27. Friederici and colleagues (2003), for example, used sentences that contained a grammatical error, and found that error-containing sentences showed greater activity in bilateral anterior STG and left IFG. Additional work has worked on dissociating syntax *per se* from verbal working memory, which is also thought to be taxed during some types of syntactically complex sentences (for example, listeners need to hold the subject of the sentence in mind longer to resolve an embedded clause). Fiebach and colleagues (2005) found frontal regions were associated with working memory more than grammatical violations, echoing similar findings of Cooke and colleagues (2002). Also consistent with this view, Friederici and colleagues (2006) found that activity in left IFG scaled with syntactic complexity when no errors were present. In more recent work, Bhattasali and colleagues (2019) examined syntactic and syntactic processing while participants listened to a short story (*The Little Prince*). They found activity in bilateral anterior temporal lobe and IFG, which they identified using a model of syntactic parsing.

28. Although not entirely consistent, a number of studies report grammatical challenges in patients with nfvPPA (including Peelle et al., 2007). In summarizing characteristics seen in patients with nfvPPA, Mesulam (2001) notes (p. 427): "Some patients display striking abnormalities of syntax (word order) and tend to misuse closed-class elements, tenses, plurals, possessives, and pronouns."

29. Stephen Wilson and colleagues (2016) examined syntactic processing in patients with primary progressive aphasia (PPA), which includes patients with nonfluent variant, semantic variant, and logopenic variant PPA. They found correlations with functional brain activity across a wide network, not limited to left inferior frontal cortex, related to performance on a sentence-picture matching task tapping

syntactic processing. These findings support the involvement of regions outside left inferior frontal cortex in syntactic processing and further underscore the usefulness of examining data from patients with neurodegenerative disease in understanding the neurobiology of language.

30. Early work showing a general relationship between frequency of oscillations in MEG and speech acoustics came from Ahissar and colleagues (2001), but modern excitement about the role of oscillatory activity in speech perception was precipitated by Luo and Poeppel (2007), who showed that the phase of neural oscillations was sentence-specific. Subsequent work has expanded to look further at speech intelligibility (Peelle et al., 2013), structure (Ding et al., 2016), and different languages (Tezcan et al., 2023).

31. As Cummins (2012) points out, as usually defined, *entrainment* refers to two periodic signals that become linked to each other. (Here, a periodic signal refers to a signal that varies regularly, like a sine wave.) Such a definition is problematic for speech, because everyday sentences are not strictly periodic. Thus the concept of entrainment, strictly defined, seems not to apply. In practice, many speech researchers think that brain signals can still adjust to the speech signal, even if the speech signal is only quasi-periodic – but this is an area of continuing discussion.

32. Important caveats to this interpretation are found in ten Oever and colleagues (2022), who point out that there are multiple interpretations to finding spectral peaks at rates matching linguistic units. One of several possibilities covered is that any regularity in a repeating string of stimuli may result in spectral peaks at multiple frequencies (ten Oever et al., 2022, figure 2).

33. Merriam-Webster's dictionary defines an *epiphenomenon* as "a secondary phenomenon accompanying another and caused by it." In other words, if some other process in the brain governed speech perception, and just happened to result in changes in oscillatory activity, we could correctly observe changes in brain oscillations, but they would not actually be *causing* changes in speech perception (and would therefore be of less interest to researchers interested in speech and language).

34. One interesting aspect to the findings is that different times were optimal for different listeners. These differences in timing may just reflect differences in electrical current spread (which introduces a delay between when the electrode delivers a current and when it has its maximal effect on auditory cortex), or perhaps individual differences in auditory processing. There is some more discussion of this study found in Peelle (2018b).

35. The phenomena suggested by Peelle and Davis (2012) include speech rate adaptation effects and word segmentation.

36. As you might recall from Chapter 4, dysarthria refers to a family of problems with speech production including difficulty with respiration, phonation, resonance, prosody, or articulation.

37. For reviews, see Giraud and Poeppel (2012), Peelle and Davis (2012), and Meyer (2018).

38. Peter Lakatos and colleagues contributed several influential studies in this domain using electrophysiological recordings in monkeys. Lakatos and colleagues (2005), for example, played noise bursts for macaque monkeys while recording electrical activity in auditory cortex using depth electrodes. They found broadly that lower-frequency activity was related to higher-frequency activity: that is, amplitude of oscillatory activity was modulated by activity at a lower frequency. They also found that some phases of oscillation that enhanced (or suppressed) responses to auditory stimuli.

39. Oded Ghitza (2011) characterizes speech processing as relying on a bank of cascading oscillations that help segment the acoustic signal into meaningful segments. One provocative piece of evidence comes from Ghitza and Greenberg (2009). They time compressed speech to one-third of its original duration, bringing intelligibility below 50 percent. They then inserted quiet pauses between the words; this did not change the acoustic information available for each word but changed the frequency with which the words appeared. Speech intelligibility was improved when the inserted pauses were periodic and of a duration that brought the speech back to its original rate. These results are consistent with an oscillatory processing mechanism that preferentially operates at the rate of normally articulated speech.

40. Elana Zion Golumbic and colleagues (2013) used ECoG to examine neural responses to a single talker and two talkers (with listeners instructed to pay attention to one of the two talkers). In auditory regions, cortical tracking of attended speech was enhanced compared to the ignored speech. They conclude (p. 988):

> Our results provide an empirical basis for the idea that selective attention in a Cocktail Party setting relies on an interplay between bottom-up sensory responses and predictive, top-down control over the timing of neuronal excitability … The product of this interaction is the formation of a dynamic neural representation of the temporal structure of the attended speech stream that functions as an amplifier and a temporal filter.

Further Reading

Davis MH, Johnsrude IS (2003) Hierarchical processing in spoken language comprehension. *Journal of Neuroscience* 23:3423–3431. https://doi.org/10.1523/JNEUROSCI.23-08-03423.2003.
  By presenting spoken sentences degraded to different levels of intelligibility using several approaches, the authors used fMRI to investigate brain regions associated with both speech intelligibility and acoustic challenge.

Pallier C, Devauchelle A-D, Dehaene S (2011) Cortical representation of the constituent structure of sentences. *Proceedings of the National Academy of Sciences* 108:2522–2527. https://doi.org/10.1073/pnas.101871110.
  Using fMRI this study identifies brain regions related to constituent structure during visual sentence processing.

Luo H, Poeppel D (2007) Phase patterns of neuronal responses reliably discriminate speech in human auditory cortex. *Neuron* 54:1001–1010. https://doi.org/10.1016/j.neuron.2007.06.004.

    Oscillatory brain responses in the theta range, measured with MEG, show reliable phase-locked responses to spoken sentences.

Rodd JM, Davis MH, Johnsrude IS (2005) The neural mechanisms of speech comprehension: fMRI studies of semantic ambiguity. *Cerebral Cortex* 15:1261–1269. https://doi.org/10.1093/cercor/bhi009.

    Responses to spoken sentences containing high-ambiguity words were compared to those without high-ambiguity words, identifying brain regions responding to semantic ambiguity.

CHAPTER NINE

Additional Forms of Language Communication

Although this book is largely organized around *spoken* communication, my intent has been to use spoken language as a starting point to buttress theoretical considerations that extend to other forms of language. In this chapter, I offer brief introductions to other forms of language communication. In a perfect world, each of these topics would get its own chapter (or own book!) – but hopefully you can at least get initial exposure to some additional fascinating areas of speech and language processing. These include other modalities of language communication as well as **paralinguistic** aspects of communication (that is, aspects of communication that complement language).

9.1 Audiovisual Speech and Lipreading

During everyday communication we are frequently able to see a talker's mouth. Visual speech information – most commonly thought of as the mouth (mouth opening, tongue, and teeth) – can aid speech understanding, especially when speech is presented in background noise. For example, if you have good hearing and hear a clearly spoken auditory-only sentence in quiet, you may have no trouble understanding what was said. However, in the presence of background noise, you might struggle to make out all the words. In these cases, adding visual speech information will improve intelligibility, sometimes rather substantially. The difference in performance between audiovisual (AV) speech and auditory-only speech is sometimes referred to as **visual enhancement**.[1]

Recognizing audiovisual speech appears to follow many of the same principles as govern auditory-only speech. As one example, the number of similar-looking words (that is, visual neighbors) affect lexical competition much the same as occurs for phonological neighbors (see Section 6.3). Just as phonemes are the basic units of auditory speech processing, **visemes** are basic units of visual speech processing. Because voicing (that is, whether vocal folds are vibrating) is not visible from a talker's face, viseme information is mostly driven by the shape and placement of a talker's mouth, tongue, and teeth (which provide information on the timing, place, and manner of articulation). Using these cues it is possible to determine the visual competitors for a target word, which act together with the auditory competitors to determine perception.[2]

A central topic in audiovisual speech processing is *multisensory integration*. That is, auditory speech information comes in through the ears (and auditory system), and visual speech information through the eyes (and visual system), and yet as listeners we have a single unified percept. Our brains must therefore somehow combine auditory and visual information during speech processing. How, and where, does this occur?

One appealing solution to this challenge is that multimodal brain regions, which have access to both auditory and visual information, act to combine information from multiple modalities into a single percept. The posterior superior temporal sulcus (pSTS) (Figure 9.1) is one region suggested to play such a role. Anatomically, the pSTS is situated in between auditory cortex and visual cortex, and it has anatomical connections to both. Keeping with this, the pSTS responds to different sensory modalities, including auditory and visual information.[3] Furthermore, in many studies of audiovisual speech processing – including with and without McGurk stimuli (see Box 9.1) – increased activity is seen in pSTS in audiovisual relative to unimodal speech conditions.

A complementary account of multisensory integration is that coordinated activity between brain regions facilitates integrative processing.[4] That is, it may be that a specialized integration region is not needed to make use of both auditory and visual speech information, but that functional connections between regions may support multisensory processing. (Structural or anatomical connectivity typically refers to axonal projections between regions that can be measured, for example, using tracer studies in animals; **functional connectivity** refers to similar

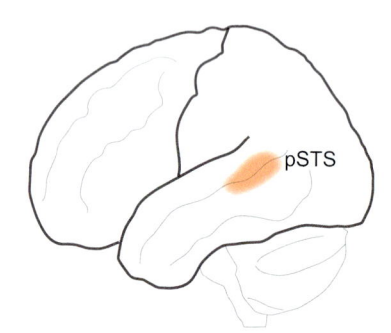

Figure 9.1 The left posterior superior temporal sulcus (pSTS), frequently associated with multisensory processing and audiovisual speech processing. https://osf.io/geqb6/ (CC-BY).

Box 9.1 What does the McGurk effect tell us about audio-visual speech processing?

Even before studying the neuroscience of language, you may have come across the **McGurk effect**. Reported by McGurk and MacDonald (1976),[8] the term refers to how we perceive speech when the auditory and visual information are incongruent. In a typical demonstration, the auditory "ba" is paired with a visual "ga," and people are asked what they hear. The auditory signal is "ba" and so you might think that regardless of what the mouth is doing, people would report hearing "ba." However, this isn't the case at all: people often report hearing a "da" (!). McGurk stimuli thus form a type of sensory illusion where many people report sensing something that is not present in the physical world. Because the illusion intrinsically depends on both auditory and visual information, the McGurk illusion is stable and is often used to assess audiovisual speech processing.[9] Individual differences in McGurk susceptibility have been related to several conditions, including childhood development, adult aging, and several special populations.

However, there are a number of problems with using McGurk stimuli to understand what happens during everyday conversation. Chief among these is the fact that it is impossible for a live human speaker to produce auditory information that is incongruent with visual information – it is *their* mouth producing the auditory information! Other potential challenges include the fact that not everyone shows a McGurk effect (but everyone *does* benefit from visual speech in noise) and that McGurk stimuli are often isolated syllables, which are only a small fraction of our daily speech input.

One way to more quantitatively assess how well McGurk susceptibility relates to visual enhancement is to measure both of these behaviors in the same people, and statistically test how strongly they are related. Van Engen and colleagues (2017) measured participants' susceptibility to the McGurk effect and their ability to identify sentences in noise (Figure 9.2). Listeners were tested in two kinds of noise at different signal-to-noise ratios (corresponding to different levels of acoustic challenge). For each condition, listeners were tested using both audio-only and audiovisual presentation. The authors found that McGurk susceptibility did not predict performance overall, nor did it interact with noise level or modality.[10]

In summary, the McGurk illusion – though a fascinating phenomenon – may not ultimately prove to be the best way of studying everyday audiovisual speech processing.[11] Instead, further work with audiovisual speech materials more representative of our daily experience is needed.

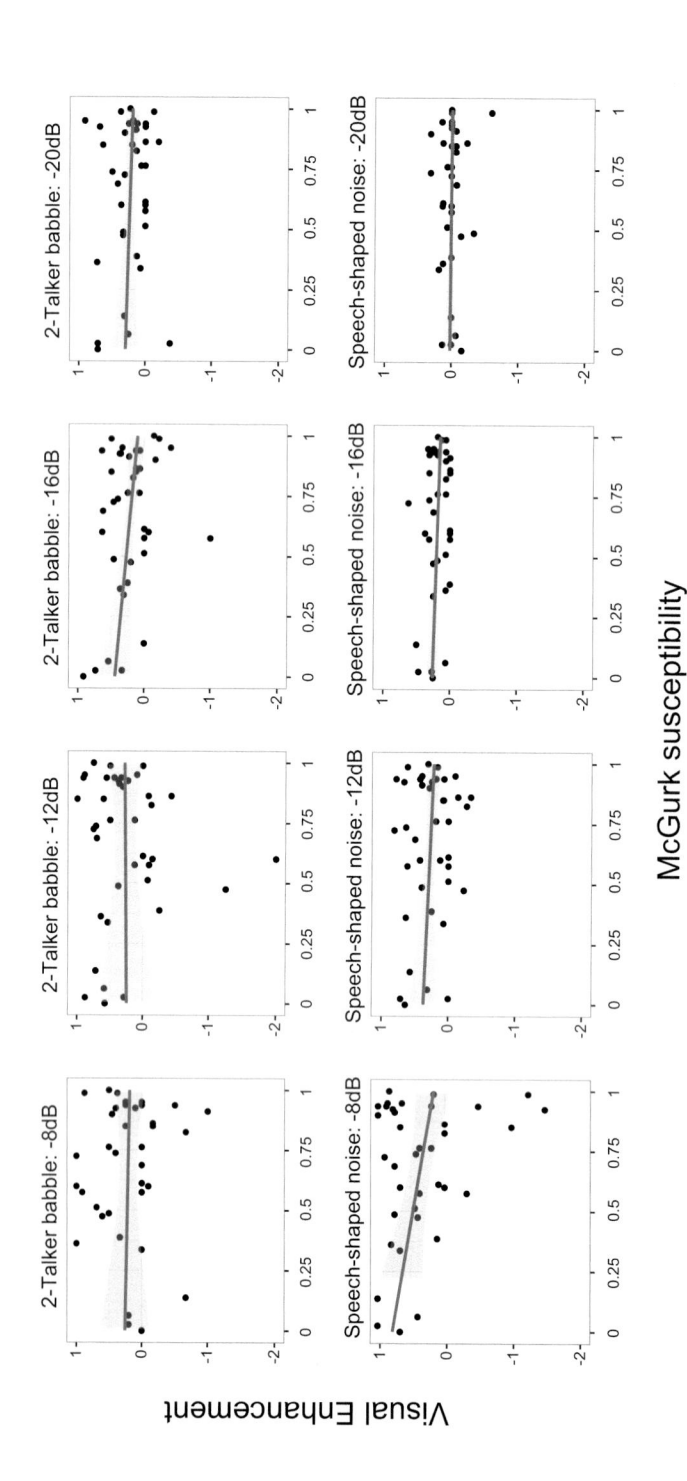

Figure 9.2 Susceptibility to the McGurk illusion does not correlate with visual benefit when listening to sentences in noise (from Van Engen et al., 2017, CC-BY).

time courses of activity observed in two regions that is suggestive of related processing, regardless of the number of synapses in between.) Observations of increased functional connectivity between auditory and visual cortices during visual-only and auditory-visual speech suggest that at least some parts of multi-sensory processing occur in a way that can affect the earliest cortical stages of sensory processing, rather than being combined to a later "integration" stage.[5]

An important facet of audiovisual speech processing is that visual speech can convey a number of different types of information. For example, being able to see the articulators of a talker may help a listener distinguish between features such as place and manner of articulation (seeing a talker's lips touch at the beginning of a word would make "bat" more likely than "cat"). In addition, a talker opening and closing their mouth corresponds to the acoustic amplitude envelope of the auditory speech signal – that is, speech tends to be louder when the mouth is more open. For connected speech (such as sentences), visual speech information therefore conveys information about speech rate and rhythm.[6] It may be that these different and complementary facets of visual speech information affect auditory speech processing in different ways.[7]

9.2 Nonverbal Vocal Communication

Many researchers interested in spoken communication focus exclusively on linguistic aspects of the signal. Partitioning speech into phonemes, words, sentences, and so on comes out of this perspective, and of course, frequently makes sense given the type of information that talkers are often trying to convey. However, nonverbal aspects of vocal communication also play hugely important roles in our everyday interactions. These are *nonverbal* because they are not concerned with words but instead with other aspects of communication, some examples of which are discussed later.

Laughter is one of the most common examples of nonverbal vocal communication.[12] Our first thought may be that as humans we tend to laugh occasionally, in response to something funny. However, in fact people tend to laugh throughout a conversation, and often laugh during, or after, their own speech – all supporting the notion that laughter is both volitional and an integral part of social interaction.[13]

Because laughter is associated with an acoustic stimulus, it is probably not surprising that the brain regions responding to laughter involve the superior temporal gyrus. Importantly, responses to laughter extend beyond primary auditory cortex, indicating some additional processing or representation is involved – that is, consistent with laughter being a meaningful communicative signal.

In everyday communication, one important aspect of interpreting laughter is knowing whether it is real or posed (for example, to tell you whether your friends *really* thought that joke you just told was funny or are just humoring you). Despite some acoustic similarities between spontaneous and volitional laughter, there are also differences, and listeners are reasonably good at telling whether laughter is authentic based on acoustic information alone.[14] The brain regions responding to laughter also differ depending on whether laughter is spontaneous or volitional, with some suggestions of executive regions such as the anterior cingulate being engaged during listening to volitional laughter.[15]

Crying is another important form of nonverbal communication that communicates important information. Interestingly, it seems that the brain regions responding to crying differ from those responding to laughter – although this is still an active area of research.[16]

In addition to emotion, another important nonverbal part of communication is identity: that is, our ability to recognize someone by their voice. A great deal of interest has been paid to regions of right STS (Figure 9.3) that typically show stronger responses to voices than to non-vocal sounds.[17] Activity in right STS relates to characteristics of individual talkers, and may represent a generalized representation of voice space (that is, a representational space capturing variability across vocal dimensions).[18] Related to these conclusions is the fact that people with damage to these regions of the right temporal lobe have difficulty recognizing voices, although the clinical picture is not completely straightforward.[19]

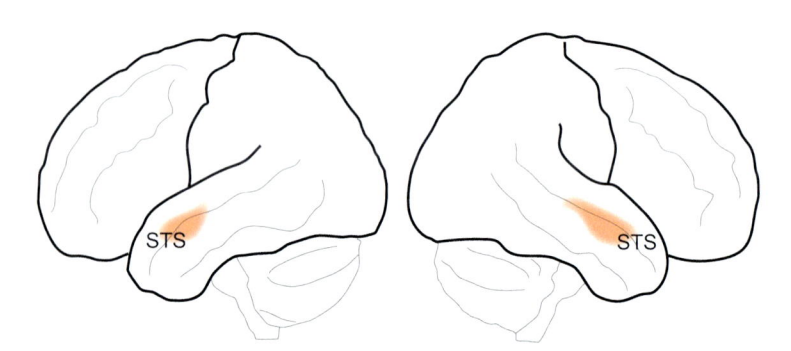

Figure 9.3 Areas responding more to voice stimuli than control conditions, sometimes termed temporal voice areas, in the STS. Although present in both hemispheres, historically those in the right hemisphere have received more focus. https://osf.io/geqb6/ (CC-BY).

9.3 Written Language

Spoken and written language share many basic principles centered around rapidly translating sensory information to a meaningful representation. We have seen how rapidly listeners process spoken words; readers are similarly rapid, with reading occurring within a couple of hundred of milliseconds. Also similar to spoken language, readers use context and prediction to facilitate understanding. A natural question is: How similar are the brain regions supporting language processing in spoken and written language?

Functional neuroimaging studies that have directly compared understanding speech and reading have identified many similarities in the brain regions involved. Although initial sensory processing is, of course, different (reading relies on visual regions, spoken language on auditory regions), much convergence is seen. Perhaps most notable is overlap in regions of posterior temporal cortex for word processing,[20] consistent with supramodal representations of lexical information.

However, the differences in brain regions across tasks are crucial, and important to understand. Differences begin from an evolutionary standpoint, from which the machinery to support vocal communication has had a much longer time to develop than that supporting written communication, which is a relatively recent invention. There is relatively good agreement that this difference has meant that to support reading we need to make use of visual abilities and systems that evolved for other tasks.[21]

A central focus in the cognitive neuroscience of reading has been a part of the ventral occipitotemporal cortex that shows strong responses to written words in literate readers, and is often termed the **visual word form area (VWFA)**.[22] For literate readers, the VWFA typically shows more activity for written words than for other visual stimuli, including objects, faces, and pseudowords. Anatomically, the VWFA is connected by the inferior longitudinal fasciculus and ventral occipital fasciculus to early visual cortex and intraparietal sulcus (involved in spatial control of attention); anterior portions of the VWFA have connections through the inferior longitudinal fasciculus and the arcuate fasciculus.[23] Interestingly, the anatomical connectivity of the VWFA appears to be in place before reading occurs, suggesting the connectivity profile of this region informs its developing functional role.[24] Thus, there has been significant interest in activity in the VWFA as it relates to the development of reading and reading difficulties.[25] However, it is also important to remember that regions beyond the VWFA contribute to reading.[26]

Because of the importance of literacy, there is intense interest in understanding the brain changes associated with learning to read and how these might be applied to improve reading education (Box 9.2 and Box 9.3).

Box 9.2 Teaching literate adults to read.

Given the importance of reading for communication and education, better understanding the cognitive and brain mechanisms involved is a high priority. However, it also presents challenges: Learning to read takes time, and different people are exposed to differing amounts of language: Even in a perfectly controlled laboratory study, participants will differ in their prior learning and exposure. The same is true of studying reading acquisition in children, where variability in experience and instruction outside of the research study can make careful experimental control challenging.

To circumvent these challenges, Jo Taylor and colleagues taught people to read an artificial language that uses a novel orthography.[27] The researchers designed 16 novel "letters" that were used to build words that had a consonant-vowel-consonant construction. The relationship between graphemes (visual word parts) and phonemes (acoustic word parts) followed a set of specific rules set by the researchers designed to mimic regularities found in real languages.

Participants first completed an exposure and learning phase in which they saw written stimuli on the screen in front of them while they heard spoken versions, then repeated each item. After learning, they completed an old-new decision task where they indicated whether an item was one they had heard before ("old") or not ("new"). Finally, during a critical generalization session, participants were shown new (that is, untrained items) and asked to read them aloud. Their accuracy could then be assessed with respect to following the spelling-sound correspondence rules established during the training portion.

Participants were generally able to transfer their learning to new items, as shown by their performance during the generalization phase. In fact, for high-frequency items with consistent grapheme-phoneme correspondence, accuracy was nearly perfect. Other results demonstrated effects of frequency and consistency, showing that participants could extract statistical regularities of spelling-sound patterns during the exposure phase. Finally, one of the amazing things about this study is that the whole experiment took under an hour, demonstrating just how quickly literate adults can learn new graphemes and grapheme-phoneme mapping. In subsequent work, participants were given additional training, and changes in representations associated with newly learned items were associated with changes in ventral occipital-temporal cortex (vOT).

Box 9.3 Teaching children to read: The view from kindergarten.

Elizabeth, a seasoned kindergarten teacher, has had a passion for children most of her adult life. She majored in early childhood education in college, and graduated licensed to teach grades kindergarten through third grade.

Earlier in her career, Elizabeth moved from teaching kindergarten to second grade. One year, a student who she thought was doing well did very poorly on his end-of-year assessments. Elizabeth was caught totally off guard and decided she needed to go back to school to figure out how to prevent this from happening again. She got her Master's in reading, and through her graduate studies was introduced to the science of reading. "I was brought into a world that was so intriguing and mind blowing ... I honestly sat for three years in classes saying 'amazing!'. It flabbergasted me."

A broad developmental cognitive neuroscience perspective has been very influential in how Elizabeth thinks about reading. She thinks about brain areas related to reading as being asleep, and her goal is to wake these areas up so they can start functioning and building the necessary pathways. And she is very aware that the same approach won't work for every child. "You have to feel them out and find out what is their hook – what gets them excited about reading?" She also often thinks of "Scarborough's Reading Rope," which emphasizes the many threads that weave together, culminating in being a skilled reader.

Elizabeth has since moved back to kindergarten teaching, where a central part of her mission is to start children off on the path to being proficient readers. "The first thing is to let them know they already are reading. They read when they see a STOP sign, or when they recognize their favorite cereal box. And then they just have to trust you, that you know what you are doing and you will take them on this journey."

When teaching reading, Elizabeth follows a straightforward approach of starting with smaller units and increasing complexity. First she teaches students about phonemes; then what happens when you put sounds together; followed by syllables, and multisyllable units. She is also a proponent of teaching children the right vocabulary to describe what they are learning: Students in her class come home to tell their parents about phonemes, digraphs, and so on. "If you talk to them about language, they learn. Kids can say the craziest names of dinosaurs, they can learn and retain these basic rules."

Elizabeth returns often to the importance of getting children excited about reading and writing. In fact, that's the top piece of advice she would give to someone considering a career in education. She finds the increased use of electronic devices by children can present some challenges in this regard. One strategy she has for instilling excitement is to model meaningful writing (for example, tied to learning and communication), as opposed to just practicing letters. The meaning ties in to motivation, which drives further learning.

Overall Elizabeth loves her job, and teaching kids to read. "I get to 'turn on' a child's brain ... I mean, that's pretty cool!"

9.4 Sign Language

The physical constraints on a language system can affect the type of information that can be conveyed, and affects the ways language can be produced. For example, spoken languages rely on the respiratory, phonatory, and articulatory systems related to speech production introduced in Chapter 4; by contrast, signed languages rely on the movements of hands, face, and torso. For those interested in the neurobiology of language, these differences provide an opportunity to observe similarities in the brain systems supporting spoken and signed languages.[28]

As with spoken language, signed language consists of a phonological inventory (signs) that occur in a structured grammatical message. Similarly, sign and word recognition are both automatic, showing similar effects on a Stroop task.[29] And signs show effects of frequency and neighborhood density (that is, based on the number of similar-looking signs as a measure of lexical competition).[30] These observations highlight the many structural similarities between perceiving speech and sign. However, there are also differences: for example, during production, speakers can hear themselves speak, but signers do not typically see themselves sign (output monitoring is done using somatosensory feedback). Unlike speech, in which vocal articulators are partially hidden, for sign articulators are fully visible for the duration of the production.

Similarities are also seen in the time course of acquisition and importance of early language experience in signed and spoken language. Children exposed to sign from an early age show similar developmental trajectories to those with comparable exposure to spoken language. However, deaf children who do not receive adequate early language exposure may fall behind. Thus, for deaf children, early exposure to sign language is critical.[31]

The similarities and differences between signed and spoken language extend to the brain systems supporting their use. Broadly speaking, however, many core language areas are involved in both signed and spoken language. For example, just as with spoken language, damage to the left hemisphere (for example, following a stroke) leads to aphasia in people who sign, whereas damage to the right hemisphere does not.[32]

Functional imaging studies are also generally consistent with a set of language networks active during signed language that closely parallels that seen in spoken language. For example, lexicosemantic processing in the temporal lobe (STS/MTG) occurs a few hundred milliseconds after word onset.[33] Such findings provide support for the conclusion that many brain regions are associated with amodal representations of language – that is, not dedicated to a single modality (such as spoken language). (Of course, given the differences in modality, there are also differences in brain systems supporting signed and spoken language. In particular, sensorimotor regions associated with skilled movement are associated with both perception and production of sign language.[34])

9.5 Gesture

Although for much of this book we have focused on the auditory portion of spoken language, users of spoken language also make use of the visual-manual modality through information conveyed by gesture.[35] Although some gestures are for emphasis, others convey semantic information. For example, making a motion like chopping vegetables with a knife while saying the word "chop," or alternating the index and middle finger on your hand while saying "walk." In these cases the gestural and spoken communication both contribute to the semantic content of the message. Moreover, appreciating a speaker's message requires integrating multimodal information in a time-dependent manner: The gesture coincides with the spoken word.[36] However, in distinction to audiovisual speech, the corresponding information across modality is semantic in nature.

Gestural communication is present in children's language development, and can even precede development seen in spoken language.[37] Gesture is thus not best viewed as somehow occurring "alongside" spoken communication but something that is tightly interwoven with it, from both evolutionary and developmental perspectives.

To understand how gestural and spoken information contribute to communication, a number of studies have manipulated the congruency of the gesture and speech. These studies show that listeners make use of both modalities; for example, by congruent gesture and speech resulting in faster and more accurate responses than incongruent gesture and speech.[38] As illustrated in Figure 9.4, brain imaging studies suggest that the regions reflecting meaning include left IFG and premotor cortex.[39] As with other multimodal forms of input, a challenge for interpretation lies in disentangling brain regions involved in sensory processing, meaning representation, and integration (if integration is necessary).

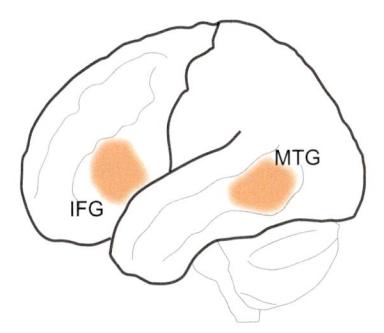

Figure 9.4 Brain regions associated with integrating meaning from gesture, including IFG and MTG. https://osf.io/geqb6/ (CC-BY).

Because gesture is communicated visually, it is associated with other visual cues, including movements of the mouth and eyes. There is mounting evidence that listeners also make use of these forms of information. For example, when speech is challenging to understand, both mouth movements and gestures aid understanding. And eye gaze – a cue to communicative intent (to whom is a speaker talking?) – modulates temporal lobe responses to gesture.[40]

9.6 Summary

- Audiovisual speech processing requires combining information from auditory and visual modalities. The posterior STS is one region implicated in this process.
- Nonverbal aspects of communication, including laughing and crying, are processed largely by superior temporal regions.
- Reading shares many aspects in common with spoken language, including speed of processing and the use of context and predictability. A region of the ventral temporal cortex, often termed the VWFA, appears to play a significant role in reading expertise.
- Sign language relies on different articulators than spoken language but shares many of the same underlying neural substrates.
- Gestures accompanying spoken language become integrated into a single meaning, relying on left hemisphere regions of inferior frontal and posterior temporal cortex to do so.

Notes

1. Sumby and Pollack (1954) are frequently cited as an early demonstration of visual speech information benefiting understanding in noise, and is a fun read. The authors used two syllable words with a spondaic stress pattern, such as "baseball," "cupcake," and so on. (A spondee is a metrical pattern with two stressed syllables. Sumby and Pollack note that "[t]hese words were chosen because they were less subject to inter-speaker variation than other classes of words examined.") The words were presented in auditory-only or audiovisual conditions in the presence of background noise at varying signal-to-noise ratios (SNRs), from −30 dB to 0 dB (and also in quiet). Of note, the speech was produced by a live talker for every participant! The visual information was varied by having the participant face the talker, or face away from the talker. Six participants were tested at a time, seated around a table and wearing headphones to present the auditory speech information. Participants performed better when they were able to see the face of the talker, supporting the importance of visual speech information in speech recognition.
2. Tye-Murray and colleagues (2007) tested listeners using a task in which words spoken in six-talker babble were presented in auditory-only, visual-only, and

audiovisual speech conditions. They found that performance in the audiovisual speech condition was not directly related to auditory-only or visual-only performance, but rather the combined constraints provided by both auditory and visual neighborhoods, or the *intersection density*. Words with a larger intersection density were associated with poorer performance than words with a smaller intersection density, analogous to effects of phonological neighborhood density in auditory-only speech processing. These findings indicate that listeners concurrently use available information from both auditory and visual modalities to constrain options during audiovisual word recognition.

3. Using fMRI, Beauchamp and colleagues (2004) presented participants with videos of tools (for example, a hammer), audio recordings of the sounds made by tools, or audiovisual movies with both components. They found some regions of pSTS responded most strongly to visual, some to auditory, and some to audiovisual presentation. The authors interpret these findings as revealing a "patchy" multisensory information. (Importantly, test-retest reliability of this patchy organization – that is, the correlation of voxel values between two independent data sets – was high, indicating the results were unlikely to be due to random fluctuations or measurement error.) These functional responses in pSTS are consistent with anatomical connections, which link pSTS to auditory, visual, and somatosensory cortex.

4. In neuroimaging, "coordinated activity" is usually equated with "functional connectivity" – that is, statistical similarities in the time series of activity in two or more brain regions (for example, a correlation of activity over time). Sometimes a distinction is made between *functional connectivity* (relationship between time series) and *effective connectivity* (a relationship mediated by task) (Friston, 2011). Functional connectivity has been proposed as a fundamental mechanism for information transfer (Fries, 2015). To study how effective connectivity might affect audiovisual speech processing, we presented participants with words that could be auditory-only, visual-only, or audiovisual (in different levels of noise) (Peelle et al., 2022). We found increased connectivity between auditory and visual cortex – and pSTS – during audiovisual relative to auditory-only conditions, suggesting that primary sensory regions (auditory and visual cortex) are functionally connected in different ways depending on the type of speech being processed.

5. In a chapter that may have my favorite title of all time ("Santa Claus, the Tooth Fairy, and auditory-visual integration: three phenomena in search of empirical support"), Sommers (2021) argues that empirical evidence for a separate integration stage in audiovisual speech processing is lacking. The evidence for this claim comes from the finding that listeners' performance on audiovisual speech tasks can be well predicted using their performance on auditory-only and visual-only speech tasks – no separate integration ability is called for. This is not to say that auditory and visual information are not *combined* in some way, only that a discrete stage (often called "integration") is not a necessary part of the process. Such a view fits well with notions of effective connectivity between sensory regions shaping perception.

6. Chandrasekaran and colleagues (2009) analyzed visual and acoustic characteristics of large speech databases, and found a correlation of 0.74 between the area of mouth opening and the acoustic amplitude envelope. These are in the range of about 3 Hz corresponding roughly to the rate of syllable production. Furthermore, they found that voicing starts 100–300 ms after mouth movements, consistent with visual speech providing a temporal attentional cue for when to start listening.

7. In Peelle and Sommers (2015) we introduced a framework for *early integration* that influences early auditory processing (e.g., in primary auditory cortex) and *late integration* that influences later stages of perception (for example, potentially in pSTS). There is a substantial amount of information suggesting visual speech affects acoustic envelope responses in auditory cortex, making this an appealing mechanism for envelope entrainment (see also Chapter 7). It may be that articulatory constraints have effects at later stages.

8. John MacDonald – who was a PhD student and research fellow with Harry McGurk in the 1970s – describes the circumstances around the original finding in a fascinating 2018 perspective. He also notes that he doesn't mind so much that the effect isn't named after him but *does* mind when he is omitted from the discovery (or his name is misspelled).

9. Basu Mallick and colleagues (2015) found that susceptibility to the McGurk effect was stable over the course of a year (that is, how participants performed on the task on their first visit was highly correlated with how they performed a year later).

10. Hickok and colleagues (2018) similarly found no evidence for a relationship between visual enhancement for phoneme perception and susceptibility to the McGurk illusion.

11. In recent years, several authors have made this point, including Alsius and colleagues (2017) and Van Engen and colleagues (2022).

12. An excellent overview of laughter in the context of human interaction comes from Scott and colleagues (2014). A special issue of the *Philosophical Transactions of the Royal Society B* titled "Cracking the laugh code: laughter through the lens of biology, psychology and neuroscience" (Volume 377, Issue 1863) is also a wealth of knowledge for readers interested in knowing more.

13. Vettin and Todt (2004) recorded long conversations between pairs of people – a total of 48 hours of conversations (!) for 10 people (five different pairs). They found that, on average, people laughed about 5.8 times for each 10 minutes of conversation – more than once every two minutes. (Interestingly, though, this number ranged from 2.3 to 12.3 – some people laugh more than others.) People laughed just as often during their conversational turns as following a conversational partner's turn (and sometimes *before* their turn).

14. Lavan and colleagues (2016) identified acoustic and perceptual properties of spontaneous and volitional laughter, including the fact that listeners differ in how they perceive the arousal, valence, and authenticity of spontaneous and volitional laughter.

(Spontaneous laughter was generated by presenting speakers with a video or audio clip of their choosing, which I always thought would be a fun recording session!)

15. McGettigan and colleagues (2015), Lavan and colleagues (2017), and Kosilo and colleagues (2021) all investigated neural responses to spontaneous and volitional laughter. Lavan and colleagues highlight the fact that spontaneous and volitional laughter differ in arousal, valence, and authenticity, and find brain regions that respond parametrically to these attributes (as opposed to a strictly categorical distinction between spontaneous and volitional laughter). These regions include portions of the STG surrounding auditory cortex, but a number of other regions as well (including anterior cingulate).

16. Nummenmaa and colleagues (2023) used fMRI to look at brain responses to laughter and crying during movie viewing. They found laughter was associated with activity in temporal cortex (particularly STG and pMTG); crying involved some of these same regions, but also thalamus, cingulate cortex, insula, and orbitofrontal cortex.

17. Belin and colleagues (2000) first noted this observation in an fMRI study where they compared responses to voices to a number of other sounds (including bells, modulated noise, and other human-made sounds such as finger snaps). That finding led to an entire area of research looking at responses to voice in the right temporal lobe, and how these might be similar to (or perhaps different than) how the visual system treats identity from faces (e.g., Yovel and Belin, 2013).

18. Latinus and colleagues (2013) characterize a framework for voice space modeled off prior observations from face perception. They used audio morphing to create average voices and found that the distance from an individual voice to its gender-associated mean related to both behavioral judgments of voice similarity and fMRI-based responses to voices.

    Rupp and colleagues (2022) use ECoG to examine acoustic responses to voice and non-voice stimuli, and find evidence for this categorical distinction in both the left and right temporal lobe.

19. As one example, Jones and colleagues (2015) tested speech and voice processing in a group of patients who had had a stroke. Participants completed two alternative forced choice tasks on voice gender (male/female) and phoneme ("pa" vs. "ta"). Patients with right hemisphere damage showed a difference in performance between voice and phoneme tasks, with voice tasks showing poorer classification. In this case, behavioral performance was most related to damage to the *frontal* lobe, rather than temporal regions. One possibility is that the role of the frontal lobe in this particular task is emphasized due to the nature of the task.

20. Marinkovic and colleagues (2003) conducted an MEG study of single-word processing. Participants were presented with words related to body parts, objects, or animals, and instructed to respond to those larger than one foot (for example, a shirt or a tiger) and not to respond to items smaller than one foot (for example, a medal or a cricket). Some of the words were repeated, allowing the researchers to

look at repetition effects. The task-related component of the task relating to size judgment is critical as it presumably engages semantic and decision-related processing, in addition to lexical processing.

21. Stanislas Dehaene encapsulates this viewpoint in a "neuronal recycling" framework (which he also applies to numbers). Dehaene and Cohen (2007) present this framework, including the following postulates (pp. 384–385):

    1. Human brain organization is subject to strong anatomical and connectional constraints inherited from evolution. Organized neural maps are present early on in infancy and bias subsequent learning.
    2. Cultural acquisitions (e.g., reading) must find their "neuronal niche," a set of circuits that are sufficiently close to the required function and sufficiently plastic as to reorient a significant fraction of their neural resources to this novel use.
    3. As cortical territories dedicated to evolutionarily older functions are invaded by novel cultural objects, their prior organization is never entirely erased. Thus, prior neural constraints exert a powerful influence on cultural acquisition and adult organization.

22. The VWFA was proposed by Cohen and colleagues (2000) following evidence for a region of the brain responding particularly strongly for written words. However, the term is not without controversy. Price and Devlin (2003) were early objectors, noting a lack of patients with pure alexia with damage limited to regions corresponding to the VWFA, and the response of the VWFA to many stimuli other than visual word form processing. They suggest instead that this region participates in a number of functions and it is important to consider the interactions of the VWFA with other regions. In this text, I adopt the term VWFA because it is still pervasive in the reading literature. However, it is worth being aware that the term may be misleading, and in fact, the debates over this region are instructive in the context of broader discussions relating to cortical localization and functional specificity. See also Hillis and colleagues (2005).

23. Yeatman and White (2021) provide a comprehensive review of the neural mechanisms supporting reading in the context of visual processing, including a distinction between two subregions of the VWFA that differ in their anatomical connectivity and functional responses.

24. Saygin and colleagues (2016) scanned children at age five (before they had learned to read fluently; a subset of the entire group) and at age eight (after they learned to read). They found that anatomical connectivity patterns at age five related to location of the VWFA at age eight; functional activity at age five did not predict VWFA location. They conclude that the anatomical connectivity of the ventral occipitotemporal cortex lays the foundation for functional specialization. See also Roy and colleagues (2024) for a large study looking at white matter development and reading.

25. In an fMRI study, Kubota and colleagues (2019) presented words and object to children and found that only skilled readers showed greater activity for words than for objects, and furthermore, word selectivity strongly correlated with reading skill across participants. These findings suggest that the word-related responses in VWFA vary from person to person and their engagement is a critical component of skilled reading.

26. Taylor and colleagues (2013) present meta-analyses of fMRI data related to reading in an effort to link theoretical frameworks for reading to available imaging data, and thus provide an excellent overview of the considerations in relating cognitive models of reading to the brain.

27. Taylor and colleagues (2011) introduced these particular stimuli. Future studies examined neural correlates (Taylor et al., 2019) and instruction style (Rastle et al., 2021).

28. Excellent reviews on the neural systems supporting signed language are found in Hickok and colleagues (1998), MacSweeney and colleagues (2008), and Emmorey (2021). Those papers also provide a perspective spanning over two decades and a nice illustration of the degree to which the field has changed over that time. For an excellent and concise overview, see Emmorey (2023).

29. In the classic Stroop effect, participants are asked to name the color of ink a word is written in, and they are slower to do so if the word is a color word (for example, the word "blue" written in red ink). These findings are often taken as strong evidence for the automaticity of reading, because even though participants do not need to read the word to perform the task, they are obligated to do so (and their performance suffers). Bosworth and colleagues (2021) used a version of the Stroop task in which hands were colored differently. Thus, a hand colored yellow could be making a sign for either "yellow" (congruent) or "purple" (incongruent). They found Stroop interference effects in both signed and spoken language, consistent with automated lexical access in sign language.

30. Caselli, Emmorey, and Cohen-Goldberg (2021) used a lexical decision task to investigate sign language processing. Participants all reported becoming deaf before the age of three years and considered themselves fluent signers of American Sign Language (ASL). They viewed signs and non-signs and indicated whether or not each item was a real sign (i.e., a standard lexical decision task). There were significant effects of sign frequency, and an interaction between frequency and density, in the response time data.

31. Lillo-Martin and Jenner (2021) provide a comprehensive review of sign language acquisition and parallels to spoken language acquisition, including in the areas of babbling, first words, and grammatical development. See also Hall (2017) for more on language deprivation in deaf children, and Caselli, Pyers, and Lieberman (2021) show that hearing parents who are learning sign alongside their deaf children provide sufficient input to support language acquisition.

32. In a case study, Kimura and colleagues (1976) report a case of a deaf man who survived a left hemisphere stroke and subsequently became aphasic (for sign language). He was additionally impaired on complex, but not simple, hand movements. Hickok and colleagues (1996) examined 23 users of sign language who had had a stroke affecting either their left or right hemisphere. They found those with damage to the left hemisphere were significantly more impaired on language tasks than those with right hemisphere damage (including more errors, lower comprehension, and poorer naming).

33. Leonard and colleagues (2012) used MEG to examine the time course of responses to signs in deaf participants and speech in hearing participants. Participants were

presented with a picture and then a word (or sign) and indicated whether the item matched the preceding picture. In the period immediately following stimulus presentation, brain responses showed modality-dependent effects (visual regions for sign language, auditory regions for speech). However, by 300–350 ms, activity converted on bilateral temporal regions, including STG and STS. These findings support language representations in the temporal lobes that do not depend on input modality.

34. Leonard and colleagues (2020) present a case study of a deaf signer who was undergoing presurgical mapping prior to removal of a brain tumor. They had the participant perform a lexical decision task on short videos showing either a real or pseudo sign, and produce signs. Electrodes along motor and somatosensory cortex – that is, pre-central gyrus, post-central gyrus, and supramarginal gyrus – showed activity related to location and handshape. A subset of these electrodes showed relationships to age of acquisition and lexical frequency, psycholinguistic attributes of words related to many aspects of behavior.

35. Özyürek (2014) provides a compelling overview of the brain systems supporting co-speech gesture, including making a persuasive case that at least some gestures convey semantic information that is processed as such by listeners.

36. Gesture phrases generally consist of three phases: the *preparation*, the *stroke* (the portion with the most semantic meaning), and the *hold* (McNeill, 1992).

37. Goldin-Meadow (2014) provides a nice overview and evidence for children's use of gesture. Among other aspects, she highlights the role of gesture in providing children practice conveying meanings and eliciting timely speech from listeners. Gestures act thus not only to "only" convey meaning but also to facilitate interpersonal interaction critical to successful communication.

38. Kelly and colleagues (2010) examined how the congruency of gestural and spoken information interacted. They primed target words (such as "chop") with gestures that were congruent (chopping), weakly incongruent (cutting), or strongly incongruent (twisting). Target words could then be presented as either speech or gesture. The authors found that congruent primes were associated with faster and more accurate performance than incongruent ones; or put another way, *incongruent* speech and gesture information resulted in much worse performance. They interpret these results as supporting an integrated systems view in which speech and gesture interact in a mutual and obligatory manner.

39. Willems and colleagues (2007) used matching and mismatching gestures in an fMRI experiment, and found that mismatching combinations resulted in increased activity in left IFG. Because the information related to the congruency is related to language, the authors interpret these findings as demonstrating a role for left IFG in both spoken and gestured language. Further work also identified a role for the left posterior temporal lobe (Willems et al., 2009) which may be related more to identifying corresponding input streams than meaning integration *per se*. See also Ösyürek and colleagues (2007) for an EEG study in which gesture and speech

mismatches were processed similarly, also consistent with a tight interaction between these modalities. See also the qualitative meta-analysis in Özyürek (2014).

40. Holler and colleagues (2015) conducted an fMRI study in which participants were listeners as part of a three-person conversation. The speaker produced gestures with their speech, which (as in prior studies) was associated with activity in left MTG and IFG relative to a speech-only condition. Critically, the speaker could also direct their gaze to the participant, or not – which further related to activity in the right MTG.

Further Reading

Cohen L, Dehaene S, Naccache L, Lehéricy S, Dehaene-Lambertz G, Hénaff MA, Michel F (2000) The visual word form area: spatial and temporal characterization of an initial stage of reading in normal subjects and posterior split-brain patients. *Brain* 123:291–307. https://doi.org/10.1093/brain/123.2.291.
  Initial description of the VWFA, a region of the fusiform gyrus that responds strongly in literate readers to written words. A good reading to pair with Price and Devlin (2003).

Lavan N, Rankin G, Lorking N, Scott S, McGettigan C (2017) Neural correlates of the affective properties of spontaneous and volitional laughter types. *Neuropsychologia* 95:30–39. https://doi.org/10.1016/j.neuropsychologia.2016.12.012.
  An fMRI study comparing neural responses to spontaneous and volitional laughter, including ratings of arousal, valence, and authenticity.

Leonard MK, Ferjan Ramirez N, Torres C, Travis KE, Hatrak M, Mayberry RI, Halgren E (2012) Signed words in the congenitally deaf evoke typical late lexicosemantic responses with no early visual responses in left superior temporal cortex. *Journal of Neuroscience* 32:9700–9705. https://doi.org/10.1523/JNEUROSCI.1002-12.2012.
  An MEG study comparing the time course of responses to signs in deaf participants and speech in hearing participants.

Marinkovic K, Dhond RP, Dale AM, Glessner M, Carr V, Halgren E (2003) Spatiotemporal dynamics of modality-specific and supramodal word processing. *Neuron* 38:487–497. https://doi.org/10.1016/S0896-6273(03)00197-1.
  An MEG study of spoken and written word processing that highlights similarities and differences in timing and localization of responses to single words.

Price CJ, Devlin JT (2003) The myth of the visual word form area. *NeuroImage* 19:473–481. https://doi.org/10.1016/S1053-8119(03)00084-3.
  Perspective on functional specialization in the fusiform gyrus, arguing that assigning a specific function (relating to processing visual word forms) may be misleading.

Willems RM, Özyürek A, Hagoort P (2007) When language meets action: the neural integration of gesture and speech. *Cerebral Cortex* 17:2322–2333. https://doi.org/10.1093/cercor/bhl141.
  Comparison of matching and mismatching speech and gesture information, suggesting involvement of left IFG in integrating gesture and speech information.

CHAPTER TEN

Language as a Whole-Brain Enterprise

Francis Schiller begins his 1979 biography of Paul Broca with the following quote (p. 1):

Paul Broca was a French surgeon-anthropologist who more than a hundred years ago identified a certain area on the convoluted surface of the human brain, approximately a square inch in size, as the central organ for speech. It is known as "Broca's area," and its destruction causes "Broca's aphasia."

Having come this far in the book, you will hopefully realize very quickly that this view does not fully agree with modern neuroscientific understanding of the neurobiology of language. A significant problem is found in what we now see as an exaggeration of the sole importance of Broca's area. Clearly the left IFG plays many important roles in language, but to say it is *the* central region for speech is an oversimplification. Without question, regions outside the left IFG play critical roles in recognizing sounds and their meanings, and conversely, people who have very healthy Broca's areas can still have severe language difficulties.

With the benefit of hindsight and decades of functional brain imaging, we might therefore feel confident in our "modern" view of language processing that does not overly simplify the processes supporting speech or language to a single brain region. Figure 10.1 shows what I hope is a more contemporary diagram showing regions of the brain implicated in language processing, which should look familiar based on preceding chapters from this book.[1]

Figure 10.1 highlights regions of the temporal lobe, left inferior frontal cortex, and others we have discussed throughout the book so far (though for space reasons, not all of them!). Is this the new "central region (network) for speech understanding"? Maybe, in the sense that these regions are consistently active in functional brain imaging studies of speech understanding, and damage to different parts of this network can cause various types of language difficulty. It is certainly an advance to have moved from a view of left-hemisphere-only Broca's area as "the speech center" to a distributed network that spans multiple regions.[2] However, this "new-and-improved" model still fails to capture the richness of what our brains do when we communicate. In this chapter, I review some other types of processes used by listeners during

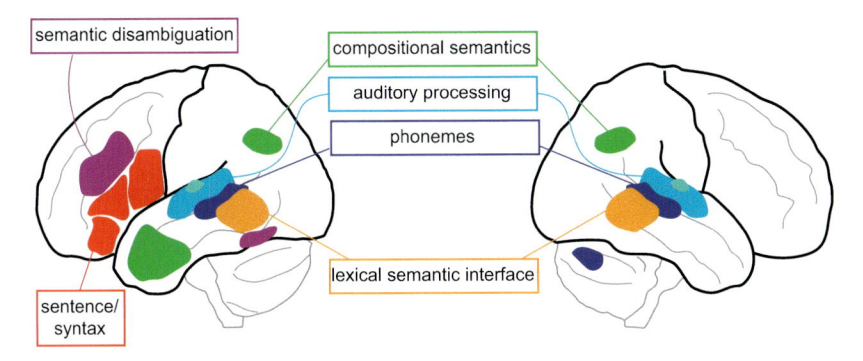

Figure 10.1 Static model of language processing in the brain informed by modern cognitive neuroscience. https://osf.io/geqb6/ (CC-BY).

spoken communication, with a goal of highlighting the flexible nature of our brains' responses to language, and the role of some regions outside traditional "language networks."

10.1 Dynamic Recruitment

For me, one of the most exciting parts of language research is that the brain networks supporting speech are not static but dynamic: They adapt to the specific challenges of a given communication situation. Figure 10.2 illustrates some of the factors affecting the demands placed on listeners during communication, including perceptual, cognitive, and linguistic aspects of communication. So, for example, trying to understand single words spoken in quiet will place different demands on a listener than trying to understand complete sentences in the middle of a noisy coffee shop – and yet, we encounter both of these situations on a regular basis. Our neuroscience-based frameworks for speech understanding should accommodate the full breadth of our communication experience. They can do so by allowing for the dynamic recruitment of different brain systems depending on the specific task and the abilities of a particular person.

While we might marvel at the flexibility of listeners to adapt to different situations, the dynamic and flexible nature of the brain can make it challenging to succinctly capture what the "main" or "central" regions supporting language are. In that sense, though, language is a prime example of principles that translate to other domains. One of the most powerful attributes of human cognition is its flexibility and ability to adapt to new situations. In this chapter, we will explore this principle in the context of language, but these few examples speak in a larger sense to the incredible flexibility of our brain.[3]

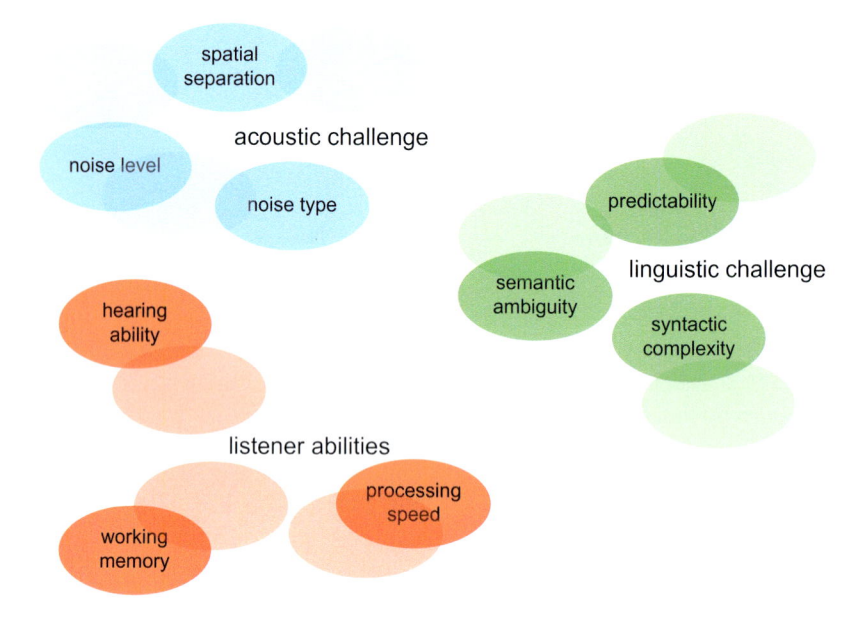

Figure 10.2 Illustration of some of the many factors affecting perceptual, cognitive, and linguistic demands faced by listeners during spoken communication. These can relate to characteristics of the content, form, or environment of the signal, as well as the individual abilities of the listener (you can imagine these in the context of the speech chain from Figure 1.1). https://osf.io/geqb6/ (CC-BY).

10.2 Acoustic Challenge

Everyday communication frequently involves an acoustic signal that is less than crystal clear. Other sources of sound in the environment might include heating or cooling fans, traffic, other people talking, music, and so on. Even in the case where the speech signal is completely clear and there is no background noise, our auditory systems must translate acoustic information into a neural signal our brains can process. Thus, the brains of listeners with hearing loss and with assistive listening devices also have to deal with acoustic challenge.

What is so challenging about "acoustic challenge"? Although the answer depends on the specific circumstance, many of these can be categorized as *degradations*, *deviations*, or *distractions*, as illustrated in Figure 10.3.[4]

A degraded speech signal is one in which the acoustic information produced by the talker never reaches the ear of a listener. If you try to have a conversation with someone using a hairdryer, the energy of the sound coming from the appliance prevents some of the vibrations of a talker's

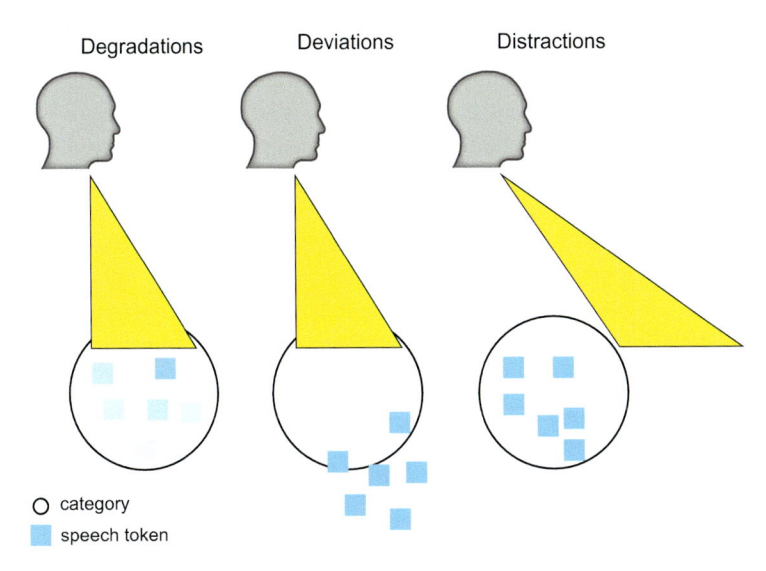

Figure 10.3 Some types of challenges during speech perception. In each panel, the circle represents a learned sound category (for example, a phoneme or word) in a listener's first language. The squares represent individual speech tokens produced by a talker, with acoustic interruptions indicated with faded colors. A listener's attention is illustrated using the yellow spotlight. In this metaphor, when the squares fully appear in a circle it indicates they are easily and accurately processed. See also Van Engen and Peelle (2014). https://osf.io/geqb6/ (CC-BY).

speech from reaching a listener's ear. If other sources of sound interrupt enough of a talker's speech, a listener will not receive enough of the signal to correctly understand every word.

By contrast, consider someone who speaks with an accent that is not your native accent.[5] In this case, the speech sounds are not missing, but they may not correspond to the speech categories you learned growing up. As with degraded speech, there is a lack of a clear match between what you hear and the speech categories your brain represents. However, unlike processes which degrade the signal (that is, prevent a clear signal from reaching the ear of a listener), in the case of accented speech the incoming speech systematically deviates from expected representations.

Finally, you might be distracted by a sound – which, in speech research, is often another talker. If you are trying to listen to what someone is saying but can hear a second talker at the same time, it takes effort to keep your attention focused on the target talker and to ignore the nontarget talker (sometimes called a "distractor"). In the real world, a target and distractor are seldom in an identical location (for example, if you are trying to hear a friend talking in a coffee shop, the other people talking are probably not in your friend's lap). Thus, information about spatial localization can help us to separate a target from distractor.[6]

And, in many real-life situations our auditory systems may deal with more than one of these challenges (for example, conversations in busy places).

There is increasing agreement that for many kinds of acoustic challenge, our brains need to recruit cognitive resources outside of the core language network[7] shown in Figure 10.1. Behavioral evidence for this extra cognitive demand comes from studies showing that listeners have trouble remembering degraded speech, even when it is intelligible.[8] Although speech and memory are often studied as separate domains, they also share common cognitive processes. Processes that operate mostly in a single domain are called *domain-specific* (or sometimes domain-preferential) cognitive processes. For example, auditory cortex processes auditory input in a tonotopic manner, and is largely devoted to auditory processing. By contrast, processes that operate across different domains of cognition are called *domain-general* cognitive processes.

One example is found in verbal working memory. Broadly speaking, **working memory** refers to the ability to store and manipulate information that is no longer available to the senses.[9] For example, I might show you some lighted shapes in different locations on the screen, one at a time, and then at the end ask you where each shape appeared. To accomplish this task, you need to remember where the shapes appeared and relate that information to the pattern you see in front of you. As the name implies, verbal working memory applies these principles but in tasks using words. In a classic task called a reading span task, participants are shown a series of sentences and asked to press a key to indicate whether or not the sentence makes sense.[10] After the list of sentences, they are asked to recall the final word of each sentence. The length of the list is increased until participants are unable to do the task – being able to remember more sentence-final words indicates better working memory ability.

The topic of verbal working memory is relevant for our present discussion because it has been suggested to be involved in both encoding verbal material to memory, and in understanding acoustically challenging speech. Because both computations rely on the same cognitive resource, allocating more processing for one process (understanding acoustically challenging speech) means there are fewer resources available for anything else a listener may want to do (such as remembering what they have heard).[11] Figure 10.4 presents a schematic of how task demands relate to cognitive resources required: As the task becomes more difficult (for example, a greater amount of background noise), more resources are required – until the task becomes *too* difficult and listeners may give up (thus allocating fewer cognitive resources).[12]

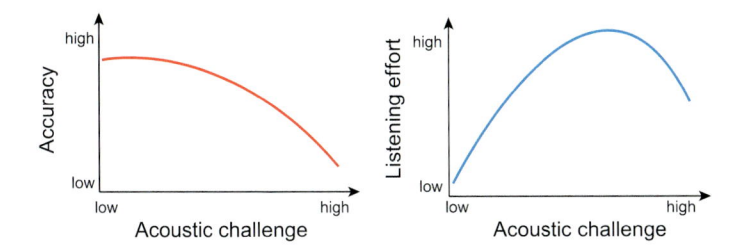

Figure 10.4 Illustration of how acoustic challenge (such as background noise or hearing loss) may affect listeners. *Left:* As acoustic challenge increases, intelligibility will decline. *Right:* As acoustic challenge increases, listeners typically exert additional cognitive effort up until the point at which the task is simply too difficult – then less effort is exerted (despite increasing challenge). https://osf.io/geqb6/ (CC-BY).

A broad category of domain-general processes come under the label of cognitive control (see Box 10.1). **Cognitive control** is central to goal-directed behavior and helps us to plan, execute, and adjust our behavior in service of our goals. For example, while driving a car, we have goal of staying on the road and avoiding pedestrians. We need to coordinate our motor behavior (including acceleration, braking, steering) in the context of other traffic and people while monitoring the environment for new information. With experience, much of this can happen automatically. But if you find yourself in a country where you drive on the other side of the road than you are used to, you will quickly notice the need to engage some additional cognitive resources!

One of the brain networks often associated with cognitive control is the **cingulo-opercular network**, which consists of the anterior cingulate cortex and bilateral frontal operculum. These regions are often active at the same time, and spontaneous "resting state" activity is strongly correlated, which suggests they may function as a unit (Box 10.2). Activity in the cingulo-opercular network is elevated, relative to rest, during task performance, and also shows an additional spike in activity following errors. Thus although this network is sometimes thought of as being centered on error detection, a more comprehensive view is that the cingulo-opercular network monitors task engagement, and helps people re-engage in a task following an error.

How does this play out during speech understanding? Consider a simple task in which you have to listen to single words presented in background noise, and repeat back what you hear (so a researcher can tell whether you

Box 10.1 Complementary perspectives on executive function.

One challenge for any construct in cognitive neuroscience is how it is best defined, both theoretically and anatomically. Although the importance of the frontal lobes for executive processing had long been appreciated, functional brain imaging brought new opportunities to study processing associated with different tasks. In 2001, John Duncan and Adrian Owen published a meta-analysis – that is, an analysis that combined data from many other studies – in which they plotted peaks of brain activity observed for a variety of cognitively demanding tasks. They found regions of the frontal lobe (dorsolateral pre-frontal cortex, anterior cingulate, frontal operculum) and parietal lobe (inferior parietal sulcus) in which numerous studies relying on different tasks all showed elevated activity. This finding, in part, led to the characterization of what Duncan termed the *multiple-demand network*.[17] A key characteristic of the multiple-demand network is that it can flexibly represent different information depending on current task goals – that is, respond to "multiple" types of cognitive demand. Much of the evidence therefore came from seeing how these regions respond to different types of tasks in both humans and nonhuman primates.

In a separate set of studies, researchers were using correlations in resting state fMRI data to define functional networks (see Box 10.2), and assigning names to these networks based on their putative function (inferred from task-based fMRI studies and lesion data). Two of these networks are the fronto-parietal network and the cingulo-opercular network (which we have already met).[18] Based on their time courses of activity, these two networks seem to play complementary roles during task-based studies. The frontoparietal network is proposed to be more involved in developing rules to govern behavior (in a laboratory task, the rule might be: press a button when I see the letter X), whereas the cingulo-opercular network relates to task engagement (and *re-engaging* in the task when attention lapses). Both of these descriptions fit nicely within the overall description of the multiple-demand network, and also anatomically align with the multiple-demand network.

A third framework for related processes is that of *cognitive control*, which is generally defined as the monitoring and adjustment of cognitive engagement to meet current goals. One framework for cognitive control, proposed by Todd Braver, involves two complementary modes of control. In this proposal, cognitive control consists of two complementary and dissociable processes: *proactive cognitive control*, which engages before engaging in a task, and *reactive cognitive control*, which is involved in error monitoring and re-engaging in the task when performance drops.[19] Generally speaking, DLPFC

Box 10.1 (cont.)

features prominently in assessments of proactive cognitive control, and anterior cingulate and frontal operculum in cases of reactive control.

The short list mentioned here is not exhaustive – there are other conventions for naming both cognitive processes related to executive function and the primary brain supporting them. The take-home message, though, is that naming cognitive functions and brain networks is not always straightforward, and different names can refer to similar (or identical) constructs. Because of the overlap in the conceptual definition and brain regions associated with each of these viewpoints, it is not an issue of picking a "correct" way to think about the issue. Rather, it is useful to understand these perspectives enough to understand the similarities and differences.

Box 10.2 Using resting state fMRI to identify brain networks.

In 1995, Bharat Biswal and colleagues published a finding that precipitated a new subfield of cognitive neuroscience.[20] Using fMRI, they measured spontaneous activity in the left motor cortex. Provocatively, they found that low-frequency spontaneous activity in the right motor cortex was strongly correlated with left motor activity – even though no motor task was being performed. This finding suggested that spontaneous activity – that is, not related to a particular task – reflects functional brain networks, and thus a new field was born: resting state fMRI.

In a typical resting state fMRI study, participants lie still in the scanner; sometimes they are instructed to keep their eyes shut, other times to look at the screen. There are no "events" or "tasks" in the sense usually used in psychology and so-called "task-based fMRI" experiments (which are what we have discussed in the rest of the book). Correlations between the time series data in different voxels are then used to infer functional connectivity: Two voxels that show a similar time course are typically interpreted as being functionally related. Furthermore, patterns of functional relationships can then be used to identify networks (sometimes called communities).

What is remarkable about brain networks identified using resting state fMRI is that they map surprisingly well onto what we know about brain function from task-based fMRI and lesion studies. For example, we know that comparable regions (that is, homologs) in the left and right hemisphere perform related functions, and resting state networks reflect this, being largely symmetrical. Resting state analysis also groups the anterior cingulate

Box 10.2 (cont.)

with the left and right frontal operculum (a "cingulo-opercular" network), which agrees with task-based data, and so on. Thus, resting state fMRI is often viewed as a method for identifying functional networks without requiring participants to perform a cognitive or perceptual task. Such a use may be particularly valuable when studying populations who might struggle with tasks, but it can also potentially be more efficient: Instead of using a motor task to identify motor regions, a visual task to identify visual regions, an auditory task to identify auditory regions, and so on, we can just use a resting state scan and pull out many of these same regions and networks.

Why would spontaneous activity at rest relate to what these networks do when active? Although this is still a topic of debate, one possibility is that when regions are co-active when engaging in a task it strengthens the connections between them, meaning that spontaneous activity in one is more likely than chance to activate another. These principles are seen at the level of individual neurons as active synapses get strengthened, often discussed in the context of Hebbian plasticity.[21] Thus, although resting state functional connectivity is using functional data, it may also capture structural differences that reflect years of lived experience and brain use.

Just like other modalities of brain imaging, networks identified using resting state functional connectivity differ from person to person.[22] Although major networks are present in everybody, their specific anatomical extent, and strength of connections between regions, differs, providing a potential tool to use for understanding individual differences in behavior.

heard the word correctly or not). The noise is difficult enough that you only get about half of the words correct. Following an error trial, functional brain imaging shows increased activity in the cingulo-opercular network (Figure 10.5). What is particularly interesting, though, is that the amount of cingulo-opercular engagement following an error helps predict accuracy on the *following* trial.[13] Cingulo-opercular activity also relates to other aspects of challenging speech processing including manipulations of attention.[14]

Another area of the brain implicated in acoustic challenge is the dorsolateral prefrontal cortex (DLPFC; corresponding roughly to the inferior frontal sulcus and middle frontal gyrus, part of the frontoparietal attention network introduced in Box 10.1). The DLPFC is engaged in a wide variety of tasks and cognitive functions, and often active when tasks are particularly challenging. During tasks in which rules need to be applied (for example, responding to

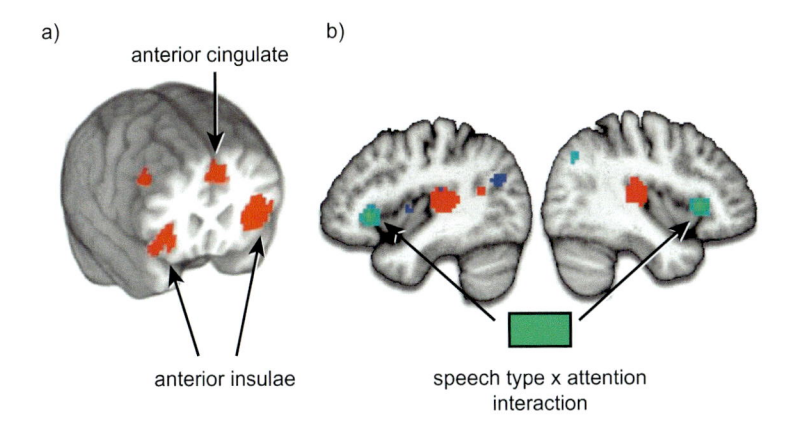

Figure 10.5 The cingulo-opercular network in the context of speech understanding. (a) Vaden and colleagues (2013) presented listeners with words in background noise and found that cingulo-opercular activity was increased in harder signal-to-noise ratios relative to easier ones. (b) Wild and colleagues (2012) presented listeners with spoken sentences that varied in acoustic clarity (manipulated with noise vocoding) and attention demands (a concurrent secondary task). The interaction between the two – where attention and speech type both influenced activity – was in the anterior insulae.

a certain shape on the screen by pressing a particular button), the DLPFC appears to represent these rules, suggesting it flexibly engages in current task goals.[15] (See Figure 10.6.)

A significant challenge of interpreting DLPFC activity during speech processing is that language-preferential and domain-general regions lie very near to each other in the frontal lobe, and their arrangement differs from person to person. When averaging results across different brains to look at an average group response – as typically done in fMRI studies – these differences can get blurred. Future work that relies on individually defined functional localizers will be critical in understanding these issues.[16]

10.3 Conversation and Turn-Taking

A key part of everyday communication is centered on the back-and-forth sharing of ideas that happens during conversation.[23] A corollary is that while listening to what a conversational partner is saying we simultaneously need to plan the content and timing of our next utterance. One study looking at turn-taking in a naturalistic conversation corpus found that 85 percent of speaking transitions could be anticipated within 750 ms![24] Remarkably, it is rare for two

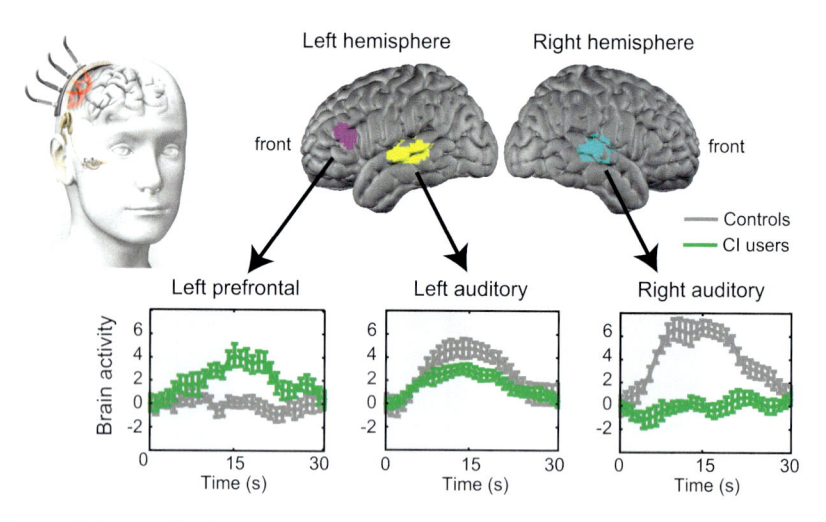

Figure 10.6 Example of DLPFC involvement in understanding speech when it is acoustically challenging. Sherafati and colleagues (2022) used optical brain imaging to look at brain responses to speech in listeners with unilateral right cochlear implants (CI) compared to listeners without. The key finding is that when listening to lists of words, listeners with CIs showed increased activity in left DLPFC, whereas listeners with normal hearing did not. These findings are all consistent with a role for DLPFC in understanding challenging speech. https://osf.io/geqb6/ (CC-BY).

people in a conversation to interrupt each other. Of course, it happens from time to time – but more often than not we are able to time our speech smoothly. These behavioral observations suggest that during conversation, listeners are using speech cues found in the unfolding utterance they are hearing to estimate how long the utterance is likely to be, and begin to plan a response.

Speech planning is an internal process that can occur in the absence of overt behavior; during conversations, it typically happens while we are listening to a conversational partner's speech. Given the necessary involvement of motor regions to speech production (Chapter 4), it therefore might not be surprising that motor regions have also been implicated in conversation.[25] As shown in Figure 10.7, these include not only left IFG but also regions of the middle frontal gyrus (MFG) not historically associated with comprehension or non-conversational speech production.[26]

Thus, regions of the frontal lobe – including regions of motor cortex, premotor cortex, and the MFG – contribute to speech production planning during conversation. The MFG in particular is interesting because it is not typically associated with speech production in non-conversational contexts.

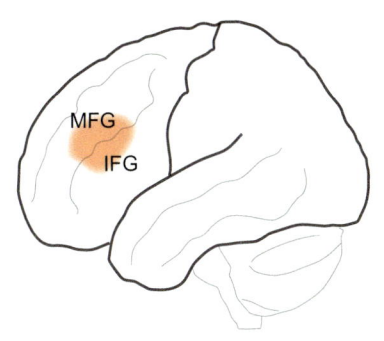

Figure 10.7 Regions of the left IFG and MFG, distinct from those associated with simple perception and production, are associated with conversation planning. https://osf.io/geqb6/ (CC-BY).

10.4 The Cerebellum

The cerebellum is a beautiful and intricate structure with approximately three to four times as many neurons as the rest of the brain,[27] and traditionally associated with motor tasks.[28] Although language-related activity has been observed in the cerebellum for decades, the cerebellum unfortunately often gets overlooked in discussions of language processing (and, embarrassingly, is sometimes omitted from brain diagrams). However, there is a long history of work looking at the cerebellum in the context of speech and language processing.

Anatomically, the cerebellum is a tightly folded layer of gray matter. Its structure consists of a number of subdivisions or lobules demarcated by fissures around a midline vermis made of white matter (*vermis* is Latin for "worm"). Structures toward the midline are considered vermal, whereas structures toward the lateral aspect are hemispheric. Although many naming schemes exist, most contemporary studies use Roman numeral designations.[29]

Historically, the cerebellum has been most associated with motor function, including **ataxia** (difficulty coordinating voluntary movement) and problems with balance, gait, and reflexes.[30] During the latter half of the twentieth century, an increasing appreciation for anatomical connections with other parts of cortex developed, and helped support the notion that the cerebellum may be involved in cognitive functions outside motor control.[31] Eventually, a growing number of reports of language difficulties associated with damage to the cerebellum began to appear.[32]

Even more recently, fMRI studies have continued to reveal much about the relationship between the cerebellum and cortex. In particular, resting state fMRI studies have identified functional connections between the cerebellum

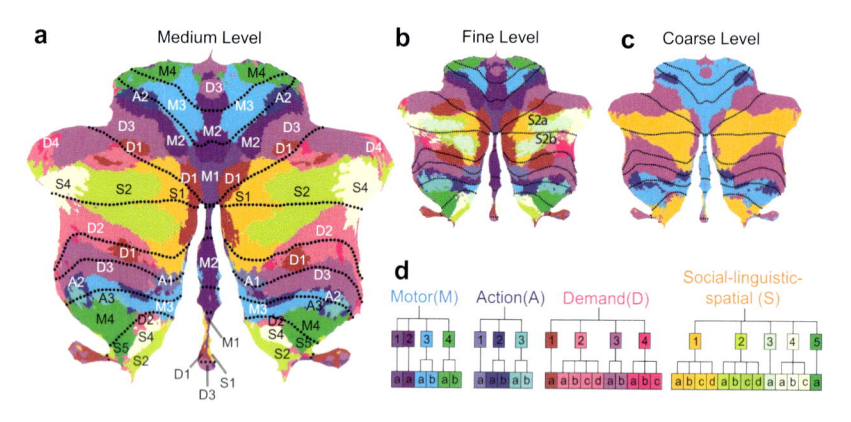

Figure 10.8 Functional subdivisions of the cerebellum based on several different data sets (including task-based and resting state functional connectivity), displayed on an inflated map of the cerebellum. The cerebellum contains ordered arrangements of maps in multiple domains, including motor, action, demand, and social-linguistic-spatial.
From Nettekoven and colleagues (2024), CC-BY.

and many areas of cortex.[33] Combining results from resting state and task-based fMRI studies provides an intricate picture of cerebellar organization that mirrors major subdivisions present in cortex (Figure 10.8).

In this context, it is perhaps not surprising that there has been steadily increasing appreciation of the role the cerebellum may play in language processing (that is, beyond its established roles in speech production). Domains in which cerebellar activity has been reported include syntactic processing, prediction, and lexical characteristics such as word frequency or lexical competition.[34]

10.5 What Parts of the Brain Support Language?

Given all that we have learned so far, perhaps now we are in a position to put it all together and produce a modern map of language in the brain. Recall Figure 10.1, which includes some (though not all) of the brain regions supporting language discussed in prior chapters of this book. Although potentially useful, I would also like to suggest that it's wrong – or at least, incomplete. The networks supporting human communication extend far beyond these traditional frontotemporal regions. The answer to the question "What parts of the brain support language?" is: *It depends*. That is, we have seen example after example of how different types of content, communication environments, or individual abilities and characteristics affect how the brain processes language. Many of these considerations reflect the level of linguistic challenge involved. For single words, factors such as the type of speech and phonological neighborhood affect processing (Chapter 6). And as we saw in Chapter 8, if sentences contain ambiguous words, or have a syntactically complex structure, our brains engage more regions (particularly of the frontal lobe) than for sentences without these features. Acoustic challenges include challenges to hearing (Chapter 5) or the use of assistive devices (Chapter 10) or the presence of background noise or other acoustic challenges (also Chapter 10). These challenges may be supported by auditory, perceptual, or cognitive processes that also vary from individual to individual. A list of some of these considerations is summarized in Figure 10.9 – the point of which is to emphasize the vast number of communicative situations we encounter on a daily basis. Furthermore, we have seen how these situations are also associated with changes in brain activity.

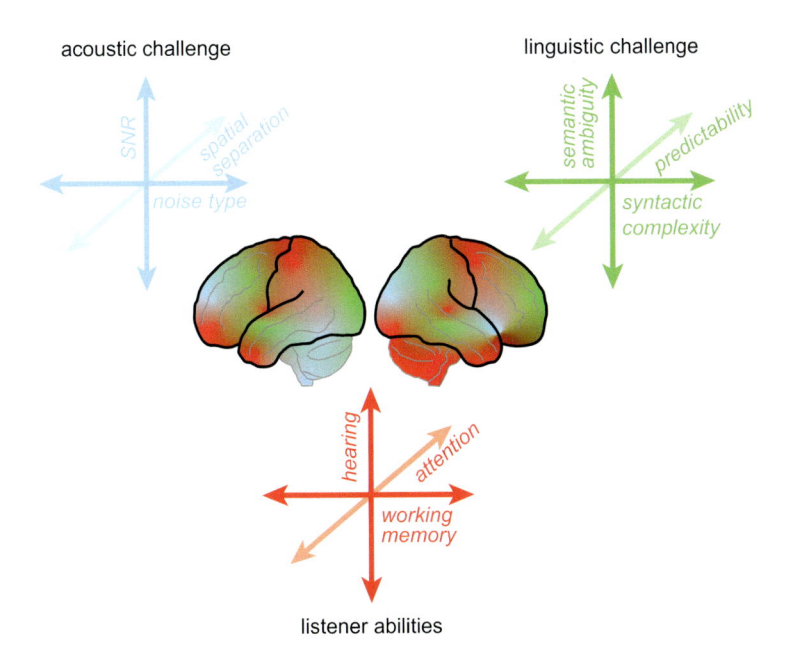

Figure 10.9 The cognitive and linguistic processes listeners need to engage depend on acoustic and linguistic characteristics of the speech and environment, cognitive and hearing abilities of the listener, and the specific task required. (The specific examples in the figure are illustrative and not intended to be a comprehensive list; similarly, the colors on the brain illustrate dynamically changing network activity, not any specific functional mapping.) https://osf.io/geqb6/ (CC-BY).

That is not to say that all regions contribute equally to language processing – the language challenges faced by people with aphasia provide ample evidence to the contrary. However, appreciating the dynamic and interconnected nature of the neural systems contributing to language processing provides a more holistic and accurate view on this remarkable feat of the human brain.

10.6 Moving from Functional Localization to Complex Systems

Perhaps due to the historical roots in functional localization, much research in the neuroscience of language continues to focus on linking different regions of the brain to specific processes supporting language processing. However, there are good reasons to think this kind of focus may not capture the complex dynamics underlying language processing.

One reason for this is the temporal nature of the speech signal. Given that rapidly varying spectro-temporal information contained in the acoustic speech signal, and associated reliance on auditory and linguistic levels of representation, the temporal dimension of processing is central to speech processing. These temporal aspects are not limited to evoked responses but also encompass ongoing rhythmic activity and long-range coupling across brain networks. That is, processing in individual brain areas is intrinsically linked to a broader network of coordinated activity.

We may take some guidance here from work in the domain of working memory – that is, representing information that is no longer available to sensory systems. Although representations of information were for many years attributed to sustained activity in prefrontal cortex, recent work has begun to reveal a picture that is potentially more complex and nuanced, relying on "activity-silent" periods in addition to periods of sustained activity. These dynamics are only observable using methods sensitive to neural dynamics, and also implicate multiple brain regions in cognitive processing.[35] It would be odd if language operated in a fundamentally different fashion.

Thus, as we consider the next research frontiers in the neuroscience of language, a deeper exploration of the temporal dynamics of distributed neural systems may be necessary to understand how we pass ideas between each other with such remarkable efficiency.

10.7 Summary

- Dynamic engagement in response to current task demands is a hallmark of neural systems. As such, static models generally fail to accurately capture brain responses to speech and language.

- Acoustic challenge during listening is associated with engagement of both DLPFC and the cingulo-opercular network.
- Processes related to conversational speech and turn-taking rely on motor and prefrontal areas.
- Many parts of the cerebellum respond to language similarly to traditional cortical language areas.
- Language-related processing can occur in every major system of the brain, depending on the specific task at hand and the individual abilities of a person.

Notes

1. Over the past two decades, many influential reviews of speech and language processing have conveyed many of these principles. Hickok and Poeppel (2007) was particularly formative in my own training, as well as Scott and Johnsrude (2003), Rauschecker and Scott (2009), and others.
2. As noted elsewhere (for example, Chapter 3), the idea of *networks* for language is not new, with formative contributions having been made by famed figures including (but not limited to) Wernicke, Lichtheim, and Geschwind.
3. Pessoa and colleagues (2022) argue that the organization of the vertebrate brain is not suited to support the sort of modular divisions we, as researchers, often use to organize our work (p. 7):

   Let us return to the question of mental categories studied in neuroscience. Are standard terms like "attention", "memory" and "decision-making" useful for studying and describing the relationship between brain and behaviour? More directly, what should the neuroscientist care about? We argue that a comparative understanding of the general vertebrate neuroarchitecture strongly constrains the classes of mental processes in vertebrates. In particular, the functions supported by the neuroarchitecture do not align themselves well with the standard decomposition. In other words, in part, our argument is that the standard decomposition would require an organization that is relatively modular. We argue, instead, that fundamental principles of the neuroarchitecture indicate that it is not.

   Similar ideas are also explored in Luiz Pessoa's (2022) provocative book *The Entangled Brain*, which proposes that it may be impossible to decompose a complex system like the brain in the manner that many cognitive neuroscientists are accustomed to thinking about.
4. Speech researchers often talk about speech understanding as involving a target (the person we are trying to understand) and a masker (the sound that is interfering with the talker). *Energetic masking* refers to situations in which the masker disrupts the acoustic information in the target. *Informational masking* refers to the case where some content of the masker is of potential interest, and causes distraction (for example, trying to hear your friend in a coffee shop while a person at the next table is sharing a story of which you can hear every word).

5. Talking about "accented speech" is a misnomer, because everyone has an accent. However, there are demonstrable differences in ease of understanding someone who has the same accent as you are most familiar with, and someone who does not. More on some challenges associated with accented speech, and how it may relate to challenges in degraded speech, is found in Van Engen and Peelle (2014).

   Weissler and colleagues (2023) discuss the use of "native" and "non-native" with respect to accent. They argue that such a framing reflects a biased view of communication (for example, if two people who are communicating do not have a common first language, which one of them is "native" and which is "non-native"?). The authors suggest that a continuum of familiarity, and sensitivity to issues of power dynamics and biases in our perspectives, will make for better research on the effects of accent.

6. Sometimes the benefit provided by spatial information is referred to as a *spatial release from masking* – in other words, the spatial localization reduces the effect of the masker. People differ in how much benefit they derive from spatial information, which is often attributed to differences in spatial sound localization abilities or attentional processes.

7. The framework for understanding effortful listening (FUEL) model (Pichora-Fuller et al., 2016) covers a wide range of factors that contribute to effort during listening, including (but not limited to) cognitive demands. Peelle (2018a) is a more focused review of behavioral and neuroimaging evidence relating to cognitive demand during listening.

8. In fact, many studies show that listeners have difficulty remembering acoustically clear speech and it comes *after* degraded speech. Perhaps the best-known early example of this work comes from Rabbitt (1968). In one study, the author presented lists of digits to participants. The second half of the list was always presented clearly; the first half of the list could be either clear or degraded. Rabbitt found that memory for the second half of the list was impaired when it followed degraded speech compared to when it followed clear speech. Because the items on the second half of the list, themselves, were clearly intelligible both times, a straightforward auditory explanation is ruled out. Rather, the memory difficulty instead seems more likely to be due to cognitive demands associated with listening to degraded speech that continue to interfere with subsequent memory encoding.

9. In Allan Baddeley's (1986) classic book *Working Memory*, Baddeley describes working memory as having three core subsystems. The central executive is responsible for the general regulation and control of cognitive processes (cf. Box 10.1); the phonological loop handles phonological and verbal information; and the visuo-spatial sketchpad stores visual or spatial information that needs to be manipulated. Although contemporary theories typically have moved beyond this particular tripartite division, Baddeley's model was enormously influential in how we think about working memory.

10. The classic citation for this task is Just and Carpenter (1980). Subsequently, many other versions of the task were developed using different sentences and modalities (i.e., spoken sentences instead of written sentences).

11. The logic assumes that cognitive resources are not unlimited but finite (a safe assumption!). The view of a limited-capacity cognitive system is both intuitive and consistent with data across many domains of cognition.

12. A famous formulation of this general effect was introduced by Robert Yerkes and John Dodson (1908) and became known as the Yerkes-Dodson Law. In brief, the idea is that performance increases with mental or physiological arousal, but only to a point – after this point, performance decreases again. The original paper was a study of how mice make choices during a discrimination task. Yerkes was also a eugenicist and racist, and he contributed a forward to Carl Brigham's 1922 book *A Study of American Intelligence*, in which he concluded: "[N]o one of us as a citizen can afford to ignore the menace of race deterioration or the evident relations of immigration to national progress and welfare." Brigham, for his part, was interested in psychometrics and intelligence and devised his own intelligence tests. On the basis of these, he concluded that immigration should be limited to protect the superior "American intelligence" (Brigham would go on to develop the SAT).

13. In a series of elegant studies, Vaden and colleagues (2013) showed this property of the cingulo-opercular network in young adults, subsequently showing similar effects in older adults (Vaden et al., 2015) and how cingulo-opercular activity relates to memory (Vaden et al., 2017). These studies extended earlier work by Eckert and colleagues implicating executive attention networks in effortful listening.

14. Adank (2012) performed a meta-analysis of neuroimaging studies of difficult speech understanding – the cingulo-opercular network shows up reliably as responding to speech difficulty across studies.

15. As one of many examples, Woolgar and colleagues (2011) used multivoxel pattern analysis (MVPA) to show responses in the multiple-demand network (including DLPFC) could distinguish between rule conditions, which were dissociated from overall difficulty (varied using a perceptual manipulation).

16. Ev Fedorenko and colleagues have done a tremendous amount of work to both highlight these problems and offer potential solutions. For example, Fedorenko and colleagues (2012) tested a large number of tasks related to language and other domains including math, working memory, and other executive tasks (such as the Stroop task). They found anatomical dissociations between regions showing selectivity for language (i.e., domain specificity) and those showing elevated responses for all difficult tasks (i.e., domain generality).

17. Duncan (2010) provides a good overview of the multiple-demand network. A basic tenet is that the multiple-demand network is key for breaking down a larger task into smaller sequential goals, and for representing information relevant for the current

goal. These types of operations appear to relate strongly to fluid intelligence (the solving of novel problems).

18. Power and Petersen (2013) provide a good review of these systems.

19. A good overview of the dual mechanisms framework is found in Braver (2012).

20. Biswal (2012) provides a fascinating personal history of the experiments leading to the publication of resting state functional connectivity (Biswal et al., 1995). Presentations about the finding, part of Biswal's PhD work, had begun earlier, including at conferences in 1993. The manuscript was rejected from the first journal to which it was submitted, but ultimately (after four rounds of review!) accepted in 1995. As of 2024 the paper now has over 10,000 citations (which is a lot!).

21. Hebbian plasticity refers to the fact that when two neurons are active at the same time, the connection between them is strengthened – that is, after repeated firing together, the effect of the presynaptic cell on the postsynaptic cell is more effective. The theory was introduced by Donald Hebb (1949) in *The Organization of Behavior*. In fact, the presynaptic cell may need to fire just before the postsynaptic cell, a fact captured in the more modern notion of spike-timing-dependent plasticity.

22. It may be that identifying these individual features requires more data than is usually acquired. Gordon and colleagues (2017) scanned 10 people for 10 hours each, and used this rich data set to identify similarities and differences not seen in prior studies. This study helped to bring about a movement toward "precision neuroimaging" (Gratton et al., 2020) that focuses on gathering a relatively large amount of data on individual participants as a way to improve reliability (and, hopefully, predictive accuracy). Participants in the Gordon and colleagues data set are sometimes referred to as the "midnight scan club" because data was collected at midnight – MRI hourly fees are high, and at Washington University in Saint Louis scanning at midnight or later resulted in a 90 percent discount! (My own attempt to take advantage of such savings were less successful, as most of my participants fell asleep while listening to sentences in the scanner . . . but that's a story for another time.)

23. Levinson (2016) provides an excellent review of the behaviors, cognitive challenges, and implications of conversational turn-taking. He also points out that turn-taking or "duetting" is present in all major branches of primates, suggesting turn-taking is part of the broader evolution of human communication.

24. This study is by de Ruiter and colleagues (2006), who recorded many hours of natural conversations between friends to mimic natural telephone conversations. They then had participants (who were not recorded) listen to the conversations and anticipate when a speaker's turn would end. Participants were remarkably good at doing so, even though they were hearing auditory-only speech samples of people they did not know.

25. Scott and colleagues (2009) provide an overview of candidate roles for motor cortex in speech perception. These include linguistic functions, task-related functions, sound-to-action functions, and involvement in joint speech (that is, speaking

in synchrony, such as reciting a pledge or creed together). They suggest that conversational turn-taking relies heavily on the motor system.

26. Castellucci and colleagues (2022) conducted an ECoG study specifically examining speech planning. They used a clever design in which the information required for a participant to make a response (and thus initiate speech motor planning) was presented early or late in an utterance, allowing the researchers to isolate planning-related activity. For example, to elicit the response "rough," the experimenter could ask either "The opposite of SOFT is what familiar word?" (critical information early in the sentence) or "What familiar word is the opposite of SOFT?" (critical information late in the sentence). Caudal portions of both the IFG and MFG showed activity related to response planning.

27. Herculano-Houzel (2010) used a method called isotropic fractionation to estimate the number of neurons in the cerebellum and neocortex in 19 species – including insectivore, rodent, and primate species (including humans) – and found a remarkable correspondence between these numbers. That is, although the sizes of brains across species varied greatly, the cerebellum contained about 3.6 times as many neurons as the neocortex. These findings lend support for the idea that the cerebellum and neocortex evolved in concert, since their proportional number of neurons scales across species. They also underscore the huge number of neurons in the cerebellum!

28. Strick and colleagues (2009) provide a comprehensive overview of nonmotor functions of the cerebellum. They also make a point that many regions of cortex are targets of cerebellar output (identified using tracing studies), suggesting a tight interplay between the cerebellum and the cortex (and many cortical targets have yet to be identified). They also enumerate three core functions associated with the cerebellum which may impact cognition more broadly: (1) timing; (2) sensorimotor imagery; (3) learning and adaptive plasticity. See also Stoodley and Schmahmann (2018) for more on cerebellar anatomy and function.

29. A detailed review of historical terminology and a prime example of "modern" (MRI-based) atlas construction is found in Schmahmann and colleagues (1999). It is also worth noting that, reminiscent of some of the localization considerations we discussed in cortex, the macroanatomical subdivisions of the cerebellum do not cleanly line up with functional subdivisions. So, as in cortex, macroanatomical landmarks are important to know but by themselves are insufficient for accurate functional localization.

30. Holmes (1917) provides an excellent example of neurological views on the cerebellum in the early twentieth century. He reviews findings in about 20 cases from gunshot injuries. The majority of these related to motor function: for example, "disturbances of muscle tone," "ataxia," "static tremor," "standing and gait," and so on. However, he also includes a section on "disturbances of speech," in which he notes difficulties with both articulation and phonation (though solidly in the domain of production, rather than perception) (p. 505):

> Speech is abnormal in most cases in which the lesions are recent and severe; it is usually slow, drawling and monotonous, but at the same time tends to be staccato and scanning. This gives it an almost typical "sing-song" character and makes it indistinct and often difficult to understand. In a few patients speech was in fact quite unintelligible for a time. In many cases the utterance is remarkably irregular and jerky, and that of many syllables, especially, as Marie has pointed out, of those that end a sentence, tends to be explosive.

31. Leiner and colleagues (1986), for example, highlight anatomical connections outside of motor cortex, and propose a more general function for the cerebellum (p. 447):

> In short, the phylogenetic data suggest that the cerebellum can be viewed as a powerful general-purpose computer, capable of being utilized for different applications in different species ... connections with the prefrontal association cortex could allow the cerebellum to extend such programming to the skilled ideational manipulations that precede planned behavior. Through such evolution of cerebellar input-output connections, the function of the cerebellum could gradually enlarge and ultimately encompass both motor and mental skills.

32. Fiez and colleagues (1992) examined performance on a variety of tasks in a patient, RC1, with a lesion to his right cerebellum following a stroke. He was discharged from the hospital two weeks after his stroke "without significant deficits noted by neurologists" and returned to full-time work in his private law practice. Six months following his stroke he reported some minor problems (occasional vertigo, handwriting less legible than it had been, increased difficulty making difficult shots in pool, "slips of the tongue"). Although the authors focused on general difficulty with error detection, one task the researchers used was a verb generation task, in which participants are shown 40 high-frequency concrete nouns, and asked to produce an appropriate verb for each noun. (This task was also used in the foundational PET study conducted by many of these same authors; Petersen et al., 1988.) Although neurologically healthy participants got faster on the task with practice, RC1 did not (suggesting difficulty with nonmotor learning). Furthermore, RC1 produced more non-verb associates to nouns than did controls, and generally produced responses which were judged by an independent set of raters to be atypical.

33. Buckner and colleagues (2011) provide an example of one such resting state parcellation. In a large data set, they found that most regions of the cerebellum showed functional connections with the cerebral cortex, and that in general the extent of the cerebellum associated with cerebral networks is proportional to the size of the cerebral network. See also Nettekoven and colleagues (2024) for a comparison of different parcellation approaches.

34. Reviews of language processing in the cerebellum are found in Murdoch (2010) and Mariën and colleagues (2014). In an fMRI study, Mechtenberg and colleagues (2024) examined cerebellar responses to a spoken narrative (a podcast), focusing on word frequency and phonological neighborhood density (that is, a measure of the number of competitors a word has). They found evidence for effects of both frequency and density in the cerebellum.

35. For a recent review see Buchsman and Miller (2022). More recent work on dynamic representations can be found in Kozachkov and colleagues (2020) and Batabyal and

colleagues (2024). I've also been heavily influenced over the years by Eve Marder's work on network properties of the stomatogastric ganglion (the *other* "STG") and how varying parameters (for example, channel conductances) can result in homeostatic behavior. I assume similar principles operate in human brains, including higher cognitive processes. For some relevant papers from computational neurobiology, see Prinz and colleagues (2004), Gjorgjieva and colleagues (2016), and Gutierrez and colleagues (2013).

Further reading

Aliko S, Wang B, Small SL, Skipper JI (2023) The entire brain, more or less, is at work: "language regions" are artefacts of averaging. bioRxiv. https://doi.org/10.1101/2023.09.01.555886.
> Using a combination of meta-analysis and looking at language data from movie watching, the authors make the argument that a much greater portion of the brain than typically associated with classic peri-Sylvian language networks are involved in language processing.

Mechtenberg H, Heffner CC, Myers EB, Guediche S (2024) The cerebellum is sensitive to the lexical properties of words during spoken language comprehension. *Neurobiology of Language* 5:757–773. https://doi.org/10.1162/nol_a_00126.
> The authors analyze activity while participants listened to a story, and identify regions of the cerebellum that respond to specific word-level characteristics (frequency and neighborhood density).

Pessoa L, Medina L, Desfilis E (2022) Refocusing neuroscience: moving away from mental categories and towards complex behaviours. *Philosophical Transactions of the Royal Society of London B: Biological Sciences* 377:20200534. https://doi.org/10.1098/rstb.2020.0534.
> A tour through several basic principles of brain organization and how these are (or are not) well suited for supporting the modular view of human cognition frequently found in textbooks (for example, separate topics on memory, emotion, language, and so on).

Sherafati A, Dwyer N, Bajracharya A, Hassanpour MS, Eggebrecht AT, Firszt JB, Culver JP, Peelle JE (2022) Prefrontal cortex supports speech perception in listeners with cochlear implants. *eLife* 11:e75323. http://doi.org/10.7554/eLife.75323.
> Example of increased recruitment of prefrontal cortex during challenging acoustic listening (specifically, adult listeners with cochlear implants listening to lists of spoken words).

Bibliography

Abbs JH, Gracco VL (1984) Control of complex motor gestures: orofacial muscle responses to load perturbations of lip during speech. *Journal of Neurophysiology* 51:705–723.

Adank P (2012) The neural bases of difficult speech comprehension and speech production: two Activation Likelihood Estimation (ALE) meta-analyses. *Brain and Language* 122:42–54.

Ahissar E, Nagarajan S, Ahissar M, Protopapas A, Mahncke H, Merzenich MM (2001) Speech comprehension is correlated with temporal response patterns recorded from auditory cortex. *Proceedings of the National Academy of Sciences* 98:13367–13372.

Aliko S, Wang B, Small SL, Skipper JI (2023) The entire brain, more or less, is at work: "language regions" are artefacts of averaging. *bioRxiv.* https://doi.org/10.1101/2023.09.01.555886.

Alm PA (2004) Stuttering and the basal ganglia circuits: a critical review of possible relations. *Journal of Communication Disorders* 37:325–369.

Alsius A, Paré M, Munhall KG (2017) Forty years after hearing lips and seeing voices: the McGurk effect revisited. *Multisensory Research* 31:111–144. http://dx.doi.org/10.1163/22134808-00002565.

Amunts K (2021) Brodmann areas. In *Encyclopedia of Evolutionary Psychological Science* (Shackelford TK, Weekes-Shackelford VA, eds.), pp 821–824. Springer International Publishing.

Amunts K, Schleicher A, Burgel U, Mohlberg H, Uylings HB, Zilles K (1999) Broca's region revisited: cytoarchitecture and intersubject variability. *Journal of Comparative Neurology* 412:319–341.

Andrews JP, Cahn N, Speidel BA, Chung JE, Levy DF, Wilson SM, Berger MS, Chang EF (2023) Dissociation of Broca's area from Broca's aphasia in patients undergoing neurosurgical resections. *Journal of Neurosurgery* 138:847–857.

Angelaki DE, Cullen KE (2008) Vestibular system: the many facets of a multimodal sense. *Annual Review of Neuroscience* 31:125–150.

Apfelbaum KS, Kutlu E, McMurray B, Kapnoula EC (2022) Don't force it! Gradient speech categorization calls for continuous categorization tasks. *The Journal of the Acoustical Society of America* 152:3728–3745.

Ardila A (2010) A review of conduction aphasia. *Current Neurology and Neuroscience Reports* 10:499–503.

Arredondo MM, Aslin RN, Werker JF (2022) Bilingualism alters infants' cortical organization for attentional orienting mechanisms. *Developmental Science* 25: e13172.

Ash S, Moore P, Antani S, McCawley G, Work M, Grossman M (2006) Trying to tell a tale: discourse impairments in progressive aphasia and frontotemporal dementia. *Neurology* 66:1405–1413.

Atta HM (1999) Edwin Smith Surgical Papyrus: the oldest known surgical treatise. *The American Surgeon* 65(12):1190–1192.

Awad M, Warren JE, Scott SK, Turkheimer FE, Wise RJS (2007) A common system for the comprehension and production of narrative speech. *Journal of Neuroscience* 27:11455–11464.

Azevedo FAC, Carvalho LRB, Grinberg LT, Farfel JM, Ferretti REL, Leite REP, Filho WJ, Lent R, Herculano-Houzel S (2009) Equal numbers of neuronal and nonneuronal cells make the human brain an isometrically scaled-up primate brain. *The Journal of Comparative Neurology* 513(5):532–541.

Baddeley AD (1986) *Working Memory.* Oxford: Clarendon Press.

Baese-Berk MM, Dilley LC, Schmidt S, Morrill TH, Pitt MA (2016) Revisiting Neil Armstrong's moon-landing quote: implications for speech perception, function word reduction, and acoustic ambiguity. *PLoS One* 11:e0155975.

Barense MD, Groen, II, Lee AC, Yeung LK, Brady SM, Gregori M, Kapur N, Bussey TJ, Saksida LM, Henson RN (2012) Intact memory for irrelevant information impairs perception in amnesia. *Neuron* 75:157–167.

Bartlett EL (2013) The organization and physiology of the auditory thalamus and its role in processing acoustic features important for speech perception. *Brain and Language* 126:29–48.

Basu Mallick D, Magnotti JF, Beauchamp MS (2015) Variability and stability in the McGurk effect: contributions of participants, stimuli, time, and response type. *Psychonomic Bulletin and Review* 22:1299–1307.

Batabyal T, Brincat SL, Donoghue JA, Lundqvist M, Mahnke MK, Miller EK (2024) Stability from subspace rotations and traveling waves. *bioRxiv.* https://doi.org/10.1101/2024.02.19.581020.

Bates E, Wilson SM, Saygin AP, Dick F, Sereno MI, Knight RT, Dronkers NF (2003) Voxel-based lesion-symptom mapping. *Nature Neuroscience* 6:448–450.

Beauchamp MS, Argall BD, Bodurka J, Duyn JH, Martin A (2004) Unraveling multisensory integration: patchy organization within human STS multisensory cortex. *Nature Neuroscience* 7:1190–1192.

Behrens TEJ, Fox P, Laird A, Smith SM (2013) What is the most interesting part of the brain? *Trends in Cognitive Sciences* 17:2–4.

Belin P, Zatorre RJ, Lafaille P, Ahad P, Pike B (2000) Voice-selective areas in human auditory cortex. *Nature* 403:309–312.

Belyk M, Carignan C, McGettigan C (2023) An open-source toolbox for measuring vocal tract shape from real-time magnetic resonance images. *Behavior Research Methods* 56:2623–2635. https://doi.org/10.3758/s13428-023-02171-9.

Belyk M, Waters S, Kanber E, Miquel ME, McGettigan C (2022) Individual differences in vocal size exaggeration. *Scientific Reports* 12:2611.

Bemis DK, Pylkkänen L (2011) Simple composition: a magnetoencephalography investigation into the comprehension of minimal linguistic phrases. *The Journal of Neuroscience* 31:2801–2814.

Bemis DK, Pylkkänen L (2013) Basic linguistic composition recruits the left anterior temporal lobe and left angular gyrus during both listening and reading. *Cerebral Cortex* 23:1859–1873.

Berker EA, Berker AH, Smith A (1986) Translation of Broca's 1865 report: localization of speech in the third left frontal convolution. *Archives of Neurology* 43:1065–1072.

Bernal B, Ardila A (2009) The role of the arcuate fasciculus in conduction aphasia. *Brain* 132:2309–2316.

Bhattasali S, Fabre M, Luh W-M, Al Saied H, Constant M, Pallier C, Brennan JR, Spreng RN, Hale J (2019) Localising memory retrieval and syntactic composition: an fMRI study of naturalistic language comprehension. *Language, Cognition and Neuroscience* 34:491–510.

Bidelman GM (2015) Multichannel recordings of the human brainstem frequency-following response: scalp topography, source generators, and distinctions from the transient ABR. *Hearing Research* 323:68–80.

Binder JR, Conant LL, Humphries CJ, Fernandino L, Simons SB, Aguilar M, Desai RH (2016) Toward a brain-based componential semantic representation. *Cognitive Neuropsychology* 33:130–174.

Binder JR, Desai RH, Graves WW, Conant LL (2009) Where is the semantic system? A critical review and meta-analysis of 120 functional neuroimaging studies. *Cerebral Cortex* 19:2767–2796.

Binder JR, Frost JA, Hammeke TA, Bellgowan PS, Springer JA, Kaufman JN, Possing ET (2000) Human temporal lobe activation by speech and nonspeech sounds. *Cerebral Cortex* 10:512–528.

Binder JR, Westbury CF, McKiernan KA, Possing ET, Medler DA (2005) Distinct brain systems for processing concrete and abstract concepts. *Journal of Cognitive Neuroscience* 17:905–917.

Binney RJ, Parker GJM, Lambon Ralph, MA (2012) Convergent connectivity and graded specialization in the rostral human temporal lobe as revealed by diffusion-weighted imaging probabilistic tractography. *Journal of Cognitive Neuroscience* 24:1998–2014.

Biswal BB (2012) Resting state fMRI: a personal history. *NeuroImage* 62:938–944.

Biswal B, Yetkin FZ, Haughton VM, Hyde JS (1995) Functional connectivity in the motor cortex of resting human brain using echo-planar MRI. *Magnetic Resonance in Medicine* 34:537–541.

Blank H, Davis MH (2016) Prediction errors but not sharpened signals simulate multivoxel fMRI patterns during speech perception. *PLoS Biology* 14: e1002577.

Blausen.com staff (2014) Medical gallery of Blausen Medical 2014. WikiJournal of Medicine 1(2). doi:10.15347/wjm/2014.010.

Bohland JW, Guenther FH (2006) An fMRI investigation of syllable sequence production. *NeuroImage* 32:821–841.

Bonner MF, Ash S, Grossman M (2010) The new classification of primary progressive aphasia into semantic, logopenic, or nonfluent/agrammatic variants. *Current Neurology and Neuroscience Reports* 10:484–490.

Bonner MF, Grossman M (2012) Gray matter density of auditory association cortex relates to knowledge of sound concepts in primary progressive aphasia. *Journal of Neuroscience* 32:7986–7991.

Bonner MF, Vesely L, Price C, Anderson C, Richmond L, Farag C, Avants B, Grossman M (2009) Reversal of the concreteness effect in semantic dementia. *Cognitive Neuropsychology* 26:568–579.

Bosworth RG, Binder EM, Tyler SC, Morford JP (2021) Automaticity of lexical access in deaf and hearing bilinguals: cross-linguistic evidence from the color Stroop task across five languages. *Cognition* 212:104659.

Bozeat S, Ralph MAL, Graham KS, Patterson K, Wilkin H, Rowland J, Rogers TT, Hodges JR (2003) A duck with four legs: investigating the structure of conceptual knowledge using picture drawing in semantic dementia. *Cognitive Neuropsychology* 20:27–47.

Bradshaw AR, Lametti DR, McGettigan C (2021) The role of sensory feedback in developmental stuttering: a review. *Neurobiology of Language* 2:308–334.

Braver TS (2012) The variable nature of cognitive control: a dual mechanisms framework. *Trends in Cognitive Sciences* 16:106–113.

Breasted JH (1930) *The Edwin Smith Surgical Papyrus*. Chicago: The University of Chicago Oriental Institute Publications. https://oi.uchicago.edu/research/publications/oip/edwin-smith-surgical-papyrus-volume-1-hieroglyphic-transliteration.

Breese EL, Hillis AE (2004) Auditory comprehension: is multiple choice really good enough? *Brain and Language* 89:3–8.

Brentari D (2019) *A Prosodic Model of Sign Language Phonology*. Cambridge, MA: MIT Press.

Brett M, Johnsrude IS, Owen AM (2002) The problem of functional localization in the human brain. *Nature Reviews Neuroscience* 3:243–249.

Brigham CC (1922) *A Study of American Intelligence*. Princeton: Princeton University Press.

Brodbeck C, Hong LE, Simon JZ (2018) Rapid transformation from auditory to linguistic representations of continuous speech. *Current Biology* 28:3976–3983.e5.

Brysbaert M, Stevens M, Mandera P, Keuleers E (2016) How many words do we know? Practical estimates of vocabulary size dependent on word definition, the degree of language input and the participant's age. *Frontiers in Psychology* 7:1116.

Buchsbaum BR, Hickok G, Humphries C (2001) Role of left posterior superior temporal gyrus in phonological processing for speech perception and production. *Cognitive Science* 25:663–678.

Buckner RL, Krienen FM, Castellanos A, Diaz JC, Yeo BT (2011) The organization of the human cerebellum estimated by intrinsic functional connectivity. *Journal of Neurophysiology* 106:2322–2345.

Bucur M, Papagno C (2021) An ALE meta-analytical review of the neural correlates of abstract and concrete words. *Scientific Reports* 11:15727.

Buschman TJ, Miller EK (2022) Working memory is complex and dynamic, like your thoughts. *Journal of Cognitive Neuroscience* 35:17–23.

Campbell KL, Samu D, Davis SW, Geerligs L, Mustafa A, Tyler LK, Cam-CAN (2016) Robust resilience of the frontotemporal syntax system to aging. *Journal of Neuroscience* 36:5214–5227.

Capitani E, Laiacona M, Mahon B, Caramazza A (2003) What are the facts of semantic category-specific deficits? A critical review of the clinical evidence. *Cognitive Neuropsychology* 20:213–261.

Caramazza A, Hillis AE, Rapp BC, Romani C (1990) The multiple semantics hypothesis: multiple confusions? *Cognitive Neuropsychology* 7:161–189.

Carey D, McGettigan C (2017) Magnetic resonance imaging of the brain and vocal tract: applications to the study of speech production and language learning. *Neuropsychologia* 98:201–211.

Caselli NK, Emmorey K, Cohen-Goldberg AM (2021) The signed mental lexicon: effects of phonological neighborhood density, iconicity, and childhood language experience. *Journal of Memory and Language* 121:104282.

Caselli N, Pyers J, Lieberman AM (2021) Deaf children of hearing parents have age-level vocabulary growth when exposed to American Sign Language by 6 months of age. *The Journal of Pediatrics* 232:229–236.

Caspers S, Geyer S, Schleicher A, Mohlberg H, Amunts K, Zilles K (2006) The human inferior parietal cortex: cytoarchitectonic parcellation and interindividual variability. *NeuroImage* 33:430–448.

Casseday JH, Fremouw T, Covey E (2002) The inferior colliculus: a hub for the central auditory system. In *Integrative Functions in the Mammalian Auditory Pathway* (Oertel D, Fay RR, Popper AN, eds.), pp 238–318. Springer Handbook on Auditory Research. New York, NY: Springer New York.

Castellucci GA, Kovach CK, Howard MA, III, Greenlee JDW, Long MA, (2022) A speech planning network for interactive language use. *Nature* 602:117–122.

Catani M, Jones DK, ffytche DH (2004) Perisylvian language networks of the human brain. *Annals of Neurology* 57:8–16.

Chandrasekaran B, Skoe E, Kraus N (2014) An integrative model of subcortical auditory plasticity. *Brain Topography* 27:539–552.

Chandrasekaran B, Tessmer R, Nike Gnanateja G (2022) Subcortical processing of speech sounds. In *Speech Perception* (Holt LL, Peelle JE, Coffin AB, Popper AN, Fay RR, eds.), pp. 13–44. Springer Handbook of Auditory Research volume 74. Springer International Publishing.

Chandrasekaran C, Trubanova A, Stillittano S, Caplier A, Ghazanfar AA (2009) The natural statistics of audiovisual speech. *PLoS Computational Biology* 5: e1000436.

Chang EF, Niziolek CA, Knight RT, Nagarajan SS, Houde JF (2013) Human cortical sensorimotor network underlying feedback control of vocal pitch. *Proceedings of the National Academy of Sciences* 110:2653–2658.

Chenausky K, Paquette S, Norton A, Schlaug G (2020) Apraxia of speech involves lesions of dorsal arcuate fasciculus and insula in patients with aphasia. *Neurology: Clinical Practice* 10:162–169.

Code C (2013) Did Leborgne have one or two speech automatisms? *Journal of the History of Neurosciences* 22:319–320.

Coffey EBJ, Nicol T, White-Schwoch T, Chandrasekaran B, Krizman J, Skoe E, Zatorre RJ, Kraus N (2019) Evolving perspectives on the sources of the frequency-following response. *Nature Communications* 10:5036.

Cohen L, Dehaene S, Naccache L, Lehéricy S, Dehaene-Lambertz G, Hénaff MA, Michel F (2000) The visual word form area: spatial and temporal characterization of an initial stage of reading in normal subjects and posterior split-brain patients. *Brain* 123:291–307.

Cooke A, Zurif EB, DeVita C, Alsop D, Koenig P, Detre J, Gee J, Pinango M, Balogh J, Grossman M (2002) Neural basis for sentence comprehension: grammatical and short-term memory components. *Human Brain Mapping* 15:80–94.

Corina DP, McBurney SL, Dodrill C, Hinshaw K, Brinkley J, Ojemann G (1999) Functional roles of Broca's area and SMG: evidence from cortical stimulation mapping in a deaf signer. *NeuroImage* 10:570–581.

Corkin S (1965) Tactually-guided maze learning in man: effects of unilateral cortical excisions and bilateral hippocampal lesions. *Neuropsychologia* 3:339–351.

Crosson B, Sadek JR, Maron L, Gokcay D, Mohr CM, Auerbach EJ, Freeman AJ, Leonard CM, Briggs RW (2001) Relative shift in activity from medial to lateral frontal cortex during internally versus externally guided word generation. *Journal of Cognitive Neuroscience* 13:272–283.

Crutch SJ (2006) Qualitatively different semantic representations for abstract and concrete words: further evidence from the semantic reading errors of deep dyslexic patients. *Neurocase* 12:91–97.

Crutch SJ, Warrington EK (2005) Abstract and concrete concepts have structurally different representational frameworks. *Brain* 128:615–627.

Cummins F (2012) Oscillators and syllables: a cautionary note. *Frontiers in Psychology* 3:364.

Cutler A, Isard SD (1980) The production of prosody. In *Language Production*, pp 245–269. Academic Press.

D'Anna CA, Zechmeister EB, Hall JW (1991) Toward a meaningful definition of vocabulary size. *Journal of Reading Behavior* 23: 109–122.

Davis MH, Di Betta AM, Macdonald MJE, Gaskell MG (2009) Learning and consolidation of novel spoken words. *Journal of Cognitive Neuroscience* 21: 803–820. https://doi.org/10.1162/jocn.2009.21059.

Davis MH, Ford MA, Kherif F, Johnsrude IS (2011) Does semantic context benefit speech understanding through "top-down" processes? Evidence from time-resolved sparse fMRI. *Journal of Cognitive Neuroscience* 23:3914–3932.

Davis MH, Gaskell MG (2009) A complementary systems account of word learning: neural and behavioural evidence. *Philosophical transactions of the Royal Society of London. Series B, Biological sciences* 364: 3773–3800.

Davis MH, Johnsrude IS (2003) Hierarchical processing in spoken language comprehension. *Journal of Neuroscience* 23:3423–3431.

Davis SW, Zhuang J, Wright P, Tyler LK (2014) Age-related sensitivity to task-related modulation of language-processing networks. *Neuropsychologia* 63:107–115.

Day BL, Fitzpatrick RC (2005) The vestibular system. *Current Biology* 15: R583–586.

de Ruiter J-P, Mitterer H, Enfield NJ (2006) Projecting the end of a speaker's turn: a cognitive cornerstone of conversation. *Language* 82:515–535.

Dehaene S, Cohen L (2007) Cultural recycling of cortical maps. *Neuron* 56:384–398.

Denes PB, Pinson EN (1993) *The Speech Chain: The Physics and Biology of Spoken Language*. Long Grove, IL: Waveland Press.

Devlin JT, Poldrack RA (2007) In praise of tedious anatomy. *NeuroImage* 37:1033–1041.

Devlin JT, Russell RP, Davis MH, Price CJ, Moss HE, Fadili MJ, Tyler LK (2002) Is there an anatomical basis for category-specificity? Semantic memory studies in PET and fMRI. *Neuropsychologia* 40:54–75.

Diachek E, Blank I, Siegelman M, Affourtit J, Fedorenko E (2020) The domain-general multiple demand (MD) network does not support core aspects of language comprehension: a large-scale fMRI investigation. *Journal of Neuroscience* 40:4536–4550.

Dick FK, Lehet MI, Callaghan MF, Keller TA, Sereno MI, Holt LL (2017) Extensive tonotopic mapping across auditory cortex is recapitulated by spectrally directed attention and systematically related to cortical myeloarchitecture. *Journal of Neuroscience* 37:12187–12201.

Dick F, Tierney AT, Lutti A, Josephs O, Sereno MI, Weiskopf N (2012) In vivo functional and myeloarchitectonic mapping of human primary auditory areas. *Journal of Neuroscience* 32:16095–16105.

Dilley LC, Pitt MA (2010) Altering context speech rate can cause words to appear and disappear. *Psychological Science* 21:1664–1670.

Ding N, Melloni L, Zhang H, Tian X, Poeppel D (2016) Cortical tracking of hierarchical linguistic structures in connected speech. *Nature Neuroscience* 19:158–164.

Dix MR, Hallpike CS (1947) The peep shows: new technique for pure-tone audiometry in young children. *British Medical Journal* 2:719–723.

Duncan J (2010) The multiple-demand (MD) system of the primate brain: mental programs for intelligent behaviour. *Trends in Cognitive Sciences* 14:172–179.

Donders, FC (1868/1969). Over de snelheid van psychische processen. (On the speed of mental processes.) (W. Koster, Trans.). In W. G. Koster, *Attention and Performance II* (pp. 412–431). Amsterdam: North Holland.

Drew PJ (2022) Neurovascular coupling: motive unknown. *Trends in Neuroscience* 45:809–819.

Drijvers L, Özyürek A (2017) Visual context enhanced: the joint contribution of iconic gestures and visible speech to degraded speech comprehension. *Journal of Speech, Language, and Hearing Research* 60:212–222.

Durfee AZ, Sheppard SM, Blake ML, Hillis AE (2021) Lesion loci of impaired affective prosody: a systematic review of evidence from stroke. *Brain and Cognition* 152:105759.

Gordon EM, Laumann TO, Gilmore AW, et al. (2017) Precision functional mapping of individual human brains. *Neuron* 95:791–807.

Devlin JT, Raley J, Tunbridge E, Lanary K, Floyer-Lea A, Narain C, Cohen I, Behrens T, Jezzard P, Matthews PM, Moore DR (2003) Functional asymmetry for auditory processing in human primary auditory cortex. *Journal of Neuroscience* 23:11516–11522.

Dockès J, Poldrack RA, Primet R, Gozukan H, Yarkoni T, Suchanek F, Thirion B, Varoquaux G (2020) NeuroQuery, comprehensive meta-analysis of human brain mapping. *eLife* 9:e53385.

Doupe AJ, Kuhl PK (1999) Birdsong and human speech: common themes and mechanisms. *Annual Review of Neuroscience* 22:567–631.

Dronkers NF (1996) A new brain region for coordinating speech articulation. *Nature* 384:159–161.

Dronkers NF (October, 2023) Lesion-symptom mapping and the neurobiology of language. Annual meeting of the Society for the Neurobiology of Language in Marseilles, France.

Dronkers NF, Plaisant O, Iba-Zizen MT, Cabanis EA (2007) Paul Broca's historic cases: high resolution MR imaging of the brains of Leborgne and Lelong. *Brain* 130:1432–1441.

Dumay N, Gaskell MG (2007) Sleep-associated changes in the mental representation of spoken words. *Psychological Science* 18(1): 35–39.

Duncan J (2010) The multiple-demand (MD) system of the primate brain: mental programs for intelligent behaviour. *Trends in Cognitive Science* 14:172–179.

Duncan J, Owen AM (2000) Common regions of the human frontal lobe recruited by diverse cognitive demands. *Trends in Neuroscience* 23:475–483.

Eggebrecht AT, Ferradal SL, Robichaux-Viehoever A, Hassanpour MS, Dehghani H, Snyder AZ, Hershey T, Culver JP (2014) Mapping distributed brain function and networks with diffuse optical tomography. *Nature Photonics* 8:448–454.

Eickhoff S, Stephan K, Mohlberg H, Grefkes C, Fink G, Amunts K, Zilles K (2005) A new SPM toolbox for combining probabilistic cytoarchitectonic maps and functional imaging data. *NeuroImage* 25:1325–1335.

Emmorey K (2021) New perspectives on the neurobiology of sign languages. *Frontiers in Communication* 6:748430.

Emmorey K (2023) Ten things you should know about sign languages. *Current Directions in Psychological Science* 32:387–394.

Evans S, Kyong JS, Rosen S, Golestani N, Warren JE, McGettigan C, Mourão-Miranda J, Wise RJS, Scott SK (2014) The pathways for intelligible speech: multivariate and univariate perspectives. *Cerebral Cortex* 24:2350–2361.

Falchier A, Clavagnier S, Barone P, Kennedy H (2002) Anatomical evidence of multimodal integration in primate striate cortex. *Journal of Neuroscience* 22:5749–5759.

Fedorenko E, Duncan J, Kanwisher NG (2012) Language-selective and domain-general regions lie side by side within Broca's area. *Current Biology* 22:2059–2062.

Fedorenko E, Hsieh P-J, Nieto-Castañón A, Whitfield-Gabrieli S, Kanwishser N (2010) New method for fMRI investigations of language: defining ROIs functionally in individual subjects. *Journal of Neurophysiology* 104:1177–1194.

Felleman DJ, Van Essen DC (1991) Distributed hierarchical processing in the primate cerebral cortex. *Cerebral Cortex* 1:1–47.

Ferreira F, Bailey KGD, Ferraro V (2002) Good-enough representations in language comprehension. *Current Directions in Psychological Science* 11:11–15.

Fiebach CJ, Schlesewsky M, Lohmann G, von Cramon DY, Friederici AD (2005) Revisiting the role of Broca's area in sentence processing: syntactic integration versus syntactic working memory. *Human Brain Mapping* 24:79–91.

Fiez JA, Petersen SE, Cheney MK, Raichle ME (1992) Impaired non-motor learning and error detection associated with cerebellar damage. A single case study. *Brain* 115:155–178.

Finger S, Roe D (1999) Does Gustave Dax deserve to be forgotten? The temporal lobe theory and other contributions of an overlooked figure in the history of language and cerebral dominance. *Brain and Language* 69:16–30.

Fischl B, Rajendran N, Busa E, Augustinack J, Hinds O, Yeo BTT, Mohlberg H, Amunts K, Zilles K (2008) Cortical folding patterns and predicting cytoarchitecture. *Cerebral Cortex* 18:1973–1980.

Flake JK, Fried EI (2020) Measurement schmeasurement: questionable measurement practices and how to avoid them. *Advances in Methods and Practices in Psychological Science* 3:456–465.

Flinker A, Korzeniewska A, Shestyuk AY, Franaszczuk PJ, Dronkers NF, Knight RT, Crone NE (2015) Redefining the role of Broca's area in speech. *Proceedings of the National Academy of Sciences* 112:2871–2875.

Flores LP (2002) Occipital lobe morphological anatomy: anatomical and surgical aspects. *Arquivos de Neuro-Psiquiatria* 60(3-A): 566–571. https://doi.org/ 10.1590/S0004-282X2002000400010.

Flurie M, Ungrady M, Reilly J (2020) Evaluating a maintenance-based treatment approach to preventing lexical dropout in progressive anomia. *Journal of Speech, Language, and Hearing Research* 63:4082–4095.

Fridriksson J, Rorden C, Elm J, Sen S, George MS, Bonilha L (2018) Transcranial direct current stimulation vs sham stimulation to treat aphasia after stroke: a randomized clinical trial. *JAMA Neurology* 75:1470–1476.

Friederici A (2018) The neural basis for human syntax: Broca's area and beyond. *Current Opinion in Behavioral Sciences* 21:88–92.

Friederici AD, Fiebach CJ, Schlesewsky M, Bornkessel ID, von Cramon DY (2006) Processing linguistic complexity and grammaticality in the left frontal cortex. *Cerebral Cortex* 16:1709–1717.

Friederici AD, Ruschemeyer SA, Hahne A, Fiebach CJ (2003) The role of left inferior frontal and superior temporal cortex in sentence comprehension: localizing syntactic and semantic processes. *Cerebral Cortex* 13:170–177.

Fries P (2015) Rhythms for cognition: communication through coherence. *Neuron* 88:220–235.

Friston K (2005) A theory of cortical responses. *Philosophical Transactions of the Royal Society B* 360:815–836.

Friston KJ (2011) Functional and effective connectivity: a review. *Brain Connectivity* 1:13–36.

Friston KJ, Price CJ, Fletcher P, Moore C, Frackowiak RS, Dolan RJ (1996) The trouble with cognitive subtraction. *NeuroImage* 4:97–104.

Gage N, Hickok G (2005) Multiregional cell assemblies, temporal binding and the representation of conceptual knowledge in cortex: a modern theory by a "classical" neurologist, Carl Wernicke. *Cortex* 41:823–832.

Gagnepain P, Henson RN, Davis MH (2012) Temporal predictive codes for spoken words in auditory cortex. *Current Biology* 22:615–621.

Garrett MF (1975) The analysis of sentence production. In *Psychology of Learning and Motivation* (Bower GH, ed.), pp 133–177. San Diego, CA: Academic Press.

Gaskell MG, Dumay N (2003) Lexical competition and the acquisition of novel words. *Cognition* 89(2):105–132.

Gazzaniga MS, Bogen JE, Sperry RW (1962) Some functional effects of sectioning the cerebral commissures in man. *Proceedings of the National Academy of Sciences* 48:1765–1769.

Gazzaniga MS, Bogen JE, Sperry RW (1965) Observations on visual perception after disconnexion of the cerebral hemispheres in man. *Brain* 88:221–236.

Geschwind N (1965a) Disconnexion syndromes in animals and man. I. *Brain* 88:237–294.

Geschwind N (1965b) Disconnexion syndromes in animals and man. II. *Brain* 88:585–644.

Ghitza O (2011) Linking speech perception and neurophysiology: speech decoding guided by cascaded oscillators locked to the input rhythm. *Frontiers in Psychology* 2:130.

Ghitza O, Greenberg S (2009) On the possible role of brain rhythms in speech perception: intelligibility of time-compressed speech with periodic and aperiodic insertions of silence. *Phonetica* 66:113–126.

Giglio L, Ostarek M, Weber K, Hagoort P (2022) Commonalities and asymmetries in the neurobiological infrastructure for language production and comprehension. *Cerebral Cortex* 32:1405–1418.

Giraud AL, Neumann K, Bachoud-Levi AC, von Gudenberg AW, Euler HA, Lanfermann H, Preibisch C (2008) Severity of dysfluency correlates with basal ganglia activity in persistent developmental stuttering. *Brain and Language* 104:190–199.

Giraud A-L, Poeppel D (2012) Cortical oscillations and speech processing: emerging computational principles and operations. *Nature Neuroscience* 15:511–517.

Gjorgjieva J, Drion G, Marder E (2016) Computational implications of biophysical diversity and multiple timescales in neurons and synapses for circuit performance. *Current Opinion in Neurobiology* 37:44–52.

Goldin-Meadow S (2014) Widening the lens: what the manual modality reveals about language, learning and cognition. *Philosophical Transactions of the Royal Society B: Biological Sciences* 369:20130295.

Goldwyn RM (1969) Guillaume Dupuytren: his character and contributions. *Bulletin of the New York Academy of Medicine* 45:750–760.

Golinkoff RM, Ma W, Song L, Hirsh-Pasek K (2013) Twenty-five years using the intermodal preferential looking paradigm to study language acquisition: what have we learned? *Perspectives in Psychological Sciences* 8:316–339.

Golfinopoulos E, Tourville JA, Bohland JW, Ghosh SS, Nieto-Castanon A, Guenther FH (2011) fMRI investigation of unexpected somatosensory feedback perturbation during speech. *NeuroImage* 55:1324–1338.

Golub JS, Brickman AM, Ciarleglio AJ, Schupf N, Luchsinger JA (2019) Association of subclinical hearing loss with cognitive performance. *JAMA Otolaryngology–Head and Neck Surgery.* http://dx.doi.org/10.1001/jamaoto.2019.3375.

Gorno-Tempini ML, Dronkers NF, Rankin KP, Ogar JM, Phengrasamy L, Rosen HJ, Johnson JK, Weiner MW, Miller BL (2004) Cognition and anatomy in three variants of primary progressive aphasia. *Annals of Neurology* 55:335–346.

Goswami U (2011) A temporal sampling framework for developmental dyslexia. *Trends in Cognitive Sciences* 15:3–10.

Gracco VL (1988) Timing factors in the coordination of speech movements. *Journal of Neuroscience* 8:4628–4639.

Gracco VL, Lofqvist A (1994) Speech motor coordination and control: evidence from lip, jaw, and laryngeal movements. *Journal of Neuroscience* 14:6585–6597.

Gratton C, Kraus BT, Greene DJ, Gordon EM, Laumann TO, Nelson SM, Dosenbach NUF, Petersen SE (2020) Defining individual-specific functional neuroanatomy for precision psychiatry. *Biological Psychiatry* 88:28–39.

Grossman M (2018) Linguistic aspects of primary progressive aphasia. *Annual Reviews of Linguistics* 4:377–403.

Grossman M, Rhee J, Moore P (2005) Sentence processing in frontotemporal dementia. *Cortex* 41:764–777.

Grossman M, Seeley WW, Boxer AL, Hillis AE, Knopman DS, Ljubenov PA, Miller B, Piguet O, Rademakers R, Whitwell JL, Zetterberg H, van Swieten JC (2023) Frontotemporal lobar degeneration. *Nature Reviews Disease Primers* 9:40.

Guenther FH (1995) Speech sound acquisition, coarticulation, and rate effects in a neural network model of speech production. *Psychological Review* 102:594–621.

Guenther FH, Ghosh SS, Tourville JA (2006) Neural modeling and imaging of the cortical interactions underlying syllable production. *Brain and Language* 96:280–301.

Gutierrez GJ, O'Leary T, Marder E (2013) Multiple mechanisms switch an electrically coupled, synaptically inhibited neuron between competing rhythmic oscillators. *Neuron* 77:845–858.

Hackett TA (2011) Information flow in the auditory cortical network. *Hearing Research* 271:133–146.

Hackett TA, Stepniewska I, Kaas JH (1998) Subdivisions of auditory cortex and ipsilateral cortical connections of the parabelt auditory cortex in macaque monkeys. *Journal of Comparative Neurology* 394:475–495.

Hall WC (2017) What you don't know can hurt you: the risk of language deprivation by impairing sign language development in deaf children. *Maternal and Child Health Journal* 21:961–965.

Hebb DO (1949) *The Organization of Behavior.* New York: Wiley & Sons.

Henke L, Lewis AG, Meyer L (2023) Fast and slow rhythms of naturalistic reading revealed by combined eye-tracking and electroencephalography. *Journal of Neuroscience* 43:4461–4469.

Henkel G (2013) History of the cochlear implant. *ENTtoday* 13. www.enttoday.org/article/history-of-the-cochlear-implant/?singlepage=1.

Henson R (2005) What can functional neuroimaging tell the experimental psychologist? *Quarterly Journal of Experimental Psychology* 58A:193–233.

Herculano-Houzel S (2010) Coordinated scaling of cortical and cerebellar numbers of neurons. *Frontiers in Neuroanatomy* 4:12.

Heynckes M, Gulban OF, De Martino F (2022) On the superior temporal gyrus by R.L. Heschl: English translation of "Über Die Vordere Quere Schläfenwindung Des Menschlichen Großhirns." *Brain Multiphysics* 3:100055.

Hickok G (2012) Computational neuroanatomy of speech production. *Nature Reviews Neuroscience* 13:135–145.

Hickok G, Bellugi U, Klima ES (1996) The neurobiology of sign language and its implications for the neural basis of language. *Nature* 381:699–702.

Hickok G, Bellugi U, Klima ES (1998) The neural organization of language: evidence from sign language aphasia. *Trends in Cognitive Sciences* 2:129–136.

Hickok G, Okada K, Barr W, Pa J, Rogalsky C, Donnelly K, Barde L, Grant A (2008) Bilateral capacity for speech sound processing in auditory comprehension: evidence from Wada procedures. *Brain and Language* 107:179–184.

Hickok G, Okada K, Serences JT (2009) Area Spt in the human planum temporale supports sensory-motor integration for speech processing. *Journal of Neurophysiology* 101:2725–2732.

Hickok G, Poeppel D (2000) Towards a functional neuroanatomy of speech perception. *Trends in Cognitive Sciences* 4:131–138.

Hickok G, Poeppel D (2004) Dorsal and ventral streams: a framework for understanding aspects of the functional anatomy of language. *Cognition* 92:67–99.

Hickok G, Poeppel D (2007) The cortical organization of speech processing. *Nature Reviews Neuroscience* 8:393–402.

Hickok G, Rogalsky C, Matchin W, Basilakos A, Cai J, Pillay S, Ferrill M, Mickelsen S, Anderson SW, Love T, Binder J, Fridriksson J (2018) Neural networks supporting audiovisual integration for speech: a large-scale lesion study. *Cortex* 103:360–371.

Hillis AE, Newhart M, Heidler J, Barker P, Herskovits E, Degaonkar M (2005) The roles of the "visual word form area" in reading. *NeuroImage* 24:548–559.

Hillis AE, Work M, Barker PB, Jacobs MA, Breese EL, Maurer K (2004) Re-examining the brain regions crucial for orchestrating speech articulation. *Brain* 127:1479–1487.

Hippocrates. *On the Sacred Disease* (Translated by Francis Adams). https://one morelibrary.com/index.php/en/books/technology/book/medicine-314/on-the-sacred-disease-2433.

Hodges JR, Patterson K (2007) Semantic dementia: a unique clinicopathological syndrome. *The Lancet Neurology* 6:1001–1014.

Holler J, Kokal I, Toni I, Hagoort P, Kelly SD, Özyürek A (2015) Eye'm talking to you: speakers' gaze direction modulates co-speech gesture processing in the right MTG. *Social Cognitive and Affective Neuroscience* 10:255–261.

Holmes G (1917) The symptoms of acute cerebellar injuries due to gunshot injuries. *Brain* 40:461–535.

Holt LL (2005) Temporally nonadjacent nonlinguistic sounds affect speech categorization. *Psychological Science* 16:305–312.

Houde JF, Jordan MI (1998) Sensorimotor adaptation in speech production. *Science* 279:1213–1216.

Hoyte KJ, Kim A, Brownell H, Wingfield A (2004) Effects of right hemisphere brain injury on the use of components of prosody for syntactic comprehension. *Brain and Language* 91:168–169.

Humphries C, Binder JR, Medler DA, Liebenthal E (2007) Time course of semantic processes during sentence comprehension: an fMRI study. *NeuroImage* 36:924–932.

Iadecola C (2017) The neurovascular unit coming of age: a journey through neurovascular coupling in health and disease. *Neuron* 96:17–42.

Idemaru K, Holt LL (2011) Word recognition reflects dimension-based statistical learning. *Journal of Experimental Psychology: Human Perception and Performance* 37:1939–1956.

Ishai A, Ungerleider LG, Martin A, Schouten JL, Haxby JV (1999) Distributed representation of objects in the human ventral visual pathway. *Proceedings of the National Academy of Sciences* 96:9379–9384.

Ishai A, Ungerleider LG, Martin A, Haxby JV (2000) The representation of objects in the human occipital and temporal cortex. *Journal of Cognitive Neuroscience* 12 Suppl 2:35–51.

James W (1890) *The Principles of Psychology.* New York: Henry Holt and Company.

Jaquemot C, Pallier C, LeBihan D, Dehaene S, Dupoux E (2003) Phonological grammar shapes the auditory cortex: a functional magnetic resonance imaging study. *The Journal of Neuroscience* 23:9541–9546.

Jerger J (2013) Why the audiogram is upside-down. *International Journal of Audiology* 52:146–150.

Jones AB, Farrall AJ, Belin P, Pernet CR (2015) Hemispheric association and dissociation of voice and speech information processing in stroke. *Cortex* 71:232–239.

Just MA, Carpenter PA (1980) A theory of reading: from eye fixations to comprehension. *Psychological Review* 87:329–354.

Kaas JH, Hackett TA, Tramo MJ (1999) Auditory processing in primate cerebral cortex. *Current Opinion in Neurobiology* 9:164–170.

Kandel E, Koester JD, Mack SH, Siegelbaum S (2021) *Principles of Neural Science, Sixth Edition*. New York: McGraw Hill.

Kanwisher N, McDermott J, Chun MM (1997) The fusiform face area: A module in human extrastriate cortex specialized for face perception. *Journal of Neuroscience* 17:4302–4311.

Kapnoula EC, Winn MB, Kong EJ, Edwards J, McMurray B (2017) Evaluating the sources and functions of gradiency in phoneme categorization: an individual differences approach. *Journal of Experimental Psychology: Human Perception and Performance* 43:1594–1611.

Kearney E, Guenther FH (2019) Articulating: the neural mechanisms of speech production. *Language, Cognition and Neuroscience* 34:1214–1229.

Keller SS, Crow T, Foundas A, Amunts K, Roberts N (2009) Broca's area: nomenclature, anatomy, typology and asymmetry. *Brain and Language* 109:29–48.

Kelly SD, Özyürek A, Maris E (2010) Two sides of the same coin: speech and gesture mutually interact to enhance comprehension. *Psychological Science* 21:260–267.

Kimura D, Battison R, Lubert B (1976) Impairment of nonlinguistic hand movements in a deaf aphasic. *Brain and Language* 3:566–571.

Kinchla RA, Wolfe JM (1979) The order of visual processing: "Top-down," "bottom-up," or "middle-out." *Perception and Psychophysics* 25:225–231.

Kong EJ, Edwards J (2016) Individual differences in categorical perception of speech: cue weighting and executive function. *Journal of Phonetics* 59:40–57.

Kösem A, Bosker HR, Takashima A, Meyer A, Jensen O, Hagoort P (2018) Neural entrainment determines the words we hear. *Current Biology* 28:2867–2875.e3.

Kosilo M, Costa M, Nuttall HE, Ferreira H, Scott S, Menéres S, Pestana J, Jerónimo R, Prata D (2021) The neural basis of authenticity recognition in laughter and crying. *Scientific Reports* 11:23750.

Kozachkov L, Lundqvist M, Slotine JJ, Miller EK (2020) Achieving stable dynamics in neural circuits. *PLoS Computational Biology* 16:e1007659.

Kraus N, Chandrasekaran B (2010) Music training for the development of auditory skills. *Nature Reviews Neuroscience* 11:599–605.

Kriegeskorte N, Mur M, Bandettini P (2008) Representational similarity analysis: connecting the branches of systems neuroscience. *Frontiers in Systems Neuroscience* 2:4.

Kriegeskorte N, Mur M, Ruff DA, Kiani R, Bodurka J, Esteky H, Tanaka K, Bandettini PA (2008) Matching categorical object representations in inferior temporal cortex of man and monkey. *Neuron* 60:1126–1141.

Krishnan A, Xu Y, Gandour J, Cariani P (2005) Encoding of pitch in the human brainstem is sensitive to language experience. *Cognitive Brain Research* 25:161–168.

Kubota EC, Joo SJ, Huber E, Yeatman JD (2019) Word selectivity in high-level visual cortex and reading skill. *Developmental Cognitive Neuroscience* 36:100593.

Kuhl PK, Williams KA, Lacerda F, Stevens KN, Lindblom B (1992) Linguistic experience alters phonetic perception in infants by 6 months of age. *Science* 255:606–608.

Kushner HI (2015) Norman Geschwind and the use of history in the (re)birth of behavioral neurology. *Journal of the History of the Neurosciences* 24:173–192.

Laird AR, Fox PM, Price CJ, Glahn DC, Uecker AM, Lancaster JL, Turkeltaub PE, Kochunov P, Fox PT (2005) ALE meta-analysis: controlling the false discovery rate and performing statistical contrasts. *Human Brain Mapping* 25:155–164.

Lakatos P, Shah AS, Knuth KH, Ulbert I, Karmos G, Schroeder CE (2005) An oscillatory hierarchy controlling neuronal excitability and stimulus processing in the auditory cortex. *Journal of Neurophysiology* 94:1904–1911.

Landauer TK, Dumais ST (1997) A solution to Plato's problem: the latent semantic analysis theory of acquisition, induction, and representation of knowledge. *Psychological Review* 104:211–240.

Lane H, Tranel B (1971) The Lombard sign and the role of hearing in speech. *Journal of Speech and Hearing Research* 14:677–709.

LaPointe, LL (2013) *Paul Broca and the Origins of Language in the Brain.* Abingdon: Plural Publishing.

Latinus M, McAleer P, Bestelmeyer PE, Belin P (2013) Norm-based coding of voice identity in human auditory cortex. *Current Biology* 23:1075–1080.

Lauterbur PC (1973) Image formation by induced local interactions: Examples employing nuclear magnetic resonance. *Nature* 242:190–191.

Lavan N, Rankin G, Lorking N, Scott S, McGettigan C (2017) Neural correlates of the affective properties of spontaneous and volitional laughter types. *Neuropsychologia* 95:30–39.

Lavan N, Scott SK, McGettigan C (2016) Laugh like you mean it: authenticity modulates acoustic, physiological and perceptual properties of laughter. *Journal of Nonverbal Behavior* 40:133–149.

Leiner HC, Leiner AL, Dow RS. Does the cerebellum contribute to mental skills? (1986) *Behavioral Neuroscience* 100:443–454.

Leonard MK, Gwilliams L, Sellers KK, Chung JE, Xu D, Mischler G, Mesgarani N, Welkenhuysen M, Dutta B, Chang EF (2023) Large-scale single-neuron speech sound encoding across the depth of human cortex. *Nature*. https://doi.org/10.1038/s41586-023-06839-2.

Leonard MK, Lucas B, Blau S, Corina DP, Chang EF (2020) Cortical encoding of manual articulatory and linguistic features in American Sign Language. *Current Biology* 30:4342–4351.

Leonard MK, Ferjan Ramirez N, Torres C, Travis KE, Hatrak M, Mayberry RI, Halgren E (2012) Signed words in the congenitally deaf evoke typical late lexicosemantic responses with no early visual responses in left superior temporal cortex. *Journal of Neuroscience* 32:9700–9705.

Levelt WJM (1989) *Speaking: From Intention to Articulation.* Cambridge, MA: MIT Press.

Levelt WJM, Roelofs A, Meyer AS (1999) A theory of lexical access in speech production. *Behavioral and Brain Sciences* 22:1–75.

Levinson SC (2016) Turn-taking in human communication: origins and implications for language processing. *Trends in Cognitive Science* 20:6–14.

Lewis JW, Van Essen DC (2000) Corticocortical connections of visual, sensorimotor, and multimodal processing areas in the parietal lobe of the macaque monkey. *Journal of Comparative Neurology* 428:112–137.

Liebenthal E, Binder JR, Spitzer SM, Possing ET, Medler DA (2005) Neural substrates of phonemic perception. *Cerebral Cortex* 15:1621–1631.

Lillo-Martin D, Henner J (2021) Acquisition of sign languages. *Annual Review of Linguistics* 7:395–419.

Lima CF, Krishnan S, Scott SK (2016) Roles of supplementary motor areas in auditory processing and auditory imagery. *Trends in Neurosciences* 39:527–542.

Limb CJ, Roy AT (2014) Technological, biological, and acoustical constraints to music perception in cochlear implant users. *Hearing Research* 308:13–26.

Lin FR, Albert M (2014) Hearing loss and dementia: who is listening? *Aging & Mental Health* 18:671–673.

Lin FR, Metter J, O'Brien RJ, Resnick SM, Zonderman AB, Ferrucci L (2011) Hearing loss and incident dementia. *Archives of Neurology* 68:214–220.

Lin FR, Yaffe K, Xia J, Xue Q-L, Harris TB, Purchase-Helzner E, Satterfield S, Ayonayon HN, Ferrucci L, Simonsick EM (2013) Hearing loss and cognitive decline in older adults. *JAMA Internal Medicine* 173:293–299.

Logothetis NK, Pauls J, Augath M, Trinath T, Oeltermann A (2001) Neurophysiological investigation of the basis of the fMRI signal. *Nature* 412:150–157.

Luce PA, Pisoni DB (1998) Recognizing spoken words: the neighborhood activation model. *Ear and Hearing* 19:1–36.

Luo H, Poeppel D (2007) Phase patterns of neuronal responses reliably discriminate speech in human auditory cortex. *Neuron* 54:1001–1010.

Lynott D, Connell L, Brysbaert M, Brand J, Carney J (2020) The Lancaster Sensorimotor Norms: multidimensional measures of perceptual and action strength for 40,000 English words. *Behavior Research Methods* 52:1271–1291.

MacDonald (2018) Hearing lips and seeing voices: the origins and development of the "McGurk Effect" and reflections on audio-visual speech perception over the last 40 years. *Multisensory Research* 31:7–18. https://brill.com/view/journals/msr/31/1-2/article-p7_2.xml.

MacGregor LJ, Gilbert RA, Balewski Z, Mitchell DJ, Erzinclioglu SW, Rodd JM, Duncan J, Fedorenko E, Davis MH (2022) Causal contributions of the domain-general (Multiple Demand) and the language-selective brain networks to perceptual and semantic challenges in speech comprehension. *Neurobiology of Language* 3:665–698.

MacSweeney M, Capek CM, Campbell R, Woll B (2008) The signing brain: the neurobiology of sign language. *Trends in Cognitive Sciences* 12:432–440.

MacSweeney M, Woll B, Campbell R, McGuire PK, David AS, Williams SC, Suckling J, Calvert GA, Brammer MJ (2002) Neural systems underlying British Sign Language and audio-visual English processing in native users. *Brain* 125:1583–1593.

Maguire EA, Gadian DG, Johnsrude IS, Good CD, Ashburner J, Frackowiak RSJ, Frith CD (2000) Navigation-related structural change in the hippocampi of taxi drivers. *Proceedings of the National Academy of Sciences* 97:4398–4403.

Mandonnet E, Sarubbo S, Petit L (2018) The nomenclature of human white matter association pathways: proposal for a systematic taxonomic anatomical classification. *Frontiers in Neuroanatomy* 12:94.

Manning L, Thomas-Anterion C (2011) Marc Dax and the discovery of the lateralisation of language in the left cerebral hemisphere. *Revue Neurologique* 167:868–872.

Marder E (2000) My word: colored chalk. *Current Biology* 10(17): R613.

Mariën P, Ackermann H, Adamaszek M, et al. (2014) Consensus paper: language and the cerebellum – an ongoing enigma. *Cerebellum* 13:386–410.

Marinkovic K, Dhond RP, Dale AM, Glessner M, Carr V, Halgren E (2003) Spatiotemporal dynamics of modality-specific and supramodal word processing. *Neuron* 38:487–497.

Marsh JT, Worden FG, Smith JC (1970) Auditory frequency-following response: neural or artifact? *Science* 169:1222–1223.

Marslen-Wilson WD (1975) Sentence perception as an interactive parallel process. *Science* 189:226–228.

Marslen-Wilson WD (1987) Functional parallelism in spoken word recognition. *Cognition* 25:71–102.

Marslen-Wilson WD, Tyler LK (1980) The temporal structure of spoken language processing. *Cognition* 8:1–71.

Mathews MS, Linskey ME, Binder DK (2008) William P. van Wagenen and the first corpus callosotomies for epilepsy. *Journal of Neurosurgery* 108:608–613.

McGettigan C, Walsh E, Jessop R, Agnew ZK, Sauter DA, Warren JE, Scott SK (2015) Individual differences in laughter perception reveal roles for mentalizing and sensorimotor systems in the evaluation of emotional authenticity. *Cerebral Cortex* 25:246–257.

McGurk H, MacDonald J (1976) Hearing lips and seeing voices. *Nature* 264:746–748.

McLaughlin DJ, Sink M, Gaunt L, Spehar B, Van Engen KJ, Sommers MS, Peelle JE (2022) Pupillometry reveals cognitive demands of lexical competition during spoken word recognition in young and older adults. *Psychonomic Bulletin and Review* 29:268–280.

McMillan CT, Corley M (2010) Cascading influences on the production of speech: evidence from articulation. *Cognition* 117:243–260.

McNeill D (1992) *Hand and Mind: What Gestures Reveal about Thought*. Chicago, IL: University of Chicago Press.

McRae K, de Sa VR, Seidenberg MS (1997) On the nature and scope of featural representations of word meaning. *Journal of Experimental Psychology: General* 126:99–130.

Mechtenberg H, Heffner CC, Myers EB, Guediche S (2024) The cerebellum is sensitive to the lexical properties of words during spoken language comprehension. *Neurobiology of Language* 5:757–773. https://doi.org/10.1162/nol_a_00126.

Mehl MR, Vazire S, Ramírez-Esparza N, Slatcher RB, Pennebaker JW (2007) Are women really more talkative than men? *Science* 317(5834): 82.

Mesgarani N, Cheung C, Johnson K, Chang EF (2014) Phonetic feature encoding in human superior temporal gyrus. *Science* 343:1006–1010.

Mesulam M-M (2001) Primary progressive aphasia. *Annals of Neurology* 49:425–432.

Meyer L (2018) The neural oscillations of speech processing and language comprehension: state of the art and emerging mechanisms. *European Journal of Neuroscience* 48:2609–2621.

Michel CM, He B (2019) Chapter 6: EEG source localization. *Handbook of Clinical Neurology* 160:85–101.

Miller JL, Grosjean F (1981) How the components of speaking rate influence perception of phonetic segments. *Journal of Experimental Psychology: Human Perception and Performance* 7:208–215.

Miller JL, Grosjean F, Lomanto C (1984) Articulation rate and its variability in spontaneous speech: a reanalysis and some implications. *Phonetica* 41: 215–225.

Milner B, Corkin S, Teuber H-L (1968) Further analysis of the hippocampal amnesic syndrome: 14-year follow-up study of H.M. *Neuropsychologia* 6:215–234.

Minagar A, Ragheb J, Kelley RE (2003) The Edwin Smith Surgical Papyrus: description and analysis of the earliest case of aphasia. *Journal of Medical Biography* 11:114–117.

Mohr JP, Pessin MS, Finkelstein S, Funkenstein HH, Duncan GW, Davis KR (1978) Broca aphasia: pathologic and clinical. *Neurology* 28:311–324.

Moerel M, De Martino F, Formisano E (2014) An anatomical and functional topography of human auditory cortical areas. *Frontiers in Neuroscience* 8:225.

Morán A, Soriano MC (2018) Improving the quality of a collective signal in a consumer EEG headset. *PLoS One* 13:e0197597.

Morrell CH, Gordon-Salant S, Pearson JD, Brant LJ, Fozard JL (1996) Age- and gender-specific reference ranges for hearing level and longitudinal changes in hearing level. *Journal of the Acoustical Society of America* 100:1949–1967.

Mosso A (1880). Sulla circolazione del cervello dell'uomo. *Atti della R. Accademia dei Lincei* 5:237–358.

Murdoch BE (2010) The cerebellum and language: historical perspective and review. *Cortex* 46:858–868.

Musacchia G, Sams M, Skoe E, Kraus N (2007) Musicians have enhanced subcortical auditory and audiovisual processing of speech and music. *Proceedings of the National Academy of Sciences* 104:15894–15898.

Narain C, Scott SK, Wise RJS, Rosen S, Leff A, Iversen SD, Matthews PM (2003) Defining a left-lateralized response specific to intelligible speech using fMRI. *Cerebral Cortex* 13:1362–1368.

Neta M, Miezin FM, Nelson SM, Dubis JW, Dosenbach NUF, Schlaggar BL, Petersen SE (2015) Spatial and temporal characteristics of error-related activity in the human brain. *Journal of Neuroscience* 35:253–266.

Nettekoven C, Zhi Da, Shahshahani L, Pino AL, Saadon-Grosman N, Buckner RL, Diedrichsen J (2024). *Nature Communications* 15:8376.

Neymotin SA, Daniels DS, Caldwell B, McDougal RA, Carnevale NT, Jas M, Moore CI, Hines ML, Hämäläinen M, Jones SR (2020) Human Neocortical Neurosolver (HNN), a new software tool for interpreting the cellular and network origin of human MEG/EEG data. *eLife* 9:e51214. http://dx.doi.org/10.7554/eLife.51214.

Nordberg A, Miniscalco C, Lohmander A, Himmelmann K (2013) Speech problems affect more than one in two children with cerebral palsy: Swedish population-based study. *Acta Paediatrica* 102:161–166.

Nummenmaa L, Malen T, Nazari-Farsani S, Seppala K, Sun L, Santavirta S, Karlsson HK, Hudson M, Hirvonen J, Sams M, Scott S, Putkinen V (2023) Decoding brain basis of laughter and crying in natural scenes. *NeuroImage* 273:120082.

Okada K, Rong F, Venezia J, Matchin W, Hsich I-H, Saberi K, Serrences JT, Hickok G (2010) Hierarchical organization of human auditory cortex: evidence from acoustic invariance in the response to intelligible speech. *Cerebral Cortex* 20:2486–2495.

Orfanidou E, Marslen-Wilson WD, Davis MH (2006) Neural response suppression predicts repetition priming of spoken words and pseudowords. *Journal of Cognitive Neuroscience* 18:1237–1252.

Özyürek A (2014) Hearing and seeing meaning in speech and gesture: insights from brain and behaviour. *Philosophical Transactions of the Royal Society B: Biological Sciences* 369:20130296.

Özyürek A, Willems RM, Kita S, Hagoort P (2007) On-line integration of semantic information from speech and gesture: insights from event-related brain potentials. *Journal of Cognitive Neuroscience* 19:605–616.

Pacharra M, Debener S, Wascher E (2017) Concealed around-the-ear EEG captures cognitive processing in a visual Simon task. *Frontiers in Human Neuroscience* 11:290.

Paivio A (1963) Learning of adjective-noun paired associates as a function of adjective-noun word order and noun abstractness. *Canadian Journal of Psychology* 17:370–379.

Paivio A (1991) Dual coding theory: retrospect and current status. *Canadian Journal of Psychology/Revue Canadienne de Psychologie* 45:255–287.

Pallier C, Devauchelle A-D, Dehaene S (2011) Cortical representation of the constituent structure of sentences. *Proceedings of the National Academy of Sciences* 108:2522–2527.

Pandya DN, Hallett M, Kmukherjee SK (1969) Intra- and interhemispheric connections of the neocortical auditory system in the rhesus monkey. *Brain Research* 14:49–65.

Panesar SS, Fernandez-Miranda J (2019) Commentary: the nomenclature of human white Matter association pathways – proposal for a systematic taxonomic anatomical classification. *Frontiers in Neuroanatomy* 13:61.

Patterson K, Nestor PJ, Rogers TT (2007) Where do you know what you know? The representation of semantic knowledge in the human brain. *Nature Reviews Neuroscience* 8:976–987.

Pearle P, Collett B, Bart K, Bilderback D, Newman D, Samuels S (2010) What Brown saw and you can too. *American Journal of Physics* 78(12):1278–1289.

Peelle JE (2012) The hemispheric lateralization of speech processing depends on what "speech" is: a hierarchical perspective. *Frontiers in Human Neuroscience* 6:309.

Peelle JE (2018a) Listening effort: how the cognitive consequences of acoustic challenge are reflected in brain and behavior. *Ear and Hearing* 39:204–214.

Peelle JE (2018b) Speech comprehension: stimulating discussions at a cocktail party. *Current Biology* 28:R68–R70.

Peelle JE, Davis MH (2012) Neural oscillations carry speech rhythm through to comprehension. *Frontiers in Psychology* 3:320.

Peelle JE, Grossman M (2008) Language processing in frontotemporal dementia: a brief review. *Language and Linguistics Compass* 2:18–35.

Peelle JE, Sommers MS (2015) Prediction and constraint in audiovisual speech perception. *Cortex* 68:169–181.

Peelle JE, Wingfield A (2005) Dissociations in perceptual learning revealed by adult age differences in adaptation to time-compressed speech. *Journal of Experimental Psychology: Human Perception and Performance* 31(6): 1315–1330.

Peelle JE, Wingfield A (2016) The neural consequences of age-related hearing loss. *Trends in Neurosciences* 39:486–497.

Peelle JE, Cooke A, Moore P, Vesely L, Grossman M (2007) Syntactic and thematic components of sentence processing in progressive nonfluent aphasia and nonaphasic frontotemporal dementia. *Journal of Neurolinguistics* 20:482–494.

Peelle JE, Johnsrude IS, Davis MH (2010) Hierarchical processing for speech in human auditory cortex and beyond. *Frontiers in Human Neuroscience* 4:51.

Peelle JE, Gross J, Davis MH (2013) Phase-locked responses to speech in human auditory cortex are enhanced during comprehension. *Cerebral Cortex* 23:1378–1387.

Peelle JE, Spehar B, Jones MS, McConkey S, Myerson J, Hale S, Sommers MS, Tye-Murray N (2022) Increased connectivity among sensory and motor regions during visual and audiovisual speech perception. *Journal of Neuroscience* 42:435–442.

Peeva MG, Guenther FH, Tourville JA, Nieto-Castanon A, Anton JL, Nazarian B, Alario FX (2010) Distinct representations of phonemes, syllables, and supra-syllabic sequences in the speech production network. *NeuroImage* 50:626–638.

Penfield W, Welch K (1951) The supplementary motor area of the cerebral cortex: a clinical and experimental study. *AMA Archives of Neurology and Psychiatry* 66:289–317.

Pessoa L (2022) *The Entangled Brain: How Perception, Cognition, and Emotion Are Woven Together.* Cambridge, MA: The MIT Press.

Pessoa L, Medina L, Desfilis E (2022) Refocusing neuroscience: moving away from mental categories and towards complex behaviours. *Philosophical Transactions of the Royal Society of London B: Biological Sciences* 377:20200534.

Petersen SE, Fox PT, Posner MI, Mintun M, Raichle ME (1988) Positron emission tomographic studies of the cortical anatomy of single-word processing. *Nature* 331:585–589.

Petkov CI, Marslen-Wilson WD (2018) Editorial overview: the evolution of language as a neurobiological system. *Current Opinion in Behavioral Sciences* 21:v–xii.

Pichora-Fuller MK, Kramer SE, Eckert MA, Edwards B, Hornsby BWY, Humes LE, Lemke U, Lunner T, Matthen M, Mackersie CL, Naylor G, Phillips NA, Richter M, Rudner M, Sommers MS, Tremblay KL, Wingfield A (2016) Hearing impairment and cognitive energy: the framework for understanding effortful listening (FUEL). *Ear and Hearing* 37:5S–27S.

Pinti P, Scholkmann F, Hamilton A, Burgess P, Tachtsidis I (2019) Current status and issues regarding pre-processing of fNIRS neuroimaging data: an investigation of diverse signal filtering methods within a general linear model framework. *Frontiers in Human Neuroscience* 12:505.

Plack CJ, Léger A, Prendergast G, Kluk K, Guest H, Munro KJ (2016) Toward a diagnostic test for hidden hearing loss. *Trends in Hearing* 20.

Poeppel D (2003) The analysis of speech in different temporal integration windows: cerebral lateralization as "asymmetric sampling in time." *Speech Communication* 41:245–255.

Poeppel D (2012) The maps problem and the mapping problem: two challenges for a cognitive neuroscience of speech and language. *Cognitive Neuropsychology* 29:34–55.

Poldrack RA (2006) Can cognitive processes be inferred from neuroimaging data? *Trends in Cognitive Sciences* 10:59–63.

Poldrack RA (2018) *The New Mind Readers: What Neuroimaging Can and Cannot Reveal about Our Thoughts.* Princeton, NJ: Princeton University Press.

Poldrack RA, Kittur A, Kalar D, Miller E, Seppa C, Gil Y, Parker DS, Sabb FW, Bilder RM (2011) The cognitive atlas: toward a knowledge foundation for cognitive neuroscience. *Frontiers in Neuroinformatics* 5:17.

Pollan M (2002) *The Botany of Desire: A Plant's-Eye View of the World.* New York: Random House Trade Paperbacks.

Port RF (1979) The influence of tempo on stop closure duration as a cue for voicing and place. *Journal of Phonetics* 7:45–56.

Portnuff CD, Fligor BJ, Arehart KH (2011) Teenage use of portable listening devices: a hazard to hearing? *Journal of the American Academy of Audiology* 22:663–677.

Poskett J (2015) National types: the transatlantic publication and reception of Crania Americana (1839). *History of Science; An Annual Review of Literature, Research and Teaching* 53(3): 264–295.

Powell DS, Oh ES, Lin FR, Deal JA (2021) Hearing impairment and cognition in an aging world. *Journal for the Association for Research in Otolaryngology* 22:387–403.

Power JD, Petersen SE (2013) Control-related systems in the human brain. *Current Opinion in Neurobiology* 23:223–228.

Price CJ, Devlin JT (2003) The myth of the visual word form area. *NeuroImage* 19:473–481.

Price AR, Bonner MF, Peelle JE, Grossman M (2015) Converging evidence for the neuroanatomic basis of combinatorial semantics in the angular gyrus. *Journal of Neuroscience* 35:3276–3284.

Price AR, McAdams H, Grossman M, Hamilton RH (2015) A meta-analysis of transcranial direct current stimulation studies examining the reliability of effects on language measures. *Brain Stimulation* 8:1093–1100.

Price AR, Peelle JE, Bonner MF, Grossman M, Hamilton R (2016) Causal evidence for a mechanism of semantic integration in the angular gyrus as revealed by high-definition transcranial direct current stimulation. *Journal of Neuroscience* 36:3829–3838.

Price CJ, Wise R, Ramsay S, Friston K, Howard D, Patterson K, Frackowiak R (1992) Regional response differences within the human auditory cortex when listening to words. *Neuroscience Letters* 146:179–182.

Prinz AA, Bucher D, Marder E (2004) Similar network activity from disparate circuit parameters. *Nature Neuroscience* 7:1345–1352.

Pylkkänen L (2019) Neural basis of basic composition: what we have learned from the red–boat studies and their extensions. *Philosophical Transactions of the Royal Society of London B: Biological Sciences* 375:20190299.

Rabbitt PMA (1968) Channel capacity, intelligibility and immediate memory. *Quarterly Journal of Experimental Psychology* 20:241–248.

Rapp B, Goldrick M (2006) Speaking words: contributions of cognitive neuropsychological research. *Cognitive Neuropsychology* 23:39–73.

Rastle K, Lally C, Davis MH, Taylor JSH (2021) The dramatic impact of explicit instruction on learning to read in a new writing system. *Psychological Science* 32:471–484.

Rauschecker JP (1998) Cortical processing of complex sounds. *Current Opinion in Neurobiology* 8(4): 516–521.

Rauschecker JP, Scott SK (2009) Maps and streams in the auditory cortex: nonhuman primates illuminate human speech processing. *Nature Neuroscience* 12:718–724.

Rauschecker JP, Tian B, Pons T, Mishkin M (1997) Serial and parallel processing in rhesus monkey auditory cortex. *Journal of Comparative Neurology* 382:89–103.

Reilly J, Flurie M, Peelle JE (2020) The English lexicon mirrors functional brain activation for a sensory hierarchy dominated by vision and audition: point-counterpoint. *Journal of Neurolinguistics* 55:100895.

Reilly J, Shain C, Borghesani V, et al. (2024) What we mean when we say semantic: toward a multidisciplinary semantic glossary. *Psychonomic Bulletin and Review.* https://doi.org/10.3758/s13423-024-02556-7.

Reilly J, Peelle JE, Garcia A, Crutch SJ (2016) Linking somatic and symbolic representation in semantic memory: the dynamic multilevel reactivation framework. *Psychonomic Bulletin and Review* 23:1002–1014.

Riecke L, Formisano E, Sorger B, Başkent D, Gaudrain E (2018) Neural entrainment to speech modulates speech intelligibility. *Current Biology* 28:161–169.

Rodd JM (2020) Settling into semantic space: an ambiguity-focused account of word-meaning access. *Perspectives in Psychological Science* 15:411–427.

Rodd JM, Cai ZG, Betts HN, Hanby B, Hutchinson C, Adler A (2016) The impact of recent and long-term experience on access to word meanings: evidence from large-scale internet-based experiments. *Journal of Memory and Language* 87:16–37.

Rodd J, Gaskell G, Marslen-Wilson W (2002) Making sense of semantic ambiguity: semantic competition in lexical access. *Journal of Memory and Language* 46:245–266.

Rodd JM, Davis MH, Johnsrude IS (2005) The neural mechanisms of speech comprehension: fMRI studies of semantic ambiguity. *Cerebral Cortex* 15:1261–1269.

Rodd JM, Johnsrude IS, Davis MH (2012) Dissociating frontotemporal contributions to semantic ambiguity resolution in spoken sentences. *Cerebral Cortex* 22:1761–1773.

Rogers CS, Jones MS, McConkey S, Spehar B, Van Engen KJ, Sommers MS, Peelle JE (2020) Age-related differences in auditory cortex activity during spoken word recognition. *Neurobiology of Language* 1:452–473.

Romanski LM, Bates JF, Goldman-Rakic PS (1999) Auditory belt and parabelt projections to the prefrontal cortex in the rhesus monkey. *Journal of Comparative Neurology* 403:141–157.

Romanski LM, Goldman-Rakic PS (2002) An auditory domain in primate prefrontal cortex. *Nature Neuroscience* 5:15–16.

Romanski LM, Tian B, Fritz J, Mishkin M, Goldma-Rakic PS, Rauschecker JP (1999) Dual streams of auditory afferents target multiple domains in the primate prefrontal cortex. *Nature Neuroscience* 2:1131–1136.

Rorden C, Karnath H-O (2004) Using human brain lesions to infer function: a relic from a past era in the fMRI age? *Nature Reviews Neuroscience* 5:813–819.

Roy CS, Sherrington CS (1890) On the regulation of the blood-supply of the brain. *Journal of Physiology* 11:85–108.

Roy E, Richie-Halford A, Kruper J, Narayan M, Bloom D, Nedelec P, Rauschecker AM, Sugrue LP, Brown TT, Jernigan TL, McCandliss BD, Rokem A, Yeatman JD (2024) White matter and literacy: a dynamic system in flux. *Developmental Cognitive Neuroscience* 65:101341.

Rupp K, Hect JL, Remick M, Ghuman A, Chandrasekaran B, Holt LL, Abel TJ (2022) Neural responses in human superior temporal cortex support coding of voice representations. *PLOS Biology* 20:e3001675.

Saenz M, Langers DR (2014) Tonotopic mapping of human auditory cortex. *Hearing Research* 307:42–52.

Sandrone S, Bacigaluppi M, Galloni MR, Cappa SF, Moro A, Catani M, Filippi M, Monti MM, Perani D, Martino G (2014) Weighing brain activity with the balance: Angelo Mosso's original manuscripts come to light. *Brain* 137:621–633.

Sandrone S, Bacigaluppi M, Galloni MR, Martino G (2012) Angelo Mosso (1846–1910). *Journal of Neurology* 259:2513–2514.

Saygin ZM, Osher DE, Norton ES, Youssoufian DA, Beach SD, Feather J, Gaab N, Gabrieli JD, Kanwisher N (2016) Connectivity precedes function in the development of the visual word form area. *Nature Neuroscience* 19:1250–1255.

Schiller F (1979) *Paul Broca*. Berkeley: University of California Press.

Schmahmann JD, Doyon J, McDonald D, Holmes C, Lavoie K, Hurwitz AS, Kabani N, Toga A, Evans A, Petrides M (1999) Three-dimensional MRI atlas of the human cerebellum in proportional stereotaxic space. *NeuroImage* 10:233–260.

Schneider DC, Foss KD, De Risio L, Hague DW, Mitek AE, McMichael M (2019) Noise-induced hearing loss in 3 working dogs. *Topics in Companion Animal Medicine* 37:100362.

Schroeder CE, Foxe J (2005) Multisensory contributions to low-level, "unisensory" processing. *Current Opinion in Neurobiology* 15:454–458.

Schroeder CE, Smiley J, Fu KG, McGinnis T, O'Connell MN, Hackett TA (2003) Anatomical mechanisms and functional implications of multisensory convergence in early cortical processing. *International Journal of Psychophysiology* 50:5–17.

Scott SK (2005) Auditory processing – speech, space and auditory objects. *Current Opinion in Neurobiology* 15(2): 197–201.

Scott SK, Blank CC, Rosen S, Wise RJS (2000) Identification of a pathway for intelligible speech in the left temporal lobe. *Brain* 123:2400–2406.

Scott SK, Johnsrude IS (2003) The neuroanatomical and functional organization of speech perception. *Trends in Neuroscience* 26:100–105.

Scott SK, Lavan N, Chen S, McGettigan C (2014) The social life of laughter. *Trends in Cognitive Sciences* 18:618–620.

Scott SK, McGettigan C, Eisner F (2009) A little more conversation, a little less action – candidate roles for the motor cortex in speech perception. *Nature Reviews Neuroscience* 10:295–302.

Scoville WB, Milner B (1957) Loss of recent memory after bilateral hippocampal lesions. *Journal of Neurology, Neurosurgery and Psychiatry* 20:11–21.

Shannon RV, Zeng F-G, Kamath V, Wygonski J, Ekelid M (1995) Speech recognition with primarily temporal cues. *Science* 270:303–304.

Shattuck-Hufnagel S (2015) Prosodic frames in speech production. In *The Handbook of Speech Production* (Redford MA, ed.), pp. 419–444. Chichester, UK: John Wiley & Sons.

SheikhBahaei S, Millwater M, Maguire GA (2023) Stuttering as a spectrum disorder: a hypothesis. *Current Research in Neurobiology* 5:100116.

Sherafati A, Dwyer N, Bajracharya A, Hassanpour MS, Eggebrecht AT, Firszt JB, Culver JP, Peelle JE (2022) Prefrontal cortex supports speech perception in listeners with cochlear implants. *eLife* 11:e75323.

Shuster BZ, Depireux DA, Mong JA, Hertzano R (2019) Sex differences in hearing: probing the role of estrogen signaling. *Journal of the Acoustical Society of America* 145:3656–3663.

Skipper JI, Devlin JT, Lametti DR (2017) The hearing ear is always found close to the speaking tongue: review of the role of the motor system in speech perception. *Brain and Language* 164:77–105.

Smith ZM, Delbutte B, Oxenham AJ (2002) Chimaeric sounds reveal dichotomies in auditory perception. *Nature* 416:87–90.

Sohoglu E, Peelle JE, Carlyon RP, Davis MH (2012) Predictive top-down integration of prior knowledge during speech perception. *Journal of Neuroscience* 32:8443–8453.

Sommers MS (2021) Santa Claus, the Tooth Fairy, and auditory-visual integration: three phenomena in search of empirical support. In *The Handbook of Speech Perception*, *Second Edition* (Pardo JS, Nygaard LC, Remez RE, Pisoni DB, eds.). Hoboken, NJ: John Wiley & Sons.

Spurzheim JG (1825) *Phrenology, or the Doctrine of the Mind: And of the Relations between Its Manifestations and the Body* (3rd edition). London: Treuttel, Wurtz, and Richter.

Stine EAL, Wingfield A, Myers SD (1990) Age differences in processing information from television news; the effects of bisensory augmentation. *Journal of Gerontology: Psychological Sciences* 45:1–8.

Stockbridge MD, Sheppard SM, Keator LM, Murray LL, Lehman Blake M, Right Hemisphere Disorders Working Group Evidence-Based Clinical Research Committee, Academy of Neurological Communication Disorders and Sciences (2022) Aprosodia subsequent to right hemisphere brain damage: a systematic review and meta-analysis. *Journal of the International Neuropsychological Society* 28:709–735.

Stoodley CJ, Schmahmann JD (2018) Chapter 4: Functional topography of the human cerebellum. *Handbook of Clinical Neurology* 154:59–70.

Strick PL, Dum RP, Fiez JA (2009) Cerebellum and nonmotor function. *Annual Reviews of Neuroscience* 32:413–434.

Sumby WH, Pollack I (1954) Visual contribution to speech intelligibility in noise. *The Journal of the Acoustical Society of America* 26:212–215.

Sweet RA, Dorph-Petersen KA, Lewis DA (2005) Mapping auditory core, lateral belt, and parabelt cortices in the human superior temporal gyrus. *Journal of Comparative Neurology* 491:270–289.

Swinney D (1979) Lexical access during sentence comprehension: (re) consideration of context effects. *Journal of Verbal Learning and Verbal Behavior* 18:645–659.

Taylor JSH, Rastle K, Davis MH (2013) Can cognitive models explain brain activation during word and pseudoword reading? A meta-analysis of 36 neuroimaging studies. *Psychological Bulletin* 139:766–791.

Taylor JSH, Davis MH, Rastle K (2019) Mapping visual symbols onto spoken language along the ventral visual stream. *Proceedings of the National Academy of Sciences* 116:17723–17728.

Taylor JSH, Plunkett K, Nation K (2011) The influence of consistency, frequency, and semantics on learning to read: an artificial orthography paradigm. *Journal of Experimental Psychology: Learning, Memory, and Cognition* 37:60–76.

ten Oever S, Kaushik K, Martin AE (2022) Inferring the nature of linguistic computations in the brain. *PLoS Computational Biology* 18:e1010269.

Tezcan F, Weissbart H, Martin AE (2023) A tradeoff between acoustic and linguistic feature encoding in spoken language comprehension. *eLife* 12: e82386.

Todman D (2009) Arnold Pick (1851–1924). *Journal of Neurology* 256:504–505.

Tong J, Binder JR, Humphries C, Mazurchuk S, Conant LL, Fernandino L (2022) A distributed network for multimodal experiential representation of concepts. *Journal of Neuroscience* 42:7121–7130.

Tremblay P, Deschamps I, Gracco VL (2016) Neurobiology of speech production: a motor control perspective. In *Neurobiology of Language* (Hickok G, Small SL, eds.), pp 741–750. New York, NY: Academic Press.

Tremblay P, Gracco VL (2006) Contribution of the frontal lobe to externally and internally specified verbal responses: fMRI evidence. *NeuroImage* 33:947–957.

Tremblay P, Gracco VL (2009) Contribution of the pre-SMA to the production of words and non-speech oral motor gestures, as revealed by repetitive transcranial magnetic stimulation (rTMS). *Brain Research* 1268:112–124.

Troche J, Crutch S, Reilly J (2014) Clustering, hierarchical organization, and the topography of abstract and concrete nouns. *Frontiers in Psychology* 5:360.

Tulving E (1972) Episodic and semantic memory. In *Organization of Memory* (Tulving E, Donaldson W, eds.). New York, NY: Academic Press.

Tye-Murray N, Sommers MS, Spehar B (2007) Auditory and visual lexical neighborhoods in audiovisual speech perception. *Trends in Amplification* 11:233–241.

Ulrich R, Mattes S, Miller J (1999) Donders's assumption of pure insertion: an evaluation on the basis of response dynamics. *Acta Psychologica* 102:43–76.

Ungerleider LG, Mishkin M (1982) Two cortical visual systems. In *Analysis of Visual Behavior* (Ingle DJ, Goodale MA, Mansfield RJW, eds.), pp. 549–586. Cambridge, MA: MIT Press.

Uttal WR (2001) *The New Phrenology*. Cambridge, MA: The MIT Press.

Utter AA, Basso MA (2008) The basal ganglia: an overview of circuits and function. *Neuroscience and Biobehavioral Reviews* 32:333–342.

Vaddiparti A, Huang R, Blihar D, Du Plessis M, Montalbano MJ, Tubbs RS, Loukas M (2021) The evolution of corpus callosotomy for epilepsy management. *World Neurosurgery* 145:455–461.

Vaden KI Jr., Kuchinsky SE, Ahlstrom JB, Dubno JR, Eckert MA (2015) Cortical activity predicts which older adults recognize speech in noise and when. *Journal of Neuroscience* 35:3929–3937.

Vaden KI Jr., Kuchinsky SE, Cute SL, Ahlstrom JB, Dubno JR, Eckert MA (2013) The cingulo-opercular network provides word-recognition benefit. *Journal of Neuroscience* 33:18979–18986.

Vaden Jr. KI, Teubner-Rhodes S, Ahlstrom JB, Dubno JR, Eckert MA (2017) Cingulo-opercular activity affects incidental memory encoding for speech in noise. *NeuroImage* 157:381–387.

Valian V (2015) Bilingualism and cognition. *Bilingualism: Language and Cognition* 18:3–24.

Van Engen KJ, McLaughlin DJ (2018) Eyes and ears: using eye tracking and pupillometry to understand challenges to speech recognition. *Hearing Research* 369:56–66.

Van Engen KJ, Peelle JE (2014) Listening effort and accented speech. *Frontiers in Human Neuroscience* 8:577.

Van Engen KJ, Xie Z, Chandrasekaran B (2017) Audiovisual sentence recognition not predicted by susceptibility to the McGurk effect. *Attention, Perception, and Psychophysics* 79:396–403.

Van Engen KJ, Dey A, Sommers MS, Peelle JE (2022) Audiovisual speech perception: moving beyond McGurk. *The Journal of the Acoustical Society of America* 152:3216–3225.

Vettin J, Todt D (2004) Laughter in conversation: features of occurrence and acoustic structure. *Journal of Nonverbal Behavior* 28:93–115.

Vickers D, De Raeve L, Graham J (2016) International survey of cochlear implant candidacy. *Cochlea Implants International* 17 Suppl 1:36–41.

Vigliocco G, Kousta S-T, Della Rosa PA, Vinson DP, Tettamanti M, Devlin JT, Cappa SF (2014) The neural representation of abstract words: the role of emotion. *Cerebral Cortex* 24:1767–1777.

Villacorta VM, Perkell JS, Guenther FH (2007) Sensorimotor adaptation to feedback perturbations of vowel acoustics and its relation to perception. *Journal of the Acoustical Society of America* 122:2306–2319.

Vogel DA, McCarthy PA, Bratt GW, Brewer C (2007) The clinical audiogram: its history and current use. *Communicative Disorders Review* 1:81–94.

Vogel I, Verschuure H, van der Ploeg CP, Brug J, Raat H (2010) Estimating adolescent risk for hearing loss based on data from a large school-based survey. *American Journal of Public Health* 100:1095–1100.

von Cramon D, Jürgens U (1983) The anterior cingulate cortex and the phonatory control in monkey and man. *Neuroscience and Biobehavioral Reviews* 7:423–425.

Wada JA (1997) Youthful season revisited. *Brain and Cognition* 33: 7–10.

Wada JA (2008) A fateful encounter: sixty years later–reflections on the Wada test. *Epilepsia* 49:726. https://doi.org/10.1111/j.1528-1167.2008.01515_6.x.

Wada J, Rasmussen T (1960) Intracarotid injection of sodium amytal for the lateralization of cerebral speech dominance. *Journal of Neurosurgery* 17:266–282.

Wang J, Conder JA, Blitzer DN, Shinkareva SV (2010) Neural representation of abstract and concrete concepts: a meta-analysis of neuroimaging studies. *Human Brain Mapping* 31:1459–1468.

Warrier C, Wong P, Penhune V, Zatorre R, Parrish T, Abrams D, Kraus N (2009) Relating structure to function: Heschl's gyrus and acoustic processing. *Journal of Neuroscience* 29:61–69.

Warrington EK (1975) The selective impairment of semantic memory. *The Quarterly Journal of Experimental Psychology* 27:635–657.

Warrington EK, Shallice T (1984) Category specific semantic impairments. *Brain* 104:829–854.

Waters GS, Caplan D (2001) Age, working memory, and on-line syntactic processing in sentence comprehension. *Psychology and Aging* 16:128–144.

Watkins KE, Smith SM, Davis S, Howell P (2008) Structural and functional abnormalities of the motor system in developmental stuttering. *Brain* 131:50–59.

Wayne RV, Johnsrude IS (2015) A review of causal mechanisms underlying the link between age-related hearing loss and cognitive decline. *Ageing Research Reviews* 23:154–166.

Weintraub S, Mesulam MM, Kramer L (1981) Disturbances in prosody: a right-hemisphere contribution to language. *Archives of Neurology* 38:742–744.

Weissler RE, Drake S, Kampf K, Diantoro C, Foster K, Kirkpatrick A, Preligera I, Wesson O, Wood A, Baese-Berk MM (2023) Examining linguistic and experimenter biases through "non-native" versus "native" speech. *Applied Psycholinguistics* 44:460–474.

Weller RE, Kaas JH (1987) Subdivisions and connections of inferior temporal cortex in owl monkeys. *Journal of Comparative Neurology* 256:137–172.

Werker JF, Polka L, Pegg JE (1997) The conditioned head turn procedure as a method for testing infant speech perception. *Early Development and Parenting* 6:171–178.

Werker JF, Tees RC (1984) Cross-language speech perception: evidence for perceptual reorganization during the first year of life. *Infant Behavior and Development* 7:49–63.

Westbury CF (2014) You can't drink a word: lexical and individual emotionality affect subjective familiarity judgments. *Journal of Psycholinguistic Research* 43:631–649.

Westbury CF, Shaoul C, Hollis G, Smithson L, Briesemeister BB, Hofmann MJ, Jacobs AM (2013) Now you see it, now you don't: on emotion, context, and the algorithmic prediction of human imageability judgments. *Frontiers in Psychology* 4:99.

White BR, Culver JP (2010) Quantitative evaluation of high-density diffuse optical tomography: in vivo resolution and mapping performance. *Journal of Biomedical Optics* 15:026006.

Wild CJ, Yusuf A, Wilson D, Peelle JE, Davis MH, Johnsrude IS (2012) Effortful listening: the processing of degraded speech depends critically on attention. *Journal of Neuroscience* 32:14010–14021.

Willems RM, Özyürek A, Hagoort P (2007) When language meets action: the neural integration of gesture and speech. *Cerebral Cortex* 17:2322–2333.

Willems RM, Özyürek A, Hagoort P (2009) Differential roles for left inferior frontal and superior temporal cortex in multimodal integration of action and language. *NeuroImage* 47:1992–2004.

Wilson SM, DeMarco AT, Henry ML, Gesierich B, Babiak M, Miller BL, Gorno-Tempini ML (2016) Variable disruption of a syntactic processing network in primary progressive aphasia. *Brain* 139:2994–3006.

Winer JA (2006) Decoding the auditory corticofugal systems. *Hearing Research* 212:1–8.

Wingfield A, Peelle JE, Grossman M (2003) Speech rate and syntactic complexity as multiplicative factors in speech comprehension by young and older adults. *Aging, Neuropsychology, and Cognition* 10:310–322.

Woolgar A, Hampshire A, Thompson R, Duncan J (2011) Adaptive coding of task-relevant information in human frontoparietal cortex. *Journal of Neuroscience* 31:14592–14599.

Woolgar A, Parr A, Cusack R, Thompson R, Nimmo-Smith I, Torralva T, Roca M, Antoun N, Manes F, Duncan J (2010) Fluid intelligence loss linked to restricted regions of damage within frontal and parietal cortex. *Proceedings of the National Academy of Sciences* 107:14899–14902.

World Health Organization (2021a) *World Report on Hearing*. Geneva: World Health Organization.

World Health Organization (2021b) *World Report on Hearing: Executive Summary*. Geneva: World Health Organization.

Wright A, Saxena S, Sheppard SM, Hillis AE (2018) Selective impairments in components of affective prosody in neurologically impaired individuals. *Brain and Cognition* 124:29–36.

Xie Z, Reetzke R, Chandrasekaran B (2017) Stability and plasticity in neural encoding of linguistically relevant pitch patterns. *Journal of Neurophysiology* 117:1407–1422.

Yarkoni T, Poldrack RA, Nichols TE, Van Essen DC, Wager TD (2011) Large-scale automated synthesis of human functional neuroimaging data. *Nature Methods* 8:665–670.

Yatham LN (2023) In Memoriam: Dr. Juhn Wada, Professor Emeritus. https://psychiatry.ubc.ca/in-memoriam-dr-juhn-wada-professor-emeritus/.

Yeatman JD, White AL (2021) Reading: the confluence of vision and language. *Annual Review of Vision Science* 7:487–517.

Yerkes RM, Dodson JD (1908) The relation of strength of stimulus to rapidity of habit-formation. *Journal of Comparative Neurology and Psychology* 18:459–482.

Young RM (1990) *Mind, Brain, and Adaptation in the Nineteenth Century: Cerebral Localization and Its Biological Context from Gall to Ferrier*. Oxford: Oxford University Press.

Yovel G, Belin P (2013) A unified coding strategy for processing faces and voices. *Trends in Cognitive Sciences* 17:263–271.

Zatorre RJ (2022) Hemispheric asymmetries for music and speech: spectrotemporal modulations and top-down influences. *Frontiers in Neuroscience* 16:1075511.

Zatorre RJ, Belin P (2001) Spectral and temporal processing in human auditory cortex. *Cerebral Cortex* 11:946–953.

Zhang W, Wang J, Fan L, Zhang Y, Fox PT, Eickhoff SB, Yu C, Jiang T (2016) Functional organization of the fusiform gyrus revealed with connectivity profiles. *Human Brain Mapping* 37:3003–3016.

Zhuang J, Randall B, Stamatakis EA, Marslen-Wilson WD, Tyler LK (2011) The interaction of lexical semantics and cohort competition in spoken word recognition: an fMRI study. *Journal of Cognitive Neuroscience* 23:3778–3790.

Zhuang J, Tyler LK, Randall B, Stamatakis EA, Marslen-Wilson WD (2014) Optimally efficient neural systems for processing spoken language. *Cerebral Cortex* 24:908–918.

Zion Golumbic E, Ding N, Bickel S, Lakatos P, Schevon CA, McKhann GM, Goodman RR, Emerson R, Mehta AD, Simon JZ, Poeppel D, Schroeder CE (2013) Mechanisms underlying selective neuronal tracking of attended speech at a "cocktail party." *Neuron* 77:980–991.

Zwaardemaker, H (1891) Der Verlust an hohen Tönen mit zunehmendem Alter. *Archiv f. Ohrenheilkunde* 32:53–56. https://doi.org/10.1007/BF01804656.

Glossary

Abstract concept – A concept that cannot be directly experienced with our senses.

Action potential – A key part of neural communication involving the propagation of an electrical signal down a neuron's axon.

Activation competition framework – Approach to spoken word recognition based on the ease with words can be distinguished from similar-sounding words (competitors).

Alternative and augmentative communication (AAC) – Strategies for facilitating communication, supplementing or replacing speech.

Adaptation – In the context of speech understanding, the ability to adjust to speech signals over time.

Aphasia – Difficulty producing or understanding language, typically due to brain damage (for example, from a stroke or neurodegenerative disease).

Apraxia – A motor disorder characterized by difficulty carrying out movements. Specific types of apraxia are classified according to the ability or body part(s) affected.

Apraxia of speech – Difficulty planning and programming speech motor output. Speech rate is slow, speech sounds are prolonged, and pauses between words are frequent.

Aprosodia – Impairment processing prosody.

Arcuate fasciculus – A bundle of white matter tracts connecting the posterior temporal lobe to the frontal lobe.

Ataxia – Neurological condition associated with a lack of muscle coordination.

Auditory brainstem response (ABR) – An electrical response to sound recording using EEG and generated in the brainstem.

Axon – In vertebrates, a long projection of a neuron that conducts action potentials away from the cell body.

Axon hillock – A thick part of the axon closest to the cell body that contains a high concentration of voltage-gated sodium channels.

Basal ganglia – A collection of nuclei located deep in the brain.

Binding problem – The challenge of linking different aspects of perception and cognition into a unified representation.

Brainstem – Connects the cerebrum of the brain to the spinal cord. It contains the midbrain, pons, and medulla oblongata.

Bottom-up processing – Computations driven largely by sensory input.

Categorical perception – The tendency to experience certain types of continuous stimuli as belonging to a discrete category.

Central sulcus – Prominent sulcus separating the parietal lobe from the frontal lobe.

Cerebral palsy – A neurodevelopmental condition associated with difficulties in motor, sensory, and cognitive domains.

Characteristic feature – Attribute of a concept that helps distinguish it from other concepts.

Cingulate gyrus – Gyrus located along the midline of the brain, directly above the corpus callosum.

Cingulo-opercular network – Brain network composed of the anterior cingulate and bilateral frontal opercula (sometimes including anterior insulae).

Cochlea – The organ of hearing located in the inner ear.

Cochlear implant – A neuroprosthetic device that electrically stimulates the auditory nerve when the cochlea is not able to do so effectively.

Cochlear nuclei –The left and right cochlear nucleus are located in the brain stem, and consist of both a ventral cochlear nucleus and a dorsal cochlear nucleus.

Cognitive control – A set of cognitive processes associated with facilitating goal-directed behavior.

Cognitive subtraction – Framework in which we can understand how more complex cognitive processes work by removing or subtracting the effect of simpler ones.

Compositional semantics – How two or more words are combined to shape meaning.

Computed tomography (CT) – A type of structural brain scan that reconstructs a three-dimensional surface based on X-rays.

Concrete concept – A concept that can be directly experienced with our senses.

Conditioned head turn procedure – Method for conducting behavioral research in infants in which children are taught to turn their head in response to novel stimuli in order to receive a reward.

Conduction aphasia – Aphasic syndrome characterized by relatively intact comprehension and fluent speech output, but difficulty with repetition. Historically associated with damage to the arcuate fasciculus.

Conductive hearing loss – Hearing loss resulting from problems with the outer or middle ear.

Converging evidence – Considering how well findings from multiple approaches support a conclusion.

Corpus callosum – A bundle of white matter tracts connecting the left hemisphere of the brain with the right hemisphere.

Cortex – The outer layer of brain tissue of the cerebrum.

Cortical thickness analysis – An approach for analyzing structural MRI images whereby the thickness of the cortex is estimated.

Corticofugal pathways – Connections from the cortex to the brainstem.

Cytoarchitecture – The architecture of cells (for example, as revealed with histological staining).

Dendrites – Processes on a neuron that receive inputs from other neurons.

Diffusion tensor imaging (DTI) – An approach to diffusion weighted imaging used to identify direction of myelin in the brain.

Diffusion-weighted imaging (DWI) – A type of magnetic resonance imaging that uses diffusion of water molecules to produce the image.

Dorsal stream – Speech processing pathway that travels up and around from auditory cortex through the arcuate fasciculus into premotor cortex.

Dual coding theory – Developed by Allan Paivio, proposes that all concepts are supported by verbal knowledge, but concrete concepts are additionally supported by nonverbal representations (hence, a dual code).

Dysarthria – Difficulty with the motor execution of speech due to weakness or problems with control of muscles used to produce speech.

Efference copy – A signal from the central nervous system sent to the periphery is an *efference*. An efference copy is thus a duplicate signal not sent to the periphery.

Electrocorticography (ECoG) – Invasive electrophysiological recordings made with surface electrodes on the human brain.

Electroencephalography (EEG) – Non-invasive electrophysiological recordings made from electrodes placed on the scalp.

Electropalatography (EPG) – Approach for measuring contact between the tongue and palate (for example, during speech production) by inserting a retainer-like sheet of electrodes in the mouth.

Epilepsy – A family of neurological disorders associated with recurrent seizures (abnormal synchronized electrical activity).

Episodic memory – Memory associated with distinct events or experiences.

Fasciculus – A bundle of white matter tracts.

Fluid intelligence – The capacity for solving novel problems. Often contrasted with crystallized intelligence, which is stored knowledge.

Fractional anisotropy (FA) – A measurement from diffusion tensor imaging reflecting the degree to which water molecules are moving in a single direction, usually interpreted as reflecting the integrity of myelin in that region.

Frequency following response (FFR) – An electrical response to sound recording using EEG and generated in the brainstem. The FFR reflects sustained fluctuations that are matched to an auditory stimulus (for example, voicing in "da").

Frontotemporal degeneration (FTD) – A family of neurodegenerative diseases associated with prominent damage to the frontal or temporal lobes. Variants of FTD that are associated with a primary language impairment are classified under primary progressive aphasia (PPA).

Functional connectivity – In the context of neuroscience, a similarity of timing of activity in two brain regions that suggests coordinated processing.

Functional MRI (fMRI) – A type of magnetic resonance imaging used to measure brain function, typically through assessing regional changes in blood flow associated with neural activity.

Functional near-infrared spectroscopy (fNIRS) – A type of functional brain imaging that uses light to estimate regional blood flow.

Fusiform face area (FFA) – Functionally defined region of the fusiform cortex that responds more strongly to faces than other visual stimuli.

Glial cells – Non-neural cells that provide support to axons. In the central nervous system, a specific type of glial cell (oligodendrocytes) provides myelin for nearby axons.

Gray matter – Portions of the central nervous system consisting largely of cell bodies and supporting cells. Because it contains relatively few myelinated axons, it appears darker in color than white matter.

Gyri (singular gyrus) – "Mountains" along the folded cortex.

Hair cells – Cells with protrusions called stereocilia that look like hairs. In the human cochlea, outer hair cells help amplify signals, and inner hair cells turn mechanical energy into a nerve impulse.

Hemispheric dominance – When one brain hemisphere plays a more central role in a process than the other. For example, people typically have one hemisphere that is dominant for language (most often the left hemisphere).

Hemodynamic response – A blood flow response. In the context of cognitive neuroscience, refers to regional changes in blood flow that are attributed to changes in brain activity.

Heschl's gyrus – Also referred to as the transverse temporal gyrus, a gyrus located along the top of the temporal lobe and the location of primary auditory cortex.

Histological staining – Placing a chemical on a surface (such as the brain) to highlight different cellular properties.

Image registration – The alignment of images with different properties (for example, size, shape, or orientation) with each other.

Inferior colliculus (IC) – Primary midbrain structure for auditory processing.

Inner ear – Contains the cochlea (dedicated to hearing) and the semicircular ducts (associated with vestibular function).

Inner hair cells – Located in the cochlea, responsible for converting mechanical energy to a nerve impulse.

Inverse problem – Generally, calculating sources from measured effects. In the context of cognitive neuroscience applies to estimating the spatial location of brain activity collected using EEG or MEG.

Lateral sulcus – The most prominent sulcus in each hemisphere of the brain, separating the frontal and parietal lobe from the temporal lobe. Also known as the lateral fissure or the Sylvian fissure.

Lateralization of function – The left or right hemisphere of the brain being more specialized for a process than the other hemisphere.

Lesion-symptom mapping – The process of relating patterns of brain damage to specific changes in behavior.

Lexical – Relating to words.

Lexical competition – During language processing, the idea that different words compete with one another until a single item is selected.

Local field potential (LFP) – The average membrane potential across a large population of neurons.

Localization of function – The view that cognitive functions can be specifically associated with one or more brain regions.

Lombard effect – Describes how talkers naturally adjust their speaking style in the presence of background noise to improve intelligibility.

Longitudinal fissure – The gap separating the left and right cerebral hemispheres.

Macroanatomy – Features of the brain visible to the naked eye or on a structural brain scan, such as sulci and gyri.

Magnetic resonance imaging (MRI) – A type of imaging relying on magnetic properties of objects (including tissue, bone, and blood) to create images.

Magnetoencephalography (MEG) – A noninvasive brain imaging approach that measures small changes in magnetic fields caused by electrical brain activity.

McGurk effect – Illusion in which the addition of incongruent visual speech changes the auditory percept.

Medial geniculate body (MGB) – Part of the auditory thalamus located between the inferior colliculus and auditory cortex.

Membrane potential – The difference in electric potential between the inside and outside of a cell (such as a neuron).

Meta-analysis – A statistical analysis that uses the results of many individual research studies to test a hypothesis.

Metalinguistic – Something *about* language. For example, a metalinguistic decision is a decision about the language you process, above and beyond simply understanding its meaning.

Microanatomy – Features of the brain not visible to the naked eye, such as different types of cells.

Middle ear – Portion of the ear consisting of the tympanic membrane and ossicles.

MNI Space – A three-dimensional atlas space for the human brain originally defined at the Montreal Neurological Institute.

Morpheme – A meaningful linguistic unit that can't be divided up into smaller units. A word like "dog" is a morpheme; so is the "s" at the end of "dogs." A free morpheme can occur as separate words, whereas a bound morpheme cannot stand on its own.

Myelin – A fatty substance that surrounds axons, providing electrical insulation. Because of its high fat content, myelin appears as white to the naked eye. Myelin is made by glial cells.

Neuron – A brain cell. Neurons have dendrites, a cell body, and an axon.

Neurotransmitter – A molecule used by a neuron to pass a signal to another cell (for example, another neuron).

Nodes of Ranvier – Gaps in the myelin sheath in myelinated axons. They are enriched in ion channels and support the propagation of the action potential along the axon.

Noise-induced hearing loss – Hearing loss resulting from excessive sound exposure.

Nucleus – A collection of brain cells that serve a specific function.

Ossicles – Consisting of the three smallest bones in the human body – the incus, malleus, and stapes – the ossicles are located in the middle ear and help amplify sound before it reaches the cochlea.

Outer ear – The external portion of the ear, including the pinna and ear canal.

Outer hair cells – In the cochlea, contribute to amplifying the incoming signal to boost the level.

Paralinguistic – Near linguistic. For example, nonverbal vocal communicative signals such as a laugh convey information even though they do not meet a formal definition of language.

Perceptual learning – In the context of speech understanding, the ability to adjust to challenging or unexpected speech signals over time.

Periodicity – The regular amplitude fluctuations in a sound wave that provide frequency information.

Phoneme – Basic unit of auditory speech (such as a consonant or vowel).

Phonotactics – Rules governing which sounds are permitted to occur together in a language.

Phrenology – The study of human abilities using the shape of the skull, which rose to prominence in the early 1800s.

Population activity – In the context of neuroscience, synchronized activity of many neurons.

Prediction error – In a predictive coding framework, the mismatch between a predicted event and the actual event.

Predictive coding – A framework for neural function postulating that the brain generates predictions about upcoming sensory input to which actual sensory inputs are compared.

Presbycusis – Age-related hearing loss (typically affecting higher frequencies more than lower frequencies).

Primary progressive aphasia (PPA) – Refers to a group of conditions resulting from neurodegenerative disease (such as frontotemporal degeneration) in which language difficulty is a central symptom.

Prosody – The timing, loudness, and inflection of speech. Also referred to as suprasegmental information because it is not constrained to individual segments (i.e., phonemes).

Real-time MRI – Structural MRI tuned to image speech production at a rapid sampling rate.

Reverse inference – In the context of functional brain imaging, the act of drawing inferences regarding cognitive function based solely on what brain regions are active. Because most brain regions are associated with multiple cognitive processes, reverse inference is prone to error.

Sensory-motor feedback – Incorporating how our sensory systems (hearing, somatosensation) perceive speech to adjust the motor programs for producing speech.

Semantic dementia – Older term for the syndrome now referred to as semantic variant primary progressive aphasia.

Semantic memory – Knowledge about the world – including people, places, facts, and concepts – that we accumulate through our lives and which is not associated with a specific event.

Semantic variant primary progressive aphasia (svPPA) – Syndrome associated with damage to the anterior temporal lobes and a profound loss of concept representation.

Sensorineural hearing loss – Hearing loss resulting from dysfunction in the inner ear, including the cochlea, associated structures, or cranial nerve VIII.

Sound localization – Identifying the direction from which a sound originates.

Spatial resolution – The level of detail about the spatial information in a signal. High spatial resolution corresponds to a small sampling area (for example, an MRI scan with 1 mm voxels has a higher spatial resolution than an MRI scan with 2 mm voxels).

Spectral information – The pattern of amplitude as a function of frequency (for example, of a sound).

Stereotactic – Occurring in a three-dimensional coordinate space.

Sublexical – Units of speech that exist at a level smaller than a word (for example, a phoneme).

Sulci (singular "sulcus") – "Valleys" along the folded cortex.

Syllable – Unit of speech which may be combined to form a word. Typically one or more consonants combined with a vowel.

Synaptic gap – The space between a presynaptic cell and the postsynaptic cell.

Temporal information – The pattern of amplitude as a function of time.

Temporal resolution – The level of detail provided about the temporal information in a signal (i.e., how rapidly a signal is sampled).

Temporal response function – A linear model of the dependency between a stimulus and a response. A predicted response can be generated by convolving the stimulus with the TRF.

Tonotopy – The ordered arrangement according to pitch, as found in the auditory system beginning with the cochlea.

Top-down processing – Computations reflecting non-sensory influences, including our expectations, memories, or attentional state.

Tracers – In the context of anatomical connectivity, substances that are absorbed by neurons and travel along axons.

Transcranial alternating current stimulation (tACS) – Application of transcranial electric stimulation using alternating current.

Transcranial direct current stimulation (tDCS) – Application of transcranial electric stimulation using direct current.

Transcranial electric stimulation (tES) – Method for noninvasive brain stimulation using weak electrical currents applied to the scalp.

Transcranial magnetic stimulation (TMS) – Method for noninvasive brain stimulation using magnetic fields that induce an electrical current.

Transverse temporal gyrus – See Heschl's gyrus.

Tympanic membrane – Also referred to as the ear drum, separates the outer ear from the middle ear.

Ventral stream – Speech processing pathway that goes from auditory cortex forward along the temporal lobe and into ventral frontal cortex.

Viseme – Basic unit of visual speech.

Visual word form area (VWFA) – A region in the ventral occipitotemporal cortex that in literate readers shows stronger responses to written words than other stimuli.

Voice onset time (VOT) – The time between the beginning of a stop consonant (like "b" or "p") and when the vocal folds begin to vibrate.

Voxel – An element of a three-dimensional image, such as an MRI or PET scan.

Voxel-based morphometry (VBM) – An approach for analyzing structural MRI images that estimates regional amounts of different tissue types (for example, gray matter).

Wada test – Use of sodium amytal to selectively disrupt processing in one hemisphere of the brain as a method to test for language dominance, developed by Dr. Juhn Wada.

Wernicke-Lichtheim model – Neuropsychological model of language function emphasizing roles for the left inferior frontal gyrus ("Broca's area"), left posterior temporal cortex ("Wernicke's area"), and the arcuate fasciculus.

White matter – Portions of the central nervous system made up largely of myelinated axons. Because of the high lipid content of the myelin, it is light in color.

Word form – The physical representation of a word (distinct from its meaning).

Working memory – A limited-capacity cognitive system for the temporary storage and manipulation of information.

External Links for Each Chapter

Chapter 1 Introduction

- A comprehensive overview of the speech chain in the context of speech science, including introduction to the main stages of speech production and comprehension: https://www.phon.ucl.ac.uk/courses/spsci/iss/week1.php
- More detail on categorical perception, including spectrograms illustrating acoustic differences between phonemes: https://pressbooks.umn.edu/sensationandperception/chapter/categorical-perception/
- An additional perspective on categorical perception and phoneme discrimination, including an opportunity to test your own perception: https://nbb.emory.edu/wyttenbach/psycog/lang/phon/index.html

Chapter 2 Methods of Cognitive Neuroscience

- Alan Alda (Discovery Channel) talks about "split brain" patients with Michael Gazzaniga: https://www.youtube.com/watch?v=Hd32_w6oqNI
- Summary of the various stages of an action potential: https://www.youtube.com/watch?v=XnksofQN8_s
- A closer view of how a synapse works: https://www.youtube.com/watch?v=OvVl8rOEncE
- A review covering the basics of EEG, including how activity in pyramidal neurons relates to the EEG signal: https://www.youtube.com/watch?v=8a5X5ABgBnU
- Introduction to the basics of MRI: https://case.edu/med/neurology/NR/MRI%20Basics.htm
- How does an MRI machine work? https://www.youtube.com/watch?v=nFkBhUYynUw
- Another overview of fMRI: https://www.youtube.com/watch?v=4UOeBM5BwdY
- Broad overview of TMS from a clinical perspective (focusing on treatment for depression): https://www.youtube.com/watch?v=d649edvxsyE

- Example of someone receiving TMS, and how it can interfere with functions such as movement and talking: https://www.youtube.com/watch?v=FMR_T0mM7Pc
- A discussion of how fNIRS works, and some experimental applications: https://www.cogneurosociety.org/fnirs_wan/

Chapter 3 A Structural Foundation: Anatomical Considerations and Primary Brain Regions

- English translation of Paul Broca's famous 1861 article on language in the brain: https://psychclassics.yorku.ca/Broca/aphemie-e.htm
- EBRAINS provides an exquisite level of detail about the structure of the human brain: https://www.ebrains.eu/brain-atlases/reference-atlases/
- \Pim Levelt talks about on the history of the neuroscience of language 1820–1922 (Language Neuroscience Podcast Episode S1E11): https://podcasts.apple.com/us/podcast/the-history-of-the-neuroscience-of-language/id1550649018?i=1000526380863
- Neuroscientist Nancy Kanwisher's "Introduction to the Human Brain" gives a broad overview of human brain science, including why we want to study the brain: https://www.youtube.com/watch?v=ba-HMvDn_vU

Chapter 4 Speech Production: The Beginning of the Speech Chain

- Information sheet from NIDCD on stuttering: https://www.nidcd.nih.gov/health/stuttering
- The thing is, I stutter: Musician Meg Washington talks about her experience as someone who stutters and how that relates to her life as a musician: https://www.youtube.com/watch?v=9MegHiL93B0
- Brief overview of some challenges people with aphasia experience, including two case studies: https://www.nm.org/healthbeat/patient-stories/what-its-like-living-with-aphasia
- What is Broca's aphasia? (From the National Aphasia Association): https://www.youtube.com/watch?v=MAvlT6L9rm8
- The evolution of augmentative and alternative communication (AAC), told with the help of a longtime user: https://www.youtube.com/watch?v=eVQJaeHEfJA

- Historical interview with a patient with Broca's aphasia demonstrating difficulties with fluent speech production: https://www.youtube.com/watch?v=f2IiMEbMnPM
- Aphasia from a caregiver perspective: https://www.youtube.com/watch?v=jqz8MDotAQQ
- Fifteen minutes of MRI voice videos, showing how the vocal tract and articulators engage during vocal production (including rapping and singing): https://www.youtube.com/watch?v=yGV8az8npZU

Chapter 5 Auditory Processing: Getting Sound from the Ear to the Brain

- "A patient's guide to the normal ear" reviews the basic structure and function of the ear: https://med.stanford.edu/ohns/education/patient-education/patients-guide-to-the-normal-ear-and-hearing.html
- A detailed description of the auditory brain stem response (ABR) and some factors affecting measurement and interpretation: https://www.interacoustics.com/academy/evoked-potentials/abr-training/auditory-brainstem-response-testing
- An in-depth look at the frequency following response (FFR) from Nina Kraus: https://www.youtube.com/watch?v=37LUDdDGidM
- Journey of sound to brain (NIDCD): https://www.youtube.com/watch?v=eQEaiZ2j9oc
- 3D animation of auditory transduction: https://www.youtube.com/watch?v=46aNGGNPm7s
- Tonotopy of an "unwound" cochlea: https://www.youtube.com/watch?v=gd5nSKNaHZ8

Chapter 6 Speech Sounds: Phonemes and Word Forms

- Comprehensive introduction to phonemes: https://cgi.luddy.indiana.edu/~gasser/HLW/PhonProcess/contexts.html
- Overview of voice onset time in the context of speech sounds: https://www.youtube.com/watch?v=KkiuV8GGKUw
- Introduction to the conditioned head turn task, used for assessing speech perception in infants: https://www.youtube.com/watch?v=X7-T3Rb2-zA
- Interview with researcher Janet Werker on child language development: https://www.youtube.com/watch?v=WvM5bqUsbu8

- TED talk from researcher Pat Kuhl on "The linguistic genius of babies": https://www.youtube.com/watch?v=G2XBIkHW954
- Friendly introduction to lexical competition and spoken word recognition: https://www.youtube.com/watch?v=nZP7pb_t4oA

Chapter 7 Word Meanings and Concept Representations

- A short description of semantic variant primary progressive aphasia (svPPA) from The Association for Frontotemporal Degeneration: https://www.theaftd.org/what-is-ftd/primary-progressive-aphasia/semantic-variant-ppa-svppa/
- Podcast with Morgan Barense on The Brain Made Plain: Links between memory and perception http://www.thebrainmadeplain.net/1
- Living with primary progressive aphasia (svPPA): https://www.youtube.com/watch?v=peWdyQzaC70
- Description of word embeddings in large language models and how these relate to high-dimensional semantic spaces: https://towardsdatascience.com/why-do-we-use-embeddings-in-nlp-2f20e1b632d2

Chapter 8 Combining Meaning across Words

- Liina Pylkkänen covers "Core Combinatory operations of language": https://www.youtube.com/watch?v=wMmRKPnhB1A
- Friendly overview of semantic composition: https://web.stanford.edu/class/linguist130a/2022/materials/ling130a-handout-01-25-composition.pdf
- Examples of ambiguity in language: https://cs.nyu.edu/~davise/ai/ambiguity.html
- Video describing different approaches to parsing sentece meaning: https://www.youtube.com/watch?v=2A-FDN7-gyo

Chapter 9 Additional Forms of Language Communication

- Bad Lip Reading (NFL) demonstrates how a visual speech gesture can be associated with many different sounds: https://www.youtube.com/watch?v=Zce-QT7MGSE
- Video demonstration of the McGurk illusion: https://www.youtube.com/watch?v=G-lN8vWm3m0
- The Enchanting Music of Sign Language: https://www.youtube.com/watch?v=2Euof4PnjDk

- Review of a relationship between gesture and language: https://cosmosma gazine.com/people/culture/language-evolution-gestures-sign/
- A perspective on how the brain learns to read from Stanislas Dehaene: https://www.youtube.com/watch?v=25GI3-kiLdo

Chapter 10 Language as a Whole-brain Enterprise

- Carolyn McGettigan discusses "the social life of voices"—how character- istics other than simply the words conveyed contribute to communication: https://www.frontiersin.org/journals/human-neuroscience/articles/10.3389/ fnhum.2015.00129/full
- Overview of the role the cerebellum plays in a n number of cognitive processes: https://www.cogneurosociety.org/cerebellum_ivry_apa/
- Introduction to simulations of speech processed by a cochlear implant: https://cochlearimplant.lab.uconn.edu/cochlear-implant-information/ sounds/
- Helen Willis: Hearing, but not as you know it (experience of listening with a cochlear implant): https://www.youtube.com/watch?v=icPsm9RnO2E

Discussion Questions

For all chapters, linking the specific topics back to the major themes (Section 1.3) often leads to interesting discussions. For example:

- How does _____ reflect the tension between stability and flexibility in language representations?
- How does _____ demonstrate the role of prediction or context in language?
- What evidence from _____ suggests a role for both bottom-up and top-down processing?
- To what degree is _____ consistent with a hierarchical account of language processing?
- How are task effects reflected in _____?
- Do the findings related to _____ support the assertion that there is no "language network"?
- To what degree does _____ suggest language processing is lateralized?

Chapter 1 Introduction

- How might language processing differ depending on the modality (for example, spoken language compared to written language)? How might environmental or evolutionary pressures shape how the brain handles these situations?

Chapter 2 Methods of Cognitive Neuroscience

- Considering all of the different cognitive neuroscience methods available, what kinds of language operations are best studied by each?
- Describe how a researcher might use two or more methods to provide converging evidence regarding a research finding. What are the critical differences between the type of information provided by each approach?

Chapter 3 A Structural Foundation

- How might the ideas of functional localization shape current cognitive neuroscience? What are the positive or negative consequences of this?
- To what degree should direct anatomical connections (that is, white matter pathways) constrain or inform our models of language function in the brain?
- How can results from animal studies inform our study of the human brain? What are the advantages and disadvantages of this type of comparative approach?

Chapter 4 Speech Production

- Alternative and Augmentative Communication (AAC) can provide language output to people who have difficulty speaking (for example, due to cerebral palsy). If you only had 20 words to use for an AAC device, what words would you pick and why?

Chapter 5 Auditory Processing

- Do the similarities of the human auditory system with other mammalian auditory systems shape how we think about speech and language processing? Why or why not?
- Wear hearing protection (such as over-the-counter foam ear plugs) for part of the day. Reflect on what you notice being different about your perceptions and experiences.

Chapter 6 Speech Sounds: Phonemes and Word Forms

- Speech sound representations need to be both stable and flexible. Come up with three examples of why each of these is important. What implications might this have for neural representations and computations?

Chapter 7 Word Meanings and Concept Representations

- Think of a word you learned in the past year (it might even be a term from this book). How did you learn the word? How long did it take you to recognize? Is it possible to learn that a sound is "a word" without knowing what it means?

Chapter 8 Combining Meaning across Words

• Come up with a list of two-word phrases that might come up in conversation. Do some differ more in how their meanings combine than others?

Chapter 9 Additional Forms of Language Communication

• Different forms of language communication have similarities and differences. What can we learn by considering more than one form of language?
• What misconceptions do you think might exist about sign language? How might these be dispelled?

Chapter 10 Language as a Whole-Brain Enterprise

• Given the totality of the evidence we have discussed, what is the best way to think about brain regions supporting language? Why or why not? (Hint: There is unlikely a single correct answer.)

Index

Printed in the United States
by Baker & Taylor Publisher Services